Java™ Game Programming For Dummies®

D0404553

`<APPLET>` Tag Attributes

Attribute	Value
CODE	**Required:** The name of the Java class file containing the compiled Applet subclass to execute.
WIDTH, HEIGHT	**Required:** The *suggested* pixel width and height of the area the browser should reserve for the applet in the Web page.
CODEBASE	The uniform resource locator (URL) of the directory or folder that contains the applet code. If CODEBASE is not specified, then the Web browser viewing the document defaults to the location of the HTML document. CODEBASE allows the applet code to be place in a different location than the HTML.
NAME	The applet name that other applets on the Web page can use to find it and communicate with it.
ALT	Text displayed by browsers that cannot run the applet. The ALT text is displayed, for instance, if the user has turned off the Java option in their browser.
ALIGN	The alignment of the applet relative to the text line containing it. This attribute works like the ALIGN attribute for the IMG tag. The possible values are top, middle, bottom, left, and right. The alignment is bottom by default.
HSPACE, VSPACE	The number of pixels of space the browser should leave around the applet on the left and right (HSPACE) and top and bottom (VSPACE).

Built-in Java Colors

Color	RGB values
Color.black	0, 0, 0
Color.blue	0, 0, 255
Color.cyan	0, 255, 255
Color.darkGray	64, 64, 64
Color.gray	128, 128, 128
Color.green	0, 255, 0
Color.lightGray	192, 192, 192
Color.magenta	255, 0, 255
Color.orange	255, 200, 0
Color.pink	255, 175, 175
Color.red	255, 0, 0
Color.white	255, 255, 255
Color.yellow	255, 255, 0

Commonly Overridden Applet Methods

Applet Method	Override It To ...
void init()	Perform any one-time initialization the applet needs before it runs.
void start()	Begin animations, processing, or threads.
void paint (Graphics g)	Draw the applet to the screen.
void stop()	Suspend animations, processing, or threads initiated in start().
void destroy()	Clean up after the applet before it quits.

Copyright © 1998 IDG Books Worldwide, Inc. All rights reserved.
Cheat Sheet $2.95 value. Item 0168-2.
For more information about IDG Books, call 1-800-762-2974.

...For Dummies: #1 Computer Book Series for Beginners

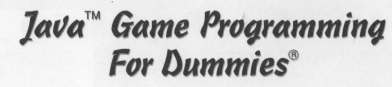

Java™ Game Programming For Dummies®

Cheat Sheet

FOR DUMMIES

COMPUTER BOOK SERIES FROM IDG

Drawing Outlined Shapes and Lines

Shape Outline	Method and Parameters
Rectangle	`drawRect(int x, int y, int width, int height)`
3-D Rectangle	`draw3DRect(int x, int y, int width, int height, boolean raised)`
Rounded Rectangle	`drawRoundRect(int x, int y, int width, int height, int arcWidth, int arcHeight)`
Oval	`drawOval(int x, int y, int width, int height)`
Arc	`drawArc(int x, int y, int width, int height, boolean raised, int startAngle, int arcAngle)`
Polygon	`drawPolygon(int[] xPoints, int[] yPoints, int nPoints)` or: `drawPolygon(Polygon poly)`
Line	`drawLine(int x1, int y1, int x2, int y2)`

Drawing Filled Shapes and Text

Filled Shape	Method and Parameters
Rectangle	`fillRect(int x, int y, int width, int height)`
3-D Rectangle	`fill3DRect(int x, int y, int width, int height, boolean raised)`
Rounded Rectangle	`fillRoundRect(int x, int y, int width, int height, int arcWidth, int arcHeight)`
Oval	`fillOval(int x, int y, int width, int height)`
Arc	`fillArc(int x, int y, int width, int height, boolean raised, int startAngle, int arcAngle)`
Polygon	`fillPolygon(int[] xPoints, int[] yPoints, int nPoints)` or: `fillPolygon(Polygon poly)`
Text String	`drawString(String str, int x, int y)`

Useful HTML Tags

Tag	Example Usage	Description
A	`<A HREF=http://www.idgbooks.com>IDG Books</A>`	The anchor tag creates a link to another document or Web page, in this case the IDG Books Web site.
APPLET	`<APPLET CODE=MyApplet WIDTH=80 HEIGHT=50></APPLET>`	Insert a Java applet, in this case an applet with the filename `MyApplet`.
IMG	`<IMG SRC="image.gif">`	Insert a GIF or JPEG image. `IMG` doesn't require an end tag.
P	`<P>This is a new paragraph</P>`	Starts a new paragraph. An end tag `</P>` is not required, but is good practice.
FONT	`<FONT SIZE=5 COLOR=RED>Big Red Text</FONT>`	Set the font size and/or color of the contained text.
TT	`<TT>Monospaced text</TT>`	The teletype tag displays the contained text using `monospaced text`.
I	`<I>Italic text</I>`	*Italicize* the contained text.
B	`<B>Bold text</B>`	Display the contained text with a **bold face font**.
U	`<U>Underlined text</U>`	Underline the contained text.

®

References for the Rest of Us!®

COMPUTER BOOK SERIES FROM IDG

Are you intimidated and confused by computers? Do you find that traditional manuals are overloaded with technical details you'll never use? Do your friends and family always call you to fix simple problems on their PCs? Then the ...*For Dummies*® computer book series from IDG Books Worldwide is for you.

...*For Dummies* books are written for those frustrated computer users who know they aren't really dumb but find that PC hardware, software, and indeed the unique vocabulary of computing make them feel helpless. ...*For Dummies* books use a lighthearted approach, a down-to-earth style, and even cartoons and humorous icons to diffuse computer novices' fears and build their confidence. Lighthearted but not lightweight, these books are a perfect survival guide for anyone forced to use a computer.

"I like my copy so much I told friends; now they bought copies."

Irene C., Orwell, Ohio

"Quick, concise, nontechnical, and humorous."

Jay A., Elburn, Illinois

"Thanks, I needed this book. Now I can sleep at night."

Robin F., British Columbia, Canada

Already, millions of satisfied readers agree. They have made ...*For Dummies* books the #1 introductory level computer book series and have written asking for more. So, if you're looking for the most fun and easy way to learn about computers, look to ...*For Dummies* books to give you a helping hand.

™

IDG BOOKS WORLDWIDE

5/97

by Wayne Holder and Doug Bell

IDG
BOOKS
WORLDWIDE

IDG Books Worldwide, Inc.
An International Data Group Company

Foster City, CA ◆ Chicago, IL ◆ Indianapolis, IN ◆ Southlake, TX

Java Game™ Programming For Dummies®

Published by
IDG Books Worldwide, Inc.
An International Data Group Company
919 E. Hillsdale Blvd.
Suite 400
Foster City, CA 94404
www.idgbooks.com (IDG Books Worldwide Web site)
www.dummies.com (Dummies Press Web site)

Copyright © 1998 IDG Books Worldwide, Inc. All rights reserved. No part of this book, including interior design, cover design, and icons, may be reproduced or transmitted in any form, by any means (electronic, photocopying, recording, or otherwise) without the prior written permission of the publisher.

Library of Congress Catalog Card No.: 98-84488

ISBN: 0-7645-0168-2

Printed in the United States of America

10 9 8 7 6 5 4 3 2 1

1O/RT/QT/ZY/IN

Distributed in the United States by IDG Books Worldwide, Inc.

Distributed by Macmillan Canada for Canada; by Transworld Publishers Limited in the United Kingdom; by IDG Norge Books for Norway; by IDG Sweden Books for Sweden; by Woodslane Pty. Ltd. for Australia; by Woodslane Enterprises Ltd. for New Zealand; by Longman Singapore Publishers Ltd. for Singapore, Malaysia, Thailand, and Indonesia; by Simron Pty. Ltd. for South Africa; by Toppan Company Ltd. for Japan; by Distribuidora Cuspide for Argentina; by Livraria Cultura for Brazil; by Ediciencia S.A. for Ecuador; by Addison-Wesley Publishing Company for Korea; by Ediciones ZETA S.C.R. Ltda. for Peru; by WS Computer Publishing Corporation, Inc., for the Philippines; by Unalis Corporation for Taiwan; by Contemporanea de Ediciones for Venezuela; by Computer Book & Magazine Store for Puerto Rico; by Express Computer Distributors for the Caribbean and West Indies. Authorized Sales Agent: Anthony Rudkin Associates for the Middle East and North Africa.

For general information on IDG Books Worldwide's books in the U.S., please call our Consumer Customer Service department at 800-762-2974. For reseller information, including discounts and premium sales, please call our Reseller Customer Service department at 800-434-3422.

For information on where to purchase IDG Books Worldwide's books outside the U.S., please contact our International Sales department at 650-655-3200 or fax 650-655-3295.

For information on foreign language translations, please contact our Foreign & Subsidiary Rights department at 650-655-3021 or fax 650-655-3281.

For sales inquiries and special prices for bulk quantities, please contact our Sales department at 650-655-3200 or write to the address above.

For information on using IDG Books Worldwide's books in the classroom or for ordering examination copies, please contact our Educational Sales department at 800-434-2086 or fax 817-251-8174.

For press review copies, author interviews, or other publicity information, please contact our Public Relations department at 650-655-3000 or fax 650-655-3299.

For authorization to photocopy items for corporate, personal, or educational use, please contact Copyright Clearance Center, 222 Rosewood Drive, Danvers, MA 01923, or fax 978-750-4470.

LIMIT OF LIABILITY/DISCLAIMER OF WARRANTY: AUTHOR AND PUBLISHER HAVE USED THEIR BEST EFFORTS IN PREPARING THIS BOOK. IDG BOOKS WORLDWIDE, INC., AND AUTHOR MAKE NO REPRESENTATIONS OR WARRANTIES WITH RESPECT TO THE ACCURACY OR COMPLETENESS OF THE CONTENTS OF THIS BOOK AND SPECIFICALLY DISCLAIM ANY IMPLIED WARRANTIES OF MERCHANTABILITY OR FITNESS FOR A PARTICULAR PURPOSE. THERE ARE NO WARRANTIES WHICH EXTEND BEYOND THE DESCRIPTIONS CONTAINED IN THIS PARAGRAPH. NO WARRANTY MAY BE CREATED OR EXTENDED BY SALES REPRESENTATIVES OR WRITTEN SALES MATERIALS. THE ACCURACY AND COMPLETENESS OF THE INFORMATION PROVIDED HEREIN AND THE OPINIONS STATED HEREIN ARE NOT GUARANTEED OR WARRANTED TO PRODUCE ANY PARTICULAR RESULTS, AND THE ADVICE AND STRATEGIES CONTAINED HEREIN MAY NOT BE SUITABLE FOR EVERY INDIVIDUAL. NEITHER IDG BOOKS WORLDWIDE, INC., NOR AUTHOR SHALL BE LIABLE FOR ANY LOSS OF PROFIT OR ANY OTHER COMMERCIAL DAMAGES, INCLUDING BUT NOT LIMITED TO SPECIAL, INCIDENTAL, CONSEQUENTIAL, OR OTHER DAMAGES.

Trademarks: All brand names and product names used in this book are trade names, service marks, trademarks, or registered trademarks of their respective owners. IDG Books Worldwide is not associated with any product or vendor mentioned in this book.

is a trademark under exclusive license to IDG Books Worldwide, Inc., from International Data Group, Inc.

About the Authors

Doug Bell is a recovering game junkie. When Doug was growing up, his parents worried about his obsession with not only playing games, but with winning them. Fortunately, about this time the first personal computers that you didn't have to build yourself became available, which rescued Doug from a certain career as a lawyer. In 1981 Doug co-founded PVC Dragon with a college buddy and entered the computer game market to pursue his passion for games. In 1984 Doug joined forces with Wayne Holder and FTL Games where he led the development of several number-one selling games, including the groundbreaking bestseller *DungeonMaster*. In late 1995 — after years of cross-platform development in Pascal, C, and assembly — Doug and Wayne jumped into Java with both feet. Doug's passion for Java quickly became an equal to his passion for games. He has written articles for *JavaWorld;* appeared on an industry panel on Java Games at Sun Microsystems's annual JavaOne conference; developed courseware and taught classes in Java programming; and, of course, co-authored this book. Doug is Vice President of Development at FTL Games, but his most important job is raising his sons Steven and Sean with his wife Kathy, an accomplished Windows programmer and mother.

Wayne Holder entered the computer revolution by building his own small computer from one of Intel's first microprocessors, the 4040, and went on to personally write the first spelling checker for Microsoft Word (later licensed to Microsoft) as well as supply spelling and grammar checkers to Kaypro, WordStar International, Philips, Xerox, Symantec, and many others. The computer game bug bit Wayne in 1983 and he jumped in by founding FTL Games. FTL Games went on to create and ship over a million units of different game titles worldwide on everything from Sega game consoles to Macs and PCs. Realizing that the Java tsunami would reshape the face of computing, Wayne and Doug paddled out to meet the wave in late 1995 and have never looked back. With the arrival of the Holder's first child, daughter Belle, in October of 1996, Wayne shifted to telecomputing and now works at home with his novelist wife Nancy who has published over 25 novels and is currently writing several original books based on the TV series *Buffy the Vampire Slayer*.

ABOUT IDG BOOKS WORLDWIDE

Welcome to the world of IDG Books Worldwide.

IDG Books Worldwide, Inc., is a subsidiary of International Data Group, the world's largest publisher of computer-related information and the leading global provider of information services on information technology. IDG was founded more than 25 years ago and now employs more than 8,500 people worldwide. IDG publishes more than 275 computer publications in over 75 countries (see listing below). More than 60 million people read one or more IDG publications each month.

Launched in 1990, IDG Books Worldwide is today the #1 publisher of best-selling computer books in the United States. We are proud to have received eight awards from the Computer Press Association in recognition of editorial excellence and three from *Computer Currents'* First Annual Readers' Choice Awards. Our best-selling *...For Dummies®* series has more than 30 million copies in print with translations in 30 languages. IDG Books Worldwide, through a joint venture with IDG's Hi-Tech Beijing, became the first U.S. publisher to publish a computer book in the People's Republic of China. In record time, IDG Books Worldwide has become the first choice for millions of readers around the world who want to learn how to better manage their businesses.

Our mission is simple: Every one of our books is designed to bring extra value and skill-building instructions to the reader. Our books are written by experts who understand and care about our readers. The knowledge base of our editorial staff comes from years of experience in publishing, education, and journalism — experience we use to produce books for the '90s. In short, we care about books, so we attract the best people. We devote special attention to details such as audience, interior design, use of icons, and illustrations. And because we use an efficient process of authoring, editing, and desktop publishing our books electronically, we can spend more time ensuring superior content and spend less time on the technicalities of making books.

You can count on our commitment to deliver high-quality books at competitive prices on topics you want to read about. At IDG Books Worldwide, we continue in the IDG tradition of delivering quality for more than 25 years. You'll find no better book on a subject than one from IDG Books Worldwide.

IDG BOOKS WORLDWIDE

John Kilcullen
CEO
IDG Books Worldwide, Inc.

Steven Berkowitz
President and Publisher
IDG Books Worldwide, Inc.

Eighth Annual Computer Press Awards ≥ 1992

Ninth Annual Computer Press Awards ≥ 1993

Tenth Annual Computer Press Awards ≥ 1994

Eleventh Annual Computer Press Awards ≥ 1995

IDG Books Worldwide, Inc., is a subsidiary of International Data Group, the world's largest publisher of computer-related information and the leading global provider of information services on information technology. International Data Group publishes over 275 computer publications in over 75 countries. Sixty million people read one or more International Data Group publications each month. International Data Group's publications include: **ARGENTINA:** Buyer's Guide, Computerworld Argentina, PC World Argentina; **AUSTRALIA:** Australian Macworld, Australian PC World, Australian Reseller News, Computerworld, IT Casebook, Network World, Publish, Webmaster; **AUSTRIA:** Computerwelt Osterreich, Networks Austria, PC Tip Austria; **BANGLADESH:** PC World Bangladesh; **BELARUS:** PC World Belarus; **BELGIUM:** Data News; **BRAZIL:** Annuário de Informática, Computerworld, Connections, Macworld, PC Player, PC World, Publish, Reseller News, Supergamepower; **BULGARIA:** Computerworld Bulgaria, Network World Bulgaria, PC & MacWorld Bulgaria; **CANADA:** CIO Canada, Client/Server World, ComputerWorld Canada, InfoWorld Canada, NetworkWorld Canada, WebWorld; **CHILE:** Computerworld Chile, PC World Chile; **COLOMBIA:** Computerworld Colombia, PC World Colombia; **COSTA RICA:** PC World Centro America; **THE CZECH AND SLOVAK REPUBLICS:** Computerworld Czechoslovakia, Macworld Czech Republic, PC World Czechoslovakia; **DENMARK:** Communications World Danmark, Computerworld Danmark, Macworld Danmark, PC World Danmark, Techworld Denmark; **DOMINICAN REPUBLIC:** PC World Republica Dominicana; **ECUADOR:** PC World Ecuador; **EGYPT:** Computerworld Middle East, PC World Middle East; **EL SALVADOR:** PC World Centro America; **FINLAND:** MikroPC, Tietoverkko, Tietoviikko; **FRANCE:** Distributique, Hebdo, Info PC, Le Monde Informatique, Macworld, Reseaux & Telecoms, WebMaster France; **GERMANY:** Computer Partner, Computerwoche, Computerwoche Extra, Computerwoche FOCUS, Global Online, Macwelt, PC Welt; **GREECE:** Amiga Computing, GamePro Greece, Multimedia World; **GUATEMALA:** PC World Centro America; **HONDURAS:** PC World Centro America; **HONG KONG:** Computerworld Hong Kong, PC World Hong Kong, Publish in Asia; **HUNGARY:** ABCD CD-ROM, Computerworld Szamitastechnika, Internetto online Magazine, PC World Hungary, PC-X Magazin Hungary; **ICELAND:** Tolvuheimur PC World Island; **INDIA:** Information Communications World, Information Systems Computerworld, PC World India, Publish in Asia; **INDONESIA:** InfoKomputer PC World, Komputek Computerworld, Publish in Asia; **IRELAND:** ComputerScope, PC Live!; **ISRAEL:** Macworld Israel, People & Computers/Computerworld; **ITALY:** Computerworld Italia, Macworld Italia, Networking Italia, PC World Italia; **JAPAN:** DTP World, Macworld Japan, Nikkei Personal Computing, OS/2 World Japan, SunWorld Japan, Windows NT World, Windows World Japan; **KENYA:** PC World East African; **KOREA:** Hi-Tech Information, Macworld Korea, PC World Korea; **MACEDONIA:** PC World Macedonia; **MALAYSIA:** Computerworld Malaysia, PC World Malaysia, Publish in Asia; **MALTA:** PC World Malta; **MEXICO:** Computerworld Mexico, PC World Mexico; **MYANMAR:** PC World Myanmar; **NETHERLANDS:** Computer! Totaal, LAN Internetworking Magazine, LAN World Buyers Guide, Macworld Netherlands, Net, WebWereld; **NEW ZEALAND:** Absolute Beginners Guide and Plain & Simple Series, Computer Buyer, Computer Industry Directory, Computerworld New Zealand, MTB, Network World, PC World New Zealand; **NICARAGUA:** PC World Centro America; **NORWAY:** Computerworld Norge, CW Rapport, Datamagasinet, Financial Rapport, Kursguide Norge, Macworld Norge, Multimediaworld Norge, PC World Ekspress Norge, PC World Nettverk, PC World Norge, PC World ProduktGuide Norge; **PAKISTAN:** Computerworld Pakistan; **PANAMA:** PC World Panama; **PEOPLE'S REPUBLIC OF CHINA:** China Computer Users, China Computerworld, China Infoworld, China Telecom World Weekly, Computer & Communication, Electronic Design China, Electronics Today, Electronics Weekly, Game Software, PC World China, Popular Computer Week, Software Weekly, Software World, Telecom World; **PERU:** Computerworld Peru, PC World Profesional Peru, PC World SoHo Peru; **PHILIPPINES:** Click!, Computerworld Philippines, PC World Philippines, Publish in Asia; **POLAND:** Computerworld Poland, Computerworld Special Report Poland, Cyber, Macworld Poland, Networld Poland, PC World Komputer; **PORTUGAL:** Cerebro/PC World, Computerworld/Correio Informático, Dealer World Portugal, Mac*In/PC*In Portugal, Multimedia World; **PUERTO RICO:** PC World Puerto Rico; **ROMANIA:** Computerworld Romania, PC World Romania, Telecom Romania; **RUSSIA:** Computerworld Russia, Mir PK, Publish, Seti; **SINGAPORE:** Computerworld Singapore, PC World Singapore, Publish in Asia; **SLOVENIA:** Monitor; **SOUTH AFRICA:** Computing SA, Network World SA, Software World SA; **SPAIN:** Communicaciones World Espana, Computerworld Espana, Dealer World Espana, Macworld Espana, PC World Espana; **SRI LANKA:** Infolink PC World; **SWEDEN:** CAP&Design, Computer Sweden, Corporate Computing Sweden, it.branschen, Macworld Sweden, MaxiData Sweden, MikroDatorn, Natverk & Kommunikation, PC World Sweden, PCaktiv, Windows World Sweden; **SWITZERLAND:** Computerworld Schweiz, Macworld Schweiz, PCtip; **TAIWAN:** Computerworld Taiwan, Macworld Taiwan, NEW ViSiON/Publish, PC World Taiwan, Windows World Taiwan; **THAILAND:** Publish in Asia, Thai Computerworld; **TURKEY:** Computerworld Turkiye, Macworld Turkiye, Network World Turkiye, PC World Turkiye; **UKRAINE:** Computerworld Kiev, Multimedia World Ukraine, PC World Ukraine; **UNITED KINGDOM:** Acorn User UK, Amiga Action UK, Amiga Computing UK, Apple Talk UK, Computing, Macworld, Parents and Computers UK, PC Advisor, PC Home, PSX Pro, The WEB; **UNITED STATES:** Cable in the Classroom, CIO Magazine, Computerworld, DOS World, Federal Computer Week, GamePro Magazine, InfoWorld, I-Way, Macworld, Network World, PC Games, PC World, Publish, Video Event, THE WEB Magazine, and WebMaster; online webzines: JavaWorld, NetscapeWorld, and SunWorld Online; **URUGUAY:** InfoWorld Uruguay; **VENEZUELA:** Computerworld Venezuela, PC World Venezuela; and **VIETNAM:** PC World Vietnam.   3/24/97

Dedication

Wayne would like to dedicate this book to his wife, Nancy, and his daughter, Belle.

Doug dedicates this book to his gracious and understanding wife, Kathy.

Publisher's Acknowledgments

We're proud of this book; please register your comments through our IDG Books Worldwide Online Registration Form located at http://my2cents.dummies.com.

Some of the people who helped bring this book to market include the following:

Acquisitions, Development, and Editorial

Project Editor: Clark Scheffy

Acquisitions Editor: Jill Pisoni

Media Development Manager: Joyce Pepple

Permissions Editor: Heather H. Dismore

Copy Editor: Kathy Ewing

Technical Editor: Garrett Pease

Editorial Manager: Mary C. Corder

Editorial Assistant: Paul Kuzmic

Production

Project Coordinator: E. Shawn Aylsworth

Layout and Graphics: Steve Arany, Cameron Booker, Lou Boudreau, Linda M. Boyer, J. Tyler Connor, Angela F. Hunckler, Jane Martin, Tom Missler, Drew R. Moore, Anna Rohrer, Brent Savage, Janet Seib, Kate Snell, Michael A. Sullivan

Proofreaders: Christine Berman, Kelli Botta, Michelle Croninger, Henry Lazarek, Rebecca Senninger, Robert Springer, Janet M. Withers

Indexer: Liz Cunningham

Special Help

Gwenette Gaddis, Copy Editor; Wendy Hatch, Copy Editor; Ted Cains, Copy Editor

General and Administrative

IDG Books Worldwide, Inc.: John Kilcullen, CEO; Steven Berkowitz, President and Publisher

IDG Books Technology Publishing: Brenda McLaughlin, Senior Vice President and Group Publisher

Dummies Technology Press and Dummies Editorial: Diane Graves Steele, Vice President and Associate Publisher; Mary Bednarek, Director of Acquisitions and Product Development; Kristin A. Cocks, Editorial Director

Dummies Trade Press: Kathleen A. Welton, Vice President and Publisher; Kevin Thornton, Acquisitions Manager

IDG Books Production for Dummies Press: Beth Jenkins Roberts, Production Director; Cindy L. Phipps, Manager of Project Coordination, Production Proofreading, and Indexing; Kathie S. Schutte, Supervisor of Page Layout; Shelley Lea, Supervisor of Graphics and Design; Debbie J. Gates, Production Systems Specialist; Robert Springer, Supervisor of Proofreading; Debbie Stailey, Special Projects Coordinator; Tony Augsburger, Supervisor of Reprints and Bluelines; Leslie Popplewell, Media Archive Coordinator

Dummies Packaging and Book Design: Patti Crane, Packaging Specialist; Kavish + Kavish, Cover Design

♦

The publisher would like to give special thanks to Patrick J. McGovern, without whom this book would not have been possible.

♦

Contents at a Glance

Introduction 1

Part I: Steppin' Out 5

Chapter 1: Follow the Bouncing Ball 7
Chapter 2: Ponglet 17
Chapter 3: Hole In One 31
Chapter 4: JavaPool 51

Part II: Up to Speed 71

Chapter 5: Sliding Blocks Brain Teaser 73
Chapter 6: Blackjack 93
Chapter 7: 2-D Maze 137
Chapter 8: 2-D Sprite Maze 173

Part III: Seven League Boots 215

Chapter 9: Modeling the Real World 217
Chapter 10: 3-D Polygon Maze 243
Chapter 11: Texture-Mapped 3-D Maze 263
Chapter 12: Advanced Imaging 285

Part IV: The Part of Tens 309

Chapter 13: Ten Secrets for Making Fun Games 311
Chapter 14: Ten Ways to Say "Game Over" 317
Chapter 15: Ten Ways to Optimize Your Java Code 323
Appendix: What's on the CD-ROM 331

Index 341

Java™ Development Kit Version 1.0.2 (Mac OS)
1.1.5 (Windows) Binary Code License 356

IDG Books Worldwide, Inc., End-User
License Agreement 358

Installation Instructions 360

Book Registration Information .... Back of Book

Cartoons at a Glance

By Rich Tennant

Fax: 978-546-7747 • E-mail: the5wave@tiac.net

Table of Contents

Introduction 1
   About This Book 1
   Who You Are 1
   About the Java Code in This Book 2
   How This Book Is Organized 2
      Part I: Steppin' Out 2
      Part II: Up to Speed 2
      Part III: Seven League Boots 3
      Part IV: The Part of Tens 3
      Appendix: About the CD-ROM 3
      CD Chapters: Fundamentals 3
   Icons Used in This Book 4

Part I: Steppin' Out 5

Chapter 1: Follow the Bouncing Ball 7
   Ticking Off the Time 7
   Making Things Move 9
      Floating the point 9
      Encapsulating the essence of a ball 9
   Setting Bounds 10
      Moving out of bounds 11
      Bouncing back 11
      Coding movement and bounce 11
      Settin' things in motion 13
   Drawing the Details 14
      Drawing offscreen 15
      Overriding the flicker 15
      Drawing the background and the ball 16
      Putting the action on the screen 16

Chapter 2: Ponglet 17
   Setting State 17
      Breaking down the task 18
      Serving the ball 20
   Up Java Creek without a Paddle 22
      Returning the serve 23
      Changing state 24
      Creating a computer opponent 24
      Rolling down the gutter 25
      He shoots, he scores! 26
      We have a winna! 26

Tracking User Input 27
    Entering the control zone 27
    Tracking the mouse 27
Displaying the State 28
    Keeping score 29
    Game over? 29

Chapter 3: Hole In One **31**
Modeling the Deceleration of a Ball 32
    Using vectors 32
    Creating a vector class 35
Starting from a Circle 36
    Creating the `Circle` class 37
    Building a `Ball` by extending `Circle` 37
    Decelerating the ball 38
    Moving the ball 39
    Staying in bounds 39
    Putting the ball 40
        Selecting the ball 40
        Executing the putt 41
        Waiting for the ball to go in 41
    Drawing the ball 41
Digging a Hole 42
    Gravitating toward the center 43
    Vectoring in 44
    Curving around the hole 44
    Coding the curve 46
        Pushing to the center 46
        Sinking the putt 47
        Spinning in the hole 47
Coding the `HoleInOne` Applet 48
    Completing the putting interface 48
    Drawing the green 49

Chapter 4: JavaPool **51**
Calculating Ball-to-Ball Collisions 52
    Passing in the night 52
    Reducing the distance 52
    Calculating position over time 53
    Calculating the distance to a collision 54
    Solving for time 56
        Two solutions? 56
        Rearrange the equation 57
        The complete set of equations (all you really need) 59
    Timing and order 60
    Checking the combinations 61
Bouncing Off the Bumpers 61
Coding the Collisions 62

Conserving Momentum 63
 Revisiting vectors 64
  What if both balls are moving? 66
  The dot product 66
   The `collide( )` method 67
   `collide( )` dissected 67
 Putting All the Pieces Together 68

Part II: Up to Speed **71**

Chapter 5: Sliding Blocks Brain Teaser **73**

Using Images In Games 74
Digital Stamp Pads 75
 Drawing while downloading 77
 Loading images with `MediaTracker` 77
  `MediaTracker.addImage( )` 78
  `MediaTracker.waitForAll( )` 78
  Loading multiple images 79
Laying Out the Game Board 79
 Reading the width and height of an `Image` 81
 Initializing `gridX`, `gridY`, `pieceWidth`, and `pieceHeight` .. 81
Crafting the Puzzle 82
 Making puzzle pieces that act like real puzzle pieces 82
 Putting the pieces together 83
Mousing the Pieces Around 85
 Selecting a puzzle piece 85
 Moving the pieces 86
 `Slide( )`ing around 87
  Checking for pieces that block the slide path with
   `Rectangle.intersects( )` 87
  Checking for the board boundaries `Rectangle.union( )` and
   `Rectangle.equals( )` 88
 Cleaning up after a move 89
Drawing the Board 90
Declaring the Puzzle Solved and Congratulating the Winner .. 91

Chapter 6: Blackjack **93**

Understanding the Blackjack Game 93
 Playing Blackjack 94
 Designing the game 95
Creating a Reusable Deck of Cards 96
 Shuffling and dealing the deck 97
 Building the `Card` class 99
  Converting cards to strings 102
  Extracting card graphics from a composite image 103
 Customizing the deck 105

Creating a User Interface with Components 106
   Using buttons 106
      Creating and placing buttons 107
      Having your game respond to buttons 108
   Reading and displaying text 108
      Displaying status and scores with labels 109
      Getting a few words from the user 109
      Creating scrolling text areas 110
   Using `Canvas` to create new components 112
      Customizing your game's appearance with `ImageButton` 112
      Displaying a hand of cards 114
Arranging the User Interface 117
   Positioning components with a `LayoutManager` 118
      FlowLayout 119
      BorderLayout 119
      GridLayout 120
      Your own LayoutManager 120
   Dividing the screen with panels 123
   Laying out a game of Blackjack 124
      The top-level applet 124
      The HTML that loads the applet 130
      The players 131
      The players' hands 134

Chapter 7: 2-D Maze **137**

Creating the `Maze` Class 138
   The `BlockMaze` subclass 139
   The `WallMaze` subclass 140
Generating a Maze 142
   Selecting an algorithm 142
   Adding to the `Maze` class 144
   Generating a wall maze 145
   Generating a block maze 149
Solving Mazes 156
   Representing the solution 156
   Keeping your left hand on the wall 157
   Using breadth-first searching to find the shortest path 159
Displaying a 2-D Maze 163
   Using the `paint( )` method 164
   Repainting the maze in a thread-friendly manner 165
   Calculating where the pixels go 166
   Knowing that block mazes are simple is half the battle 167
   Displaying a wall maze 167
   Displaying a solution 169
Putting the maze on the screen 170
   Using a thread to animate, generate, and solve a maze 170
   Reviewing parameters in the `MazeApplet` class 171

Chapter 8: 2-D Sprite Maze **173**

Gentleman, Start Your Sprite Engines! 174
  Implementing a sprite 174
  Putting sprites in their place 176
  Moving sprites around the play field 178
  Resolving collisions 179
  Displaying sprites 180
  Animating sprites 181
A Sprite Framework 183
  The `SpriteEngine` class 184
    Keeping track of all the sprites 188
    Drawing sprites layer by layer 189
    Moving sprites and detecting collisions 190
      Improving the accuracy of collision detection 190
      Selecting a movement frame rate 192
  The `BackgroundSpriteEngine` class 194
  Sprite events and handling them 194
  Sprite control 195
Computer Adversaries 197
  Using random intelligence to make adversaries smarter 197
  Using a breadth-first search for adversary navigation 198
  Prioritizing adversary goals 198
The Sprite Maze Game 200
  Implementing a cast of sprites 201
    Running into a wall 202
    Animating maze runners 202
    Animating an adversary who shoots to kill 204
    Whizzing bullets 205
  Building on the `BlockMaze` class 206
    Initializing the game 210
    Overriding `drawSquare()` 210
    Giving the player control 211
    Keeping things moving 211
    Chasing the player 212
  Finalizing the Sprite Maze applet 212

Part III: Seven League Boots *215*

Chapter 9: Modeling the Real World **217**

Making Things Happen at the Right Time with a Timeline 217
  A heap of events 218
  Adding events to the timeline 219
  Processing events in order 221
  Changing the future: Removing events before they happen 222
    Removing events 222
    Searching the timeline 222
Playing Sounds 223

Matching Animations to Game Events with Scripts 224
    Interfacing the programmer and the artist 225
    Writing a script 225
    Reading scripts from text files 227
    Looping an animation 228
    Adding random behavior 228
    Adding special effects and other goodies 230
    Understanding the code 231
        Organizing scripts by action 231
        Filling a script with frames 233
        Implementing an `AnimFrame` 238
            `SoundFrame` 238
            `BranchFrame` 239
        Putting the code to work: The `ScriptSprite` class 240

Chapter 10: 3-D Polygon Maze 243

Moving into Three Dimensions 243
    Calculating perspective 243
        Calculating the height of a wall 247
        Finding the x-axis intersection 247
        Expanding the grid into 3 dimensions 247
        Sizing up the screen 247
    Drawing the Maze 248
        The painter's algorithm 248
        Draw from the outside in 248
        Deeper is wider 249
Creating a Rat's-Eye View 250
    Writing `GridView` 250
    Coding `MazeMap` 252
    Coding `PolyMaze` 253
Adding Shading, Light Effects, and a Reason to Solve the Maze 255
    Updating `MazeMap` 257
    Updating `PolyMaze` 258
Running a Random Maze 259
    Extending from `BlockMaze` 259
    Sizing the maze in your HTML 260

Chapter 11: Texture-Mapped 3-D Maze 263

Mapping Some Texture 263
Scaling Images 264
Tiling Textures 268
Texture Mapping a 3-D Maze 269
    Introducing Mr. Bresenham 270
    Experimenting with Bresenham 271
    Extending a `TexView` class from `GridView` 273
        Loading textures 273
        Overriding `drawSq( )` 273
        Alternating wall textures 274

Drawing front walls 275
    Calculating the front wall's texture offset 275
    Creating the front wall image 276
    Clipping to the view 276
    Slicing a column of texture 277
Drawing side walls 278
    Calculating the side wall's texture offset 279
    Tracing the side-wall edges 280
    Masking the side walls 280
Darkening the walls 280
    Computing a darkened color table 280
    Shading the walls 281
    Shading the side walls 282
Assembling the Pieces 283

Chapter 12: Advanced Imaging **285**

Drawing Partially Transparent Images 286
    Creating new images with `MemoryImageSource` 286
    Coding an `AlphaGradient` 287
    Blending the edges of images with alpha masking 289
        Creating alpha information from a GIF image 289
        Using `PixelGrabber` 290
Antialiasing in Java 293
    Rendering to subpixels 293
    Reading from offscreen images 294
    Shrinking text 296
Drawing Direct 297
    The `ImageProducer` interface 298
    Coding an `ImageProducer` 298
    Dancing the `ImageProducer` tango 299
    Demoing `DirectImage` 301
Modifying GIF Images 304
    Getting at the raw image data with the
       `ImageConsumer` interface 304
    Recoloring a GIF Image 307

Part IV: The Part of Tens **309**

Chapter 13: Ten Secrets for Making Fun Games **311**

Knowing What Players Want 311
Understanding What Makes a Game Addictive 312
Start Easy and Then Increase Difficulty 312
Making It Easy to "Step In" 313
Enhancing the Player's Suspension of Disbelief 313
Making the Player Feel Smart 314
What Did I Do Wrong? The Player Should Always Know 314

Cheating Spoils the Fun 315
Your Friend, Mr. Random Number 315
Playtesting 316

Chapter 14: Ten Ways to Say "Game Over" 317

Fading to Black 317
Rolling the Credits 318
Providing an Instant Replay 318
Scoring and Points: the Competitive Obsession 319
Marking Levels of Achievement 319
Ranking One Player against Another 320
Reusing Game Code to Make an Ending Animation 320
Offering a Practice Round 321
Losing Should Even Be Fun 321
Thanking Players for an Enjoyable Game 321

Chapter 15: Ten Ways to Optimize Your Java Code 323

Code Profiling: Finding Where the Time Goes 323
A Shifty Divide 324
Inline Methods with the Compiler 325
Do Once, Use Often 325
Faster Variables 326
A Faster Loop 327
Faster Methods 328
Reduce the Cost of Synchronizing 328
Beware of Large Array Initializers 329
The Fastest Way to Copy Arrays 330

Appendix: What's on the CD-ROM 331

System Requirements 331
Using the CD with Microsoft Windows 95 or NT 4.0 332
Using the CD with Mac OS 333
Getting to the Content 333
Installing Programs 334
What You'll Find 335
    The Java Development Kit 335
    Microsoft Internet Explorer 4.0 336
    Adobe Acrobat Reader 336
    CD Bonus Chapters 336
       CD Chapter 1: An Applet a Day 336
       CD Chapter 2: Using Threads 337
       CD Chapter 3: Getting Savvy with Graphics 337
       CD Chapter 4: Adding Color to Cool 337
       CD Chapter 5: User Input 337
    Applets and More Applets 337
    Chinese Checkers for Java 339

GoldWave 3.24 339
SoundForge XP 4.0d Demo 339
SoundApp 2.4.4 339
SoundHack 0.872 340
If You've Got Problems (Of the CD Kind) 340

Index *341*

Java™ *Development Kit Version 1.0.2 (Mac OS)*
1.1.5 (Windows) Binary Code License *356*

IDG Books Worldwide, Inc., End-User
License Agreement *358*

Installation Instructions *360*

Book Registration Information .... *Back of Book*

Introduction

*W*elcome to *Java Game Programming For Dummies*. This book takes you from writing your first, basic game applets all the way through advanced, texture-mapped 3-D. Along the way, you see and apply all the under-the-hood techniques like maze generation, collision detection, and sprites that put the red meat in your game stew.

About This Book

This book shows you the techniques that make games tick, and gives you dozens of working Java code examples. In addition, each example is backed up by detailed explanations that fully deconstruct the code so that you can see how everything works. You can start from these working examples and customize them, use the parts to create entirely new games, or simply use them as a source of ideas for writing your own custom game code.

While this book does, where necessary, discuss a little theory, the real heart of the book is intended more like a hands-on auto shop class than a physics lecture. After all, understanding how a water pump works is a lot easier if you can hold one in your hand and see where it fits on a real car engine. Likewise, understanding game code is a lot easier if you can examine each part of the code in detail and see where it fits in the overall structure of a working program.

Who You Are

We wrote this book in such a way that it is accessible to all levels of Java programmers. If you are fairly new to Java, you can copy the code in this book and, with the tips and instruction we give (and a little adventure), easily customize the games we present. You can, for example, take the JavaPool applet in Chapter 4 and easily figure out how to change the color of the pool table and balls, tweak the speed of play, and so on. If you find that this book is really beyond your understanding, buy it anyway and then also buy *Java Programming For Dummies* by Donald J. Koosis and David Koosis (IDG Books Worldwide, Inc.) — no seriously, this book doesn't go into detail about the most basic stuff, so if you've never touched Java before, you may want to start with the Koosis' book.

On the other hand, you experienced programmers can find a whole load of tips and game-specific programming techniques in this book. You can also copy and tweak the code we present, as well as get exposure to many game programming techniques to use in creating your own Java games.

About the Java Code in This Book

All the code examples in this book are coded as Java applets so that they can be used with Java-enabled Web browsers and published on the Web. At the time of this writing, the current release of Java is release 1.1.5 with version 1.2 just appearing as a developer release. Java versions 1.1 and later add many new features, such as a completely new event model, but many Web browsers have yet to fully incorporate these new features. Therefore, the applets in this book are coded to be compatible with the earlier Java 1.0.2 standard so that they work with the widest variety of Web browsers.

How This Book Is Organized

This book is divided into three major parts, each covering a progressively more involved array of game programming techniques. We then include three more elements, each with useful tips and additional information. As with all ...*For Dummies* books, you can pretty much dip in and out of chapters to find information. The only exception is that in some cases, a later section uses material or pieces of code from earlier chapters. We always alert you to these cases when they arise so that you know where to look, and you can always just go to the CD-ROM and pull in the necessary code if you need to.

Part I: Steppin' Out

This part covers the basics of animation and simulation and shows you how to program imaginary objects to obey physical rules, such as momentum, acceleration and rebounding from collisions. In this part, you create a Ping-Pong game, putting green, and pool table while exploring some advanced concepts, such as vector math, in a fun, straightforward way.

Part II: Up to Speed

This next part introduces the techniques you need to create professional-quality games. Moving beyond the simple, solid-colored graphics of Part I,

Part II shows you how to use multicolor images in your games. Starting with a logic puzzle, you progress to a multiplayer blackjack game, master 2-D sprites, and combine sprites with code to generate random mazes and create a maze chase game.

Part III: Seven League Boots

This part moves you beyond the flat world of 2-D games into the realm of 3-D flat-shaded and texture-mapped graphics, and shows you how to create several different styles of 3-D maze games. You also experiment with a variety of advanced game programming techniques, such as using timelines, employing animation scripts, playing sounds, and using the alpha channel to create spectacular image effects — all in 100 percent Java.

Part IV: The Part of Tens

If you've previously read any *...For Dummies* books, you know that this section is intended to pull together a variety of useful facts and other goodies that just don't fit anyplace else. This book includes "Ten Secrets for Making Fun Games," "Ten Ways to Say Game Over" and "Ten Ways to Optimize Your Java Code."

Appendix: About the CD-ROM

The last section in this book contains information on the programs and applets included on the *Java Game Programming For Dummies* CD-ROM.

CD Chapters: Fundamentals

The CD-ROM included with this book contains an additional five chapters of the book in a part called "Fundamentals" which is provided as Adobe Acrobat PDF files on the CD-ROM. These chapters cover many aspects of Java that are particularly useful for game programming, but not necessarily specific to game programming. If you're still new to coding Java and want to brush up on the fine points of applets, threads, graphics, color, user input, or basic HTML, you should check out these chapters. Whenever we discuss topics that rely on information in the CD Chapters, we also include a helpful reference to the appropriate chapter.

Icons Used in This Book

The tip icon marks information that can save you time or keep you out of trouble.

This icon introduces a special technique or programming trick that can help you program games like the pros.

This icon points out Java 1.1 differences from Java 1.02.

This icon points out Java 1.2 differences from Java 1.1 or Java 1.02.

This icon marks important information that you need to understand and use later.

Danger, Will Robinson! Ignore this icon at your own peril because the advice given can often save you from making a serious error. However, with appropriate attention, you'll have smooth sailing ahead.

This icon introduces a technical term that can help you find information on this topic in other reference books. You can also sprinkle these terms into your daily conversation to impress your friends.

This icon refers you to stuff you can find on the *Java Game Programming For Dummies* CD-ROM included at the back of this book.

This icon points out technical details that may be interesting to you, but which are not essential to understanding the topic under discussion.

Part I
Steppin' Out

The 5th Wave — By Rich Tennant

"WE SHOULD HAVE THIS FIXED IN VERSION 2."

In this part . . .

Simulation is at the heart of many computer games because many of them are adapted from games you can play in the real world. Simulation is a tricky subject, though, because you can't put real balls and Ping-Pong paddles into a computer game program. Instead, you have to write code that mimics how these objects act in the real world. Simulation is as much an art as it is a science, and Part I gives you a good solid foundation in both the craft and the technique of simulation.

Chapter 1

Follow the Bouncing Ball

- -

In This Chapter

▶ Making things animate

▶ Modeling motion

▶ Handling boundary collisions

▶ Reducing flicker with double buffering

- -

*M*oving objects across the screen is one of the basic skills you need to create action games. The way you simulate motion in a computer game is fairly simple: First, you break time down into a small unit, such as $1/30$ second. Then, between each tiny tick of time, you move the object a small amount. When you repeat this process quickly enough, the small steps of movement blend together to create the illusion of motion.

This chapter discusses the various details and techniques used for animating and modeling a bouncing ball. The completed applet and applet code is on the *Java Game Programming For Dummies* CD-ROM.

Ticking Off the Time

Java's Thread class lets you easily construct a program that slices time into tiny intervals using method sleep() to rest for specified intervals of time. You create a Thread and then use a loop that alternates between doing something, such as updating the position of your object, and sleeping. The framework code you need to set up this alternation is

```
public class Bounce extends Applet implements Runnable {
  private Thread    ticker;
  private boolean   running = false;

  public void run () {
    while (running) {
      repaint();
```

(continued)

(continued)

```
      try {
        ticker.sleep(1000 / 15);
      } catch (InterruptedException e) { }
    }
  }

  public synchronized void start () {
    if (ticker == null || !ticker.isAlive()) {
      running = true;
      ticker = new Thread(this);
      ticker.setPriority(Thread.MIN_PRIORITY + 1);
      ticker.start();
    }
  }

  public synchronized void stop () {
    running = false;
  }
}
```

This applet extends the `Runnable` interface so that it can start the new `ticker` Thread in the applet's `start()` method. The `start()` method also sets the `boolean` variable `running` to `true` to tell the `run()` method to continue to `sleep()` and loop for as long as `running` remains `true`. When it's time for the animation to stop, the `stop()` method sets `running` to `false` and the `run()` method exits.

If the browser calls the `start()` method again after it has stopped the applet, the `isAlive()` method returns `false` to indicate that the `ticker Thread` is no longer running. In response, the code creates a new `Thread` to restart the animation.

Your animation code needs to respect the applet's life cycle as described in the previous paragraph; otherwise the animation can continue to run — even after the user leaves the page containing your applet — and waste CPU cycles.

The calculation `1000 / 30` inside the call to `sleep()` sets the animation rate for the applet. The `sleep()` method expects to be told how long to sleep in units of 1 millisecond. A millisecond is one 1,000th of a second, so dividing 1,000 by 30 calculates a time in milliseconds that results in the animation repeating roughly 30 times a second.

The previous code example provides the applet with a *heartbeat,* so to speak, to drive the animation. However, the sole task of the timing loop in `run()` is simply to sleep and to call `repaint()`. You need additional code to make the applet compute and display the next step, or `frame`, in the animation.

Making Things Move

The position of an image in two dimensions can be specified with the x and y coordinates of the image. In order to make the image move, you specify an additional set of x and y values that define the amount to add to the image's original position for the next frame; think of these as *delta x* and *delta y* values (the Greek letter delta [Δ] is used in math and physics to indicate the *difference* between two values). You can simply add the proper values of delta x and delta y to the starting x and y position to specify motion in any direction and at any speed.

For example, say you have an image of a ball at point 1,1. If you then specify a delta x value of 1 and a delta y value of 1, the ball would move to position 2,2 for the next frame; 3,3 for the frame after that, and so on. If your delta x value is 2 and your delta y value is 2, the ball moves in the same direction, only twice as fast (or twice as far, depending on how you think about it) for each new frame.

The x and y coordinates in Java use the upper-left corner of the applet screen as the origin (0,0) and describe x and y locations in terms of pixels.

Floating the point

The best way to specify delta x and delta y values is with `float`-type rather than `int`-type values. That way, your objects aren't limited to movement of a whole pixel per frame, nor are they limited to moving in directions that can only be expressed in terms of `int`-type values. Not so long ago, people used fixed point math to do fractional calculations, and many books in print still recommend this practice. However, all modern CPUs now include special floating point calculation features so that using floating point (`float`) values for fractional calculations is quicker.

Encapsulating the essence of a ball

Now that you understand the basics, you're ready to write code to use the ideas presented in this chapter and create a Java class to represent a ball that can move:

```
class Ball {
    public float   x, y, dx, dy;
    private Color  color;
    private int    size;
```

(continued)

(continued)

```
Ball (float x, float y, float dx, float dy, int size,
        Color color) {
    this.x = x;
    this.y = y;
    this.dx = dx;
    this.dy = dy;
    this.color = color;
    this.size = size;
}

public void draw (Graphics g) {
    g.setColor(color);
    g.fillOval((int) x, (int) y, size, size);
}
}
```

The constructor for Ball is straightforward. It simply copies the ball's initial x,y position values, dx,dy delta values, and color and size into the class variables x, y, dx, dy, color, and size, respectively.

Ball also defines a draw() method that you can call to make the ball draw itself to a Graphics context. The code is really not much more than calls to setColor() and fillOval(), but note that the float values x and y must be cast to int in the call to fillOval() to avoid a compile error. Whenever you intentionally reduce the precision of a number, you must use a cast to tell the compiler that you are doing so intentionally.

Setting Bounds

The final thing you need to add to your Ball class is code to keep the ball inside the bounds of the applet's screen area; you can add code that detects when the ball reaches one of the boundaries and then responds by reversing the appropriate delta value. Reversing either the delta x or delta y value reverses the x or y direction of the ball's movement, respectively; doing so at the boundary of the applet makes the ball appear to bounce off the boundary.

The top boundary of an applet is y=0, and the left boundary of an applet is x=0. The width and height of an applet are set by the applet's WIDTH and HEIGHT attributes in the <APPLET> HTML tags used to place the applet, as explained in CD Chapter 1.

Moving out of bounds

If the bouncing ball's x position becomes less than the boundary's x position (x < bounds.x), the ball just collided with the left boundary. If the ball's y position becomes less than the boundary's y position (y < bounds.y), the ball just collided with the top edge. Detecting a collision between the ball and the lower and right edges is only slightly more complicated. The right edge is computed by adding bounds.x to bounds.width. You compare this sum to the ball's x position plus its size (x + size > bounds.x + bounds.width) to check for a collision on the right side. Likewise, you compare the ball's y position plus its size to bounds.y plus bounds.height (y + size > bounds.y + bounds.height) to see if the ball collided with the bottom edge.

Bouncing back

When you detect that the ball's position has moved out of bounds, you need to reverse the sign of dx (if the ball collided with the left or right edges), or dy (if the ball collided with the top or bottom edges). Reversing the sign of dx or dy reverses the ball's movement in the given direction, thus making it appear to bounce back from the collision. However, because you can't catch a collision with a boundary until after the ball has actually moved *out* of bounds, you need to move the ball back in bounds to a spot that makes it appear as if it really bounced off the boundary edge.

After crossing the boundary edge, the ball wants to appear some distance beyond the edge. If the ball had actually bounced off the edge, it would have, instead, moved that same distance back in the other direction. Because a bounce is the action you actually want to create, you need to move the ball from its projected out-of-bounds position to the desired "bounced" position. You do this by moving the ball back by *twice* the distance it traveled out of bounds, as shown in Figure 1-1.

If the ball bounced off the left edge, this distance is 2 * (x - bounds.x). Likewise, if the ball bounced off the top edge, this distance is 2 * (y - bounds.y). When the ball bounces off the right edge, the distance is 2 * ((x + size)-(bounds.x + bounds.width)) and it's 2 * ((y + size) - (bounds.y - bounds.height)) when it bounces off the bottom edge.

Coding movement and bounce

Your next job is to take all these different collision detection and bounce handling calculations and convert them into code. The most convenient place to put this code is in a new method called move() that you can add to your Ball class. Here's the complete code for move():

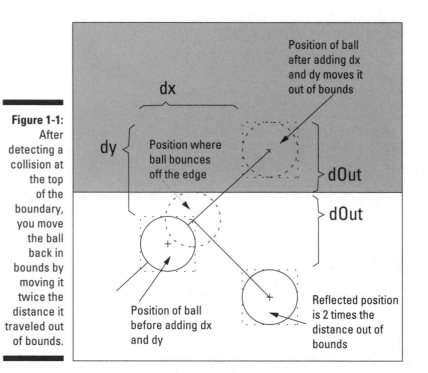

Figure 1-1:
After detecting a collision at the top of the boundary, you move the ball back in bounds by moving it twice the distance it traveled out of bounds.

```
public void move (Rectangle bounds) {
   // Add velocity values dx/dy to position to get
   // ball s new position
   x += dx;
   y += dy;
   // Check for collision with left edge
   if (x < bounds.x && dx < 0) {
      dx = -dx;
      x -= 2 * (x - bounds.x);
   }
   // Check for collision with right edge
   else if ((x + size) > (bounds.x + bounds.width) &&
            dx > 0) {
      dx = -dx;
      x -= 2 * ((x + size) - (bounds.x + bounds.width));
   }
   // Check for collision with top edge
   if (y < bounds.y && dy < 0) {
      dy = -dy;
      y -= 2 * (y - bounds.y);
   }
   // Check for collision with bottom edge
```

```
  else if ((y + size) > (bounds.y + bounds.height) &&
         dy > 0) {
    dy = -dy;
    y -= 2 * ((y + size) - (bounds.y + bounds.height));
  }
}
```

The move() method starts by adding the dx and dy delta values to the ball's x and y position values to update the ball's position. This calculation may move the ball out of bounds, so move() then checks the new position against the left and right bounds and then the top and bottom bounds.

 You may notice that each collision test code case not only checks the ball's position, but also checks to see if dx and dy are less than or greater than zero, depending on the case. This extra bit of checking adds a fail-safe feature to the code that prevents a ball from getting stuck should you accidentally initialize it in a position where it's already colliding with an edge. Without this check, a ball in collision with an edge may not be able to move away from the edge before colliding with the edge again. This would cause the ball's direction to reverse, then reverse again, on and on, forever.

To avoid this problem when checking for a collision with the left edge, the code also verifies that dx is less than zero. Similarly, the code makes sure that dy is less than zero when checking the top edge for a collision. A collision with the right edge requires that dx be greater than zero, and a bottom edge collision makes sure dy is also greater than zero. The code ignores collisions where dx or dy do not match these tests.

Settin' things in motion

Now you're ready to create a Ball object initialized with values that move and bounce it around inside the applet's draw area. You should add the variables as class variables (inside the Bounce class, but not inside a method) and initialize them in the applet's init() method, like this:

```
private Rectangle  bounds;
private Ball       ball;
private int        width, height;

public void init() {
  width = width = size().width;
  height = size().height;
bounds = new Rectangle(width, height);
  // Initialize Ball position and velocity
  ball = new Ball(width / 3f, height / 4f, 1.5f,
              2.3f, 12, Color.blue);
}
```

The new instance of Ball is saved in the variable ball. The starting position for ball is set to an x position that is 1/3 of the way in from the left boundary, and a y position that is 1/4 of the way down from the top boundary. The dx value is set to 1.5f (you add an f suffix to a number in order to create a floating point constant) and the dy to 1.3f. You can initialize the ball's position to any value you choose, but the calculations width/3f and height/4f and the values 1.5f and 1.3f set the ball's position inside the bounds of the applet and start it moving slowly down and to the right.

The init() method also records the applet's size in int variables called width and height. Then, init() uses these values to create a Rectangle object named bounds. The applet later passes the bounds object to Ball's move() method, which uses it to check for collisions with the edges of the applet.

Drawing the Details

The next step is to add code to the applet to draw ball on the screen. Also, just so things aren't too boring, you may want to draw a simple background pattern so that you can more easily see ball move. Here's the code for a paint() method that draws a 2 x 2 checkerboard pattern for the background, animates ball by calling move(), and draws ball into the background by calling draw():

```java
public void paint (Graphics g) {
  if (offscr == null) {
    offscreenImage = createImage(width, height);
    offscr = offscreenImage.getGraphics();
  }
  // Draw checkerboard background
  int x2 = width >> 1;
  int y2 = height >> 1;
  offscr.setColor(Color.gray);
  offscr.fillRect(0, 0, x2, y2);
  offscr.fillRect(x2, y2, width - x2, height - y2);
  offscr.setColor(Color.white);
  offscr.fillRect(x2, 0, width - x2, height - y2);
  offscr.fillRect(0, y2, x2, y2);
  ball.move(bounds);
  ball.draw(offscr);
  g.drawImage(offscreenImage, 0, 0, null);
}
```

Examine this code carefully — it includes a few new things that you may not have seen before, as the following sections explain.

Drawing offscreen

First, much of the code in paint() methods doesn't draw directly to the screen. Notice that the code to draw the background pattern uses a series of setColor() and fillRect() calls that aren't prefixed with the Graphics context g that you normally use. Instead, the paint() method starts by creating an *offscreen Image,* like this:

```
if (offscr == null) {
   offscreenImage = createImage(width, height);
   offscr = offscreenImage.getGraphics();
}
```

You draw into an offscreen Image so that you can construct the entire image, containing the background pattern and the image of the ball (both of which need to be redrawn each frame), before you draw it to the screen. Using an offscreen image helps reduce the flicker that results if you draw the pattern and ball directly to the screen.

Creating an offscreen Image that you can draw to is done in two steps: First, you create an offscreen Image sized the same as the applet, like this:

```
offscreenImage = createImage(width, height);
```

After you have an offscreen Image, you can get a Graphics context for this Image, like this:

```
offscr = offscreenImage.getGraphics();
```

You only need to perform this step once, so you can declare class variables at the top of the applet to hold the reference to these two objects, like this:

```
private Image      offscreenImage;
private Graphics   offscr;
```

The listing for the complete applet on the CD-ROM shows where to place these two variable declarations.

Overriding the flicker

All applets have a method called update() that, by default, clears the screen before paint() is called. In many cases, you want the screen cleared before paint() is called, and so this default behavior can be useful. But, when you use an offscreen Image and then draw this offscreen Image to the screen, the old Image is erased and the new Image is drawn (as you can see by the momentary screen flicker). Because you're drawing over the applet's entire visible area with the offscreen Image, the update() method screen clear is unnecessary.

To remove the screen clear caused by the default version of update(), you write a new update() method in your applet. Your new update() omits the screen clear code and, instead, simply calls paint(), like this:

```
public void update (Graphics g) {
  paint(g);
}
```

Drawing the background and the ball

The code to draw the 2 x 2 checkerboard pattern computes two variables x2 and y2 that are the center points of the offscreen Image. The code then uses the values for x2 and y2 to draw the upper-left and lower-right sections in gray, and the upper-right and lower-left sections in white.

Next, the code calls the methods in Ball to move ball to its new position and draw ball onto the offscreen Image, like this:

```
ball.move(bounds);
ball.draw(offscr);
```

Putting the action on the screen

The final step is to copy this Image onto the screen. Here's the code you need:

```
g.drawImage(offscreenImage, 0, 0, null);
```

Figure 1-2 shows your completed applet in action.

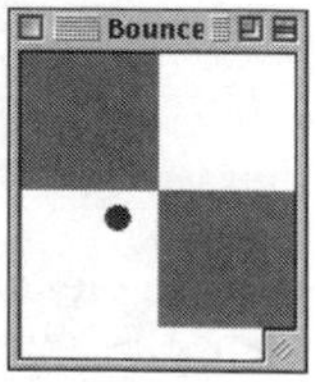

Figure 1-2:
The completed Bounce applet.

The code for your completed applet, with all the details discussed in this chapter filled in, is on the *Java Game Programming For Dummies* CD-ROM.

Chapter 2

Ponglet

In This Chapter

▶ Designing with state

▶ Using the mouse

▶ Keeping score

▶ Creating a computer opponent

*O*ften, the hardest thing to do when creating a computer program is to decide how to organize all its different actions. You know that each separate action is really quite simple by itself, but making them all work smoothly together can be confusing. Fortunately, managing all those program actions is actually fairly easy.

And, to prove it, in this chapter you're going to create your own Ping-Pong applet (Ponglet), complete with mouse controls, score display, and a computer opponent. The techniques you use to work with and organize the different actions in the Ponglet game are equally useful for many other games you may create.

As you go through the examples and read about the techniques presented in this chapter, you may want to follow along with the complete code for the Ponglet applet included on the *Java Game Programming For Dummies* CD-ROM.

Setting State

Imagine that you are a robot, and your job is to perform a series of tasks that take five minutes each, but every six minutes your power is switched off, and you forget everything. However, you have a detailed book of instructions on how to do your job. Each page in the book is organized like this:

Step 1: IMPORTANT: You have only five minutes to complete this task.

Step 2: The description of the task.

Step 3: When task is complete, turn to page *xx*, and wait.

Each time you wake up, you are on the page that you turned to in Step 3 and you see the next task to perform (having now forgotten the wait command), and you do it. Then, by turning to the next page, you set up the next task to perform when you wake up again. The page you select serves to set the *state* of your brain when you wake up. Organizing a task in this fashion is called *state-driven design*.

The key to state-driven design is how the task is organized. The obvious difficulty for the robot is deciding how to break up a complex job into a set of tasks that can each be completed in five minutes or less. The advantage, when you break up a job this way, is that each individual task is so simple that you don't need to keep track of any other details.

Breaking down the task

When you play Ping-Pong, you go through a series of sequential steps. First, your opponent waits for you to get ready. Then, your opponent serves and you scramble to return the serve. Then, your opponent tries to hit your return. This process continues until one player misses. After one player misses, the score of the other player is advanced, and you both get ready for the next round. Finally, after one of you has enough points, the winner of the round is declared, and the victor gets a moment to bask in the glory.

The different steps, or *states,* in a game of table tennis can be described as wait, serve, return, player1 scores, player2 scores, player1 wins, player2 wins. Of course, unlike the robot example earlier in this chapter, the states of the table tennis game can appear in a variety of different sequences as the game is played.

In a computer simulation of table tennis, each state is a separate action that you need to animate, and each animated action takes a different amount of time to complete. For example, the *serve* state lasts until the ball travels down to where the returning player hits or misses the ball.

In the bouncing ball example in Chapter 1, the ball bounces around indefinitely or at least until you stop the applet. So the animation loop consists entirely of code to move the ball and check for collisions. However, in the case of a Ponglet game, there are some states where the ball isn't visible, such as when the ball has moved off the table. Therefore, the code to draw the ball needs to check the current game state before it draws.

One way of structuring all this is to define constants for every possible state and a variable to keep track of what state the game is currently in. Then the code in `paint()` and the control code in `run()` can check the current state to decide what to paint to the screen and what task the game should perform.

The code that goes in run() is going to be the most complex, so you want to think out a clean way to organize it. Using a switch statement turns out to be a nice approach. You can use the current state variable to select which case to execute. This code goes inside a while (running) loop that uses sleep() to set the animation frame rate. Here's the complete run() framework for Ponglet:

```
public void run () {
  while (running) {
    switch (gstate) {
    case WAIT:
      break;
    case SERVE:
      break;
    case RETURN:
      break;
    case PGUTTER:
      break;
    case GGUTTER:
      break;
    case PSCORE:
      break;
    case GSCORE:
      break;
    case PWON:
    case GWON:
      break;
    }
    repaint();
    try {
      ticker.sleep(1000 / 30);
    } catch (InterruptedException e) { ; }
  }
}
```

Note that there is no break between the PWON and GWON states because you want your code to do the same thing for both states. Therefore, when the switch statement selects the PWON state, the code will *fall through* to the GWON state.

The *states* that we discuss in the earlier example of a table tennis game are analogous to the case statements in this code. The key to dealing with these case statements is in the code that you add to complete the case statements (this code is missing here — you add it a little later in this chapter).

This code includes a few new states not mentioned in the table tennis example, such as PGUTTER and GGUTTER. The reason for these particular case statements becomes clear as you work through the sections in this chapter and fill in the missing code.

First, though, here are the definitions for the state constants and the `gstate` variable:

```
private static final int   WAIT = 1;
private static final int   SERVE = 2;
private static final int   RETURN = 4;
private static final int   PGUTTER = 8;
private static final int   GGUTTER = 16;
private static final int   PSCORE = 32;
private static final int   GSCORE = 64;
private static final int   PWON = 128;
private static final int   GWON = 256;
private int                gstate = WAIT;
```

Note that the declaration of the variable `gstate` initializes `gstate` to the value `WAIT`. This is necessary so that the first case that is executed when the `run()` method starts will be the `WAIT` case.

Serving the ball

The `WAIT` state is responsible for serving the ball and then setting `gstate` to `SERVE`. Here's the code you need for the `WAIT` case:

```
case WAIT:
  if (!mouse_in)
    delay = 20;
  else if ( delay < 0) {
    // Serve the ball
    int sLoc = rndInt(table.width - ballSize) +
                      (ballSize >> 1);
    ball = new Ball(sLoc, -ballSize, rnd(5f) + 0.5f,
                    rnd(4f) + 3f, ballSize, Color.blue);
    gstate = SERVE;
    win_show = 100;
    delay = 20;
  }
  break;
```

The test `if (!mouse_in)` checks to see whether the player is ready to play and has moved the mouse pointer into the control area (the area of the applet's screen that tracks the player's mouse movements — more about this later in the section "Entering the control zone"). After the player moves the mouse to the control area, the delay value counts down, and the code in the `else if` block serves the ball.

The value sLoc computes a random location from which to serve the ball, and this value is passed to the constructor for Ball. This code is nearly identical to the Ball class in Chapter 1, except that it only checks for bounces off the left and right bounds. Here's the complete code:

```
class Ball {
  public  float   x, y, dx, dy;
  public  int     size, radius;
  private Color   color;
Ball (float x, float y, float dx, float dy,
        int size, Color color) {

    this.x = x;
    this.y = y;
    this.dx = dx;
    this.dy = dy;
    this.color = color;
    this.size = size;
    radius = size >> 1;
  }

  public void move (Rectangle bd) {
    // Add velocity to position to get new position
    x += dx;
    y += dy;
    // Check for collision with bounding Rectangle
    if ((x < bd.x  &&  dx < 0f)  ||
        ((x + size) > (bd.x + bd.width)  &&  dx > 0f))
      x += (dx = -dx);
  }

  public void draw (Graphics g) {
    g.setColor(color);
    g.fillOval((int) x - radius, (int) y - radius,
            size, size);
  }
 }
 }
```

The code in WAIT that serves the ball also calls two new methods rndInt() and rnd() that generate random int and float values. WAIT uses these methods to generate a random velocity (speed) for the ball and to serve it from a random point along the top edge of the applet window. The rndInt(nn) method generates a random int (integer) between 0 and nn. The rnd(nn) method generates a random float (floating-point value) that is greater than or equal to 0 and less than nn. Here's how you need to write these two methods:

```
public float rnd (float range) {
   return (float) Math.random() * range;
}

public int rndInt (int range) {
   return (int) (Math.random() * range);
}
```

Up Java Creek without a Paddle

Okay — the ball is in motion and headed across the table toward you — time to add code for a Paddle object that you can use to return the serve. Here's the code:

```
class Paddle {
   public int     x, y, width, height;
   private Color  color;

   Paddle (int x, int y, int width, int height,
           Color color) {
      this.x = x;
      this.y = y;
      this.width = width;
      this.height = height;
      this.color = color;
   }

   public void move (int x, Rectangle bd) {
      if (x > (width >> 1)  &&  x < (bd.width - (width >> 1)))
         this.x = x;
   }

   public int checkReturn (Ball ball, boolean plyr,
                           int r1, int r2, int r3) {
      if (plyr  &&  ball.y > (y - ball.radius) ||
          !plyr  &&  ball.y < (y + ball.radius)) {
         if ((int) Math.abs(ball.x - x) < (width / 2  +
                                           ball.radius)) {
            ball.dy = -ball.dy;
            // Put a little  english  on the ball
            ball.dx += (int) (ball.dx * Math.abs(ball.x - x) /
                              (width / 2));
            return r2;
         }
         else
```

```
        return r3;
    }
    return r1;
}

public void draw (Graphics g) {
    g.setColor(color);
    g.fillRect(x - (width >> 1), y, width, height);
}
}
```

Paddle is structured similarly to the Ball class; it has values to record its x and y position, width, height, and Color. However, because Paddle doesn't move on its own, its move() method is called by the mouse input code, as we cover in the "Entering the control zone" section a little later in this chapter.

Returning the serve

The checkReturn() may look a little complicated at first, but its main job is simply to check whether the ball hits the paddle. You use the same code to create a paddle for the player and also for the computer. The boolean parameter plyr is true if checkReturn() is checking the player's paddle; otherwise, it checks the computer's paddle.

The first bit of code in checkReturn() checks to see whether the ball has reached the position on the table where the ball collides with the paddle. The code for the player's paddle is

```
ball.y > (y - ball.radius)
```

and the code for the computer's paddle is

```
ball.y < (y + ball.radius)
```

If the ball is in position to be hit by the paddle, the code checks to see whether the x position of the paddle is correct to connect with the ball. The code for this check is

```
(int) Math.abs(ball.x - x) < (width / 2  + ball.radius)
```

If the ball does connect with the paddle, the code needs to reverse the dy value for the ball to send it back across the table, like this:

```
ball.dy = -ball.dy;
```

However, the game would be pretty boring if the ball simply reversed direction (dy value is reversed) and retraced its original path every time the player's paddle hit the ball. You can add code to tweak the dx value and apply a little *English* to the ball, like this:

```
ball.dx += (int) (ball.dx * Math.abs(ball.x - x) /
                  (width / 2))
```

You can play with the (width / 2) value to change the *feel* of the paddle and how it returns the ball.

Finally, checkReturn() returns one of three different parameter values, r1, r2, or r3, depending on the results of its checks. checkReturn() returns the value that is passed in r1 if the ball hasn't yet reached the paddle, r2 if the ball reached the paddle and the paddle hit the ball, and r3 if the ball reached the paddle but the paddle missed the ball.

Changing state

Now that you've created the Paddle class, you can add code to call it. You need to call it to check the player's paddle when in the SERVE state and to check the computer's paddle when in the RETURN state. Here's the code you need to add to the SERVE case to call checkReturn(). This code goes in the SERVE case in the switch statement because the SERVE case is the case the code will call when gstate equals SERVE.

```
case SERVE:
  // Check for ball in position for player to hit
  gstate = pPaddle.checkReturn(ball, true, SERVE, RETURN,
                              PGUTTER);
  if (gstate == RETURN)
    gPaddle = new Paddle((int) (trackX = width / 2), 3,
                        20, 3, Color.red);
  break;
```

When the player hits the ball, the call to checkReturn() sets gstate to RETURN. If the player missed the ball, gstate is set to PGUTTER. When gstate is set to RETURN, the code also creates a new Paddle object for the computer to use to try and return the ball.

Creating a computer opponent

Time to create a simple computer opponent to play against. You can start out by making the computer fairly easy to beat, but you can easily tweak the program to make the computer harder to beat — it's your choice!

When the player hits the ball, the code in the SERVE case instantiates a paddle for the computer and changes gstate to RETURN. You now need to put code in the RETURN case to control the computer's paddle. Here's that code:

```
case RETURN:
  // Implement our simple-minded computer opponent
  if (Math.abs(gPaddle.x - ball.x) >= 1)
    gPaddle.move((int) (trackX += (gPaddle.x < ball.x ?
                         1.5f : -1.5f)), table);
  // Check for ball in position for game to hit
  gstate = gPaddle.checkReturn(ball, false, RETURN, SERVE,
                         GGUTTER);

  break;
```

The code for the computer opponent simply tries to move the paddle to intercept the ball. However, the computer is limited in how fast it can move the paddle by the two constants 1.5f and -1.5f. These constants are added or subtracted from the paddle position each animation tick in order to make the paddle attempt to track the ball.

Set to 1.5f and -1.5f, the paddle can only move 1.5 pixels per tick in either direction. Make these constants larger if you want your computer opponent to be able to move the paddle faster and, therefore, be a more difficult opponent.

Rolling down the gutter

In the case where the player or the computer misses the ball, you need to wait until the ball moves off the table before serving the next ball. The PGUTTER state waits for the computer's scoring ball to move off the player's side of the table. It then sets gstate to GSCORE to record the score. Here's the code:

```
case PGUTTER:
  // Wait for computer s scoring ball to move off table
  if ((int) ball.y > (table.height + ball.radius))
    gstate = GSCORE;
  break;
The code for GGUTTER is nearly identical:
case GGUTTER:
  // Wait for player s scoring ball to move off table
  if ((int) ball.y < (table.y - ball.radius))
    gstate = PSCORE;
  break;
```

He shoots, he scores!

After scoring a point, the PSCORE case increments the player's score and checks whether the player has scored a total of 10 points (the criteria for declaring a winner). If the player has won, gstate is set to PWON. If the player has not yet reached a score of 10, gstate is set back to WAIT to wait to serve the next ball. Here's the code:

```
case PSCORE:
  // Increment player s score and check if she has won
  gstate = (++pScore >= MAX_SCORE ? PWON : WAIT);
break;
```

This code uses Java's ++ prefix increment operator to advance pScore to the new point before checking to see if pScore has reached MAX_SCORE. If pScore equals MAX_SCORE, the code sets gstate to PWON, else it sets gstate to WAIT.

If the computer scores, the code in the GSCORE case is nearly identical:

```
case GSCORE:
  // Increment computer s score and check if it has won
  gstate = (++gScore >= MAX_SCORE ? GWON : WAIT);
  break;
```

We have a winna!

When the player or the computer wins the game, you need to provide time to bask in the thrill of victory. To provide this time, code in the WAIT case initializes a variable called win_show to a value of 100. The code also counts down win show's value in the code for the PWON and GWON states. The code is the same for both states, so the case statements fall through, like this:

```
case PWON:
case GWON:
  // Delay while we show who won
  if ( win_show < 0) {
    gstate = WAIT;
    gScore = pScore = 0;
  }
```

Tracking User Input

Now that you have constructed the game logic, you need to add code to handle input from the user.

Entering the control zone

First, the game draws a small area at the bottom of the applet that serves as the control area for the mouse. Moving the mouse pointer into this area causes the player's paddle to start tracking the mouse's movement to the left or right. To track when the mouse has moved into this area, you need to override the mouseEnter() method, like this:

```
public boolean mouseEnter (Event evt, int x, int y) {
  pPaddle.move(x, table);
  mouse_in = true;
  return true;
}
```

The call to pPaddle.move(x, table) sets the position of the paddle to match the mouse's x position when mouseEnter() is called. The boolean variable mouse_in is set to true to indicate that the game can start. Code in the paint() method also checks mouse_in so that it knows when to draw the player's paddle.

You also need to override mouseExit() to provide code to set mouse_in to false in case the player moves the mouse out of the control area. This resets the delay counter in the WAIT state so that the game doesn't serve the ball until the player has had a chance to get ready (by moving the mouse back into the control area). Here's the code for mouseExit():

```
public boolean mouseExit (Event evt, int x, int y) {
  mouse_in = false;
  return true;
}
```

Tracking the mouse

Finally, you also need to override the mouseMove() method to update the position of the player's paddle whenever the mouse moves, like this:

```
public boolean mouseMove (Event evt, int x, int y) {
  pPaddle.move(x, table);
  return true;
}
```

Displaying the State

Now you're in the home stretch. Your final task is to add code to draw the Ping-Pong table, the ball, the paddles, the score, and the control area. You can put most of the new code into the paint() method for the applet.

Start with the same framework code that you used to create the bouncing ball example in Chapter 1. You can use the same code from Chapter 1 that draws to an offscreen Image in order to reduce flicker in the animation. You can also borrow the code that draws a checkerboard background image, or you can invent your own creative background pattern.

Here's the borrowed framework code:

```
public void paint (Graphics g) {
  if (offscr == null) {
    offscreenImage = createImage(width, height);
    offscr = offscreenImage.getGraphics();
  }
  // Fill offscreen buffer with a background B/W checkerboard
  int x2 = table.width >> 1;
  int y2 = table.height >> 1;
  offscr.setColor(Color.gray);
  offscr.fillRect(0, 0, x2, y2);
  offscr.fillRect(x2, y2, table.width - x2,
                  table.height - y2);
  offscr.setColor(Color.white);
  offscr.fillRect(x2, 0, table.width - x2,
                  table.height - y2);
  offscr.fillRect(0, y2, x2, y2);
  g.drawImage(offscreenImage, 0, 0, this);
}
```

Your new code goes into the paint() method just before the call to drawImage() at the end of paint().

You also need to initialize a few variables in the applet's init() method to create a font for displaying the score and to handle a few other details for the preceding sections. Here's the code you need to write for init():

```
public void init() {
  width = size().width;
  height = size().height;
  // Set up table and mouse control area dimensions
  table = new Rectangle(width, width);
  msePad = new Dimension(width, height - width);
```

```
    pPaddle = new Paddle(width >> 1, table.height - 6, 20,
                        3, Color.black);
    player = new Point(width - width / 4, 5);
    game = new Point(width / 4, 5);
    // Create offscreen Image
    offscreenImage = createImage(width, height);
    offscr = offscreenImage.getGraphics();
    // Setup text font for displaying the score
    font = new Font( TimesRoman , Font.PLAIN, 14);
    fontMet = getFontMetrics(font);
    fontHeight = fontMet.getAscent();
}
```

Keeping score

Next, you can add code to paint() to draw the score, like this:

```
// Draw Scores
offscr.setFont(font);
centerText(offscr, game, Color.white,    + gScore);
centerText(offscr, player, Color.gray,    + pScore);
```

This code uses a new method called centerText() to center the code on the screen locations given by the Point objects game and player. Here's the code for centerText():

```
private void centerText (Graphics g, Point loc, Color clr,
                        String str) {
  g.setColor(clr);
  g.drawString(str, loc.x - (fontMet.stringWidth(str) / 2,
            loc.y + fontHeight);
}
```

The Point parameter loc specifies a location for centerText() to center the score passed in the String str and draw it in Color clr. The FontMetrics object fontMet is called to compute the width of the string. The value fontHeight is added to the y value of loc so that the string is centered relative to the top center of the text.

Game over?

If the game is over, you need to declare the winner. The following code displays the string "Win" beneath the winning player's score. Add this code after the code to draw the score:

```
if ((gstate & (PWON | GWON)) != 0) {
  Point winner = gstate == GWON ? game : player;
  Point loc = new Point(winner.x, winner.y + 15);
  centerText(offscr, loc, Color.black, Win );
}
```

If the game isn't over, you need code to draw the ball and the paddles. You can add this code to an `else` statement that follows the code to declare a winner:

```
else {
    // Draw ball
  if ((gstate & (SERVE | RETURN | PGUTTER)) != 0)
    ball.draw(offscr);
  // Draw player s paddle
  if (mouse_in || (gstate & (SERVE | RETURN | PGUTTER | GGUTTER))) != 0)
    pPaddle.draw(offscr);
  // Draw computer s paddle
  if (gstate == RETURN)
    gPaddle.draw(offscr);
}
```

Finally, you need to add code to draw the mouse control pad at the bottom of the screen. This code also needs to prompt the player to move the mouse into the control area to start the game, like this:

```
// Fill in mouse pad area
offscr.setColor(Color.yellow);
offscr.fillRect(0, msePad.width, table.width,
                msePad.height);
if (!mouse_in) {
  Point loc = new Point(table.width >> 1, table.height +
                ((msePad.height - fontHeight) >> 1));
  centerText(offscr, loc, Color.black, Move Mouse Here );
}
```

Figure 2-1 shows the completed Ponglet applet in action. You can find the complete code for Ponglet on the *Java Game Programming For Dummies* CD-ROM included with the book.

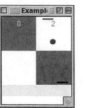

Figure 2-1:
Here's
how the
completed
Ponglet
game looks.

Chapter 3

Hole In One

● ●

In This Chapter

▶ Simulating golf

▶ Making a click-and-drag putt interface

▶ Faking the physics of a ball

● ●

*P*erhaps you play golf as a personal pastime. Or maybe you've putted a few holes of the miniature variety down at the family fun center. If you have, you're in good company: Golf is a hugely popular sport in the United States, around the world, and even off the world. (Golf has the distinction of being possibly the only game played on the surface of the moon, as Alan Shepard did on February 6, 1971, during the Apollo XIV mission. Reportedly, Shepard hit his first shot about 400 yards and then badly shanked his second.)

Golf is also popular as a computer game. Dozens of versions of computer golf have appeared over the years. Some of these games present fanciful versions of the miniaturized game, some bear the names of famous players or golf courses, and some claim to be accurate simulations that model the physics and aerodynamics of real golf.

In this chapter, you won't be tackling anything as lofty as trying to calculate the wind forces on a golf ball in flight. Instead, this chapter's goal is to explore how to simplify the simulation of one aspect of golf, in this case putting, by faking the calculations just well enough to get a result that feels realistic. By the end of the chapter you'll be ready to turn this knowledge into your own HoleInOne applet.

This chapter describes all the techniques used in the HoleInOne applet. The complete code and ready-to-use applet is included on the *Java Game Programming For Dummies* CD-ROM at the back of this book.

Faking physics

Don't be shocked by the idea of faking the calculations for a game. In truth, all calculations that claim to simulate a real phenomenon are really just faking it — you can never take every single variable into account (and even if you do, El Niño is just around the corner). Some calculations just happen to be less fake than others.

Your goal should be to fake (perhaps *simplify* sounds better) the calculations well enough to create a realistic and *fun* golf simulation, while avoiding needless complications.

Think of the unpredictability of a golf ball rolling across a grassy surface. Just a single blade of grass at the edge of the hole could prevent the ball from falling in. But do you really spoil the simulation if you treat the hole as a perfectly round, sharp-edged circle? Naah — it works just fine, as this chapter shows.

Modeling the Deceleration of a Ball

Chapters 1 and 2 show code that simulates a ball that bounces around the screen and that moves at a constant speed. In the real world, balls behave differently. For example, a golf ball starts out moving at a certain speed proportional to how hard it's hit by the putter. And immediately after the ball is hit, it starts to slow down as it travels toward the hole. This slow-down, or more formally, *deceleration,* is the result of a variety of forces acting on the ball, but deceleration of a golf ball is mostly caused by the rolling friction of the grass.

When real objects decelerate (or accelerate), Sir Isaac Newton's famous second law gets involved. Mr. Newton says that the deceleration of a real golf ball is proportional to the forces acting on it divided by the mass of the ball. Simulated golf balls don't have real mass, of course, and they don't have real forces acting on them either, but you do need some type of calculation to *simulate* Sir Newton's law in action.

The code in Chapters 1 and 2 moves the ball by adding values called dx and dy to the ball's x,y position. Therefore, you've certainly deduced that slowing the motion of the ball is going to require you to reduce the dx and dy values. Before you start working out the details, though, you may want to consider *vector math,* a new way to do these types of motion calculations.

Using vectors

A *vector* (not to be confused with the java.util class of the same name) is another name for a pair of dx and dy values. You can think of a vector as representing the difference between two points; the dx and dy values form a vector because they represent the difference between two points along the path of the ball.

You can slow the movement of your golf ball by reducing the distance it travels in each successive animation frame. However, the tricky part is reducing the distance the ball travels without changing the direction it's moving.

If you think of dx and dy as proportional to the length of two sides of a right triangle (see Figure 3-1), the distance a ball travels when you add dx and dy is proportional to the length of the diagonal side of the same triangle. To compute the length of the diagonal you use the formula for the lengths of sides of right triangles, discovered by one Mr. Pythagoras:

$$a^2 + b^2 = c^2$$

Figure 3-1:
Compute the distance between two points dx and dy using a version of the Pythagorean theorem.

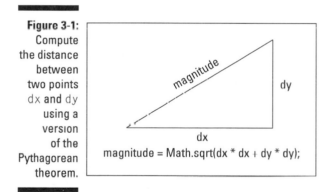

magnitude = Math.sqrt(dx * dx + dy * dy);

By rearranging this formula, you can compute the length of the diagonal as

```
Math.sqrt(dx * dx + dy * dy)
```

The length of a vector's diagonal is commonly called the *magnitude* of the vector.

Vector magnitude is important because it's the key to understanding how to decelerate your golf ball. You can visualize what happens when you reduce the magnitude of a vector by examining the relationship between the three nested triangles in Figure 3-2.

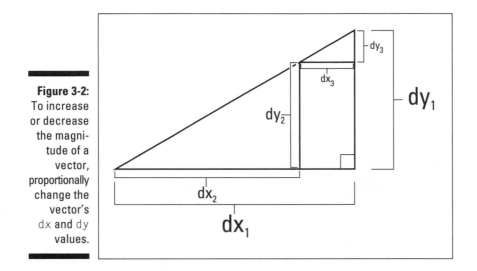

Figure 3-2:
To increase
or decrease
the magni-
tude of a
vector,
proportionally
change the
vector's
dx and dy
values.

The biggest triangle, with sides dx_1/dy_1, has a diagonal that is as long as the other two triangles combined. To reduce the biggest triangle so that it has a diagonal as long as the next smaller triangle, shown with sides dx_2/dy_2, you have to subtract the lengths of the sides of the smallest triangle, dx_3/dy_3, from the sides of dx_1/dy_1.

However, notice that you subtract more from dx_1 than you do from dy_1. If you were to subtract the same amount from dx_1 and dy_2, you would change the *shape* of the triangle rather than just the length of the diagonal (or more specifically, *hypotenuse*). To keep the shape of the triangle the same, you need to maintain the same ratio between the lengths of the sides defined by dx and dy.

The secret to keeping the ratio of dx and dy the same is to divide dx and dy by the magnitude of the vector formed by dx and dy:

```
dx =  dx / Math.sqrt(dx * dx + dy * dy)
dy =  dy / Math.sqrt(dx * dx + dy * dy)
```

Dividing by the magnitude changes dx and dy into a *unit vector* (see the following techno term icon), with values for dx and dy ranging from 0 to 1. The unit vector represents the direction the ball is moving, independent from the ball's speed. And because you divide dx and dy by the same number, you maintain the same ratio between dx and dy and therefore the same direction for the ball. For example, when the ball's movement is completely vertical (dx = 0), the value of dy divided by the magnitude of the vector is 1, *regardless of how fast the ball is moving.*

When you divide a vector's dx and dy values by its magnitude, you get a new type of vector called a *unit vector*. The magnitude of a unit vector is always 1, hence the name. Unit vectors are used extensively in 2-D and 3-D graphics calculations because they can be used to represent a direction independent of speed.

You can also use a unit vector to calculate how to decelerate your ball without altering its direction. First, you calculate a unit vector from the ball's current motion vector. Then, because the magnitude of this unit vector is 1, you can scale it to any size you want by multiplying its dx and dy values by a value that represents the magnitude of the vector you want to create. Then, you simply subtract this vector from your original motion vector, and voilà! you've reduced the speed of the ball while keeping it moving in the same direction.

Creating a vector class

The golf simulation in this chapter uses vectors extensively to do many of the motion calculations, and you need code to perform the basic vector math operations, such as adding one vector to another, computing a unit vector, and so on. So why not bundle up all these methods into a useful new utility class called Vec2D, like this:

```java
public class Vec2D {
  public float  dx, dy;

  public void setVec (float dx, float dy) {
    this.dx = dx;
    this.dy = dy;
  }

  public float mag () {
    return (float) Math.sqrt(dx * dx + dy * dy);
  }

  public void addVec (Vec2D vec) {
    dx += vec.dx;
    dy += vec.dy;
  }

  public void subVec (Vec2D vec) {
    dx -= vec.dx;
    dy -= vec.dy;
  }
```

(continued)

(continued)

```
public void unitVec () {
    float mag = mag();
    setVec(dx / mag, dy / mag);
}


public void mulVec (float scale) {
    setVec(dx * scale, dy * scale);
}
}
```

Vec2D defines internal dx and dy values so that you can create a Vec2D object whenever you need to keep track of a vector quantity. For example, you can create a Vec2D object called vel to control the motion of your golf ball. Then, after you have this Vec2D object, you can call the methods on it, such as setVec() to set the direction and speed of the ball by setting the dx and dy values in vel.

The methods addVec() and subVec() in Vec2D are used to add or subtract one vector from another. You use these methods in the Golf game to apply forces to the moving ball, such as the deceleration effect of friction and the force of gravity acting to push the ball into the hole whenever the ball crosses the edge of the rim.

The method unitVec() converts a vector into a unit vector. You can use this method in combination with mulVec() to proportionally scale the dx and dy values in a vector by the float parameter passed to it by mulVec(). Notice that unitVec() is coded to use the method mag() that returns the magnitude of the vector.

With just these six vector operations, you can simulate all the motion dynamics needed to create a nice putting simulation. So now that you have these code elements ready to go, move on to the next section where we present the code that uses these elements to simulate the golf ball and the hole on the putting green.

Starting from a Circle

Your golf simulation requires code to simulate both a ball and a hole in the putting green. The code for simulating a hole shares many things in common with the code for a ball. For example, to calculate when the ball rolls into the hole, you need code to compute the distance between the hole and the ball. So thinking along object-oriented lines, why not start by creating a common base class called Circle to contain the code that is common to both a hole and a ball?

Creating the `Circle` *class*

Your `Circle` class needs to define `x`, `y`, and `diam` values to store its location and size. It also needs to have a constructor to initialize these values. And to simplify some of the calculations you need to do in your `Ball` class, you need the constructor to initialize a value for the `radius` of the circle. Finally, you need code to compute the distance from one point to another; you can put this code into a method called `dist()`. Here's the complete code for `Circle`:

```
class Circle {
  public float      x, y;
  protected float  radius;
  protected int     diam;

Circle (int x, int y, int diam) {
    this.x = x;
    this.y = y;
    radius = (float) (this.diam = diam) / 2;
  }

  protected float dist (Circle loc) {
    float xSq = loc.x   x;
    float ySq = loc.y - y;
    return (float) Math.sqrt((xSq * xSq) + (ySq * ySq));
  }
}
```

Building a `Ball` *by extending* `Circle`

Next, you can extend `Circle` to create a new class called `Ball`. You put code in `Ball` essentially to do the same thing as the bouncing ball in Chapter 1, but you can use your new `Vec2D` class (see "Creating a vector class," earlier in this chapter) to do the motion calculations. The new features in `Vec2D` also help you handle decelerating the ball as it moves. You can start by declaring the basic class, like this:

```
class Ball extends Circle {
  public Vec2D      vel = new Vec2D();
  private Vec2D     tvec = new Vec2D();
  public boolean    sunk = false;

  Ball (int x, int y, int diam) {
    super(x, y, diam);
  }
}
```

In addition to the constructor, this code defines two Vec2D objects: vel and tvec. The code for the Golf game uses vel to hold the ball's dx and dy values and tvec as a temporary variable to do your deceleration calculations. You use the boolean flag sunk to keep track of when the ball falls into the hole. In addition, you use sunk in both Ball's draw() method and in the code you write to implement the hole.

Decelerating the ball

The next job to tackle is the code to handle decelerating the ball. You use this code in two different places, so you may as well put it into its own method called decel(). decel() takes a single parameter called val that specifies the amount you want to subtract from the vector's magnitude.

Your decel() code needs to start by checking that the magnitude of the ball's vel vector isn't less than val. If vel is less than val, the ball has slowed so much that if you were to further slow down the ball by subtracting the amount in val from vel, the ball would start to roll backward. To avoid having the ball roll backward, you can simply set the vel vector to zero. However, if the magnitude is greater than or equal to val (meaning that the ball has not yet rolled to a stop), you can go ahead and do the deceleration calculation, like this:

```
public void decel (float val) {
  if (val >= vel.mag())
    vel.setVec(0, 0);
  else {
    tvec.setVec(vel.dx, vel.dy);
    tvec.unitVec();
    tvec.mulVec(val);
    vel.subVec(tvec);
  }
}
```

The deceleration code starts by initializing a temporary Vec2D object called tvec. It initializes by calling setVec() and passing vel's dx and dy values, which gives you a copy of vel in tvec.

Next, you call the unitVec() method to convert tvec into a unit vector. Then you call mulVec() to shrink this vector down to the same magnitude as val. Finally, you subtract this scaled vector from vel by calling subVec().

Moving the ball

Now that you've conquered deceleration, you can write the code to implement Ball's move() method. This method is the one your applet calls to advance the ball's position on each frame of the animation. Your move() method takes two parameters: The first parameter, bd, specifies the bounds of the applet. You need bd to detect when the ball needs to bounce off the edges of the applet so that it doesn't roll out of the applet's play field.

The second parameter, friction, specifies how much to decelerate the ball for each frame of animation. You use friction to call decel() in order to update the ball's deceleration, like this:

```
decel(friction);
```

Calling decel() updates vel to account for deceleration, after which you can add vel to the ball's position to move the ball. You need to modify the ball's position in one other place in your code, so you may as well create a method in Ball for this purpose: You can call it addPos(). addPos() needs to take a Vec2D object as its input parameter. When you call addVec(), addVec() should add the dx and dy values in the vector to the ball's position, like this:

```
public void addPos (Vec2D vel) {
   x += vel.dx;
   y += vel.dy;
}
```

After you code addVec(), you can add the code to move() to call it, like this:

```
addPos(vel);
```

Staying in bounds

After advancing the ball, move() must check whether the ball has moved out of bounds, which move() does by comparing the ball's position to the bd parameter. (bd, remember, is the bounds of the applet.) The code to do this comparison is nearly identical to the code in the "Bouncing back" section of Chapter 1, except that you add the decel() in order to slow the ball's movement when it bounces off an edge, like this:

```
boolean hitEdge;
if (hitEdge = (x < bd.x + radius ||
              (x + radius) > (bd.x + bd.width)))
```

(continued)

(continued)

```
   x += (vel.dx = -vel.dx);
if (hitEdge |= (y < bd.y + radius ||
                (y + radius) > (bd.x + bd.height)))
   y += (vel.dy = -vel.dy);
if (hitEdge)
  decel(vel.mag() * .8f);
```

You use the boolean flag hitEdge to signal that the ball has bounced off a vertical or horizontal edge. Then, you use the decel() method to reduce the ball's speed by 80 percent after a rebound by multiplying vel's current magnitude by .8.

Putting the ball

You also need to add code to Ball to support a mouse-driven, click-and-drag putt interface. Using this interface, the player can click on the ball to select it. Then, while holding down the mouse button, the player can drag the mouse cursor back in the direction opposite from the hole, as shown in Figure 3-3. Doing so draws a rubber-band line from the mouse's current position to the ball. The player can then use this line to aim a putt. The player makes the putt by releasing the mouse button. The length of the rubber-band line when the button is released indicates the force of the putt.

Figure 3-3:
The golf
game
interface
uses a
rubber-
band style
display to
control the
direction
and force
of a putt.

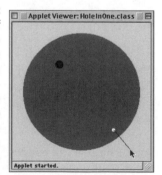

Selecting the ball

The Ball class needs several methods to support this interface. First, you need a method called touches() to detect when the user clicks the ball:

```
public boolean touches (int mx, int my) {
   return (new Circle(mx, my, 0)).dist(this) < radius;
}
```

When you call `touches()`, you pass it two `int` parameters called `mx` and `my` to indicate where the user clicked. You use these values to create a new `Circle` object located in the spot where the user clicked. Then you can call `Circle`'s `dist()` method to calculate the distance from this point to the center of the ball. If this distance is less than the ball's `radius`, `touches()` returns `true`, indicating that the user has clicked the ball.

Executing the putt

To actually make a putt, your applet calls a method in `Ball` called `putt()` and passes it a `Point` object called `ptr` that indicates the location of the mouse when the mouse button is released. `Point` is a class in `java.awt`. Creating a `Point` object (in this example, `ptr`) is a convenient way to pass x,y values as a single parameter. Using these values, `putt()` calls `setVec()` to set the ball's `vel` variable in order to put the ball in motion. Here's the code for `putt()`:

```
public void putt (Point ptr) {
  vel.setVec((x - ptr.x) / 20, (y - ptr.y) / 20);
}
```

Notice that the speed of the putt is defined as the difference between the mouse's position and the ball's position, divided by 20. Dividing by 20 provides greater resolution for aiming the putt without imparting too much force to the ball. However, you can adjust this value to suit your own preferences.

Waiting for the ball to go in

You need a final method to support the putting interface: `moving()`. The Golf applet calls `moving()` in order to check the `dx` and `dy` values in `vel` and returns `true` if the ball is currently in motion. Your interface code can use this method to prevent the player from trying to select the ball while it is still in motion from the last shot. Here's the code:

```
public boolean moving () {
  return vel.dx != 0  || vel.dy != 0;
}
```

Drawing the ball

The last bit of code you need to add to `Ball` is a `draw()` method. To add a nice 3-D effect, you can code `draw()` to put a shadow beneath the ball. You can create a shadow by drawing a dark gray circle offset two pixels down and to the right of the ball.

Fictitious Force?

If you tie a rock to a string and whirl it around your head you can demonstrate *centrifugal* force. However, centrifugal force isn't really a force at all. You are merely seeing the result of the ball's inertia as it orbits around your head. However, for the sake of convenience, you pretend that a real force is pulling on the rock. This type of pretend force is called, appropriately, a *fictitious force*.

Why invent a fictitious force? Well, sometimes simulating a fictitious force is easier than computing all the effects of real forces — such is the case for your golf simulation. There isn't a real force that pulls the ball toward the center of the hole, but the calculations get a lot simpler if you pretend such a force exists.

The shadow needs to be drawn before the ball; however, you don't want a shadow when the ball is in the hole. You can check the state of the sunk flag to see whether the ball is in the hole, and if so, not draw the shadow. Also, when the ball is in the hole, it looks better to draw it in light gray in order to simulate the darkness of looking down into a real golf hole. Here's the code for draw():

```
public void draw (Graphics g) {
  if (!sunk) {
    g.setColor(Color.darkGray);
    g.fillOval((int) (x - radius) + 2,
               (int) (y - radius) + 2, diam, diam);
  }
  g.setColor(sunk ? Color.lightGray : Color.white);
  g.fillOval((int) (x - radius), (int) (y - radius),
             diam, diam);
}
```

Digging a Hole

Now that you have code (the Ball class) to simulate the golf ball, the next step is to create code for the hole in the form of a Hole class. Hole is a little trickier to create than Ball because the physics of how a real golf ball interacts with a real hole are far from simple. However, by using your new Vec2D code and by faking the calculations, you can get nice results without too much work.

Hole, just like Ball, extends from Circle. Inside Hole you can write a constructor that sets the position and size of the hole. Hole also requires a temporary vector for its calculations, so you can go ahead and declare a Vec2D object called tvec for this purpose. And because the draw() method for Hole is so simple, you can go ahead and write it, too:

```java
class Hole extends Circle {
  Vec2D    tvec = new Vec2D();

  Hole (int x, int y, int diam) {
    super(x, y, diam);
  }

  public void draw (Graphics g) {
    g.setColor(Color.black);
    g.fillOval((int) (x - radius),
               (int) (y - radius), diam, diam);
  }
}
```

Gravitating toward the center

When the ball is sailing across the green, nowhere near the hole, the hole has no influence on the motion of the ball. However, when the ball strays close enough to the edge of the hole, gravity, using the hole as a lever, tries to push the ball into the hole. If the ball is moving fast enough and is at a sufficient distance from the hole's center, the ball escapes the force pulling it in. If not, gravity wins, and the ball is captured, spinning around futilely at the bottom of the hole until it slows to a stop.

The force of gravity normally can only push a ball down against the grass. However, when the center of gravity of the ball is inside the radius of the hole, the force of gravity gets redirected by the lip of the hole and creates a *fictitious* force that seems to push the ball toward the center of the hole. In your simulated golf game, this happens whenever the distance from the center of the ball to the center of the hole is less than the radius of the hole, as shown in Figure 3-4.

If you were to more closely simulate the forces acting on the ball, you'd have to consider that the fictitious force acting on the ball changes as the ball moves closer toward the center of the hole. This happens because the edge acts like a ramp that gets steeper and steeper as the ball topples into it. You could add code to simulate this, but you don't need to be this precise in order to get a realistic result. The important part is that the ball reacts as if a force is pushing it toward the center of the hole.

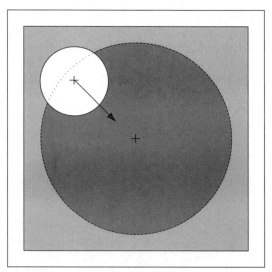

Figure 3-4:
Gravity
pushes the
ball down
against the
edge of the
hole, which
acts like
a fictitious
force
pushing the
ball toward
the center.

Vectoring in

When you animate the ball by adding the `vel` vector to the ball's position, you use `vel` to simulate the force of the putter acting on the ball and the ball's resulting momentum pushing it in a particular direction. The fictitious force pushing the ball to the center of the hole can also be represented by a vector. However, the effect of the hole doesn't replace `vel`'s effect on the ball. Instead, the hole's effect gets added to `vel` and changes the direction of the force created by the ball's momentum.

You can simulate the effect of combining two different forces by adding the vectors that represent those two forces. And, as Figure 3-5 shows, when you add two vectors, you get a new vector that represents their combined forces. The new vector can have a greater magnitude than the two vectors you add, or it can produce a vector that has an equal or lesser magnitude, depending on the values of the two vectors you add.

Curving around the hole

In the case of a fast moving ball that only grazes the edge of the hole, the fictitious force acting to push the ball into the hole is much weaker than the force of the ball's momentum. So the combined force only manages to deflect the ball's path. However, because the fictitious force deflects the ball in the direction of the hole's center, the force keeps on pushing on the ball as long as it stays near the hole. As Figure 3-6 shows, even this weaker force can manage to redirect the ball's path into one that curves around the lip of the hole. And this curved path may even move the ball closer to the center of the hole and wind up causing the ball to spiral in. If not, the ball's path eventually leads away from the hole, and the ball travels off in a new direction.

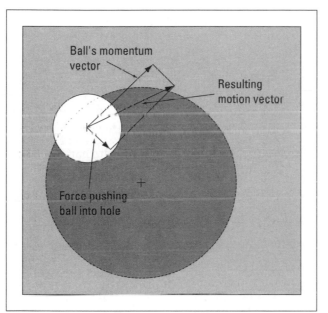

Figure 3-5:
The result of adding two vectors is a new vector that combines the effects of the original two.

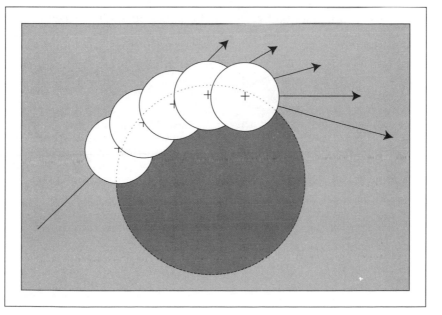

Figure 3-6:
If the distance and speed are correct, the combination of the force pushing the ball into the hole and the ball's motion can cause the ball to follow a curved path around the hole.

Coding the curve

Now that you've got the theory down, you're ready to start converting it into real code. You can start by adding a method to Hole called influence() in which you put the code that computes the fictitious force acting to push the ball into the hole. You also need to put code in influence() to detect when the ball has been captured by the hole, and in turn set the sunk flag to true. Also, although not strictly necessary, it's fun to add code that simulates the effect of a sunk ball bouncing around in the hole until it settles to a stop.

Your influence() code starts by computing two values to which you need to refer in several places in the code. The first value, distIn, must be set to the radius of the hole minus the radius of the ball. The second value, hbDist, must be set to the distance from the center of the ball to the center of the hole; you can determine this distance by calling the Circle method dist(). These values are used to determine if the ball has strayed close enough to the hole that the fictitious force should begin acting on it.

If the hbDist is less than the radius of the hole and greater than distIn, then the fictitious force should act on the ball. If hbDist is greater than the radius of the hole, then the ball's center of gravity is not inside the diameter of the hole, and the fictitious force has no effect on the ball. If hbDist is less than distIn, then the ball has fallen completely into the hole and is no longer in contact with the lip of the hole, so the fictitious force should stop acting on the ball.

Pushing to the center

Whenever the fictitious force is acting on the ball, you can simulate its effect by computing a unit vector that points from the ball's center to the center of the hole. You can use the Vec2D object tvec to do the computation, like this:

```
tvec.setVec(x - ball.x, y - ball.y);
tvec.unitVec();
```

You can then multiply this unit vector by some number in order to increase or decrease the force of gravity pulling the ball into the hole, but the force of the unchanged unit vector turns out to be just about right for this simulation. So you can use addVec() to add this new vector to the ball's momentum vector vel, like this:

```
ball.vel.addVec(tvec);
```

Sinking the putt

Next, you need to add the code that detects when the ball is sunk. At its heart, this check looks to see whether the distance from the ball's center to the hole's center (hbDist) is less than the radius of the hole minus the radius of the ball (distIn). But for a little extra realism, you want to first make sure that the ball isn't moving too fast to simply skip *over* the hole. Skipping over is what a real ball does, even if it is hit to the dead center of the hole.

You can check for a reasonable speed by comparing the magnitude of vel to the hole's radius. This comparison isn't a precise calculation, but it works reasonably well. The result of these checks set the ball's sunk flag, like this:

```
ball.sunk |= ball.vel.mag() < radius && hbDist < distIn;
```

The code sets the radius of the hole at 15 pixels, so if the magnitude of the ball's movement vector is greater than or equal to 15, then the ball is moving too fast to go in.

Spinning in the hole

Even after the ball drops into the hole, the ball's momentum vector still tries to make it move. A real golf ball bounces off the sides of the hole, but your Hole class doesn't yet include any code to simulate this. So unless you add more code, the Java golf ball would simply keep moving as if the hole weren't there.

The way you can simulate a ball bouncing off the inside of a circular hole is similar to the approach you use in the section "Staying in bounds" in order to make the ball bounce off the edges of applet's display area (see Chapter 1). In effect, you wait until the ball has moved outside the bounds of the hole and then compute a new location and path for the ball that mimics the path the ball would have taken if it had bounced off the sides of a real hole.

The first step tests whether the ball has been sunk. If it has, the code needs to check whether the ball has moved beyond the bounds of the hole:

```
if (ball.sunk && hbDist > distIn) {

}
```

Next, you need to write code to go between the { } brackets to calculate the position to which the ball should move after it bounces off the sides of the hole. You also need to calculate the new direction the ball will be moving after this bounce and change the ball's vel vector to make the ball move in that new direction. The calculations to do this so that the movement is modeled on the real life behavior of a ball can get quite complex. However, because this effect is only for show, you can just fake it.

Step one in faking it is to update the ball's velocity vector `vel` to simulate a bounce off the sides. A real ball bounces off the sides of a hole on a path that is related to the angle between the point where the ball touches the side of the hole and a radial line between the center of the hole and this point. However, just calculating the point of intersection requires more math than you need to use here.

Instead, you can simply compute a vector to apply a force to the ball that pushes it back toward the center of the hole by an amount proportional to the distance the ball has strayed outside the hole. Here's the code:

```
tvec.setVec(x - ball.x, y - ball.y);
tvec.mulVec((hbDist - distIn) / hbDist);
ball.vel.addVec(tvec);
```

You also need to update the ball's position to make it appear that it bounced off the sides. Again, you can resort to sheer fakery by simply moving the ball back toward the center of the hole by an amount proportional to how far the ball moved beyond the bounds of the hole. Here's the code:

```
tvec.setVec(x - ball.x, y - ball.y);
float m2 = tvec.mag() - distIn;
tvec.unitVec();
tvec.mulVec(m2);
ball.addPos(tvec);
```

Coding the `HoleInOne` *Applet*

Now that you've accomplished the hard part — that of writing the code that simulates the ball and the hole — the code to complete the applet is a straightforward exercise. You mostly need to fill in the details that follow from the work you've already done in Chapters 1 and 2. For example, you need to create a `run()` method and `Thread` to handle the animation. The complete code is on the CD-ROM included with this book, so you can look there if you've forgotten any details.

Completing the putting interface

You still need to add the applet side of the code in order to complete the rubber-band putting interface. As discussed in the earlier section "Putting the ball," your code must use a `Point` object to record the position of the mouse and pass it to the `putt()` method in `Ball`. And you need to override the applet methods `mouseDown()`, `mouseDrag()`, and `mouseUp()` to implement the full mouse interface. Here's the complete code for these three methods:

```
public boolean mouseDown (Event evt, int x, int y) {
  if (ball.sunk) {
    ball = new Ball(x, y, BALL_SIZE);
    repaint();
  }
  if (!ball.moving()  &&  (select = ball.touches(x, y))) {
    putt = new Point(x, y);
    repaint();
  }
  return true;
}

public boolean mouseUp (Event evt, int x, int y) {
  if (select) {
    ball.putt(putt);
    repaint();
  }
  select = false;
  return true;
}

public boolean mouseDrag (Event evt, int x, int y) {
  if (select) {
    putt = new Point(x, y);
    repaint();
  }
  return true;
}
```

Drawing the green

You can customize the code you write for the applet's `paint()` method so
that it draws the green in any shape you desire, but here's code that draws a
simple circular green. This code also includes the code to draw the rubber-
band, putt-control line:

```
public void paint (Graphics g) {
  if (offscr == null) {
    offscreenImage = createImage(width, height);
    offscr = offscreenImage.getGraphics();
  }
  offscr.setColor(roughColor);
  offscr.fillRect(0, 0, width, height);
  offscr.setColor(greenColor);
```

(continued)

(continued)

```
    offscr.fillOval(gap / 2, gap / 2, width - gap,
                    height - gap);
  hole.draw(offscr);
  ball.draw(offscr);
  if (select) {
    offscr.setColor(Color.black);
    offscr.drawLine((int) ball.x, (int) ball.y,
                    (int) putt.x, (int) putt.y);
  }
  g.drawImage(offscreenImage, 0, 0, this);
}
```

The complete code for HoleInOne is included on the *Java Game Programming For Dummies* CD-ROM at the back of this book.

Chapter 4

JavaPool

● ●

In This Chapter

▶ The mathematics of detecting collisions

▶ Simulating pool

▶ Modeling billiard ball physics

● ●

The game of billiards certainly appeals to barflies and pool hustlers still eyein' the color of the next guy's money. It also appeals to physicists because it demonstrates, in a fun way, some of the basic laws that make the universe work. For example, when a billiard ball smacks, dead center, into another billiard ball, the moving ball comes to a complete stop. The second ball steals the first ball's momentum and travels off at nearly the same velocity as the first ball — basic physics demonstrated with elegant simplicity.

This chapter shows you how to create a simplified game of billiards in Java. However, the main point of this chapter is to introduce you to the art and science of *collision detection*. Because of the math involved, programmers often regard collision detection as one of the more difficult problems lurking in game design. However, the goal of this chapter is to get you past the math and down to useful techniques that you can use to get results.

This chapter also shows you how to simulate the physical laws that control how one billiard ball bounces off another. Simulating billiards and programming collision detection requires a bit of math, but don't panic; the math isn't that hard to use, even if you don't understand all the physics behind it. In the end, all equations turn back into Java code so that only your computer has to worry about them.

This chapter largely deals with the concepts you need to understand to write code that can detect and handle collisions. The full code for the applet described in this chapter is contained on the *Java Game Programming For Dummies* CD-ROM.

Calculating Ball-to-Ball Collisions

Chapters 1 and 3 show you how to simulate balls that move, bounce off fixed boundaries, and fall into holes on a simulated golf green. However, simulating the interaction of billiard balls is a little more complicated because billiard balls bounce off *each other,* not just static boundaries or holes. This is tricky to simulate because you have to compute both the exact moment when two balls collide and the exact point at which they touch in order to simulate properly the rebound from the collision.

Passing in the night

Before you think *too* much about billiard balls, start by imagining two ocean liners sailing across the sea. One liner is heading in a northeast direction and the other is heading in a southeast direction. Further, the path each is traveling crosses the other's path at some distance in front of their present locations.

If both ships are the same distance from this intersection (crossing point) and if both ships are traveling at the same speed, it's obvious that the two ships arrive at the intersecting point at exactly the same time. In other words, the ships are on a collision course (man the lifeboats).

If one ship is just a ship's length closer or farther from the point of intersection, the two ships won't collide. Instead, the closer ship passes the intersection point, just as the other ship arrives at it. The passengers scream, but the ships don't collide. Likewise, if one ship travels sufficiently slower or faster than the other, the two ships don't collide because the faster ship clears the intersection point before the slower ship arrives.

In between the possibility of one ship passing the intersection point before the other arrives and a full on collision, is a tiny window of time where the slower or more distant ship reaches the intersection point before the other ship completely passes it. Exactly when the slower or more distant ship arrives determines where it hits the other ship. If it arrives at nearly the same time as the other ship arrives, it rams into the front of the other ship. If the slower, or more distant ship arrives just slightly before the other ship passes the intersection point, it clips the rear of the other ship.

Reducing the distance

As the two ships approach the point where their paths cross, the distance between the two ships gets smaller and smaller. Conversely, after one of the ships passes the intersection point, the distance between the ships starts to increase. All this decreasing and increasing of distance means that there must be a point in time at which the distance between the ships is as small as it's going to get.

If this distance is small enough, both ships will try to sail into the same place at the same time and means that the ships are doomed to collide. However, if this distance is large enough, both ships can pass without a collision. In between these two distances, you need to know the shape and size of each ship in order to calculate how close the ships can pass before risking a collision.

You see the obvious parallel between ships on an ocean and billiard balls on a pool table, of course. However, unlike ships, billiard balls are spheres of the same size, and calculating how close two billiard balls can get to each other without colliding is much easier than a ship shape. Because real billiard balls are never exact spheres, this distance, measured from the center of one ball to the center of the other, is just a hair larger than twice the radius of a billiard ball. However, for your pool simulation you can simplify this to simply twice the radius.

Calculating position over time

Imagine a billiard ball rolling across the felt surface of a real pool table at a constant speed. Then, imagine a ruler lying on the table parallel to the path of the billiard ball, as shown in Figure 4-1. At time zero, the ball is at position 1 on the diagram, and the ball is moving at a speed that carries it to position 4 one second later. Therefore, you know that in 1/4 second, the ball arrives at position 2 and in 1/2 second, the ball reaches position 3. In other words, the distance the ball travels is proportional to time.

If you know the position of the ball at any two points and you also know the time it takes for the ball to travel between those two points, you can calculate the position of the ball at any point in time. For example, suppose that you know that the coordinates for the ball when it is in position 1 are x=10 and y=20 and that the coordinates for the ball when it is at position 2 are x=12 and y=17. You know that it takes 1/4 second for the ball to travel from position 1 to position 2, and you also know that it takes 1 full second for the ball to travel from position 1 to position 4. This means that in 1/4 second, the x value of the ball's position increases by 2 and the y values decreases by 3. In one full second, the x value increases by 8 (4×2) and the y value decreases by 12 (4×3.) Therefore, in one second, the ball reaches coordinates x=18, y=7.

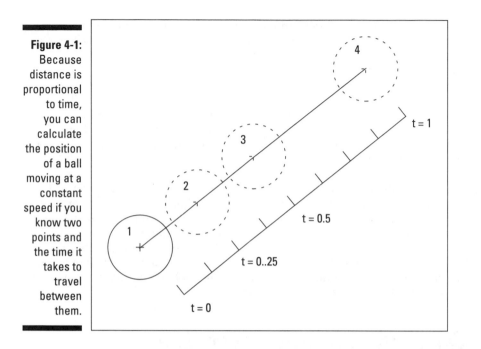

Figure 4-1:
Because
distance is
proportional
to time,
you can
calculate
the position
of a ball
moving at a
constant
speed if you
know two
points and
the time it
takes to
travel
between
them.

When you animate a moving ball, you add dx and dy to the ball's x and y position values at each tick of the animation. This means that in one animation tick, the ball moves from coordinate x, y to coordinate x + dx, y + dy. Therefore, in three ticks of the animation clock, the ball moves to coordinate x + 3 × dx, y + 3 × dy. If you replace a specific number of ticks with the variable t to represent any number of animation ticks, you can easily write equations for x and y to calculate the position of the ball at a new point in time nx, ny like this:

nx = x + dx × t;

ny = y + dx × t;

Calculating the distance to a collision

Chapter 3 covers using the relationship $a^2 + b^2 = c^2$ (the Pythagorean Theorem) to calculate the distance between two points. You may recall that the distance between two points point1 and point2 is the square root of $(point1.x - point2.x)^2 + (point1.y - point2.y)^2$. This formula is called the *distance formula*. Now that you know how to calculate the position of a moving ball over time, you can use this formula to compute the distance between two moving balls, b1 and b2, over time.

Ball b1's current position is given by b1.x, b1.y, and ball b2's current position is given by b2.x, b2.y. For each animation tick, ball b1 adds b1.dx to its x position and b1.dy to its y position. Likewise, ball b2 adds b2.dx and b2.dy to its x and y position. Therefore, the x and y coordinates of ball b1 at point t in time is x = b1.x + b1.dx × t, y = b1.y + b1.dy × t and the coordinate for ball b2 at the same point in time is x = b2.x + b2.dx × t, y = b2.y + b2.dy × t.

Combining the formula to compute the distance between two points and the formulas for the position of balls b1 and b2 over time produces this formula that computes the distance d between ball b1 and b2 at time t:

$$d = sqrt((b1.x + b1.dx \times t) - (b2.x + b2.dx \times t))^2 +$$

$$sqrt((b1.y + b1.dy \times t) - (b2.y + b2.dy \times t))^2$$

Think of this equation as a formula for computing *distance over time*. It's a rather large formula, but it's really just an expanded form of the distance formula listed at the start of this section. The difference is that the expression (b1.x + b1.dx × t) replaces p1.x in the original formula, (b2.x + b2.dx × t) replaces p2.x, (b1.y + b1.dy × t) replaces p1.y, and (b2.y + b2.dy × t) replaces p2.y.

Using this formula, you can take any two moving balls and calculate the distance between them at any future point in time. For example, you can use this formula to see whether two balls collide in the next tick of the animation clock by computing the distance and checking whether it is less than twice the radius of the balls.

However, using the formula in this fashion isn't a foolproof solution. For example, Figure 4-2 shows the paths of two moving balls. Ball A moves from A1 to A2 in one tick of the animation clock, and ball B moves from B1 to B2. The distance between the balls at A1/B1 isn't close enough to collide, and the same is true at A2/B2. As Figure 4-2 shows, the two balls should have collided at the position shown by the dotted outlines. However, the code can fail to detect this if it only checks for collisions at fixed time intervals.

You can try to solve this "missed collision" problem by using a loop to check the distance between the two balls at points in time even closer together than a single animation tick. However, unless you were to loop until you were checking extremely tiny distances, computing the exact time one ball hits another would be difficult. You need to know the exact time to calculate the exact location of each ball when the collision happens. If you don't know the exact position of both balls at the moment of collision, you can't properly calculate the result of the collision. Even a small error in position can make a big difference in the direction and speed of the balls after the collision.

Figure 4-2:
Some
potential
collisions
would take
place
between
the time
intervals
used to
animate
movement,
which
results in
the collision
being
missed.

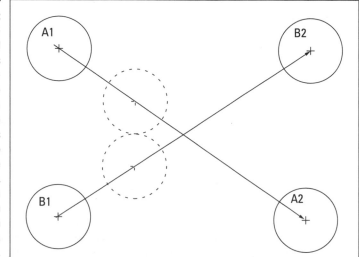

Solving for time

If you still remember any high-school algebra, you probably recall that formulas — like the one presented in the previous section for computing distance over time — can be rearranged to solve for specific values. From the position, direction, and velocity information for two objects at a specified time, the distance-over-time formula calculates the distance separating the two objects.

You already know that the only distance you care about is the distance at which two balls collide, which is twice a ball's radius. So what you want is an equation that assumes d = radius × 2 and solves for time.

Two solutions?

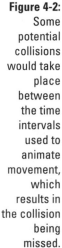

Although your algebra may be a bit too rusty to figure out how to solve the distance-over-time equation for time, some quite sophisticated computer programs are available that can do it for you. One such program, Mathematica 3.0 from Wolfram Research (www.mathematica.com), takes only a few seconds to figure out the correct solution. With the solved equation, you can spend time working on your code rather than digging through your old math textbooks.

However, before you start examining this equation, you need to know that it actually has *two* possible solutions that solve for time when d = radius × 2, as demonstrated in Figure 4-3.

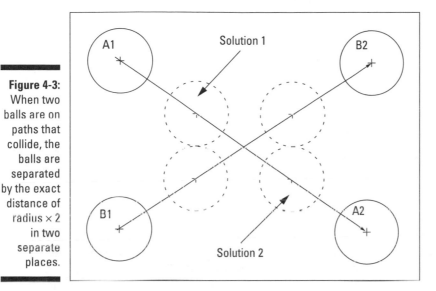

Figure 4-3:
When two
balls are on
paths that
collide, the
balls are
separated
by the exact
distance of
radius × 2
in two
separate
places.

In Figure 4-3, ball A is moving from A1 to A2, and ball B is moving from B1 to B2. As the balls approach the intersection point, the distance between the balls becomes equal to radius × 2 at the point marked *Solution 1*. However, as Figure 4-3 shows, at another place on the path marked as *Solution 2*, the distance between the balls is also equal to radius × 2. Physically, only Solution 1 makes any sense because the balls collide at that point and can never reach the position for Solution 2 unless they pass through one another. Solution 2 is a perfectly valid mathematical solution, it just doesn't make sense for a pair of solid billiard balls.

Rearrange the equation

To solve the distance-over-time formula for t, you first rearrange the equation into a *polynomial equation* of the form

General
form of a
polynomial
equation.

$$a \times t^2 + b \times t + c = 0$$

Rearranging the distance-over-time formula into a fully expanded polynomial form produces

The distance-over-time formula from the previous section, expanded here into the general polynomial form.

$$\left((b1.x - b2.x)^2 + (b1.dy - b2.dy)^2\right) \times t^2 +$$

$$2 \times \left((b1.x - b2.x) \times (b1.x - b2.x) \times (b1.dx - b2.y) \times (b1.dy - b2.dy)\right) \times t +$$

$$\left((b1.x - b2.x)^2 + (b1.y - b2.y)^2 - (b1.radius + b2.radius)^2\right) = 0$$

Note: This equation is broken into three lines to show the parts that correspond to the a, b, and c terms of the polynomial form.

You then solve this polynomial equation using the *quadratic formula*. The general form of the quadratic formula is

The quadratic formula.

$$t = \frac{-b \pm \sqrt{b^2 - 4ac}}{2a}$$

The strange ± notation shows how you get two solutions to the equation. Solution 1 results when you *subtract* the subexpression

The subexpression in the quadratic formula that gives you the two possible solutions.

$$\sqrt{b^2 - 4ac}$$

and Solution 2 results from *adding* the same subexpression. Given that you know that you only want to find the first collision, you need only Solution 1.

The complete set of equations (all you really need)

The values a, b, and c in the quadratic formula are only placeholders for the real subexpressions, which you pull from the polynomial form of the distance-over-time formula. You can, in turn, reduce these equations to a simpler set by noting the repeated subexpressions in the fully expanded polynomial form. The complete set of calculations for a, b, and c, when calculated for your two balls b1 and b2, is as follows:

$$d = b1.radius + b2.radius$$

$$ddx = b1.dx - b2.dx$$

$$ddy = b1.dy - b2.dy$$

$$distx = b1.x - b2.x$$

$$disty = b1.y - b2.y$$

$$a = ddx^2 + ddy^2$$

$$b = 2 \times (dx \times ddx + dy \times ddy)$$

$$c = dx^2 + dy^2 - d^2$$

Note: The values d, ddx, ddy, distx, and disty are simply intermediate values that show how to avoid duplicate calculations in the equations that calculate the values for a, b, and c.

Then you can plug these computed values for a, b, and c into the Solution 1 version of the quadratic formula to precisely calculate the time t when two balls first collide, like this:

Solution 1 with the values for a, b, and c plugged in.

$$t = \frac{\left(-b - \sqrt{b \times b - 4ac}\right)}{2a}$$

If the value of t that you compute with this formula is exactly zero, the balls are at the point of collision. If the value of t is *greater* than zero but *less than* 1, the balls collide at some point before the balls reach their respective x + dx and y + dy positions, that is, some time before the next frame in the animation.

You can also use the value of t to compute the precise positions where b1 and b2 collide by multiplying each ball's dx and dy values by t and adding the result to each ball's x and y values, like this:

nb1.x = b1.x + b1.dx × t

nb1.y = b1.y + b1.dx × t

nb2.x = b2.x + b2.dx × t

nb2.y = b2.y + b2.dx × t

nb1.x / nb1.y represents the position where ball b1 collides with ball b2, and nb2.x / nb2.y represents the position where ball b2 collides with ball b1.

Timing and order

The solution worked out in the previous sections is a great way to calculate the precise time and place where two balls collide. What happens, though, when you have more than two balls on a collision course? With two balls you only had to calculate when they would collide. With three balls you have three different ways for the balls to collide. With four balls you have six different possible collisions, and the combinations climb faster as you add more balls.

Also, when two balls collide, the collision sends the balls off in new directions. This means that your code needs to redo all your collision calculations to consider the new courses of the two balls that collided. However, instead of being a *problem,* this fact leads to the key idea at the center of the billiards simulation. At any given moment, you only need to calculate when the *next* collision is going to take place; it doesn't matter which balls are involved. If you know the *time* of the next collision, you can run the motion simulation forward to that point in time, calculate the result of the collision that occurs, and then repeat the process.

You can find the first collision between a set of balls by computing the collision times for the different combinations of balls and then selecting the shortest time. Take three balls for example: balls b1 and b2 can collide, balls b2 and b3 can collide, and balls b1 and b3 can collide. Whichever pair of balls collides first becomes the next collision that your code needs to handle, and in the meantime, the code can proceed smoothly through the motion simulation for the balls.

Of course, all three balls can collide at the exact same time as well, which may seem to complicate things. However, arbitrarily picking one pair of balls to handle first works just fine for a game simulation because the calculations all happen so fast that the player doesn't notice.

Checking the combinations

Finding the collision times for different combinations of balls requires a method to figure out which combinations of balls to check. The obvious approach is to use two nested loops, like this:

```
for (int ii = 0; ii < numBalls; ii++)
  for (jj = 0; jj < numBalls; jj++)
    // check ball[ii] to ball[jj]
```

However, this approach isn't optimal. First of all, it checks for a ball colliding with itself. In addition, it checks mirror combinations, such as comparing ball[0] to ball[1] and ball[1] to ball[0]. Here's a more efficient way to arrange your loops:

```
for (int ii = 1; ii < numBalls; ii++)
  for (jj = 0; jj < ii; jj++)
    // check ball[ii] to ball[jj]
```

By changing the first loop to start at 1 and by changing the second loop's comparison test to jj < ii, you create a loop that checks each combination only once.

You can see the complete code for checking all the different combinations of balls and edges in the JavaPool applet's updateBalls() method in the listing on the *Java Game Programming For Dummies* CD-ROM.

Bouncing Off the Bumpers

Chapters 1, 2, and 3 introduce a simple technique to detect and handle a collision between the ball and the applet boundary. However, the technique in those chapters isn't suitable for your pool applet because it can only detect and process collisions *after* they've occurred. Instead, you need a new method that works like your ball-to-ball collision code and computes the time when a ball hits an edge so that you can decide if the first collision that happens is a ball-to-ball collision or a ball-to-wall collision.

Computing when a ball hits an edge is much easier than computing when a ball hits another ball. First, a moving ball, always eventually hits an edge (unless of course, the ball slows down to a stop before reaching an edge — but more on that later in the "Putting All the Pieces Together" section). Second, the sign of the ball's dx and dy values limits which edge the ball can hit. For example, if the dx value is positive, the ball is moving to the right and can hit the right edge but can't ever hit the left edge. Likewise, if the sign of dy is positive, the ball can hit the bottom edge but not the top edge.

After you know which edge (left, right, top, or bottom) the ball can hit, you can compute the distance to each edge and then divide by dx or dy, respectively, to get the time to reach each edge. For example, the time to reach the left or right edge is the distance to the edge divided by dx. Likewise, the time to reach the top or bottom edge is the distance to the edge divided by dy. The next ball-to-wall collision is the one with the shorter time to collision.

Ball-to-wall collisions are different from ball-to-ball collisions, but your pool simulation code will have to watch for both types of collisions at the same time. At any given moment, the code needs to know what type of collision will happen next and how to handle it — the next section shows you how.

Coding the Collisions

Now you need to convert your collision math into code. You can use an approach similar to the one discussed in Chapter 3 and extend a new Ball class from the Circle class and extend Circle from the Point2D class.

The code for Ball is similar to the Ball class in Chapter 3 except that it contains several new methods to compute ball-to-ball and ball-to-wall collisions. The method to compute ball-to-ball collisions is called pathIntercept(), and it contains code that uses your new formula to compute the time one ball hits another. Here's the code for pathIntercept():

```
public float pathIntercept (Ball b) {
  float d = radius + b.radius;
  float ddx = vel.dx - b.vel.dx;
  float ddy = vel.dy - b.vel.dy;
  float dx = x - b.x;
  float dy = y - b.y;
  float A = ddx * ddx + ddy * ddy;
  float B = 2 * (dx * ddx + dy * ddy);
  float C = dx * dx + dy * dy - d * d;
  return (-B - (float) Math.sqrt(B*B - 4*A*C)) / (2*A);
}
```

The code to compute the time for a ball to collide with an edge goes into a new method called edgeIntercept(). Here's the code:

```
public float edgeIntercept (Rectangle bd) {
  if (vel.dx >= 0)
    hCol = (bd.width + bd.x - x - radius) / vel.dx;
  else
    hCol = (bd.x - x + radius) / vel.dx;
```

```
  if (vel.dy >= 0)
    vCol = (bd.height + bd.y - y - radius) / vel.dy;
  else
    vCol = (bd.y - y + radius) / vel.dy;
  return Math.min(hCol, vCol);
}
```

You need to declare hCol and vCol as class variables so that you can use the values to compute the new direction for a ball that bounces off an edge. Then, code a method called bounce() that uses these values to compute the result of an edge bounce. Here's the code for bounce():

```
public void bounce (float t) {
  if (t == hCol)
    vel.dx = -vel.dx;
  if (t == vCol)
    vel.dy = -vel.dy;
}
```

Notice that bounce() accepts a single float parameter called t. bounce() that uses t to decide if the ball bounces off a left/right edge, a top/bottom edge, or both. Your code needs to calculate the time to the next collision, run the simulation forward to this point in time, and then resolve that collision. (This stuff is all covered in the "Timing and order" section, later in this chapter.)

The code only calls bounce() when the next collision is a ball-to-wall collision, and so hCol and vCol values are set by edgeIntercept() just prior to calling bounce(). Therefore, if bounce()'s t parameter passes in the same time value returned by edgeIntercept(), you compare this time value to hCol and vCol to determine if the ball bounced off a left/right or top/bottom edge, or both.

After you know which edge the ball bounces off of, you handle the collision by reversing the appropriate dx or dy value in the ball's vel vector. For a collision on a left/right edge, you reverse dx, and for a collision along a top/bottom edge, you reverse dy. (See Chapter 1 for more details.)

Conserving Momentum

Handling a ball-to-ball collision is a bit more complicated than handling a ball-to-wall collision. When one ball collides with another, Newton's law of *conservation of momentum* controls how each ball reacts, and you need to write code that simulates this behavior.

The momentum of a moving object is equal to the object's mass times its velocity. When two objects collide, if you calculate the sum of the momentum of the two objects before and after the collision, the law of conservation of momentum says that you have to get the same sum in both cases (minus friction, of course). To appear realistic, your collision calculations must maintain this balance (you don't want to break the *law,* do you?).

Imagine that a moving ball strikes a stationary ball and that at the point of collision, the stationary ball is exactly 45 degrees to the right of the path of the moving ball. After the collision, the previously stationary ball moves off at the 45 degree angle. Conversely, the path of the moving ball is deflected 45 degrees to the left of its original direction. The law of conservation of momentum tells you that the sum of the momentum of both balls after the collision is equal to the momentum of the moving ball before the collision. However, because you are working in two dimensions, you need to vector math to calculate the velocity of both balls after the collision.

Because billiard balls all have the same mass, you can assign all your simulated billiard balls a mass of one and greatly simplify your calculations (one times any value equals the same value). This trick means that you can use a ball's *velocity* as its *momentum.*

Revisiting vectors

Chapter 3 demonstrates that the result of adding two vectors is a new vector that combines the effects of the original two. This same principle also applies in reverse. If you add the velocity vectors for the two balls *after* the collision, you must get a value that exactly equals the velocity vector of the moving ball *before* the collision. Figure 4-4 graphically illustrates conservation of momentum by using a vector diagram to show how adding the velocity vectors for the balls after the collision produces a vector that equals the original moving ball's velocity vector.

To determine the velocities of the two balls after the collision, you need to compute how momentum is redistributed. As Figure 4-5 shows, the transfer of momentum from the moving ball to the stationary ball is proportional to the cosine of the angle formed by a line drawn between the centers of the balls at the moment of impact and the line defined by the motion of the moving ball. Conversely, the momentum retained by the moving ball is proportional to the sine of this same angle.

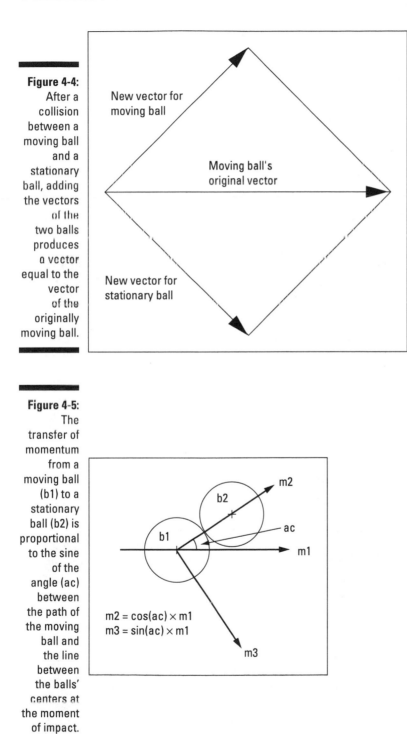

Figure 4-4:
After a collision between a moving ball and a stationary ball, adding the vectors of the two balls produces a vector equal to the vector of the originally moving ball.

New vector for moving ball

Moving ball's original vector

New vector for stationary ball

Figure 4-5:
The transfer of momentum from a moving ball (b1) to a stationary ball (b2) is proportional to the sine of the angle (ac) between the path of the moving ball and the line between the balls' centers at the moment of impact.

m2

b2

ac

b1

m1

$m2 = \cos(ac) \times m1$
$m3 = \sin(ac) \times m1$

m3

For example, in the case where the moving ball hits in the dead center of the moving ball, this angle is zero. Therefore, cos(0) equals 1 and sin(0) equals 0, and the stationary ball receives all the momentum from the moving ball and the previously moving ball comes to a complete stop. Likewise, if the moving ball barely grazes the stationary ball, the angle between the centers is nearly 90 degrees with respect to the path of the ball. Therefore, because the cosine of an angle close to 90 degrees is a very small number, very little of the moving ball's momentum transfers to the stationary ball.

What if both balls are moving?

You may be wondering how to deal with distributing momentum if *both* balls are moving before the collision. Easy: You can pretend that one ball is stationary simply by calculating the collision in that ball's *frame of reference*. For example, if you were riding in a tiny helicopter that was exactly matching the speed of one of the moving balls, a physicist would say you were in that ball's frame of reference. From your aerial perspective, the collision would appear to have happened between a moving ball and a stationary ball. Albert Einstein's theory of relativity says that the laws of physics have to look valid no matter where you observe from.

With the following approach, you convert the problem of two moving balls, ball A and ball B, into one where you always have one moving ball and one stationary ball:

1. **Subtract ball A's velocity vector from ball B.**

2. **Set ball A's velocity vector to zero.**

   This is the same as subtracting the ball A's vector from itself.

3. **Compute the collision as though ball A (with the modified vector) strikes a stationary ball A.**

4. **Add ball A's original vector back to both balls.**

The code to perform these calculations is fairly simple to write using a slightly improved and expanded version of the Vec2D class from Chapter 3. The main addition is a new method called dotProd() that calculates the *dot product* of two vectors.

The dot product

The *dot product* is what you get when you multiply the first vector's dx value times the second vector's dx value and then add this to the first vector's dy value times the second vector's dy value. This may seem like a strange calculation, but when both vectors are *unit vectors* (unit vectors are explained in Chapter 3), the dot product is just a fast way to compute the cosine of the angle between the two vectors.

The `collide()` *method*

Use this dot product trick to write a new method called `collide()` for your `Ball` class. `collide` computes the result of a collision between two balls. You call `collide()` by passing it a reference to a second ball. For example, to collide ball b1 with ball b2 you write:

```
b1.collide(b2)
```

Here's the code for `collide()`:

```
public void collide (Ball b) {
  // Calculate collision in b's reference frame
  float mv = vel.subVec(b.vel).mag();
  Vec2D v12 = (new Vec2D(this, b)).unitVec();
  Vec2D v1c = vel.copy().unitVec();
float cos = v1c.dotProd(v12);
  vel.subVec(v12.mulVec(cos * mv)).addVec(b.vel);
  b.vel.addVec(v12);
}
```

This code is made more compact by a revision to the `Vec2D` class (see "Creating a vector class" in Chapter 3) which changes any method that previously returned `void` to instead return a reference to the same object. This trick means that you can combine several calls to successive `Vec2D` methods into a single statement. For example, instead of writing

```
vel.subVec(b.vel);
float mv = vel.mag();
```

you can write the more compact

```
float mv = vel.subVec(b.vel).mag();
```

`collide()` *dissected*

After you understand this new way of writing vector code, you can examine how `collide()` works in more detail. The first line of code

```
float mv = vel.subVec(b.vel).mag();
```

makes the collision calculation relative to ball b's frame of reference. It does this by subtracting its velocity vector from the current ball's velocity vector. This code also calculates the magnitude of the current ball's velocity vector *after* subtracting ball b's vector and saves this in the variable `mv`.

The code then creates two new `Vec2D` objects: `v12` and `v1c`. The code that creates `v12` uses a new `Vec2D` constructor, takes references to two `Point2D` objects, and creates a vector that is the difference between the two `Point2D` objects. The code then converts this difference to a unit vector. The following line of code accomplishes these steps:

```
Vec2D v12 = (new Vec2D(this, b)).unitVec();
```

Next, the code creates the `v1c` `Vec2D` object by copying the current ball's `vel` vector and converting the copy to a unit vector, like this:

```
Vec2D v1c = vel.copy().unitVec();
```

The code then calculates the cosine of the angle between `v12` and `v1c` by computing the dot product, like this:

```
float cos = v1c.dotProd(v12);
```

Next, the code sets the magnitude of `v12` to equal `mv * cos`. Before this calculation, `v12` is a unit vector that points along a line from `b` to the current ball. Adjusting the magnitude to `cos * mv` converts `v12` into a vector that represents the amount of momentum to be transferred from the current ball to ball `b`.

In the next step, the code subtracts `v12` from the current ball's `vel` vector. Doing so removes the momentum from the current ball — the same momentum that the code later transfers to ball `b` in the next step. Then, the code restores the current ball's original frame of reference by adding back the original, unmodified vector for ball `b`. All these steps are accomplished in this line of code:

```
vel.subVec(v12.mulVec(cos * mv)).addVec(b.vel);
```

Finally, the code transfers the momentum taken from the current ball to ball `b` and restores its original frame of reference by adding `v12` to ball `b`'s original `vel` vector, like this:

```
b.vel.addVec(v12);
```

Putting All the Pieces Together

Much of the code for the `JavaPool` applet is copied directly from the `HoleInOne` applet in Chapter 3, so there's no point in describing it again here. However, there is new code to watch for.

First, the JavaPool applet creates and maintains a list of active Ball objects using the Vector object balls. resetTable() creates four balls and adds them to the empty Vector list. It adds a white cue ball and arranges three colored balls into a triangular shape that resembles a rack of billiard balls.

The controlling code for JavaPool applet is the code in the method updateBalls(). The code in updateBalls() is based on the ideas discussed earlier in the "Timing and order" section. For each tick of the animation, updateBalls() calls each ball's edgeIntercept() and pathIntercept() methods to see whether a collision occurs during the current animation tick. If updateBalls() finds a collision, it processes the collision by calling bounce() or collide(), depending on the type of collision — ball-to-ball or ball-to-wall, respectively — it finds.

When updateBalls() can't find any more collisions that occur during the current animation cycle, it calls each ball's decel() method to simulate slowing the ball's motion due to friction. updateBalls() also checks to see whether each ball is close enough to the hole to fall in or be influenced by it by calling the Hole method influence(). (See the section "Digging a Hole" in Chapter 3 for the whole hole story.) If influence() returns true, the code knows that the ball has fallen into the hole and removes it from the list of active balls.

The interface for shooting a ball is identical to the click-and-drag interface described in Chapter 3, except that with the JavaPool interface you can select and shoot any of the four balls. The applet's init() method also creates a pocket hole in the lower-left corner of the applet. You can move this hole to another location by changing the values passed to the constructor.

The completed JavaPool applet is shown in Figure 4-6.

You can find the completed JavaPool applet and the complete code for the applet on the *Java Game Programming For Dummies* CD-ROM.

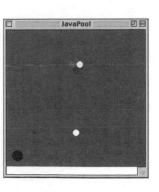

Figure 4-6:
The completed JavaPool applet shows three racked balls, a cue ball, and a pocket hole in the lower-left corner.

Part II
Up to Speed

The 5th Wave   By Rich Tennant

LET'S JUST KEEP THE CURSOR ON THE COMPUTER SCREEN, YOUNG MAN, AND OFF YOUR BROTHERS FOREHEAD! NOW LOWER HIM GENTLY BACK INTO HIS CRIB.

In this part . . .

Producing a professional-quality game means mastering more than just the basics of game coding. A finished game must attend to a myriad of practical details while also serving up a heaping measure of eye appeal and style. Part II shows you how to apply spit and polish to your core game logic in order to create that professional look.

Part II also delves into the ins and outs of mazes by showing you how to create them and how to solve them. Mazes are an integral part of many games, and the maze code this part presents is used to create some of the games in both Part II and Part III.

Chapter 5

Sliding Blocks Brain Teaser

. . . .

In This Chapter

▶ Spicing up your games with images

▶ Using the `MediaTracker` class

▶ Programming puzzle logic

▶ Implementing a *click and drag* interface

. . . .

*I*n the 1870s, an American named Sam Loyd drove the world crazy with a new type of game called a *Sliding Block Puzzle*. Sam arranged 15 wooden tiles in a 4×4 grid in a small cardboard box. Because Loyd left out a tile, the box had room for you to slide one tile past another, and by a series of moves, rearrange the order of tiles.

Each tile was numbered, and the box started with tile number 1 in the upper-left corner. The sequence continued to the right and then down, but the last two numbers, 14 and 15, were reversed, as shown in Figure 5-1. Thus, Loyd called his invention the 14-15 puzzle and offered a prize of $1,000 to the first person who could solve the puzzle by putting all the numbers in sequence.

The blocks in Loyd's puzzle can be arranged in over 600 billion ways, but each rearrangement of the tiles can result only from an even number of exchanges between the blocks. Therefore, Loyd's fiendish little puzzle is impossible to solve, and the $1,000 prize, was never claimed.

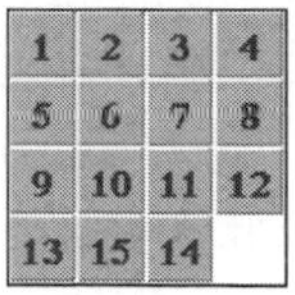

Figure 5-1:
Sam Loyd's
impossible
puzzle.

In this chapter, we show you how to construct your own sliding block puzzle. This puzzle is difficult to solve, but unlike sneaky Sam's puzzle, it does have a solution. And instead of using Sam's numbers, the puzzle in this chapter has sliding blocks with colorful images.

The puzzle presented in this chapter simulates a set of wooden blocks that slide around inside a recessed rectangular area cut into a game board. You move puzzle pieces by clicking and dragging with the mouse, but the particular arrangement of the pieces (see Figure 5-2) constrains how the pieces can move. Solving the puzzle requires the player to discover the sequence of moves needed to relocate the large square piece from the top center of the board to the winning position at the bottom center.

Figure 5-2:
The starting position for the Sliding Block Brain Teaser.

This chapter covers all the techniques used in the Sliding Blocks Brain Teaser applet. The complete code and ready-to-run applet is on the *Java Game Programming For Dummies* CD-ROM included with this book.

Using Images in Games

To paraphrase an old saw: When programming games, one picture can be far cooler than a thousand `fillRect()` calls. Besides, modern game players expect games to have snazzy graphics, which usually means using fancy artwork rather than plain, solid colors. With modern tools, like Adobe Photoshop, you can easily create custom pictures to use in your games, even if you aren't the next Rembrandt.

The puzzle we present in this chapter uses GIF (Graphics Interchange Format — one of two graphics formats used on the World Wide Web) images to create the illusion that the puzzle is constructed from wooden blocks. These pieces slide around on a puzzle board, which is also made to resemble wood.

The puzzle uses puzzle pieces in three different sizes. If you think of the smallest pieces as 1×1 unit squares, the remaining two sizes of pieces are 1×2 and 2×2. These pieces slide around in a recessed rectangular area on the puzzle board. Using the 1×1 puzzle pieces as a unit, the size of this rectangular area is four puzzle-piece units wide by five puzzle-piece units high.

The puzzle pieces and the puzzle board shown in Figure 5-2 are all constructed in Photoshop using a third-party plug-in called PhotoTools (from Extensis Corporation) that modifies a background texture, in this case a picture of wood grain, to create the look of beveled edges similar to the effect created by the fill3DRect() in the Graphics class (see CD Chapter 3 for more information). This effect creates a raised look on the pieces, as if they were cut with a routing tool. The effect is reversed to create the recessed look of the rectangular area that holds the pieces. The same effect is also used on the outside edge of the puzzle board, except that the plug-in is set to create a rounded bevel.

You can easily create your own graphics to replace the files provided on the *Java Game Programming For Dummies* CD by using the included GIF files as templates. You need to construct 10 different piece files to replace the files piece0.gif through piece9.gif. You can also replace the game board by creating your own board.gif file. You can use almost any image editing program that can save files in the GIF format.

Digital Stamp Pads

Using Image in Java is like having a digital stamp pad that you can use to stamp down copies of a picture onto a Graphics context. In this case, the stamp pad is an Image object, and you stamp it using the drawImage() method provided in the Graphics class. However, before you can call drawImage(), you first have to load an image file and create a Java Image object. You can create an Image object by loading files from a Web server or from your hard disk.

To create an Image object, you use a method called getImage() that is provided in the Applet class. When you call getImage(), you pass it a URL parameter (Universal Resource Locator, or more simply, Web address) that tells getImage() where to find an image file. Usually the image file is located on a Web server, but it can also come from your hard drive if you only need to run your applet on your computer. getImage() loads the data from this image file and uses it to construct an Image object.

You can also call getImage() and pass it a URL and a string that specifies the name of an image file. The string is appended to the URL to specify the exact location of the file. This form of getImage() can be conveniently used with two other Applet methods called getCodeBase() and getDocumentBase(). Calling getCodeBase() returns a URL that points to the directory on the Web server from which the applet was loaded. Calling getDocumentBase() returns a URL that points to the directory from which the HTML document that created the applet was loaded. So you can easily fetch an Image from the same directory that contains an applet's class files like this:

```
Image img = getImage(getCodeBase(), pic.gif );
```

After you have an `Image`, you can draw it to a `Graphics` context by calling the `Graphics` method `drawImage()`. Here's an example of a simple applet that fetches an `Image` using `getImage()` and then draws the same `Image` with `drawImage()`:

```java
import java.awt.*;
import java.applet.Applet;

public class Example extends Applet {
  Image  coffee;
  public void init() {
    coffee = getImage(getCodeBase(),  coffee.gif );
  }

  public void paint (Graphics g) {
    g.drawImage(coffee, 0, 0, null);
  }
}
```

Choosing GIF or JPEG

You can use `getImage()` to fetch an `Image` from a file encoded in the GIF format, but you can also call `getImage()` to fetch a JPEG encoded `Image`. The code is basically the same in either case; you just pass the name of the image file, whether it be JPEG or GIF. JPEG files let you use images that contain millions of colors, whereas GIF files have a limit of 256 colors. However, JPEG's larger color palette may sometimes be a disadvantage.

Some people may want to play your games on systems that can only display 256 colors. In this case, Java has to convert a JPEG before it can display it. This conversion process, called *dithering*, can produce a grainy, undesirable result. You are best off testing your games on a 256-color system to make sure that you like the result. To completely avoid dithering, you need to be careful to create your GIF files using only the 216-color *browser-safe* palette. (CD Chapter 4 covers the ins and outs of the browser-safe palette.)

If you use Adobe Photoshop to create your GIF files, you can convert any type of image to the 216-color browser-safe palette. If you are starting with a JPEG file and want to convert it to a GIF file, simply select Image⇨Mode⇨ Indexed Color. Then in the dialog box that appears, set the palette option to Web. You can also let Photoshop predither the image by selecting something other than None for the Dither option in the same dialog box.

In this code, drawImage() gets passed four parameters. The first parameter is the reference to the Image object you want drawImage() to draw. The next two parameters are the x and y offset that tell drawImage() where to position the upper-left corner of the Image. In this example, the Image is drawn exactly in the upper-left corner at 0,0 (the origin) of the applet's screen area.

The last parameter (null) passed to drawImage() is used to pass a reference to an ImageObserver. ImageObserver is an interface you can implement in your applet if you want the applet to be notified of the status of an Image while it is downloading. However, you don't need this capability for the applet in this chapter and can simply pass null when you call drawImage().

Drawing while downloading

When you try the previous applet, you may notice a strange thing, depending on how fast your browser or applet viewer loads images. When you call getImage(), it returns almost immediately, passing back a reference to an Image object. However, the Image hasn't actually been loaded at this point and doesn't start to load until the first time drawImage() is called. To make things even stranger, drawImage() attempts to draw an Image even when the Image isn't fully loaded.

According to the developers of Java, Java's incremental display of images as they are loaded is a "feature," not a bug. The intent is to let you duplicate the effect of a browser displaying an image while it is still loading it. However, for many game applications this can be a real nuisance.

One way to solve this problem is to use the ImageObserver interface, mentioned earlier in this chapter, to write code that keeps track of the status of the images you are fetching and determines when all of them have been fully loaded. An even simpler solution is to use Java's MediaTracker class to manage image loading and keep track of when the images are loaded, as the next section explains.

Loading images with MediaTracker

The MediaTracker class lets you construct a list of images you have requested with getImage(). After this list is complete, you can tell MediaTracker to start loading all of them and to wait until all the images have been loaded before proceeding.

The first step in using `MediaTracker` is to create a new `MediaTracker` object, like this:

```
MediaTracker tracker = new MediaTracker(this);
```

The `this` parameter passed to the `MediaTracker` constructor is a reference to the applet that needs to use the images. `MediaTracker` uses this parameter to register with the code that actually loads the images.

MediaTracker.addImage()

After you have a new `MediaTracker` object, you can start making a list of images for `MediaTracker` to manage. You add an image to the list by calling MediaTracker's `addImage()` method. Here's an example:

```
Image boardImage = getImage(getCodeBase(), board.gif );
tracker.addImage(boardImage, board.gif ), 0);
```

Notice that you still need to call `getImage()` to request the `Image` you want. However, you then also call `addImage()` to add the `Image` to the list of images your `MediaTracker` is managing.

When you call `addImage()`, you are required to give it an `int` parameter that specifies an ID value for the `Image` you are telling `MediaTracker` to track. `MediaTracker` supports several different methods for monitoring image loading. For example, the `MediaTracker` method `waitForID()` waits for all images that were assigned a particular ID value to load before it returns. However, it's usually easier to call the `MediaTracker` method `waitForAll()`, which doesn't return until all the images you added with `addImage()` are loaded. If you use `waitForAll()`, it doesn't matter what ID value you pass to `addImage()`.

MediaTracker.waitForAll()

After you add all the images to your `MediaTracker` object, you call the method `waitForAll()` to start loading the images and wait for loading to finish. This call doesn't return until all the images you added with `addImage()` are fully loaded and ready to use. However, the `waitForAll()` method has one more detail you have to handle.

The `waitForAll()` method specifies that it can throw an `InterruptedException`. This exception isn't currently implemented in Java 1.0.2, but you still need to provide a `try/catch` block so that the code compiles properly, like this:

```
try {
  tracker.waitForAll();
} catch (InterruptedException e) { ; }
```

Loading multiple images

The sliding blocks puzzle has 11 different images that you need to load — 10 puzzle pieces plus the puzzle board. The image for the puzzle board is called board.gif; the images for the puzzle pieces are named piece0.gif through piece9.gif. You can simplify the code to load the puzzle pieces by taking advantage of the sequential naming of the puzzle piece files. Code a loop and then use *string concatenation* (fancy lingo meaning to combine multiple strings into one) to create the name of each file from the loop counter variable. For example, if you have an int variable called ii and the current value of ii is zero, the following code creates the string piece0.gif:

```
String fname = piece + ii + .gif ;
```

Using this string concatenation trick, here is the code you need to load the puzzle board and all 10 puzzle pieces:

```
MediaTracker tracker = new MediaTracker(this);
boardImage = getImage(getCodeBase(),  board.gif );
tracker.addImage(boardImage, 0);
for (int ii = 0; ii < 10; ii++) {
  pieceImages[ii] = getImage(getCodeBase(),
                            piece + ii + .gif );
  tracker.addImage(pieceImages[ii], 0);
}
try {
  tracker.waitForAll();
} catch (InterruptedException e) { ; }
```

You can put this code in the init() method of the puzzle applet. You also need to declare boardImage and the pieces[] array as class variables, like this:

```
private Image       offscreenImage, boardImage;
private Image[]     pieceImages = new Image[10];
```

Laying Out the Game Board

The design of the puzzle board, shown in Figure 5-3, aligns all the puzzle pieces onto an invisible 4×5 grid to make calculating how to draw each puzzle piece onto the board as easy as possible. The origin (upper-left corner) of the grid is offset from the applet's origin by the values specified in the variables gridX and gridY. The width and height of a grid square is specified by the variables pieceWidth and pieceHeight.

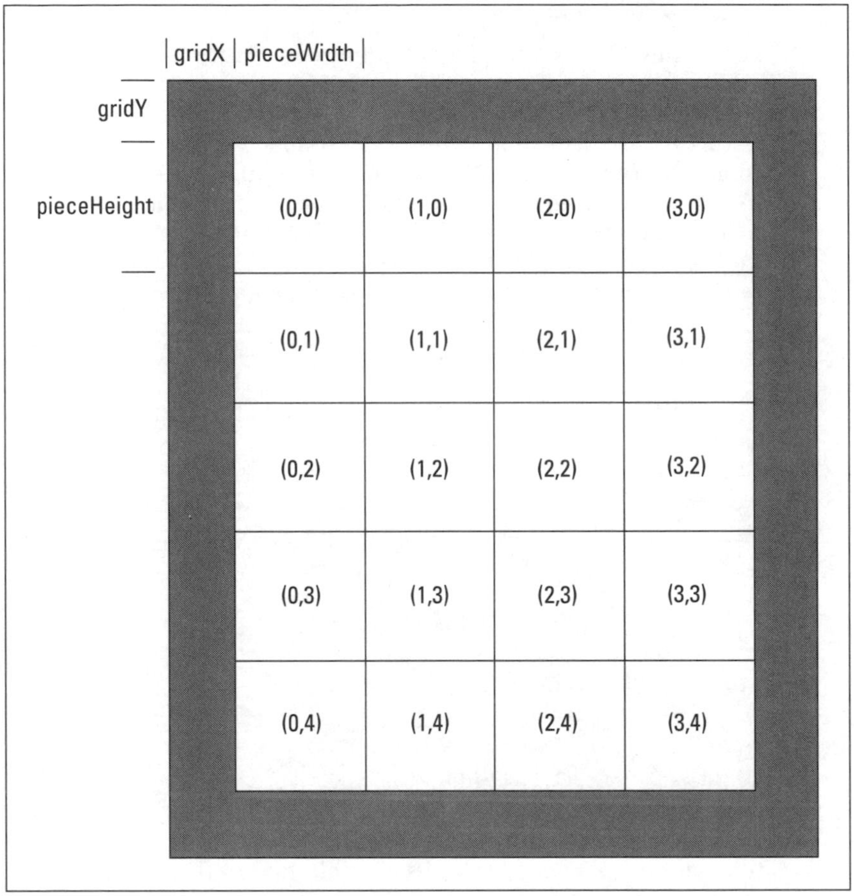

| gridX | pieceWidth |

gridY

pieceHeight

(0,0)	(1,0)	(2,0)	(3,0)
(0,1)	(1,1)	(2,1)	(3,1)
(0,2)	(1,2)	(2,2)	(3,2)
(0,3)	(1,3)	(2,3)	(3,3)
(0,4)	(1,4)	(2,4)	(3,4)

Figure 5-3:
All the puzzle pieces on the game board align to an invisible 4 × 5 grid centered in the middle of the board.

The grid squares are arranged such that grid square x=0, y=0 is the upper-left square, and x=3, y=4 is the lower-right square, as shown in Figure 5-3. When you draw a puzzle piece onto the board, you calculate the upper-left corner for any grid square from these four variables, `gridX`, `gridY`, `pieceWidth`, and `pieceHeight`, using the following formulas:

imageX = gridX × pieceWidth + gridX

imageY = gridY × pieceHeight + gridY

However, you can't apply these formulas until you know the proper values to assign to `gridX`, `gridY`, `pieceWidth`, and `pieceHeight`. You can write the code to initialize these values from constants, but this means you can't change the size of the puzzle graphics without recompiling the code. Instead, because the size of the grid square is equal to the size of the smallest puzzle piece, you can initialize `pieceWidth` and `pieceHeight` by reading the width and height of one of the puzzle piece images.

Reading the width and height of an Image

The Image class contains methods called getWidth() and getHeight() that determine the width and height of an Image. For example, to read the width and height of the game board Image boardImage, use the following code:

```
int width = boardImage.getWidth(null);
int height = boardImage.getHeight(null);
```

 Due to the design of the Java AWT, you can't reliably read an Image's width and height until the Image has been fully loaded. This isn't a problem when you use MediaTracker to wait for an Image to fully load before you use it — a very good reason to always use MediaTracker to load your Images.

Initializing gridX, gridY, pieceWidth, *and* pieceHeight

Using getWidth() and getHeight() lets you initialize pieceWidth and pieceHeight by reading the width and height of one of the small puzzle piece images. The earlier section "Loading multiple images" shows code that loads all the puzzle piece image files and saves references to the Image objects in an Image[] array called pieceImages. pieceImages[5] contains a reference to the image file piece5.gif, which is one of the small puzzle pieces. Read the width and height of pieceImages[5] to initialize pieceWidth and pieceHeight, like this:

```
int pieceWidth = pieceImages[5].getWidth(null);
int pieceHeight = pieceImages[5].getHeight(null);
```

You still haven't initialized gridX or gridY, but you can easily calculate these values from the width and height of the game board image boardImage and pieceWidth and pieceHeight. Because the grid is centered in the middle of the game board, you calculate gridX by subtracting the width of the grid from the width of the game board (boardImage) and then divide the result by two. The width of the grid is 4 × pieceWidth, so you calculate gridX like this:

```
int gridX = (boardImage.getWidth(null) -
            (pieceWidth * 4)) / 2;
```

You calculate gridY using nearly identical code:

```
int gridY = (boardImage.getHeight(null) -
            (pieceHeight * 5)) / 2;
```

Crafting the Puzzle

To make the puzzle work, you need to construct a class to encapsulate the logic that handles each individual puzzle piece. This new class, called `Piece`, needs to contain a constructor to *instantiate* (create and define) the pieces needed by the puzzle, code to draw the `Image` that represents the piece on the board, and code to handle sliding the piece from place to place on the board.

Making puzzle pieces that act like real puzzle pieces

One of the trickiest aspects of coding the puzzle is designing the logic that makes the puzzle pieces act like real puzzle pieces placed on a real board. For example, when you try to slide a puzzle in the direction of an adjacent piece, the adjacent piece either blocks the first piece from moving, or, if that piece is able to slide in the same direction, is pushed along.

To accomplish this, each puzzle piece needs to know its size and current position and be able to check the size and position of the other pieces. In addition, you need to have some way to monitor when one piece pushes another piece.

Thankfully, the Java AWT includes a built-in class called `Rectangle` that is designed to represent a movable rectangular area. `Rectangle` includes code that can check whether one rectangular area overlaps or *intersects* another rectangular area and greatly simplifies your task of creating the logic of sliding puzzle pieces. `Rectangle`'s built-in features make it the perfect superclass for your new `Piece` class.

Starting with `Rectangle`, you can easily code the beginnings of your new `Piece` class, including code to draw the image of the puzzle piece, like this:

```
class Piece extends Rectangle {
  private Image pic;
  Piece (int bx, int by, Rectangle grid, Image img) {
    super(bx * grid.width + grid.x,
         by * grid.height + grid.y,
        img.getWidth(null), img.getHeight(null));
    pic = img;
  }
```

```
  public void draw (Graphics g) {
    g.drawImage(pic, x, y, null);
  }
}
```

The first two parameters to Piece, bx and by, specify the location of the
piece on the invisible 4 × 5 grid shown in Figure 5-3. For example, to position
a piece in the upper-left position on the grid, specify bx = 0 and by = 0.

Even though you specify the location of a piece on the grid, the piece can't
calculate where to draw the Image that represents the piece unless it knows
the values you computed for gridX, gridY, pieceWidth, and pHyt. You could
pass these parameters to the constructor for Piece in four int parameters.
However, it's easier to create a Rectangle object from these four values and
pass a reference to this object to Piece in a parameter called grid.

The last parameter for Piece, img, is a reference to the Image that represents the piece on the board. The constructor saves this reference in the
variable pic, which is used by Piece's draw() method. The constructor
calls img.getWidth() and img.getHeight() to determine the size of the
Image and passes this to the superclass constructor, along with the pixel
position. Therefore, after a piece is instantiated, Piece's x and y values
record the pixel position of the piece on the board, and the Piece's width
and height values give the real size of the Piece, in pixels.

Piece's draw() method, as shown in the code in this section, uses the
Image variable pic and the x and y pixel position values to draw the image
that represents the piece onto the game board.

Putting the pieces together

Now that you can instantiate a puzzle piece, you're ready to finish the
applet's init() method by adding the code to instantiate all the pieces for
the puzzle. Here's the completed code for init() along with all the needed
class variables for the puzzle applet:

```
public class Puzzle extends Applet {
    private Image       offscreenImage, boardImage;
    private Image[]     pieceImages = new Image[10];
    private Graphics    offscr;
    private Piece[]     pieces = new Piece[10];
    private Piece       picked = null;
    private Rectangle   grid, clickArea;
    private Font        bbCourier = new Font( Courier ,
                                         Font.BOLD, 48);
```

(continued)

(continued)

```
 private String     winMsg = Win! ;
 private  Point     selectedPiece, winLocation;
 // The pcs[] array specifies the starting position of the
 // different puzzle pieces on the 4x5 grid.
private int[][]     pcs = {{1,0},{0,0},{0,2},{3,0},{3,2},
                           {0,4},{1,3},{2,3},{3,4},{1,2}};public void init() {
   MediaTracker tracker = new MediaTracker(this);
   boardImage = getImage(getCodeBase(),  board.gif );
   tracker.addImage(boardImage, 0);
   for (int ii = 0; ii < 10; ii++) {
     pieceImages[ii] = getImage(getCodeBase(),
                         piece + ii + .GIF );
     tracker.addImage(pieceImages[ii], 0);
   }
   try {
     tracker.waitForAll();
   } catch (InterruptedException e) { ; }
   int pieceWidth = pieceImages[5].getWidth(null);
   int pieceHeight = pieceImages[5].getHeight(null);
   int gridX = (boardImage.getWidth(null) -
             (pieceWidth * 4)) / 2;
   int gridY = (boardimage.getHeight(null) -
             (pieceHeight * 5)) / 2;
   grid = new Rectangle(gridX, gridY,
                       pieceWidth, pieceHeight);
   winLocation = new Point(pieceWidth + gridX,
                       3 * pieceHeight + gridY);
   clickArea = new Rectangle(gridX, gridY,
                       4 * pieceWidth,
                       5 * pieceHeight);
   for (int ii = 0; ii < 10; ii++)
     pieces[ii] = new Piece(pcs[ii][0], pcs[ii][1],
                       grid, pieceImages[ii]);
   offscreenImage = createImage(size().width,
                       size().height);
   offscr = offscreenImage.getGraphics();
   repaint();
 }
}
```

The puzzle pieces are instantiated inside the last `for` loop. The values in the `pcs[][]` array define the starting position for each piece. Notice also how `grid` is initialized using the values computed for `gridX`, `gridY`, `pieceWidth`, and `pieceHeight`.

The puzzle uses an offscreen Image to draw the puzzle graphics, as set up by the calls to createImage() and getGraphics(). (See the section "Drawing offscreen" in Chapter 1 for more on creating offscreen Images.) However, notice the call to repaint() in the last line of init(). In many examples, you don't need this call, but because MediaTracker can take some time to load all the images and because Java is *multithreaded* (see CD Chapter 2), paint() is almost certainly called before the graphics are loaded. So you need to call repaint() to schedule another call to paint() after the images are loaded so that they actually appear onscreen.

The Rectangle object clickArea is created for use in the interface, as described in the next section.

Mousing the Pieces Around

To make your puzzle easy to play (or playable at all, for that matter), you need to create an interface. Probably the easiest way to come up with an interface is to create simple code that lets the user click a piece and then, while holding the mouse button down, drag the piece to a new position.

Selecting a puzzle piece

The first step in implementing your user interface, that of detecting when the user has clicked on a piece to select it, is implemented by overriding the mouseDown() method, like this:

```
public boolean mouseDown (Event evt, int x, int y) {
  if (clickArea.inside(x, y)) {
    for (int ii = 0; ii < pieces.length; ii++) {
      if (pieces[ii].inside(x, y)) {
        picked = pieces[ii];
        selectedPiece = new Point(x, y);
        break;
      }
    }
  }
  return true;
```

This code first checks whether the user clicks the mouse inside the puzzle board's recessed area. The applet's init() method, described in the earlier section "Putting the pieces together," creates a Rectangle called clickArea that defines the boundaries of the area where the pieces can move. The Rectangle class has a method called inside() that returns true if a point, defined by its two x and y parameters, is inside the rectangle.

Next, the code uses a `for` loop to iterate through the list of pieces and, again, uses the `inside()` method to check whether the user clicks the mouse inside this piece. If the mouse is clicked inside a piece, the reference for that `Piece` is copied to the `picked` variable, and the location where the user clicked is recorded by creating the `Point` object `selectedPiece` and passing the x and y location of the click to the `Point` constructor.

A `Point` is an AWT class that holds the values of an x,y pair.

Moving the pieces

Next, you override the `mouseDrag()` method so that you can track the movement of the mouse while the mouse button is held down. However, you need to make sure that you only try to track the mouse when a puzzle piece is selected. So the code starts by testing to see if `picked != null` and `selectedPiece != null`.

Your users can drag the mouse in any direction, including diagonally, but the code to slide the pieces is simpler if you constrain the mouse to moving either vertically or horizontally. You can divide the code into separate sections to handle movement along each axis like this:

```
public boolean mouseDrag (Event evt, int x, int y) {
  if (picked != null  &&  selectedPiece != null) {
    int  dx, dy;
    while ((dx = limit(x - selectedPiece.x)) != 0  &&
           picked.slide(pieces, dx, 0, clickArea)) {
      selectedPiece.translate(dx, 0);
    }
    while ((dy = limit(y - selectedPiece.y)) != 0  &&
           picked.slide(pieces, 0, dy, clickArea)) {
      selectedPiece.translate(0, dy);
    }
    repaint();
  }
  return true;
}
```

Taking the horizontal movement first, the code calls a small helper method called `limit()` that constrains the movement to stepping by a single pixel, or not at all, by limiting the movement to ±1 or zero. Here's the code for limit:

```
private int limit (int val) {
  return (val > 0 ? 1 : (val < 0 ? -1 : 0));
}
```

If you're not familiar with it, `limit()`'s use of the conditional operator (? :) in the `return` statement may look strange. However, this is just a more compact way of writing:

```
if (val > 0)
  return 1;
else {
  if (val < 0)
    return -1;
  else
    return 0;
}
```

Inside `mouseDrag()`, the code computes the difference between the original location where the user clicked the mouse to select the piece, which is held in the `Point` value `selectedPiece`, and the current position of the mouse, which is passed to `mouseDrag()` in the x and y parameters. Then, `mouseDrag()` uses two `while` loops to move the piece, one pixel at a time, until the position of the piece matches the current location of the mouse. The first `while` loop handles moving the piece left or right, and the second `while` loop controls movement up or down.

The `while` loops also have to handle one other important detail: As the user drags the piece around on the game board, the piece the user is moving may bump into another piece. If the piece does bump into another piece, the code needs to check if the piece that the selected piece bumped into blocks further movement of the selected piece or if the selected piece can push the blocking piece out of the way. The check to determine if the selected piece moves a blocking piece or is blocked by it is determined by a new method called `slide()`.

`Slide()`*ing around*

Writing `slide()` is the trickiest bit of code in this book so far, but it isn't that hard to write if you break the problem down into simpler steps. The key is to leverage several of the methods provided in `Rectangle`.

Checking for pieces that block the slide path *with* `Rectangle.intersects()`

Given two rectangles, the `Rectangle` method `intersects()` returns `true` if one `Rectangle` overlaps or *intersects* the other. You can use `intersects()` to determine whether the player is trying to move one puzzle piece on top of another by creating a new `Rectangle` that holds the new position for the piece (the one that indicates the move the player intends to make) and then coding a loop that checks this new position against all the other puzzle pieces in the game. If the new position `Rectangle` intersects with any other puzzle piece, the piece that the player wants to move is potentially blocked from moving.

Of course, you also need to check whether the puzzle piece that is potentially blocking the player's move is itself able to slide in the same direction. You can check this potential movement by allowing `Piece` to recursively call itself and attempt to move the blocking puzzle piece. Then, if the blocking piece is able to move, you allow the original piece to move as well. The neat trick about the way the code makes this check recursively is that it allows a blocking puzzle piece, in turn, to move a puzzle piece that blocks it, and so on — as though the code walks down the line and checks all the pieces in a given direction to see whether they can move.

Checking for the board boundaries `Rectangle.union()` *and* `Rectangle.equals()`

After the code lets the player move a piece, it also needs to make sure that the move doesn't push the piece beyond the bounds of the playing area on the board. The `Rectangle` class provides a simple way to check for the piece's position in the form of two additional methods: `union()` and `equals()`.

The `union()` method starts with two `Rectangles` and creates a new `Rectangle` that is as large as the smallest `Rectangle` you can draw that would contain both the original rectangles. The `equals()` method compares two `Rectangles` and returns `true` if both `Rectangles` describe exactly the same rectangular area. Using these two methods, you can easily check whether a piece is trying to move outside the bounds of the playing area, as shown in the following code where `bd` is the `Rectangle` that describes the bounds of the board and `np` is a `Rectangle` object that describes the new position for the piece:

```
if (bd.union(np).equals(bd))
```

Recursion

When a method calls itself, that is a *recursive* call. Writing recursive code is not something you do every day, but there are some types of calculations that are easier to accomplish if you use recursion. The classic example is using recursion to compute factorials, like this:

```
int factorial (int n) {
  if (n > 1)
    return n * factorial(n - 1);
  else
    return 1;
}
```

This statement is false only if Rectangle np goes outside the bounds of bd and causes bd.union(np) to return a Rectangle larger than bd. Note that np is created by adding dx and dy to the current position of the piece. The variables x, y, width, and height are inherited from the Rectangle class from which Piece extends.

Now that you understand the basic approach, here's the complete code for slide():

```
public boolean slide (Piece[] pp, int dx, int dy,
                      Rectangle bd) {
  Rectangle np = new Rectangle(x + dx, y + dy,
                                width, height);
  for (int jj = 0; jj < pp.length; jj++) {
    if (this != pp[jj] &&  pp[jj].intersects(np)) {
      if (pp[jj].slide(pp, dx, dy, bd))
        continue;
      return false;
    }
  }
  if (bd.union(np).equals(bd)) {
    translate(dx, dy);
    return true;
  }
  return false;
}
```

The final step in moving a puzzle piece is the call to translate(), which moves the position of the Piece to the same location that your code just checked (as we discuss earlier in this section). Notice that the code only allows translate() to happen when all the other checks have passed, the puzzle piece has space to move, and the move keeps the piece on the board.

Cleaning up after a move

One last step is "cleaning up" after the player releases the mouse button. To keep the layout of the puzzle pieces nice and tidy, and also to simplify the check for solving the puzzle, you need to add code to slide the pieces to the closest grid position when the player releases the mouse button after a move. You can put this code in mouseUp() like this:

```
public boolean mouseUp (Event evt, int x, int y) {
  for (int ii = 0; ii < pieces.length; ii++)
    pieces[ii].snap(grid);
  picked = null;
  repaint();
  return true;
}
```

The code in mouseUp() uses a loop to adjust every puzzle piece on the board by getting the reference to each piece from the pieces[] array and calling a new Piece method called snap(). You need to add code for snap() to the Piece class, like this:

```
public void snap (Rectangle grid) {
  move(((x - grid.x + grid.width / 2) / grid.width) *
       grid.width + grid.x,
     ((y - grid.y + grid.height / 2) / grid.height) *
       grid.height + grid.y);
}
```

snap() calculates the grid position closest to the current location of a piece and calls the Rectangle method move() to move the piece to this location. The Rectangle parameter grid passes in the values for gridX and gridY (described in the section "Laying Out the Game Board") in grid.x and grid.y and the width and height of a grid square in grid.width and grid.height.

The calculation (x - grid.x + grid.width / 2) computes the position of the center of the piece on the x axis and the calculation (y - grid.y + grid.height / 2) does the same on the y axis. Then, dividing by grid.width and grid.height, respectively, computes the closest position in grid coordinates (take a look back at Figure 5-3). Finally, multiplying the x axis value by grid.width and adding grid.x (gridX) converts the piece's horizontal position on the grid back to a pixel position on the game board. Likewise, multiplying by grid.height and adding grid.y (gridY) converts the vertical grid position back to a pixel position.

Drawing the Board

You're best off drawing the board to an offscreen Image and then copying this Image to the screen to get smooth screen updates (see "Drawing offscreen" in Chapter 1 for more info). Draw the board first and then draw the puzzle pieces on top of the board with a loop to call each piece's draw() method:

```
public void paint (Graphics g) {
  if (offscr != null) {
    offscr.drawImage(boardImage, 0, 0, null);
    for (int ii = 0; ii < pieces.length; ii++)
      pieces[ii].draw(offscr);
    g.drawImage(offscreenImage, 0, 0, this);
  }
}
```

And when drawing to an offscreen Image, you need to always override
update() to remove the flicker that it can cause:

```
public void update (Graphics g) {
  paint(g);
}
```

Declaring the Puzzle Solved and Congratulating the Winner

Finally, you need to add code to determine when the player has solved the
puzzle and to display an appropriate congratulatory message. As we cover
in the "Putting pieces together" section earlier in this chapter, you use the
init() method to create a Point object called winLocation that contains
the upper-left pixel coordinates for a 2 × 2 square in the winning location.
winLocation thus allows your code to check for a solved puzzle simply by
checking whether the 2 × 2 sized puzzle piece (which is the first entry in the
pieces[] array) has moved to the same location as winLocation, like this:

```
if (pieces[0].x == winLocation.x  &&
    pieces[0].y == winLocation.y)
```

Next, you need to display a nice simple message like "Win!" to herald the
success of the player. You can display such a message by adapting the code
from CD Chapter 3 that displays centered text. However, to create a nice
effect and help make the text stand out against the somewhat busy background of the puzzle board, you may also want to put a shadow beneath the
text. You can add a shadow by drawing the text twice: First, set the draw
color to black and draw the text offset down and to the right by a few pixels.
Then, set the color of the text, in this case yellow, and draw the text at the
centered position.

This new code, along with the `winLocation` check, is best added to the `paint()` method just after the `for` loop that draws the pieces. Here's the code:

```
if (pieces[0].x == winLocation.x  &&
    pieces[0].y == winLocation.y) {
  FontMetrics fm = offscr.getFontMetrics(bbCourier);
  offscr.setFont(bbCourier );
  int strHyt = fm.getAscent();
  int xOffset = (size().width - fm.stringWidth(winMsg)) / 2;
  int yOffset = (size().height - strHyt) / 2 + strHyt;
  offscr.setColor(Color.black);
  offscr.drawString(winMsg , xOffset + 3, yOffset + 3);
  offscr.setColor(Color.yellow);
  offscr.drawString(winMsg , xOffset, yOffset);
}
```

The solved puzzle is shown in Figure 5-4. Have fun trying to solve the puzzle yourself!

The complete code for the Sliding Blocks puzzle is on the *Java Game Programming For Dummies* CD-ROM included with this book.

Figure 5-4:
The puzzle
solved.

Chapter 6

Blackjack

· ·

In This Chapter

▶ Building a complete game of Blackjack

▶ Programming the fundamentals of card games

▶ Extracting graphics from composite images

▶ Creating a user interface using AWT components

▶ Arranging AWT components on the screen

· ·

Card games make fantastic Java games: They are relatively easy to program and are great for playing on a computer, whether by single or multiple players. You can create Java card games from any of the popular card games you're already familiar with, or you can invent your own.

All most card games require is a deck of cards and a playing surface. In this chapter, we present a complete game of Blackjack to demonstrate a reusable deck of cards, and show how to create a playing surface using the standard `Component` classes from the *Abstract Window Toolkit* (AWT). We also show you how to use the `button` and `text` components, and how to arrange various components on the screen using the AWT's `LayoutManager` classes; both of these techniques are applicable to many types of games.

Understanding the Blackjack Game

Blackjack (also called Twenty-One) is the most popular casino card game in the United States. The Blackjack dealer plays against one or more players, and in the casino version of Blackjack, the house rules strictly regulate the dealer's options for play. The dealer's predictable behavior makes Blackjack an excellent choice for a computer card game: You can make the computer play the role of dealer and easily program a strict set of dealer actions.

Playing Blackjack

The object in Blackjack is to end up with a hand that scores higher than the dealer's hand without going over 21. A hand's score is the sum of the values of all the cards in the hand, using the following point values for the cards:

- **Face cards (Jack, Queen, and King)** are each worth 10 points.

- **2 through 10** are worth points equal to the face value of the card.

- **Ace** is worth 11 points, except when the addition of 11 points makes the player's hand total more than 21 points, in which case the **Ace** is worth 1 point.

Each player places a bet to begin play. Next the dealer deals one card face-down to everyone at the table, including herself. Then the dealer deals a second card face-down to each player and a second card *face-up* to herself. Each player then has an opportunity to receive additional cards dealt face up one at a time (be *hit*) until either the cards in his hand exceed 21 points (the hand *busts*) or he declines additional cards (*stand*). After all players receive any additional cards they want, if any, the dealer exposes her face-down card and then takes cards according to the house rules — typically hitting the hand until it busts or totals at least 17 points.

The player loses his bet if he busts (goes over 21) or if the dealer's hand totals more than the player's hand. The dealer returns the bet if the player and dealer have hands with the same point totals and pays the player an amount equal to the bet if the dealer busts or the player's hand is higher than the dealer's hand.

In addition, Blackjack has a few special situations:

Blackjack's Special Situations

Blackjack	A *Blackjack,* or *natural,* is a hand that totals 21 points after the first two cards (an **Ace** counting as 11 points and a **10** or a **face card**). If a player has a natural and the dealer doesn't, the player wins 1 1/2 times the initial bet, and gets back his original bet as well. A natural beats a non-natural 21.
Double Down	After the first two cards are dealt, a player may opt to *double down,* which means the player doubles his bet and takes a single additional card. Some casinos restrict doubling down to when the player's hand totals 10 or 11.

Split	A player may *split* a hand consisting of two cards with the same point value into two hands, thereby doubling the chance for a win (or a loss, of course). The player puts the two hands side by side on the table and places a bet on the new hand equal to the original bet. The player then plays each hand normally, except that if a split hand totals 21 after two cards, it doesn't count as a natural.

Designing the game

The first step in designing an object-oriented program (***Remember:*** Java is an object-oriented programming language) is to look at the objects being modeled by the program. Figure 6-1 shows the objects in a real game of Blackjack.

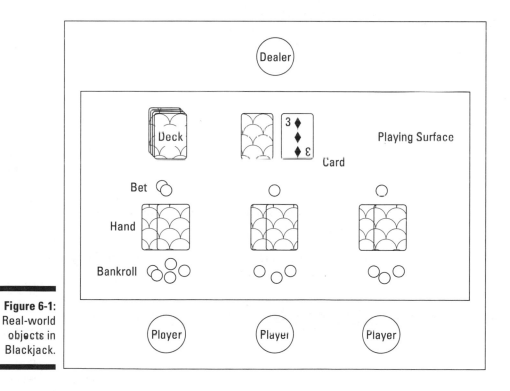

Figure 6-1: Real-world objects in Blackjack.

After you identify the objects your game needs to model, you need to organize the objects according to their relationships and functions in the game. Although programming challenges usually have more than one solution, the elements typically suggest certain logical relationships that, in turn, suggest the most elegant way to program them. The Blackjack game presented in this chapter organizes the elements of Blackjack, as shown in Figure 6-2.

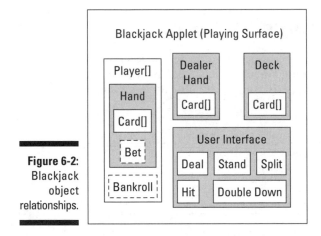

Figure 6-2:
Blackjack
object
relationships.

As Figure 6-2 shows, the Blackjack Applet provides the playing surface and contains an array of player objects, a dealer hand object, a deck object, and a user interface. The deck and dealer hand objects each contain an array of card objects. Each player object contains a player hand object and a bankroll. The player hand contains an array of card objects and a bet. The user interface is a panel component that contains the button objects for the various options available to the player. The fact that the object relationships for Blackjack look similar to the layout of the real-world "objects" is no coincidence: The game design is derived from the real-world objects.

Creating a Reusable Deck of Cards

A deck of cards is a common element to all card games (bet you didn't know *that*), and many of the techniques presented in this section can be applied to any card game you want to program. You can even create specialized decks (for example, Pinochle or Poker with the Joker added) with minor changes here and there, as we explain a bit later in this chapter.

One of the powerful aspects of object-oriented programming is how it facilitates reusing code. This section shows how to create a reusable Deck class that you can use in any card game that uses a standard deck. This section also presents the Card objects that the Deck class shuffles and deals.

Shuffling and dealing the deck

The Deck class uses an array to keep track of the cards in the deck. Rather than actually remove cards from the array as they are dealt, the Deck class maintains an index to the last card in the card array and deals cards from the end of the array. As each card is dealt, the index to the last card in the array is decremented. The complete Deck class is:

```java
import java.util.NoSuchElementException;
public class Deck {
  protected Card[]  cards;
  protected int     top;
  protected int     packs;

  public int getSize () { return top; }    //# undealt cards
  public int getPacks () { return packs; } //# packs in deck
  public int packSize () { return 52; }    //# cards in pack
  public Deck () { this(1); }
  public Deck (int packs) {
    if ((this.packs = packs) > 0) {
      top = packs * packSize();
      cards = new Card[top];
reshuffle();
    }
  }

  // Fills the deck with cards and shuffles
  public synchronized void reshuffle () {
    top = 0;
    for (int packs = this.packs;  --packs >= 0; )
      for (int suit = Card.CLUB; suit <= Card.SPADE; suit++)
        for (int rank = Card.ACE; rank <= Card.KING; rank++)
          cards[top++] = new Card(rank, suit);
    shuffle();
  }

  // Shuffles the undealt cards in the deck
  public synchronized void shuffle () {
    if (top > 1)
      for (int ii = top;  --ii >= 0; ) {
        int rnd = (int) (Math.random() * top);
        Card temp = cards[ii];
        cards[ii] = cards[rnd];
        cards[rnd] = temp;
      }
  }
```

(continued)

(continued)

```
// Deals the top card from the deck
public Card deal () throws NoSuchElementException {
  return deal(0);
}


// Deals a card from the deck. <pos> is relative to the
// top of the deck (0 = top, 1 = second from top, etc.)
public synchronized Card deal (int pos)
  throws NoSuchElementException
{
  Card c = peek(pos);
  if (pos > 0)  // deal card from middle of deck
    System.arraycopy(cards, top - pos,
                     cards, top - pos - 1, pos);
  top--;
  return c;
}


// Returns the top card from the deck without dealing it
public Card peek () throws NoSuchElementException {
  return peek(0);
}


// Returns a card from the deck without dealing it.
// <pos> is relative to the top of the deck (0 = top)
public synchronized Card peek (int pos)
  throws NoSuchElementException
{
  if (pos < 0)
throw new NoSuchElementException();
  try { return cards[top - (pos + 1)]; }
  catch (IndexOutOfBoundsException e) {
    throw new NoSuchElementException();
  }
}
} // end class Deck
```

The algorithm used in `Deck.shuffle()` works by swapping each card in the deck with another randomly selected card. This swapping randomizes the deck after a single pass through the deck and is much simpler than simulating a real shuffle.

The deal() and peek() methods fetch cards from the deck. deal() removes the fetched cards from the deck, but peek() does not. Both deal() and peek() are *overloaded* methods, meaning that they are given alternate versions with different parameters. One version operates on the top card in the deck; the other version accepts a parameter specifying the card position. The Blackjack applet doesn't use peek() or the ability to deal from the middle of the deck; neither is necessary for a functioning Blackjack game. However, other computer card games, like Solitaire, use these methods to cycle through the deck multiple times and play cards from arbitrary positions.

Notice that instead of defining its own subclass of Exception to indicate when a requested card is unavailable, Deck uses the standard java.util.NoSuchElementException class included as part of the Java API. Using this standard class eliminates your having to write and the player's web browser having to download extra code to define a class to handle unavailable cards.

Some card games, including Blackjack, use a deck built from combining several packs of cards. The Deck class supports multipack decks by overloading the Deck() constructor to accept the number of packs to use.

Building the Card class

Each card must remember just two things: its *suit* (**Club, Diamond, Heart, Spade**) and its *rank* (**Ace, 2, 3, 4, 5, 6, 7, 8, 9, 10, Jack, Queen, King**). You can give cards the following capabilities to make working with them as easy as possible:

- ✔ **Assign the suits and ranks to** static final **variables.**
- ✔ **Override** Object.toString() **so that a card can display its name.**
- ✔ **Have cards draw themselves to a specified** Graphics **context.**
- ✔ **Override** Object.equals() **so that cards can compare themselves.**

The resulting Card class is

```
import java.awt.*;
import java.applet.Applet;

public class Card {
  public static final int
      CLUB = 0, DIAMOND = 1, HEART = 2, SPADE = 3;
```

(continued)

(continued)

```
public static final int
    JOKER = 0, ACE = 1, TWO = 2, THREE = 3, FOUR = 4,
    FIVE = 5, SIX = 6, SEVEN = 7, EIGHT = 8, NINE = 9,
    TEN = 10, JACK = 11, QUEEN = 12, KING = 13;
private static final String[] suitNames =
    { Club , Diamond , Heart , Spade };
private static final String[] rankNames =
    { Joker , Ace , Two , Three , Four , Five ,
      Six , Seven , Eight , Nine , Ten , Jack ,
      Queen , King };
private static Image cardsImage;
private static int  cardWidth, cardHeight;  // in pixels
private int rank;
private int suit;

public final int getRank () { return rank; }
public final int getSuit () { return suit; }
public Card (int rank, int suit) {
  if ((this.rank = rank) != JOKER)
    this.suit = suit;
}

public final String getSuitName () {
  return rank == JOKER ?    : suitNames[suit];
}
public final String getPluralSuitName () {
  return rank == JOKER ?    : suitNames[suit] + s ;
}
public final String getRankName () {
  return rankNames[rank];
}
public final String getPluralRankName () {
  return rankNames[rank] + (rank == SIX ? es  :  s );
}
public final String getArticle () {
  return rank == ACE || rank == EIGHT ? an   : a ;
}

public final boolean isRed () {
  return suit == DIAMOND || suit == HEART;
}
public final boolean isFace () {
  return rank >= JACK;
}
```

```
public static int getCardWidth ()   { return cardWidth; }
public static int getCardHeight ()  { return cardHeight; }
/* If not currently loaded, then loads and inits the
 * cards.gif  image. This image is laid out as a 14 wide
 * by 4 tall grid of card images laid out as:
 *   JOKER    A 2 3 4 5 6 7 8 9 10 J Q K  (CLUBS)
 *   CARDBACK A 2 3 4 5 6 7 8 9 10 J Q K  (DIAMONDS)
 *   BLANK    A 2 3 4 5 6 7 8 9 10 J Q K  (HEARTS)
 *   BLANK    A 2 3 4 5 6 7 8 9 10 J Q K  (SPADES)
 */
public static synchronized void initGraphics(Applet app) {
  if (cardsImage == null) {
    MediaTracker tracker = new MediaTracker(app);
    cardsImage = app.getImage(app.getCodeBase(),
                              cards.gif );
    tracker.addImage(cardsImage, 0);
    try { tracker.waitForAll(); }
    catch (InterruptedException e) {}
    cardWidth = cardsImage.getWidth(app) / 14;
    cardHeight = cardsImage.getHeight(app) / 4;
  }
}


public static void drawCardBack (Graphics g,
                                 int x, int y) {
  // card back is second card down in first column
  doDraw(g, x, y, 0, cardHeight);
}


private static void doDraw (Graphics g, int x, int y,
                            int xoff, int yoff) {
  if (cardsImage != null) {
    Graphics gcopy = g.create();
    gcopy.clipRect(x, y, cardWidth, cardHeight);
    gcopy.drawImage(cardsImage, x - xoff, y - yoff, null);
    gcopy.dispose();
  }
}


public void draw (Graphics g, int x, int y) {
  doDraw(g, x, y, rank * cardWidth, suit * cardHeight);
}
```

(continued)

(continued)

```
public String toString () {
  StringBuffer buf = new StringBuffer(rankNames[rank]);
  if (rank != JOKER)
    buf.append( of ).append(getPluralSuitName());
  return buf.toString();
}

public boolean equals (Object obj) {
  if (obj instanceof Card) {
    Card c = (Card)obj;
    return c.rank == rank && c.suit == suit;
  }
  return false;
}

public int hashCode () {
  return (rank << 2) + suit;
}
} // end class Card
```

The Card class supports **Jokers** even though Blackjack does not use a **Joker.** Card is a general-purpose class useful for all kinds of games, including those that use a **Joker.**

Converting cards to strings

Most computer games use an image of a card to represent a card on screen, but sometimes cards need to be displayed as text. For example, if you are trying to develop and debug a game, you may want the cards to appear as text so that you can work out the process of the game before creating the images for the cards.

To convert cards to strings, override Object.toString() so that it implicitly converts an object to a string when using the + string concatenation operator. A Card object has methods for returning the plural and singular names of its suit and rank. Card uses these methods in toString() to construct and return the name of the card.

For example, the following code displays **The card is an Ace of Spades**:

```
Card c = new Card(Card.ACE, Card.SPADE);
System.out.println( The card is  + c.getArticle() + c);
```

Overriding `equals()`

Notice that `Card` overrides both `Object.equals()` and `Object.hashCode()`. The `Vector`, `Hashtable`, and other data structure classes use `equals()`. A `Vector` is like an array that automatically grows as new objects are added to it. A `Hashtable` is a vector where the objects are located by using a key object, such as a string, instead of an index. `Hashtable` uses a *hash code* (an integer) — calculated by calling the `hashCode()` method for the key object — to find the object in the hash table. You need to maintain certain relationships between `equals()` and `hashCode()` in order for an object to work correctly with these data structures. While the `Card` objects work fine with the array used by the `Deck` class, the games that use the `Card` class may place `Card` objects in `Vectors` or `Hashtables`. So whenever you override `equals()` or `hashCode()`, you must make sure that the following expressions remain true:

```
a.equals(b) == b.equals(a)
if (a.equals(b))
    a.hashCode() == b.hashCode()
```

In addition, both `equals()` and `hashCode()` need to return consistent results throughout the lifetime of the object. The data structures use `equals()` and `hashCode()` to organize and find the objects placed in the data structure. If the result of `equals()` or `hashCode()` changes, the object could become "lost" in the data structure. You use *immutable* (unchangeable) attributes to calculate the hash code and perform the equality comparison consistently. For example, the `Card` class uses the `suit` and `rank` attributes in both `equals()` and `hashCode()` but never changes their values after the `Card()` constructor runs.

Extracting card graphics from a composite image

`Card` contains several methods that load and display card graphics. Instead of loading 54 individual images (52 cards plus a joker and a card back), the methods in `Card` use a *composite image* (a single large image that contains all the individual images) and then extract a piece of the composite image to draw the particular card to the screen, as shown in Figure 6-3. Think of the composite image as a quilt of card "patches" from which the code extracts the necessary patch to display.

A single large image downloads faster, requires less memory to store, and is easier to create and edit than multiple small images. It also keeps all the images for a deck of cards encapsulated in a single object, and that fits well with an object-oriented design.

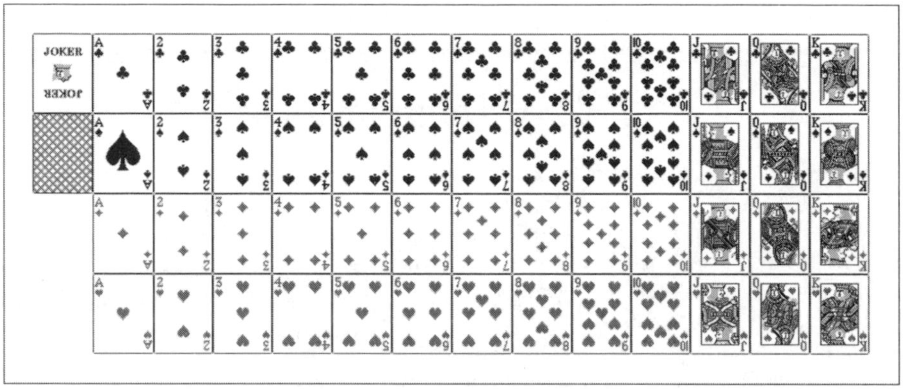

Figure 6-3:
The
"cards.gif"
composite
image.

Four rows of 14 card images — one row for each suit — combine to form the composite image. You call the static method `initGraphics()` to load the combined image. `initGraphics()` uses the `MediaTracker` class discussed in Chapter 5 to load the `cardsImage` image. `initGraphics()` calculates the width (`cardWidth`) of an individual card by dividing the composite image's width by 14 and the height (`cardHeight`) by dividing the composite's height by 4.

To draw a single card rather than the entire `cardsImage` graphic, you need to define a *clipping region* to restrict where the graphics context draws pixels. To understand how a clipping region works, imagine that the graphics context is a piece of paper. To create a clipping region take another piece of paper the same size, cut a rectangular hole in it, and position it over the first piece of paper. Now when you draw on the graphics context, you can only draw within the clipping region. To draw a card from the `cardsImage` graphic, you make the clipping region the size of a single card, then position `cardsImage` to line up the desired card with the clipping region and call `drawImage()` to draw the card. Figure 6-4 shows what this clipping image looks like if `cardsImage` is a third piece of paper and you place it between the other two sheets of paper.

The `draw()` and `drawCardBack()` methods use `cardWidth` and `cardHeight` to calculate the x,y pixel coordinates of the upper-left corner of the image to extract from `cardsImage`. These methods pass the x,y pixel coordinates to `doDraw()`, which uses them as the offsets for positioning `cardsImage` so that the card to be drawn is in the correct place relative to the clipping region. `doDraw()` sets the clipping region and draws the card using the following code:

```
Graphics gcopy = g.create();
   gcopy.clipRect(x, y, cardWidth, cardHeight);
   gcopy.drawImage(cardsImage, x - xoff, y - yoff, null);
   gcopy.dispose();
```

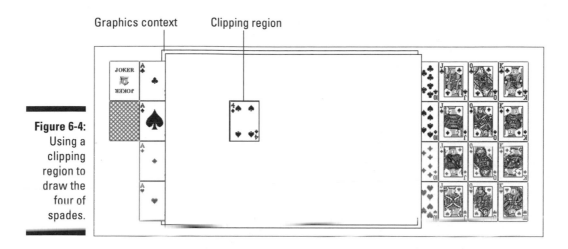

Graphics context   Clipping region

Figure 6-4:
Using a
clipping
region to
draw the
four of
spades.

The clipRect() call sets the upper-left corner of the clipping region to the specified x and y coordinates and sets the width and height of the region to the dimensions of a single card. drawImage() accepts the position for the upper-left corner of cardsImage. You calculate the position of cardsImage relative to the clipping region by subtracting the x and y offsets within cardsImage (xoff and yoff) of the upper-left corner of the card to draw.

Setting the clipping region of a graphics context is an irreversible operation. Each subsequent call to clipRect() sets the clipping region to the intersection of the current clipping region and the new region, which means that you can never enlarge the clipping region. In order to keep from permanently setting the main clipping region of the component, the preceding code from doDraw() obtains a temporary copy of the graphics context, sets the clipping region in the copy, and performs the draw operations using the copy. The code obtains a copy of the graphics context by calling the context's create() method. After it finishes with the temporary copy, the code calls its dispose() method so that the Java Virtual Machine (JVM) can reclaim its memory.

Java 1.1 adds the setClip() method to the Graphics class and allows the clipping area to be more flexibly resized. You don't need to make a copy of the graphics context before using setClip(). However, until Java 1.1 becomes more widely used, use clipRect() for maximum portability.

Customizing the deck

You can give the cards in the deck custom graphics by creating a new cards.gif image. The Card class automatically calculates the size of the cards based on the image.

In addition, you can extend the Deck class to play Poker with a joker in the deck or to play games such as Pinochle that use a nonstandard deck of cards. You override packSize() and reshuffle() to initialize the custom deck. A Pinochle deck has 48 cards — two of each suit of the ranks nine through ace. You implement a Pinochle deck like this:

```
public class PinochleDeck extends Deck {
  public PinochleDeck ()          { super(); }
  public PinochleDeck (int packs) { super(packs); }
  public int packSize ()          { return 48; }
  public synchronized void reshuffle () {
    top = 0;
    for (int packs = this.packs * 2;  --packs >= 0; )
      for (int suit = Card.CLUB; suit <= Card.SPADE; suit++)
      {
        for (int rank = Card.NINE; rank <= Card.KING; rank++)
          cards[top++] = new Card(rank, suit);
        cards[top++] = new Card(Card.ACE, suit);
      }
    shuffle();
  }
}  // end class PinochleDeck
```

Creating a User Interface with Components

You create a user interface in Java from AWT components. Component is an abstract class in the java.awt package that embodies all the common functions of user interface elements. You build your interface from the subclasses of Component: Button, Canvas, Checkbox, Choice, Label, List, Scrollbar, TextArea, and TextField.

Using buttons

Buttons are a common interface element. You use buttons to represent an action the user can perform. Unlike menus, which also represent available actions, a button is

 ✔ **Visible, so the user doesn't have to look through menus to determine what actions are available.**

 ✔ **Convenient, because it requires a single mouse click to perform the associated action.**

You use the Button class in the java.awt package to add buttons to your game.

Creating and placing buttons

In order to create a button, you invoke the Button() constructor and pass it a string to use as the button label. The button automatically adjusts its size to fit the label. Optionally, you can omit the string in the constructor call and call the button's setLabel() method to set the label string.

```
Button dealButton = new Button( Deal );
Button cancel = new Button();
cancel.setLabel( Cancel   + operation);
```

After you create a button, you must call add() to add the button to a Container component — a Panel, Applet, Window, Frame, or Dialog — in order to use it. After adding components to a container, you need to call the container's layout() or validate() method to tell the container to arrange its components and set their sizes. layout() arranges the current container; validate() arranges the current container as well as any containers *inside* the current container.

Component peers

You don't usually subclass Button or most other components to create custom versions. Only Canvas and the container components — Panel, Applet, Window, Frame, Dialog, and FileDialog — are designed to be extended. The reason is that each AWT component has a platform-specific *component peer*.

A component peer is a class that connects an AWT component such as a button to the platform's native implementation. The peers

then draw the component and handle the component events. So for example, Microsoft Windows implements the ButtonPeer using a Windows button, and Apple Computer's MacOS implements the ButtonPeer using a Mac button, and so on. The component peer feature is why Java buttons on a Mac look different than Java buttons on a PC. The two figures below show the same applet (Colored Applet) running in Netscape Navigator 3.0, one in Windows 95, a PC, and one on a Mac running OS 8.

Having your game respond to buttons

Button **converts a mouse click into an** ACTION_EVENT. **You override** Component.action() **in the parent container in order to handle action events. You identify the button that generated the event in** action() **by comparing the** Event.target **field to the** Button **object or, alternately, by comparing the** Event.arg **field to the button label string.**

Here is an example of an applet creating and responding to a button:

```
import java.awt.*;
public class ColoredApplet extends java.applet.Applet {
  private Button red = new Button( Red );
  private Button blue = new Button( Blue );
  public void init () {
    add(red);
    add(blue);
    layout();
  }

  public boolean action (Event evt, Object arg) {
    if (evt.target == red)
      setBackground(Color.red);
    else if ( Blue .equals(arg))
      setBackground(Color.blue);
    repaint();
    return true;
  }
} // end class ColoredApplet
```

Notice that the action() **method in** ColoredApplet **uses the** evt.target field to find the red **button and uses the** arg **parameter to identify the** blue button. We include both techniques in the example just to show both ways of checking. However, the evt.target **way is faster, because comparing object references is less work than comparing strings.**

Reading and displaying text

At some point, most programs need to display text or collect information entered by the user. Java 1.0 provides three components for displaying text: TextField, TextArea, **and** Label. **The Blackjack applet uses labels to display each player's name and current bankroll.** TextField **and** TextArea **also accept text typed by the user.** TextField **displays and accepts a single line of text;** TextArea **creates a scrollable, editable text area that displays multiple lines. This section shows how to use each of these components.**

Displaying status and scores with labels

You use a Label component to display text in a container. The program code can change the text in a label, but the user cannot edit the text on screen. You can use labels to display things such as game scores or to create, well . . . *labels* such as those used to describe on-screen buttons or other objects. You create a label and add it to a container like this:

```
import java.awt.*;
public class ScoreLabel extends java.applet.Applet {
  private int    score;
  private Label scoreDisplay;

  public void init () {
    add(new Label( Score ));
    add(scoreDisplay = new Label(     0 , Label.RIGHT));
    layout();
  }

  public boolean mouseDown (Event evt, int x, int y) {
    scoreDisplay.setText(Integer.toString(score += x));
    return true;
  }
} // end class ScoreLabel
```

This example initially sets the scoreDisplay label to a right-aligned string with several leading zeros, as shown in Figure 6-5. The spaces cause the label to automatically set its size to be larger than the space required for just the 0 character. The RIGHT alignment positions the label text from the right edge of the label so that additional digits appear on the left. You align a label to the LEFT, CENTER, or RIGHT — the default alignment is LEFT.

Figure 6-5:
The
ScoreLabel
applet.

Getting a few words from the user

Use a TextField component to collect a single line of text from the user. As with other components, you add a text field to a Container component. You override action() in the container to detect when the user enters text.

TextField is a subclass of TextComponent. A TextComponent supports the normal cut, copy, paste, and text edit functions of the underlying operating system (OS). Table 6-1 lists some of the TextComponent methods for working with text.

Table 6-1	TextComponent Methods
Method	*Use This Method to . . .*
getText()	Retrieve the current text from the component.
setText(str)	Set the value of the component's text to the string str.
getSelectedText()	Retrieve the currently selected text in the component.
select(start, end)	Set the component's selection to the characters from offset start to offset end, inclusive.
setEditable(edit)	If the boolean parameter edit is false, user editing is disabled for the component; otherwise editing is enabled.

The offset of a character is the position in a string of that character, starting from 0 and counting up. For example, the letter "n" has an offset of 3 in the word "Barney."

Creating scrolling text areas

You use a TextArea to create editable and scrollable text displays. As is TextField, TextArea is a subclass of TextComponent and has all the text editing features listed in Table 6-1. TextArea also has the three additional methods for working with the text, listed in Table 6-2.

Table 6-2	Additional TextArea Methods
Method	*Use This Method to . . .*
appendText(str)	Append the string str to the end of the area's current text.
insertText(str, pos)	Insert the string str at the character offset pos.
replaceText(str, start, end)	Replace the text from character offset start to offset end, inclusive, with the string str.

The following example uses a `Label`, `TextField`, and `TextArea`:

```
import java.awt.*;
public class ListEntry extends java.applet.Applet {
  static final String newline =

                  System.getProperty( line.separator );
  private TextArea    list = new TextArea(5, 20);
  private TextField   entry = new TextField(20);

  public void init () {
    list.setEditable(false);
    add(list);
    add(new Label( Name: , Label.RIGHT));
    add(entry);
  }

  public boolean action (Event evt, Object arg) {
    if (evt.target == entry) {
      list.appendText(entry.getText() + newline);
      entry.selectAll();
      return true;
    }
    return false;
  }
} // end class ListEntry
```

`ListEntry` creates a `TextArea` that holds five lines of approximately 20 characters each and a `TextField` that holds a single line of approximately 20 characters. The AWT calls `ListEntry.action()` when the user presses the Enter or Return key in the `entry` text field. `action()` appends the `entry` text to the `list` text area and selects the text in `entry` so that the next text that the user types replaces the current text. Figure 6-6 shows the program running.

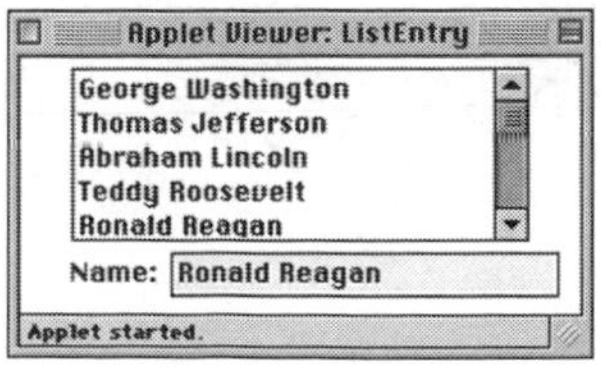

Figure 6-6:
The
`ListEntry`
applet.

The `System.getProperty( line.separator )` call in the preceding example gets the *system-dependent* character string used to separate lines of text. You would think that operating systems would standardize on something as simple and basic as a line separator, but they don't. Under UNIX-based operating systems, the separator is a linefeed character (\n); under Mac OS, the separator is a carriage return character (\r); and under DOS and Windows operating systems, the separator is a carriage return followed by a linefeed (\r\n).

Using `Canvas` *to create new components*

A `Canvas` component is a way to create your own component — it provides all the hooks to collect user events and draw itself, but the default canvas is basically a blank slate. You can use `Canvas` to create your game's playfield, displays, and just about anything else that you want to display a certain way.

Customizing your game's appearance with `ImageButton`

The AWT components are functional but not particularly colorful. You can design your own custom components by subclassing the `Canvas` component. The simplest and probably the most useful component to customize is `Button`. The following `ImageButton` class uses two images — the pressed and unpressed button images — rather than the standard button with a text label:

```
import java.awt.*;
public class ImageButton extends Canvas implements Runnable {
  private ThreadGroup tg;
  private Image[]     img = new Image[2]; //up = 0, down = 1
  private int         imgndx;             //index into img[]

  public ImageButton (Image up, Image down) {
    tg = Thread.currentThread().getThreadGroup();
    img[0] = up;
    img[1] = down;
  }

  public synchronized Dimension minimumSize () {
    int x = Math.max(img[0].getWidth(null),
                     img[1].getWidth(null));
    int y = Math.max(img[0].getHeight(null),
                     img[1].getHeight(null));
    return new Dimension(x < 0 ? 10 : x, y < 0 ? 10 : y);
  }
```

```
public Dimension preferredSize () {
  return minimumSize();
}

public void paint (Graphics g) {
  if (img[imgndx] != null)
    g.drawImage(img[imgndx], 0, 0, this);
}

public void update (Graphics g) {
  paint(g);
}

public synchronized void run () {
  imgndx = 1;
  repaint();
  Component p = getParent();
  if (p != null)
    p.postEvent(new Event(this, Event.ACTION_EVENT,
                          img[0]));
try { Thread.sleep(200); }  // press for 1/5 second
  catch (InterruptedException e) {}
  imgndx = 0;
  repaint();
}


public synchronized boolean mouseDown (Event evt,
                                       int x, int y) {
  (new Thread(tg, this)).start();
  return true;
}
}  // end class ImageButton
```

The following are the key points for implementing `ImageButton`:

- ✔ ImageButton **overrides** Component.preferredSize() **and** Component.minimumSize() **in order to have the button automatically size itself to the size of the largest image.**

- ✔ mouseDown() **spawns a thread to animate the button press so that it doesn't perform the animation in the AWT Interface thread.** (CD Chapter 2 explains what the AWT Interface thread is and how to spawn threads from mouseDown() and other event handlers.)

- ✔ mouseDown() **and** run() **are** synchronized **to prevent the animation from being interrupted.** Synchronization prevents mouse clicks from being processed faster than the animation rate.

✔ `run()` **passes an** `ACTION_EVENT` **to the parent container's**
`postEvent()` **method so that you handle** `ImageButton` **events in the**
same way as `Button` **events.** Because an `ImageButton` doesn't have a
label string, it uses the "up" image for the `Event.arg` field.

✔ **The button animation is state-driven;** `run()` **sets the** `imgndx` **variable**
to change the state, and `paint()` **uses** `imgndx` **to display the current**
state.

Java 1.2 has something called *lightweight components* that support custom
appearances without having to re-create the entire functionality of the
component.

Displaying a hand of cards

The Blackjack computer game extends `Canvas` to create a displayable hand
of cards, as shown in Figure 6-7.

Figure 6-7:
A
BlackjackHand
with four
cards.

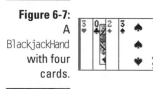

The `BlackjackHand` class includes both the code for displaying the hand
and for handling the details of a Blackjack hand — dealing cards to the hand,
calculating the value of the hand, testing for a Blackjack (natural), and so
on. The `BlackjackHand` class is

```java
import java.awt.*;
import java.util.*;

class BlackjackHand extends Canvas {
  protected int      horizInset;
  protected boolean  soft;
  protected Vector   hand = new Vector(6);
  private boolean    exposed, active;
  private Image      offscreenImage;
  private Graphics   offscr;
  public Dimension preferredSize () {
    return new Dimension((Card.getCardWidth() + horizInset)
                    * 2, Card.getCardHeight());

  }
```

```
BlackjackHand () {
  resize(preferredSize());
}


int cardCount ()                 { return hand.size(); }
protected boolean isDealer () { return true; }
boolean blackjack () {  // is a blackjack?
  return hand.size() == 2 && value() == 21;
}


boolean isSoft () {  // has an 11-point ace in the hand?
  value();  // sets <soft> field
  return soft;
}


void setActive (boolean on) {  // highlight this hand
  active = on;
  repaint();
}


void expose () {  // expose the dealer s hole card
  exposed = true;
  repaint();
}


void clearHand () {  // remove all cards from hand
  hand.removeAllElements();
  exposed = active = soft = false;
  repaint();
  Thread.yield();
}


void deal (Card card) {  // deal a card to the hand
  hand.addElement(card);
  repaint();
}


public void paint (Graphics g) {
  if (offscreenImage == null) {
    offscreenImage = createImage(size().width,
                                 size().height);
    offscr = offscreenImage.getGraphics();
  }
```

(continued)

(continued)

```
    offscr.setColor(active ? Color.yellow : Color.gray);
    offscr.fillRect(0, 0, size().width, size().height);
    int handsize = hand.size();
    if (handsize > 0) {
      int overlap = Math.min(Card.getCardWidth(),
                   (size().width - Card.getCardWidth() -
                   2*horizInset) / Math.max(1, handsize-1));
      Enumeration deal = hand.elements();
      int xoff = horizInset;
      while (deal.hasMoreElements()) {
        Card card = (Card)deal.nextElement();
        if (!exposed && isDealer() && xoff == horizInset)
          Card.drawCardBack(offscr, xoff, 0);
        else
          card.draw(offscr, xoff, 0);
        xoff += overlap;
      }
    }
    g.drawImage(offscreenImage, 0, 0, this);
  }

  public void update (Graphics g) { paint(g); }
  // returns the point value for the hand
  int value () {
    int val = 0;
    boolean ace = false;
    for (int ii = hand.size();  --ii >= 0; ) {
      int v = value(ii);
      val += v;
      if (v == Card.ACE) ace = true;
    }
    if (soft = (val <= 11 && ace))
      val += 10;
    return val;
  }

  // returns base point value of card <cardNum> in the hand
  protected int value (int cardNum) {
    int rank = ((Card)hand.elementAt(cardNum)).getRank();
    return Math.min(Card.TEN, rank);  // face cards are 10's
  }
}  // end class BlackjackHand
```

Here are the key elements in BlackjackHand:

- ✔ BlackjackHand **extends** java.awt.Canvas **so that it can display itself on the screen.**

- ✔ **The** BlackjackHand() **constructor sets the size of the canvas — necessary because by default a canvas is zero pixels wide and zero pixels tall.**

- ✔ **The** java.util.Vector **field** hand **stores the cards. (Remember, a** Vector **works like an array that automatically resizes itself as more objects are added to it.)** Using a vector allows a hand to accept any number of cards dealt to it. deal() adds cards to the vector and clearHand() removes all the cards from the vector.

- ✔ BlackjackHand **overrides** paint() **to create the display for the hand.** If necessary, paint() overlaps the cards to fit within the display area — this makes the cards look like they are "fanned out" on the table, as shown back in Figure 6-1.

- ✔ paint() **uses the graphics context** offscr **to draw to the offscreen image.** offscreenImage.paint() copies the offscreen image to the screen to smoothly draw the hand to the screen in a single operation. paint() initializes the offscreen buffer the first time it runs. (Chapter 1 discusses the details of using an offscreen image.)

- ✔ horizInset **holds the number of pixels to inset the hand from the left and right edges of the canvas.** The Blackjack applet uses the inset space to highlight the active hand. setActive() sets or clears the hand's active state.

Arranging the User Interface

Like the Web pages in which Java runs, Java configures its screen area to fit the available space and allows a Java applet to automatically adapt to smaller or larger screens. Creating an interface that configures itself presents challenges. On the one hand, you don't have to worry about specifying the pixel location of each interface component. On the other hand, trying to get your game to look just the way you want can be frustrating. Compounding this frustration is the fact that the size and look of the individual components vary between platforms. But rest assured, with a little work you can create a user interface that looks good and intelligently configures itself to fit a variety of screen sizes.

Positioning components with a LayoutManager

The AWT uses classes that implement the java.awt.LayoutManager interface to determine what size to make AWT components and where to place them. Each container — a Panel, Applet, Window, Frame, Dialog, or FileDialog — has its own *layout manager* to accomplish this task.

A layout manager positions each of the components in the container and can also set the sizes of the contained components. The layout manager calls a component's move() method to position the component, calls resize() to set the component's size, and calls reshape() to set both the size and position. Most layout managers use the component's preferredSize() and minimumSize() methods to determine its dimensions, but some layout managers ignore these suggested sizes (see Table 6-3).

You can subclass Label, Button, and other AWT components to override the preferredSize() and minimumSize() methods. By doing so, you can explicitly control the size of the laid-out component.

The AWT provides five layout managers — BorderLayout, CardLayout, FlowLayout, GridLayout, GridBagLayout. Table 6-3 lists types of layout managers assigned by default to each type of container.

Table 6-3	Default Layout Managers	
Container	*Layout Manager*	*Comments*
Panel	FlowLayout	
Applet	FlowLayout	
Window	BorderLayout	(ignores suggested size)
Frame	BorderLayout	(ignores suggested size)
Dialog	BorderLayout	(ignores suggested size)
FileDialog	null	

A container can have a null layout manager for which you must explicitly position its components. A container with a layout that doesn't need to adapt to different screen sizes — for example, a container that conforms to a background graphic — may be best with a null layout manager.

If you want to use a different layout manager than the default, pass the new layout manager to the container's setLayout() method. For example, if you want to have an applet use a BorderLayout, place the following in the applet's init() method:

```
setLayout(new BorderLayout());
```

If you change a container's layout manager after it has already been laid out, you need to tell the container. To do so, call invalidate() to tell the container to invalidate its current layout and then call validate() to have the container recursively layout itself along with any nested containers.

FlowLayout

You use a FlowLayout manager to arrange the components from left to right and top to bottom. Each horizontal row aligns its components LEFT, CENTER, or RIGHT. The default alignment is CENTER.

The following code produces the applet that Figure 6-8 shows:

```
public class Flow extends java.applet.Applet {
  public void init () {
    for (int i = 1;  i < 10;  i++)
      add(new java.awt.Button(Integer.toString(i)));
  }
}
```

Figure 6-8:
An applet
using
FlowLayout.

BorderLayout

BorderLayout arranges as many as five components: one along each of the four sides and one in the center of the container. You call the container's add() method with the name of the location (North , South , East , West , or Center) at which to add a component to a BorderLayout container. If you don't specify a location, the layout manager places the component in the center location.

BorderLayout resizes the components according to the following rules:

- ✔ **The north and south components use their preferred height but are resized as wide as the container.**

- ✔ **The east and west components use their preferred width but are resized to be as tall as the container minus the heights of the north and south components.**

> ✓ **The center component is resized to fill the remaining space not used by the other components in the container.** It is as tall as the east and west components, and as wide as the container minus the widths of the east and west components.

The following code produces the applet shown in Figure 6-9:

```
public class Border extends java.applet.Applet {
  public void init () {
    setLayout(new java.awt.BorderLayout());
    add( North ,  new java.awt.Button( North ));
    add( East ,   new java.awt.Button( East ));
    add( West ,   new java.awt.Button( West ));
    add( South ,  new java.awt.Button( South ));
    add( Center , new java.awt.Button( Center ));
  }
}
```

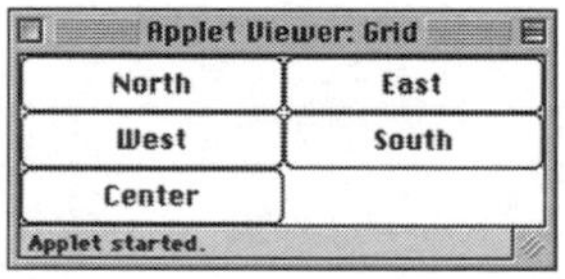

Figure 6-9:
An applet
using
BorderLayout.

GridLayout

You use a GridLayout to arrange all the components on an evenly spaced grid. GridLayout resizes each component to fit the grid. You can create the applet Figure 6-10 shows by replacing the setLayout() call in the preceding Border example with

```
setLayout(new java.awt.GridLayout(0,2));
```

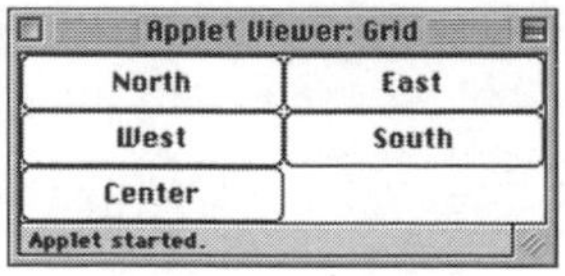

Figure 6-10:
An applet
using
GridLayout.

Your own LayoutManager

If none of the layout managers supplied by the AWT is right for your container, you can always write your own. You create a layout manager by implementing the LayoutManager interface in your class.

A layout manager needs to do two things:

✔ **Determine the preferred and minimum sizes needed to layout the components in a container.**

✔ **Lay out a container's components, which requires positioning and possibly sizing the components.**

The Blackjack applet uses a custom layout manager to arrange the hands for a player. A Blackjack player starts out with a single hand of cards. When a player splits a hand, the hand becomes two new hands. (**Remember:** The player may *split* a hand into two hands if the first two cards have the same point value.) Further, the player can potentially split either or both of the new hands. Because it takes a lot of space to display each hand, reserving space for the unlikely possibility that each player would end up with four hands more than doubles the size of the applet. A better solution is to overlap the hands to cover up part of the hand, as Figure 6-11 shows.

Figure 6-11:
Laying out
split hands.

The following custom layout manager lays out the hands as Figure 6-11 shows:

```
import java.awt.*;

class PlayerHandLayout implements LayoutManager {
  private BlackjackPlayer player;
  private float overlap;
  public PlayerHandLayout (BlackjackPlayer player,
                           float overlap) {
    this.player = player;
    this.overlap = overlap;
  }

  public void addLayoutComponent (String nm, Component c) {}
  public void removeLayoutComponent (Component c) {}
  public Dimension preferredLayoutSize (Container parent) {
    Dimension ds = ((BlackjackHand)parent.getComponent(0)). preferredSize();
    int numHands = parent.countComponents();
    if (numHands <= 2)
      return new Dimension(ds.width, ds.height * numHands);
```

(continued)

(continued)

```
    else
      return new Dimension(ds.width, (ds.height * 2) +
            (numHands - 2) * (int)(overlap * ds.height));
  }


  public Dimension minimumLayoutSize (Container parent) {
    return preferredLayoutSize(parent);
  }


  public void layoutContainer (Container parent) {
    Dimension hsize = ((BlackjackHand)parent.getComponent(0)).preferredSize();
    int numHands = parent.countComponents();
    int h, y = 0;
    for (int ii = 0;  ii < numHands;  ii++) {
      if (ii == player.getHandIndex()  ||
          ii == player.getActiveHandCount()-1)
        h = hsize.height;
      else
        h = (int)(hsize.height * overlap);
      parent.getComponent(ii).
          reshape(0, y, hsize.width, hsize.height);
      y += h;
    }
  }
}  // end class PlayerHandLayout
```

The prevalent aspects of PlayerHandLayout are

✔ **The** BlackjackPlayer **passes a reference to itself and the vertical** overlap **ratio to the** PlayerHandLayout() **constructor.** layoutContainer() uses player to access information about the hand.

✔ layoutContainer() **leaves the active hand exposed so that it's easier to recognize.** Figure 6-12 shows the layout of four split hands where the second hand is the exposed, active hand.

✔ layoutContainer() **calls** reshape() **to set the size of overlapped hands to the size of the exposed area of the hand.** Using reshape() is important, because you can't rely on the draw order to obscure other hands; the AWT doesn't guarantee any particular draw order for the components.

✔ `preferredLayoutSize()` **calculates the dimensions needed to display** `numHands` **hands by assuming two exposed hands: the active hand and the last hand.** If the active hand is the last hand, only one hand is exposed, but the calculation still sets the size of the hands as if two hands were exposed. The result of this calculation allows the container to size itself based on the maximum number of hands a player can have.

✔ **Layouts such as** `BorderLayout`, **which separate the components into different named groups, use the** `addLayoutComponent()` **and** `removeLayoutComponent()` **methods to organize the components into groups.** However, `PlayerHandLayout` doesn't use these methods and just needs to include empty methods to complete the `LayoutManager` interface.

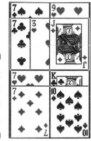

Figure 6-12:
Exposing
the active
hand.

Dividing the screen with panels

Frequently, you cannot arrange an applet or other container with a single layout manager. In these cases, you can arrange your interface hierarchically by grouping components within `Panel` containers and using the panel's layout manager to arrange the components inside the panel. The panel itself is a single component arranged by the layout manager for the container containing the panel.

For example, consider an applet with four groups of radio buttons and several standard buttons. You can use these steps to arrange the radio buttons into separate columns and the standard buttons into a row across the bottom:

1. Create a panel for each column of radio buttons.

Give each of these panels a `GridLayout(0, 1)` layout manager. Add the radio button `Checkbox` components to their respective groups.

2. Create a panel to hold the radio button column panels.

Leave its layout manager set to the default `FlowLayout`. Add the column panels to this group.

3. Create a panel for the standard buttons.

Leave its layout manager set to the default `FlowLayout`. Add the `Button` components to this group.

4. Give the applet a `BorderLayout` layout manager.

Add the panel from Step 2 to the `Center` location of the border layout. Add the panel from Step 3 to the `South` location of the border layout.

Figure 6-13 shows the hierarchical organization these steps produce.

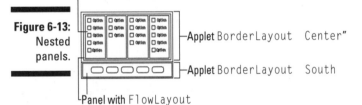

Figure 6-13: Nested panels.

You can also arrange this example with a `GridBagLayout`. A `GridBagLayout` is a powerful layout manager for creating complex arrangements. Unfortunately, using a `GridBagLayout` is a fairly complicated process, and nested panels, as in this example, are usually easier to create and maintain.

Laying out a game of Blackjack

Figure 6-2 earlier in this chapter shows the logical organization of the Blackjack applet. This organization translates to a physical organization on the screen, as Figure 6-14 shows.

The top-level applet

The Blackjack applet that implements the top level of the game is as follows:

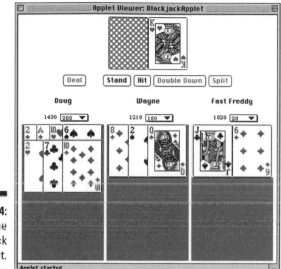

Figure 6-14:
The
Blackjack
applet.

```
import java.awt.*;
import java.util.StringTokenizer;
public class BlackjackApplet extends java.applet.Applet
  implements Runnable
{
  private Deck            deck;
  private BlackjackHand    dealer, lastActive;
  private BlackjackPlayer[] players;
  private int              curPlayer;
  private Button           newdeal, stand, hit, doubledown,
                           split;
  private ThreadGroup      appTG;
  private Panel            dpan, ppan, bpan;

  public void init () {
    int      numPlayers = 1, deckSize = 1, bankroll = 0;
    String   param;
    String[] names = null;
    Thread curT = Thread.currentThread();
    appTG = curT.getThreadGroup();
    curT.setPriority(curT.getPriority() - 1);
    setLayout(new BorderLayout());
```

(continued)

(continued)

```
  if ((param = getParameter( PLAYERS )) != null) {
    StringTokenizer st = new StringTokenizer(param, , );
    names = new String[st.countTokens()];
    for (numPlayers = 0; st.hasMoreTokens(); numPlayers++)
      names[numPlayers] = st.nextToken();
  }

  Card.initGraphics(this);    // load the card images
  deck = new Deck(deckSize);
  players = new BlackjackPlayer[numPlayers];
  dpan = new Panel();
  dpan.add(dealer = new BlackjackHand());
  add( North , dpan);
  bpan = new Panel();
  add( Center , bpan);
  bpan.add(newdeal    = new Button( Deal ));
  bpan.add(new Label(    ));
  bpan.add(stand      = new Button( Stand ));
  bpan.add(hit        = new Button( Hit ));
  bpan.add(doubledown = new Button( Double Down ));
  bpan.add(split      = new Button( Split ));
  setButtons(null);
  ppan = new Panel();
  add( South , ppan);
  for (int ii = 0;  ii < numPlayers;  ii++)
    players[ii] = new BlackjackPlayer(ppan,
          names == null ? null : names[ii], bankroll);
}

public boolean action (Event evt, Object what) {
  if (evt.target == newdeal)
    new Thread(appTG, this).start();
  else {
    BlackjackPlayer player = getPlayer();
    if (evt.target == stand)
      nextHand(false);
    else {
      BlackjackPlayerHand hand = player.getHand();
      if (evt.target == hit) {
        hand.deal(deal());
        if (hand.value() > 21)
          nextHand(false);
        else
          setButtons(player);
      }
```

```
          else if (evt.target == doubledown) {
              hand.deal(deal());
              player.addToBankroll(-hand.bet);
              hand.bet <<= 1;
              nextHand(false);
          }
          else if (evt.target == split) {
              BlackjackPlayerHand splitHand =
                              player.newHand(hand.bet);
              hand.split(splitHand);
              hand.deal(deal());
              splitHand.deal(deal());
              setButtons(player);
          }
          else
              return super.action(evt, what);
      }
  }
  return true;
}

public synchronized void run () {
  newDeal();
  newDeal.disable();
  try {
    BlackjackPlayerHand hand;
    for (int card = 2;  --card >= 0; ) {
      for (int pp = 0;  pp < players.length;  pp++)
        if ((hand = players[pp].getHand()) != null) {
          hand.deal(deal());
          Thread.sleep(500);
        }
      dealer.deal(deal());
      Thread.sleep(500);
    }
    if ((hand = nextHand(true)) != null) {
      setButtons(getPlayer());
      wait();  // wait for players to play their hands
    }
    setButtons(null);
    dealer.expose();
    Thread.sleep(1000);
    if (hand != null)
      while (dealer.value() <= 16) {
        dealer.deal(deal());
        Thread.sleep(500);
```

(continued)

(continued)

```
        }
    }
    catch (InterruptedException e) {}
    for (int pp = 0;  pp < players.length;  pp++)
        players[pp].resolveDeal(dealer);
    newdeal.enable();
}

BlackjackPlayer getPlayer () {
    return curPlayer >= players.length ?
            null : players[curPlayer];
}

BlackjackPlayer nextPlayer () {
    curPlayer++;
    return getPlayer();
}

BlackjackPlayerHand nextHand (boolean firstHand) {
    BlackjackPlayer      player = null;
    BlackjackPlayerHand hand = null;
    if (dealer.blackjack())
        curPlayer = players.length;
    else if ((player = getPlayer()) != null)
        hand = firstHand ?
                player.getHand() : player.nextHand();
    while (player != null  && hand == null)
        if ((player = nextPlayer()) != null)
            hand = player.getHand();
    if (player == null) {
        setButtons(null);
        synchronized (this) { notify(); }  // deal to dealer
        return null;
    }
    if (hand.blackjack())  // skip this hand
        return nextHand(false);
    setButtons(player);
    return hand;
}

boolean newDeal () {
    int    ii = players.length;
    boolean shuffled;
    curPlayer = 0;
    if (shuffled = (deck.getSize() < ii * 3 + 3))
        deck.reshuffle();
```

```
    dealer.clearHand();
    while (--ii >= 0) {
      players[ii].clearHands();
      players[ii].newHand(0);
    }
    newdeal.enable();
    setButtons(null);
    return shuffled;
  }

  private void setButtons (BlackjackPlayer player) {
    if (lastActive != null) {
      lastActive.setActive(false);
      lastActive = null;
    }
    stand.disable();
    hit.disable();
    split.disable();
    doubledown.disable();
    if (player != null) {
      BlackjackPlayerHand hand = player.getHand();
      if (hand != null) {
        (lastActive = hand).setActive(true);
        stand.enable();
        int val = hand.value();
        if (val < 21)
          hit.enable();
        if (player.getBankroll() >= hand.bet) {
          if (player.canSplit() && hand.canSplit())
            split.enable();
          if (val <= 11 && hand.cardCount() == 2)
            doubledown.enable();
        }
      }
    }
    Thread.yield();
  }

  private Card deal () {
    try { return deck.deal(); }
    catch (NoSuchElementException e) {
      deck.reshuffle();
      return deal();
    }
  }
} // end class BlackjackApplet
```

The HTML that loads the applet

The HyperText Markup Language (HTML) document invokes the Blackjack applet using the following applet tag:

```
<APPLET CODE=BlackjackApplet WIDTH=480 HEIGHT=460>
<PARAM NAME= PLAYERS  VALUE= Doug,Wayne,Fast Freddy >
</APPLET>
```

The `BlackjackApplet` gets going like this:

1. **HTML passes the player names to the applet.**

   The applet automatically adjusts the layout for more or fewer players.

2. **The applet uses a** `BorderLayout` **to divide the applet into the dealer's hand at the top (** `North` **), the button controls in the middle (** `Center` **), and the players at the bottom (** `South` **).**

3. `init()` **creates a panel for each of the** `BorderLayout` **locations to hold the individual components.**

   The `North` location contains only the dealer's hand, but still uses a panel in order to prevent the border layout from resizing the dealer's hand, and cause border layout to resize the panel instead. Each of these panels uses the default `FlowLayout` manager.

4. `setButtons()` **enables and disables the buttons to match the legal options for a given point in the game.**

   The state-driven approach determines by examining the state of the game the required state of the buttons.

5. `deal()` **deals cards from the deck and automatically reshuffles if the cards have all been dealt.**

6. **The applet spawns a new thread when the user presses the Deal button.**

   The thread controls the tempo of the deal from the `run()` method.

7. **After** `run()` **deals the initial hands, the applet's Deal thread needs to wait for the players to play their hands.**

   `run()` calls `wait()` on the applet and waits for `action()` to handle the user options.

8. `nextHand()` **determines the next hand to play and sets it as the active hand.**

   If the next hand is the dealer's hand, `nextHand()` calls `notify()` to wake up the Deal thread. When the Deal thread wakes up, `run()` plays the dealer's hand, settles the bets with each player, enables the Deal button, and exits the thread.

The players

Each player requires additional user interface elements:

- ✔ Labels **to display the player's name and current bankroll**
- ✔ A Choice **selector to allow the amount of the next bet to be selected**
- ✔ A Panel **to display the player's Blackjack hand(s)**

BlackjackPlayer panel groups together these interface elements. A BlackjackPlayer also includes all the necessary methods and fields for keeping track of a player. The following code implements BlackjackPlayer:

```java
import java.awt.*;

class BlackjackPlayer extends Panel {
  public static final int STANDARD_BET = 10;
  public static final int STANDARD_BANKROLL = 1000;
  private static int[]    betAmount =
                {1, 5, 10, 20, 30, 50, 100, 200, 500, 1000};
  private static int      playerCount;
  private String          name;
  private int             lastBet, bankroll, curHand,
                          numHands;
private final BlackjackPlayerHand[]
                          hands = new BlackjackPlayerHand[4];
  private Label           bankrollLabel;
  private Choice          betEntry;
  private Panel           handsPanel;

  BlackjackPlayerHand getHand () {
    return curHand >= numHands ? null : hands[curHand];
  }

  int getHandIndex () {
    return curHand >= numHands ? -1 : curHand;
  }

  BlackjackPlayerHand nextHand () {
    curHand++;
    handsPanel.layout();
    return getHand();
  }

  int getBankroll () { return bankroll; }
  int getActiveHandCount () { return numHands; }
```

(continued)

(continued)

```
boolean canSplit () { return numHands < hands.length; }
BlackjackPlayer (Container parent) {
  this(parent, null, STANDARD_BANKROLL);
}

BlackjackPlayer (Container parent, String name,
                 int bankroll) {
  parent.add(this);
  setLayout(new BorderLayout());
  playerCount++;
  if (name == null)
    name = Player  + playerCount;
  add( North , new Label(this.name = name, Label.CENTER));
  if (bankroll <= 0)
    bankroll = STANDARD_BANKROLL;
  String bankStr = Integer.toString(bankroll);
  Font font = new Font( Courier , Font.PLAIN, 10);
  bankrollLabel = new Label(bankStr, Label.RIGHT);
  betEntry = new Choice();
  for (int ii = 0;  ii < betAmount.length;  ii++)
    betEntry.addItem(Integer.toString(betAmount[ii]));
  bankrollLabel.setFont(font);
  betEntry.setFont(font);
  Panel pbank = new Panel();
  add( Center , pbank);
  pbank.add(bankrollLabel);
  pbank.add(betEntry);
  addToBankroll(bankroll);
  setBet(STANDARD_BET);

  handsPanel = new Panel();
  handsPanel.setLayout(new PlayerHandLayout(this, .30f));
  handsPanel.setBackground(Color.gray);
  add( South , handsPanel);
  for (int hh = 0;  hh < hands.length;  hh++)
    handsPanel.add(hands[hh] =
        new BlackjackPlayerHand(this));
}

public boolean action (Event evt, Object what) {
  if (evt.target == betEntry)
    setBet(Integer.parseInt(betEntry.getSelectedItem()));
```

```
    else
      return super.action(evt, what);
    return true;
  }

  synchronized void clearHands () {
    while (numHands > 0)
      hands[--numHands].clearHand();
    curHand = 0;
    handsPanel.layout();
  }

  synchronized void resolveDeal (BlackjackHand dealer) {
    for (int hh = numHands;  --hh >= 0; )
      addToBankroll(hands[hh].winnings(dealer));
  }

  synchronized BlackjackPlayerHand newHand (int bet) {
    BlackjackPlayerHand result = null;
    if (bet == 0)
      bet = lastBet;
    if (numHands < hands.length && (bet = setBet(bet)) > 0){
      result = hands[numHands++];
      addToBankroll(-(result.bet - bet));
      handsPanel.layout();
    }
    return result;
  }

  int setBet (int bet) {
    if (bet > bankroll)
      for (int i = betAmount.length;
          i > 0 && (bet = betAmount[--i]) > bankroll; );
    betEntry.select(Integer.toString(bet));
    return lastBet = bet;
  }

  void addToBankroll (int amount) {
    this.bankroll += amount;
    bankrollLabel.setText(Integer.toString(this.bankroll));
  }
}  // end class BlackjackPlayer
```

The responsibilities of a BlackjackPlayer are

- A BlackjackPlayer **can have up to four hands active at once.** The hands[] array field stores all the hands.

- **BlackjackPlayer uses a BorderLayout and places the name label in the** North **location, the current bankroll and the bet selector in the** Center **, and the player's Blackjack hands in the** South **.**

- getHand() **and** nextHand() **return and update the current active hand.** newHand() activates a new hand after first checking that the player has enough money to cover the bet.

- **The** addToBankroll() **and** setBet() **methods manage the player's money.** These methods are responsible for making sure that the player never gambles money he doesn't have.

- BlackjackPlayer **overrides** action() **to handle the events from the** Choice **selector used to set the player's next bet.**

The players' hands

The hand for a player is a specialized case of the BlackjackHand that the dealer uses, as discussed earlier in this chapter. On top of the dealer's hand's function, the player's hand has to handle the additional duties of wagering and splitting. The BlackjackPlayerHand extends the BlackjackHand like this:

```java
import java.awt.*;

class BlackjackPlayerHand extends BlackjackHand {
  int bet;
  private boolean hasSplit;

  BlackjackPlayerHand (Container parent) {
    super();
    horizInset = 3;
    parent.add(this);
  }

  protected boolean isDealer () { return false; }
  boolean blackjack () {
    return !hasSplit && super.blackjack();
  }

  boolean canSplit () {
    return hand.size() == 2 && value(0) == value(1);
  }
```

```
void clearHand () {
  super.clearHand();
  hasSplit = false;
}

void split (BlackjackPlayerHand splitHand) {
  splitHand.deal((Card)hand.elementAt(1));
  hand.removeElementAt(1);
  hasSplit = splitHand.hasSplit = true;
}

int winnings (BlackjackHand dealer) {
  int hval = value();
  if (hval <= 21) {
    if (blackjack()) {
      if (dealer.blackjack())
        return bet;
      else
        return (bet << 1) + (bet >> 1);
    }
    else {
      int dval = dealer.value();
      if (dval > 21  ||  dval < hval)
        return bet << 1;
      else if (dval == hval  &&  !dealer.blackjack())
        return bet;
    }
  }
  return 0;
}
} // end class BlackjackPlayerHand
```

Chapter 7

2-D Maze

In This Chapter

▶ Creating block and wall mazes

▶ Generating random mazes

▶ Solving mazes using the right-hand rule

▶ Solving mazes using breadth-first searching

▶ Displaying 2-D mazes

Computer games are about challenges that the game player attempts to overcome. A maze is a confusing, intricate network of passages. The challenge of finding your way around a maze makes computer games and mazes a perfect match. In one form or another, many games base their game environments on a maze. Here are some examples of the types of mazes computer games use:

✔ **Adventure games use *graph mazes* in which locations in the environment connect to each other in an arbitrary arrangement.** Any point on the graph can connect to any other point. These mazes have less to do with representing a physical structure than with organizing the sequence in which the game is played.

✔ **Games like *PacMan* and *DungeonMaster* use a *block grid maze* in which a flat grid of uniform rectangles defines the maze.** Each square is either open (a floor) or closed (a solid wall).

✔ ***Wizardry,* one of the original fantasy role-playing games, uses a *wall grid maze* in which a flat grid of uniform rectangles defines the maze.** The edges of the rectangles define the walls, and the planes of the rectangles define the floor and ceiling.

✔ **Games like *Doom* use an *extruded polygon maze* in which adjacent polygonal columns define the regions in the game.** The bottom and top surfaces of the polygonal column define the floor and ceiling, and the sides of the columns define the walls. (Doom varies the height of the floor and ceiling polygons in order to effectively create the illusion of a 3-D maze, but the actual topography of the maze is two-dimensional.)

This chapter shows how to create block and wall grid mazes and how to find a path between two locations in a maze. Chapter 8 uses the block maze from this chapter as a playing field for "intelligent" computer adversaries called *sprites* that incorporate the capability of navigating a maze.

Creating the Maze *Class*

You use a two-dimensional array to represent grid mazes. Wall and block mazes (both types use a grid) have many common features, so the mazes this chapter presents use a common abstract class named Maze. Maze extends the Canvas component from the java.awt package so that a maze can display itself. The WallMaze and BlockMaze classes extend Maze to implement the features specific to each type of maze.

You can extend an *abstract class,* but you can't instantiate (have objects created from) the class. You use abstract classes as superclasses to implement common functionality for subclasses. An abstract class can contain *abstract methods.* Abstract methods don't have implementations and simply define methods that must be implemented by nonabstract subclasses.

The Maze class uses a two-dimensional array of bytes (a byte holds an 8-bit value in the range –128 to 127) to represent the maze. Each byte in the array represents a single rectangle in the grid that makes up the maze. The values in the array have different meaning in the WallMaze and BlockMaze subclasses. However, both classes reserve the high bit (the bit corresponding to the value 0x80) in each byte for the display code in Maze. The display code (the methods in Maze involved with drawing the maze on the screen) uses the high bit as a DIRTY flag to keep track of which squares have changed since paint() drew them on the screen — when the high bit is set to one, the square is "dirty" and needs to be drawn. (The "Displaying a 2-D Maze" section later in this chapter discusses how Maze uses the DIRTY flag.)

Computers store values using *binary numbers* composed of a series of *bits* set to 0 or 1. The bits are ordered from the high bit on the left to the low bit on the right. Sometimes it is useful to use the individual bits to store several values in a single number.

The declaration of the Maze class starts with the following:

```
import java.awt.*;

abstract class Maze extends Canvas {
  static final byte TOP    = 0x01;
```

```
static final byte RIGHT  = 0x02;
static final byte BOTTOM = 0x04;
static final byte LEFT   = 0x08;
static final byte DIRTY  = (byte) 0x80;


protected byte[][] maze;

protected abstract byte initSq ();
}
```

Maze also contains a clearMaze() method for initializing a blank maze.
Because wall and block mazes use different values for the squares in the
maze[][] array, Maze defines the abstract method initSq() to return the
initial value for the squares with this line:

```
protected abstract byte initSq ();
```

Declaring initSq() as an abstract method requires that any classes that
extend the Maze class must implement initSq().

The complete source code for the Maze class is on the *Java Game Programming For Dummies* CD-ROM at the back of this book.

The BlockMaze *subclass*

Each square in a block maze is either floor or wall. Figure 7-1 shows an
example of a block maze.

Figure 7-1:
A block
maze.

To extend Maze to implement a block maze, you implement the abstract
method initSq() that Maze defines. The portion of the BlockMaze class
responsible for representing the maze looks like this:

```
public class BlockMaze extends Maze {
  public static final byte WALL = 0, FLOOR = 1;
  protected byte initSq () { return (byte) (WALL | DIRTY); }
} // end class BlockMaze
```

The code (WALL | DIRTY) "ORs" the DIRTY flag with the WALL value to set the high bit and indicate that the code has changed the square since the last time the maze displayed the square, or in this case, has set a square that has never been displayed.

The WallMaze *subclass*

Each square in a wall maze needs to keep track of which sides of the square have walls and which sides are open. Figure 7-2 shows an example of a wall maze.

Figure 7-2:
A wall
maze.

You give squares the capability to keep track of themselves by setting or clearing a different bit for each wall in the byte for the maze[][] grid square. You set the bit when the wall exists and clear the bit when the wall is open. The LEFT, RIGHT, TOP, and BOTTOM static final variables in Maze define the bit values used in maze[][]. The portion of the WallMaze class responsible for representing the maze looks like

```
public class WallMaze extends Maze {
  public static final byte BLOCKED =
              (byte) (TOP | RIGHT | BOTTOM | LEFT);

  protected byte initSq () {
    return (byte) (BLOCKED | DIRTY);
  }
} // end class WallMaze
```

You display a square with all walls set as a solid wall. The static final BLOCKED variable holds the value with all the walls set — a solid wall is BLOCKED on all sides. initSq() creates its return value from BLOCKED.

Note that because squares share walls with adjacent squares, maze[][] records every interior wall in the two squares that share it. (We define an interior wall as a wall between two squares as opposed to an exterior wall on the edge of the maze.) Recording the wall in two places means that you must always change both squares when setting or clearing a wall. Although this approach is redundant and therefore susceptible to errors, it makes checking for walls easier than if `maze[][]` were to record the walls in only one square. Given that a game typically changes the maze much less frequently than it checks the state of the maze, making checking the maze easier than changing it is a good trade-off.

TECHNICAL STUFF

Working with bits

People count using decimal numbers. Each digit in a decimal number can be one of the ten values from 0 to 9. The decimal counting system is called *base 10* because it has ten digits. People probably use decimal numbers because our counting system arose from primitive people counting on their fingers. You (most likely) have ten fingers and can represent ten different values by holding up some number of your fingers.

Computers don't have fingers to count on — at least not yet — and instead use a series of on/off values as a counting system. Every value stored in a computer is composed of *bits*. Each bit is either an off value or an on value. By convention, an off bit represents the value 0 and an on bit represents 1. The computer represents values larger than 1 by combining bits to form *base 2* or *binary* numbers.

Java doesn't have a representation for using binary numbers in your code, but it does have one for *hexadecimal (base 16)* numbers. In the hexadecimal counting system, each digit is one of the values from 0 to 9 or from A to F where A = 10, B = 11, and so on. A hexadecimal digit represents exactly four binary digits so, converting between hexadecimal and binary numbers is relatively easy. You indicate a hexadecimal number in Java by beginning the number with a zero followed by an x, like this:

```
0x0  0x10  0xA1B2C3  0xDEADBEEF  0x17
```

For example, the decimal number 23 is 10111 in binary and 0x17 in hexadecimal. 23 stands for 2 tens and 3 ones; 10111 stands for 1 sixteen, 0 eights, 1 four, 1 two, and 1 one; and 0x17 stands for 1 sixteen and 7 ones.

```
20+3 = 23₁₀ = 10100011   10111₂ = 16+7 = 17₁₆
```

You use the "bitwise" operators &, |, ^, ~, <<, >>, and >>> to work with individual bits and the "or" (|) operator to set or combine bits:

```
x |= 1  // sets the ones bit in x
```

You use the "and" (&) operator to clear or test bits:

```
(x & 1) != 0  // true if the ones bit in
  x is set
x &= 1  // clears all bits in x except the
  ones bit
```

You use the "exclusive-or" (^) operator to toggle bits:

```
x ^= 1  // toggle the ones bit in x (0-
  >1, 1 >0)
```

You use the "bitwise complement" (~) operator to toggle all the bits in a value:

```
x &= ~1  // clears the ones bit in x
```

You use the "left shift" operator (<<) to move all the bits in the value to the left:

```
x <<= 1  // equivalent to x *= 2 (10111 <<
  1 = 101110)
```

You use the "right shift" operator (>>) to move all the bits in the value to the right:

```
x >>= 1  // equivalent to x /= 2 (10111 >>
  1 = 1011)
```

Generating a Maze

One way to add infinite variety to your game is to randomly generate the game environment. The problem with random-generated environments is that they tend to be less interesting than hand-crafted environments. However, when the central element in the game environment is a maze, you have some good reasons to use a randomly generated maze rather than a hand-crafted maze:

- ✔ **To prevent players in a multiplayer game from gaining or losing advantage due to familiarity with the terrain.**

- ✔ **To connect hand-crafted environments with sections of randomly generated mazes so that each time the player plays the game, or perhaps each time they enter the section with the generated maze, the maze is different.**

- ✔ **To create environments that extend indefinitely.**

- ✔ **To reduce download time by creating the environment on the player's browser instead of downloading it.**

- ✔ **Because solving the maze *is* the game.**

 The code in this section generates mazes that start on the left edge and finish on the right edge. The only reason the maze generation uses start and finish squares is to make the animations for generating and solving the maze more interesting. You can arbitrarily select start and finish squares, if you even need them, after generating the maze.

Selecting an algorithm

You can use a number of different algorithms to generate mazes. The most important consideration when selecting an algorithm is what type of maze you want to generate. Some of the questions to consider when selecting a maze generation algorithm are

- ✔ **Do you want to be able to navigate between any two points in the maze?**

- ✔ **Do you want the maze to connect back on itself so that it has more than one path between two points in the maze? If so, how much interconnection do you want?**

- ✔ **Do you want rooms or open spaces in the maze?**

- ✔ **Do you want a dense maze or a sparse maze?**

> ✓ **Do you want to favor straight hallways or twisty passages?**
>
> ✓ **Do you want lots of branching passageways or longer stretches between branches?**

This section shows you how to implement two different maze generation algorithms: one for generating wall mazes and one for block mazes. Both of these algorithms create dense mazes that allow navigation between any two points in the maze.

The wall maze algorithm creates mazes that have a single path between any two points in the maze, are constructed entirely of passages with no open space, and favor twisty passages with moderate branching.

The block maze algorithm is configurable: You can change the settings for the generator in order to produce generated mazes with different characteristics. The default settings create mazes that allow multiple paths between points, have small rooms and open spaces, and favor straighter passages with lots of branching.

Wall mazes and block mazes impose different constraints on the generator. In particular, block mazes are a little trickier to generate because you have to leave room in the grid to create walls. Wall mazes can place a wall between any two squares on the grid, so you don't need to reserve squares on the grid to separate passages.

In general terms, the algorithm for generating a maze is

1. **Initialize the maze so that every square is a solid wall.**

2. **Select a square in which to start the maze.**

3. **Extend the path from the selected square to an adjacent square.**

4. **Select a square on the current path.**

   Frequently, the algorithm selects the adjacent square from Step 3 in order to continue along the same path.

5. **Repeat Steps 3 and 4 until done.**

   The algorithm may consider the maze done when all squares have been included, or may use a combination of criteria to decide to call it quits.

The wall maze and block maze generation algorithms are both based on this general maze-generating algorithm, but the specific details of each algorithm vary. In particular, the algorithms differ in how they choose the adjacent square in Step 3 and how they select a new square in Step 4.

Adding to the Maze *class*

You add the common methods and fields needed to generate mazes to the Maze superclass. (The "Creating the Maze Class" section earlier in this chapter presents the Maze class.) You add the specific generation algorithms to the WallMaze and BlockMaze subclasses. Here are the fields and methods you add to the Maze superclass to keep track of which squares are "dirty" and need to be redrawn by paintOffscreenImage():

```
protected int minXdirty, minYdirty, maxXdirty, maxYdirty;

protected int dirtySquare (int x, int y) {
  if (x < minXdirty) minXdirty = x;
  if (x > maxXdirty) maxXdirty = x;
  if (y < minYdirty) minYdirty = y;
  if (y > maxYdirty) maxYdirty = y;
  return maze[x][y] |= DIRTY;
}
```

The (minXdirty, minYdirty) and (maxXdirty, maxYdirty) fields keep track of the upper-left and lower-right limits of the squares that have changed — and are therefore "dirty" — since paintOffscreenImage() drew them. The dirtySquare() method maintains the "dirty" fields. You use the "dirty" fields and methods to minimize the work done to redraw the screen. The "Displaying a 2-D Maze" section later in this chapter shows how the dirty fields help minimize redraw time.

If you don't keep track of which part of the maze has changed, you have to draw the entire maze each time it changes, and the animation rate slows down dramatically under most Web browsers and Java runtimes.

You also add declarations to Maze for the following abstract methods that must be implemented by subclasses of Maze:

```
abstract boolean isOpen (int x, int y);
abstract void generate (boolean displaySearch);
```

The abstract method isOpen() defines a method to test a square in the maze grid in order to determine whether it's a solid wall. Each type of maze implements a different test.

Maze defines the abstract method generate(), which the classes that extend Maze implement in order to generate the maze. generate() accepts a boolean parameter of true if you want the maze to display its progress as it builds itself. You pass false to generate() if you don't want the progress of the maze displayed as it's built.

Generating a wall maze

Here are the steps the WallMaze class uses to generate a maze:

1. **Set all the squares in the maze grid to the** BLOCKED **state.**

2. **Randomly select a square on the left edge of the maze as the current square, clear the wall on the left side of the square, and set** lastSide **to** LEFT.

3. **Randomly choose a sequence to rotate through the remaining sides (the sides other than** lastSide**) of the current square.**

4. **Set** nextSide **to the next selected side in the rotation.**

5. **If a** BLOCKED **square lies adjacent to the** nextSide **of the current square, go to Step 9.**

6. **If more sides remain in the rotation sequence decided on in Step 3, go to Step 4.**

7. **You get to this step when the current square isn't adjacent to any** BLOCKED **squares. Randomly select a non-**BLOCKED **square (a square already added to the maze) as the current square.**

   This creates a new branch in the maze by starting a path at the newly selected square.

8. **Set** lastSide **to one of the open sides of the selected square and go to Step 3.**

9. **You get to this step when you have found a square to add to the maze. Remove the wall between the current square and the square adjacent to its** nextSide.

10. **Set the new current square to the adjacent square and set** lastSide **to the wall of this square removed in Step 9.**

    This sets lastSide to the side opposite nextSide. For example, if nextSide is TOP, the new lastSide is BOTTOM.

11. **If any** BLOCKED **squares remain in the maze grid, go to Step 3, otherwise you're done.**

The WallMaze class implements the abstract methods isOpen() and generate() defined in the Maze superclass like this:

```
public boolean isOpen (int x, int y) {
  return inBounds(x, y) && sqr(x, y) != BLOCKED;
}
```

(continued)

(continued)

```
public synchronized void generate
  (boolean displayConstruction)
{
  int xx, yy, sq, lastSide = LEFT;
  int count = mzWid * mzHyt, threshold = count / 8;
  // Step #1 - initialize the maze
  clearMaze();
  if (displayConstruction)
    showMaze(true);
  // Step #2 - select and set the starting square
  startX = xx = 0;
  startY = yy = rint(mzHyt);
  sq = (byte) ((BLOCKED | DIRTY) & ~LEFT);
  while (--count >= 0) {
    // Step #3 - choose a sequence to rotate thru the sides
    int nextSide, nx = 0, ny = 0, nsq;
    int scnt = 3;  // # of sides left to try in current sqr
    int sideInc = rint(3);  // offset from  lastSide  to try
    boolean branch = false, found = false;
    do {
      // Step #4 - set  nextSide  to direction to search
      nsq = 0;
      if ((nextSide = lastSide << (sideInc + 1)) > BLOCKED)
        nextSide >>= 4;
      switch (nextSide) {  // get next square to add to maze
        case TOP:
          if (yy > 0)
            nsq = sqr(nx = xx, ny = yy - 1);
          break;
        case BOTTOM:
          if (yy < mzHyt - 1)
(#1         nsq = sqr(nx = xx, ny = yy + 1);
          break;
        case LEFT:
          if (xx > 0)
            nsq = sqr(nx = xx - 1, ny = yy);
          break;
        case RIGHT:
          if (xx < mzWid - 1)
            nsq = sqr(nx = xx + 1, ny = yy);
          else if (finishX < 0) {  // mark sqr as maze exit
            found = branch = true;
            finishX = xx;  finishY = yy;
          }
          break;
```

```
        }
        if (!found) {
          if (nsq == BLOCKED)      // unused square, use it
            found = true;          // Step #5 - add the square
          else if (--scnt > 0)     // try next direction
            sideInc = (sideInc + 1) % 3; // Step #6 - new side
          else  // dead end, start a new branch
            branch = true;         // goto step #7 below
        }
        if (found || branch) {
          // Step #9 - add the square to the maze
          // sq contains the current square which was either
          // inited in step #2 before the main loop, or set in
          // step #9a below.  If found then the nextSide
          // wall is cleared in sq before setting maze[][]
          maze[xx][yy] = (byte)
                          (found ? (sq & ~nextSide) : sq);
          dirtySquare(xx, yy);
          if (displayConstruction)
            showMaze(false);
          if (branch) {
            // Step #7 - select a square to branch from
            if (count < threshold) {
              // exhaustively search for remaining squares
              sq = BLOCKED;
SEARCH:       for (xx = 0;  xx < mzWid;  xx++)
                for (yy = 0;  yy < mzHyt;  yy++)
                  if (sqr(xx, yy) == BLOCKED) {
                    int dir = rint(4);
                    for (int ii = 4;  --ii >= 0; ) {
                      nx = xx;  ny = yy;
                      switch (dir = ++dir & 3) {
                        case 0: nx--;  break;
                        case 1: nx++;  break;
                        case 2: ny--;  break;
                        case 3: ny++;  break;
                      }
                      if (inBounds(nx, ny) &&
                          (sq = sqr(nx, ny)) != BLOCKED) {
                        xx = nx;  yy = ny;
                        break SEARCH; // found sqr for branch
                      }
                    }
                  }
              if (sq == BLOCKED)
                break;  // maze done
```

(continued)

(continued)

```
        }
        else { // randomly search for a sqr for new branch
          do {
            xx = rint(mzWid);
            yy = rint(mzHyt);
            sq = sqr(xx, yy);
          } while (sq == BLOCKED);
        }
        // Step #8 - set  lastSide  to an open side
        for (lastSide = 1;  (lastSide & sq) != 0; )
          lastSide <<= 1;
        scnt = 3;
        sideInc = rint(3);
        branch = found = false;
      }
    }
  } while (!found);
  // Step #10 - init the new square and set  lastSide
  if ((lastSide = nextSide << 2) > BLOCKED)
    lastSide >>= 4;
  sq = nsq & ~lastSide;  // Step #9a
  xx = nx;  yy = ny;
  if (!displayConstruction  &&  (count & 0xFF) == 0)
    Thread.yield();  // give some time to other threads
  // Step #11 - check for more squares (at top of loop)
}

if (finishX < 0) {  // no exit square selected, do it now
  maze[xx = mzWid - 1][yy = rint(mzHyt)] &= (byte)~RIGHT;
  dirtySquare(xx, yy);
  if (displayConstruction)
    showMaze(false);
}
if (!displayConstruction)
  repaint();
}  // generate()
```

Notice that each time the code modifies the maze[][] array, it calls dirtySquare() to tell the display code that it needs to redraw the square. Also, if displayConstruction is true, the code calls showMaze() to display the maze after it adds a square to the maze. You call showMaze() to animate the progress of the maze generation. (The "Displaying a 2-D Maze" section later in the chapter discusses how showMaze() works.)

Step 7 in generate() employs two different strategies for picking a random square from which to start a new branch. When lots of BLOCKED squares remain, generate() randomly selects squares in the grid until it finds an unblocked square. Using random selection creates more interesting and varied mazes. When the number of BLOCKED squares remaining in maze[][] falls below the threshold level — arbitrarily set to 1/8 of the total grid squares — the code uses an exhaustive search to find the remaining BLOCKED squares. An exhaustive search quickly adds the remaining squares to the maze, additions that could take a long time to make randomly.

Generating a block maze

The block maze algorithm maintains a list of squares that it must explore. The algorithm adds squares to the list as it adds them to the maze grid. Each square in the list keeps track of the unexplored directions from itself. Each square also remembers the direction in which the search was proceeding when the particular square was added to the list so that the algorithm can give a preference to continuing to search in the same direction. Each entry in the list is an object of the Sqr class shown here:

```
class Sqr {
  private boolean t, b, l, r;  // top, bottom, left, right
  private int      dir;        // direction square entered
  int              x, y;       // coordinates of square

  Sqr (int x, int y, int dir,
       boolean t, boolean b, boolean l, boolean r) {
    this.x = x;  this.y = y;  this.dir = dir;
    this.t = t;  this.b = b;  this.l = l;  this.r = r;
  }

  // open() returns a count of the unexplored directions
  int open () {
    return (t ? 1:0) + (b ? 1:0) + (r ? 1:0) + (l ? 1:0);
  }

  int select (int n, boolean sameDir) {
    // Step #6b - select dir to explore and mark as explored
    if (sameDir)  // try to expand in dir square was entered
      switch (dir) {
        case Maze.TOP:   if (t) { t = false; return dir; }
                         break;
```

(continued)

(continued)

```
        case Maze.BOTTOM: if (b) { b = false; return dir; }
                          break;
        case Maze.LEFT:   if (l) { l = false; return dir; }
                          break;
        case Maze.RIGHT:  if (r) { r = false; return dir; }
                          break;
    }
    // return the  n th unexplored direction
    if      (t && --n < 0) { t = false; return Maze.TOP; }
    else if (b && --n < 0) { b = false; return Maze.BOTTOM;}
    else if (r && --n < 0) { r = false; return Maze.RIGHT; }
    else                   { l = false; return Maze.LEFT; }
    }
}  // end class Sqr
```

The open() method in the Sqr class returns the number of unexplored directions from the square. select() returns an unexplored direction and then marks the direction as explored.

Here are the steps the BlockMaze class uses to generate a maze:

1. **Set all the squares in the maze grid to** WALL.

2. **Randomly select a noncorner square on the left edge of the maze and set the square to** FLOOR. **Create a** Sqr **object with the** RIGHT **direction unexplored and add it to the list of available squares.**

3. **If the list of available squares is empty, you're done.**

4. **Select a square to explore from the list of available squares.**

5. **If less than two unexplored directions are available from the square, remove the square from the list of available squares.**

   The single remaining direction is the last direction to explore, so you remove the square from the list.

6. **Select a direction to explore from the square and mark the direction as explored.**

7. **Check to see whether you need to add the square in the selected direction to the maze grid.**

   If the answer is "yes," add the square to the maze and to the list of available squares. When adding the square to the list of available squares, mark all of the directions to explore from the square to the directions that contain adjacent WALL squares.

8. **Go to Step 3.**

The `BlockMaze` class implements the abstract methods `isOpen()` and `generate()` defined in the `Maze` superclass. `generate()` in turn uses the `private` method `tryDir()`. `tryDir()` uses the `private` methods `blocked()`, `noDiag()`, and an overloaded version of `isOpen()`. (Remember, an overloaded version of a method is an alternate method that accepts different parameters.) Here are fields and methods you add to `BlockMaze` to generate mazes:

```
private Vector pending;   // list of available Sqr objects
private int strt =  70;   // prob of exploring from same sqr
private int sdir =  60;   // prob of exploring in same dir
private int thru =  90;   // prob of blocking thru loop
private int side =  60;   // prob of blocking wide area
private int diag = 100;   // prob of blocking diag connection
private int dens =  15;   // prob of leaving areas unexplored

public boolean isOpen (int x, int y) {
  return inBounds(x, y)  &&  sqr(x, y) == FLOOR;
}

private boolean isOpen (int x, int y, int allowProb) {
  return prob(allowProb)  &&  isOpen(x, y);
}

private boolean blocked (int x, int y) {
  return inBounds(x, y)  &&  sqr(x, y) == WALL;
}

private boolean noDiag (int x, int y, int dx, int dy) {
  return blocked(x + dx, y) && blocked(x, y + dy) &&
        isOpen(x + dx, y + dy, diag);
}

private boolean tryDir (int x, int y, int dir) {
  // Step #7 - check if adjacent square in direction  dir
  //            should be added to the maze
  switch (dir) {
    case TOP:
      y--;
      if (isOpen(x, y-1, thru) ||
          isOpen(x-1, y, side) || isOpen(x+1, y, side) ||
          noDiag(x, y, -1, -1) || noDiag(x, y, 1, -1))
        return false;
      break;
```

(continued)

(continued)

```
    case BOTTOM:
      y++;
      if (isOpen(x, y+1, thru) ||
          isOpen(x-1, y, side) || isOpen(x+1, y, side) ||
          noDiag(x, y, -1, 1) || noDiag(x, y, 1, 1))
        return false;
      break;
    case LEFT:
      x--;
      if (isOpen(x-1, y, thru) ||
          isOpen(x, y-1, side) || isOpen(x, y+1, side) ||
          noDiag(x, y, -1, -1) || noDiag(x, y, -1, 1))
        return false;
      break;
    case RIGHT:
      x++;
      if (isOpen(x+1, y, thru) ||
          isOpen(x, y-1, side) || isOpen(x, y+1, side) ||
          noDiag(x, y, 1, -1) || noDiag(x, y, 1, 1))
        return false;
      break;
  }
  if (finishX < 0  && x == mzWid-1) {
    finishX = x;  finishY = y;  // found exit
  }
  else if (x <= 0 || x >= mzWid-1 || y <= 0 || y >= mzHyt-1)
    return false;  // square on border or out of bounds
  else {
    Sqr sq = new Sqr(x, y, dir,
                     blocked(x, y-1), blocked(x, y+1),
                     blocked(x-1, y), blocked(x+1, y));
    // if pruning density, replace last pending Sqr
    if (pending.size() > 10  && prob(dens))
      pending.setElementAt(sq, pending.size() - 1);
    else  // not pruning, add pending Sqr to list
      pending.addElement(sq);
  }
  maze[x][y] = FLOOR;
  dirtySquare(x, y);
  return true;
}
```

```
public synchronized void generate
  (boolean displayConstruction)
{
  int free, idx;
  // Step #1 - initialize the maze
  clearMaze();
  if (displayConstruction)
    showMaze(true);
  // Step #2 - select and set the starting square
  pending = new Vector();
  maze[startX = 0][startY = rint(mzHyt - 2) + 1] = FLOOR;
  dirtySquare(startX, startY);
  pending.addElement(new Sqr(startX, startY, RIGHT,
                            false, false, false, true));
  // Step #3 - loop until list of squares is empty
  while (!pending.isEmpty()) {
    // Step #4 - select a square to explore
    if (prob(strt))
      idx = pending.size() - 1;   // continue with last Sqr
    else
      idx = rint(pending.size()); // choose random Sqr
    Sqr next = (Sqr) pending.elementAt(idx);
    // Step #5 - remove square if no more sides to explore
    // Also randomly remove squares to reduce maze density.
    if ((free = next.open()) <= 1 ||
        (pending.size() > 10 && prob(dens)))
      pending.removeElementAt(idx);
    if (free > 0) {
      // Step #6a - select a direction to explore
      if (tryDir(next.x, next.y,
                 next.select(rint(free), prob(sdir))))
        if (displayConstruction)
          showMaze(false);
    }
    // Step #8 - explore another square
  }
  if (!displayConstruction)
    repaint();
} // generate()
```

The key to generating an interesting block maze is how Step 7 in the method tryDir() decides whether to add a square to the maze. tryDir() looks at the squares surrounding the new square candidate. Figure 7-3 shows the operations tryDir() performs when the dir parameter is RIGHT.

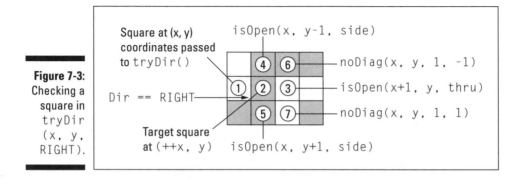

Figure 7-3: Checking a square in tryDir (x, y, RIGHT).

Here is the code from the `tryDir()` switch statement:

```
case RIGHT:
  x++;
  if (isOpen(x+1, y, thru) ||
      isOpen(x, y-1, side) || isOpen(x, y+1, side) ||
      noDiag(x, y, 1, -1) || noDiag(x, y, 1, 1))
    return false;
  break;
```

The first thing the code does is increment x to adjust the (x, y) coordinates from the current square (square 1 in Figure 7-3) to the new square candidate (square 2). Working from the candidate square, the code calls `isOpen(x+1, y, thru)` to check whether the square to the right (square 3) is a floor square. Here is the `isOpen()` method:

```
private boolean isOpen (int x, int y, int allowProb) {
  return prob(allowProb)  &&  isOpen(x, y);
}
```

The `thru` parameter specifies the probability (from 0 to 100) that `isOpen()` returns `true` regardless of whether or not the square is open. Because `thru` is 90 and square 3 in Figure 7-3 is open, there is a 90 percent chance that `prob(90)` returns `true` and a 90 percent chance that the first call to `isOpen()` returns `true`. If `isOpen()` returns `true`, `tryDir()` returns `false` and doesn't use the square.

Even if `tryDir()` decides not to use the square this time, the square could still be selected when evaluated from another direction. For example, square 2 in Figure 7-3 could be selected when moving to the LEFT from square 3.

Assuming that the first test beats the odds and isOpen() returns false, the next check isOpen(x, y-1, side) looks to see whether the square to the top (square 4 in Figure 7-3) is open. The side probability is 80 percent, but because square 4 is a wall, isOpen() returns false regardless of the results of the probability test. The next check is for the other side at the bottom (square 5); square 5 is also a wall square, so isOpen() again returns false.

The last two checks are looking to see whether using square 2 creates two diagonally opposed open squares, as shown in Figure 7-4.

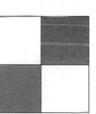

Figure 7-4:
Diagonally
opposed
open
squares.

The test noDiag(x, y, 1, -1) checks to see whether using square 2 creates diagonally opposed open squares between squares 2 and 6 in Figure 7-3. The noDiag() test is

```
private boolean noDiag (int x, int y, int dx, int dy) {
    return blocked(x + dx, y) && blocked(x, y + dy) &&
           isOpen(x + dx, y + dy, diag);
}
```

noDiag() first checks that both of the other opposing corners (squares 4 and 3 from Figure 7-3 in this case) are wall squares. If they are, it checks whether the diagonal square (square 6) is open. However, because BlockMaze sets the diag probability to 100, tryDir() never uses a square that creates diagonally opposed open squares.

Although diagonally opposed open squares don't create a faulty maze, they are aesthetically undesirable, at least when viewed from overhead.

Table 7-1 shows all the settings that you can tinker with to change the characteristics of the maze that BlockMaze generates. You change the settings by changing the initialization values of the private fields in the BlockMaze class.

Table 7-1		BlockMaze **Maze Generation Settings**
Field	*Default*	*Increasing This Value Generates a Maze That . . .*
strt	70	has longer uninterrupted passageways
sdir	60	has straighter passageways with fewer turns
thru	90	has fewer loops and alternate paths
side	60	has fewer open areas and fewer areas wider than the passageway
diag	100	allows fewer diagonally opposed squares like the squares shown in Figure 7-4
dens	15	has more walls and a lower path density

Solving Mazes

You solve a maze by finding a path between two points in the maze. Games need to solve mazes in order to allow computer adversaries to navigate through the maze. This section shows how to implement algorithms to find a path through the maze. Chapter 8 discusses how to use the capability to navigate through mazes to instill "artificial intelligence" in your computer opponents.

Representing the solution

You declare the following two-dimensional array of bytes in the Maze class to keep track of a maze solution:

```
protected byte[][] path;
```

Each entry in the array records the sides of the corresponding maze square through which the solution passes. You mark a path in the array by setting the bit for the corresponding side. The static final fields LEFT, RIGHT, TOP, and BOTTOM in the Maze class define the bits. For example, if the path enters the left side of the square and exits out the top, the entry in path[][] is (LEFT | TOP).

You add the following methods to the Maze class to define the methods for traversing the maze:

```
abstract boolean traverse (int startX, int startY,
                           int finishX, int finishY,
                           boolean displaySearch);

public boolean traverse (boolean displaySearch) {
  return traverse(startX, startY, finishX, finishY,
            displaySearch);
}
```

The classes that extend Maze must implement the abstract method traverse(). You declare the overloaded traverse(boolean displaySearch) method to use as a shortcut for traversing from the start and finish squares of the maze.

Keeping your left hand on the wall

A relatively simple yet effective strategy for traversing a maze is to keep your left or right hand in contact with the wall as you move through the maze. Keeping your left hand on the wall causes you to take all the left-hand branches. When you reach a dead end, your hand sweeps along the dead-end wall and you start walking back down the path. Figure 7-5 shows traversing a maze while keeping the left hand on the wall.

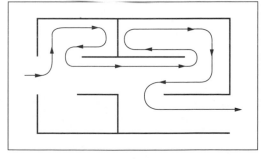

Figure 7-5:
Traversing
a maze
using the
left-hand
rule.

The left-hand (or right-hand) rule only works reliably for mazes with a single solution between any two points. If a maze has more than one solution, you can end up traveling in an endless circle if you follow the left-hand rule. To see why you can move in an endless circle, consider a hallway with a column in the middle. Your objective in this simple maze is to get from one end of the hall to the other with two solutions: You can go around the column to the left or to the right. If you happen to start your search with your hand on the column, you perpetually walk around the column; your hand never leaves the column, and you never reach the goal of the maze.

The `WallMaze` class implements the left-hand rule traversal algorithm like this:

```
public synchronized boolean traverse
  (int xx, int yy, int fx, int fy, boolean displaySearch)
{
  if (!inBounds(xx, yy)  ||  !inBounds(fx, fy))
    return false;
  int     count = 0, sq = maze[xx][yy];
  int     side = LEFT, sx = xx, sy = yy;
  boolean solve = (xx == startX && yy == startY &&
                   fx == finishX && fy == finishY);
  resetPath();
  if (solve) {  // mark path to enter maze
    path[xx][yy] = LEFT;
    dirtySquare(xx, yy);
    side = TOP;
  }
  while (xx != fx  ||  yy != fy) {
    while ((sq & side) != 0)  // search for direction to try
      if ((side <<= 1) > BLOCKED)
        side = TOP;
    path[xx][yy] ^= side;  // set exit from current square
    dirtySquare(xx, yy);
    switch (side) {  // set entrance to new square
      case LEFT:   path[--xx][yy] ^= RIGHT;   side = BOTTOM;
                   break;
      case TOP:    path[xx][--yy] ^= BOTTOM;  side = LEFT;
                   break;
      case RIGHT:  path[++xx][yy] ^= LEFT;    side = TOP;
                   break;
      case BOTTOM: path[xx][++yy] ^= TOP;     side = RIGHT;
                   break;
    }
    sq = dirtySquare(xx, yy);
    if (xx == sx  && yy == sy  && side == LEFT) {
      // we ve searched the entire maze and we re back at
      // the starting square, so there s no solution
      resetPath();
      if (displayPath)
        repaint();
      return false;
    }
    if (displaySearch)
      showMaze(false);
    else if ((++count & 0xFF) == 0)
      Thread.yield();
```

```
    }
    if (solve) {  // mark path to exit maze
      path[xx][yy] |= RIGHT;
      dirtySquare(xx, yy);
    }
    if (displayPath)
      repaint();
    return true;
  } // traverse()
```

Notice that traverse() marks a square in the path using the exclusive-or operator (^=). Remember that you use the exclusive-or operator to toggle bits: A zero bit becomes a one and a one becomes a zero. This toggling means that the first time traverse() marks a path in a square, the code sets the bit for the path to one. As traverse() backtracks down a dead-end path, this same instruction toggles the one and clears the path to zero, effectively erasing the dead-end path from the path[][] array.

Using breadth-first searching to find the shortest path

You use a breadth-first search to find the shortest path between two points in a maze. Unlike the left-hand rule, a breadth-first search is designed to find the optimal solution in a maze with multiple paths between two squares. Breadth-first searching works by taking one step at a time on each possible path before taking a second step on any path. The search proceeds simultaneously along all paths that have not been *pruned*. You prune a path (eliminate it from future searching) when the search reaches a dead end or a square that has already been searched. Because all search paths are the same length, you know that when you find the destination square, you've also found the shortest path.

You use a two-dimensional array the same size as the maze grid to keep track of which squares have been searched. You declare and allocate the array like this:

```
byte[][] graph = new byte[mzWid][mzHyt];
```

First, you initialize each entry in the graph[][] array to zero. Next, set the entry in graph[][] for the square where the search starts to –1. As you search, you record in graph[][] the direction to move in order to return to the previous square on the path. This record creates a backwards-pointing graph that you can follow to get back to the square where the search was begun. Figure 7-6 shows the breadth-first search path through a maze and the resulting graph[][] array.

Figure 7-6:
A breadth-first search path and corresponding graph array.

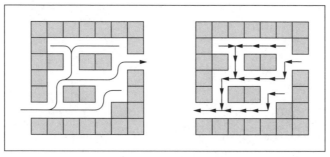

While searching, you maintain a queue of squares waiting to be searched. After you add a square to the search path and set the corresponding entry in graph[][], you add the square to the queue. Each iteration of the search pulls the next square out of the queue and checks each direction to see whether the search path can be extended to the square in that direction. You add any squares you find to the search path, set the corresponding entry in graph[][], and place them in the queue. This cycle continues until either you find the destination square, in which case you've solved the maze, or the queue is empty, in which case the maze has no solution.

A *queue* is a first in, first out (FIFO) data structure, which means that the first item put into the queue is the first item removed from the queue and that you add items to the queue at one end and take them out at the other. The term queue means "a waiting line," and like a line at the Department of Motor Vehicles, the first person in line is the first person served.

Here is the breadth-first traverse() method for the BlockMaze class:

```
public synchronized boolean traverse
  (int sx, int sy, int fx, int fy, boolean displaySearch)
{
  if (!inBounds(sx, sy) || !inBounds(fx, fy))
    return false;
  int       dir, xx = sx, yy = sy, count = 0;
  int       qhead, qtail, qsize = (mzWid + mzHyt - 1) * 2;
  short[][] queue = new short[qsize][2];  // 0 = x, 1 = y
  byte[][]  graph = new byte[mzWid][mzHyt];
  boolean   solve = (xx == startX && yy == startY &&
                     fx == finishX && fy == finishY);
  if (displaySearch) {
    resetPath();
    if (solve) {
      path[sx][sy] = LEFT;
      dirtySquare(sx, sy);
    }
    showMaze(false);
```

```
    }
  graph[xx][yy] = -1;
  queue[0][0] = (short)xx;   queue[0][1] = (short)yy;
  qtail = 0;   qhead = 1;
TRAVERSE:
  for (;;) {
    if (qhead == qtail) {   // empty queue: unsolvable maze
      resetPath();
      if (displayPath)
        repaint();
      return false;
    }
    xx = queue[qtail][0];   yy = queue[qtail][1];
    qtail = (qtail + 1) % qsize;
    int qstart = qhead;
    for (dir = TOP;  dir <= LEFT;  dir <<= 1) {
      int ndir = 0, nx = xx, ny = yy;
      switch (dir) {
        case TOP:     ny--;  ndir = BOTTOM;  break;
        case RIGHT:   nx++;  ndir = LEFT;    break;
        case BOTTOM:  ny++;  ndir = TOP;     break;
        case LEFT:    nx--;  ndir = RIGHT;   break;
      }
      if (inBounds(nx, ny) &&
          graph[nx][ny] == 0  &&  maze[nx][ny] == FLOOR)
      {   // extend the search path in direction  dir
        graph[nx][ny] = (byte)ndir;  // point to prev square
        if (displaySearch) {
          path[xx][yy] |= dir;
          dirtySquare(xx, yy);
          path[nx][ny] |= ndir;
          dirtySquare(nx, ny);
        }
        if (nx == fx  &&  ny == fy)  // found solution
          break TRAVERSE;
        queue[qhead][0] = (short)nx;
        queue[qhead][1] = (short)ny;
        qhead = (qhead + 1) % qsize;
      }
    }
    if (displaySearch) {
      if (qhead == qstart) {   // dead end, backtrack
        while (path[xx][yy] -= graph[xx][yy]) {
          path[xx][yy] = 0;
          dirtySquare(xx, yy);
```

(continued)

(continued)

```
        switch (graph[xx][yy]) {
          case TOP:    path[xx][--yy] &= (byte)~BOTTOM;
                       break;
          case RIGHT:  path[++xx][yy] &= (byte)~LEFT;
                       break;
          case BOTTOM: path[xx][++yy] &= (byte)~TOP;
                       break;
          case LEFT:   path[--xx][yy] &= (byte)~RIGHT;
                       break;
        }
        dirtySquare(xx, yy);
      }
    }
    showMaze(false);
  }
  else if ((++count & 0xFF) == 0)
    Thread.yield();
}
if (displaySearch) {
  if (solve) {
    path[xx][yy] |= RIGHT;
    dirtySquare(xx, yy);
  }
  showMaze(false);
}

// reconstruct path by following graph
// from finish to start
resetPath();
if (solve)
  path[fx][fy] = RIGHT;
while ((dir = graph[fx][fy]) != -1) {
  path[fx][fy] |= (byte)dir;
  switch (dir) {
    case TOP:    path[fx][--fy] = BOTTOM;  break;
    case RIGHT:  path[++fx][fy] = LEFT;    break;
    case BOTTOM: path[fx][++fy] = TOP;     break;
    case LEFT:   path[--fx][fy] = RIGHT;   break;
  }
}
if (solve)
  path[fx][fy] |= LEFT;
if (displayPath)
  repaint();
return true;
}
```

Notice in the preceding code that after you find a solution, you reconstruct the path by following graph[][] from the destination square to the starting square.

Displaying a 2-D Maze

The Maze class extends java.awt.Canvas to give it a display area. You draw the maze by overriding the paint() method inherited from Canvas.

Because most of the work to draw a wall maze or a block maze is the same, the Maze class overrides paint() to do the drawing. As far as the paint() method is concerned, the only difference between the two Maze subclasses, BlockMaze and WallMaze, is in the actual drawing of a square. paint() calls drawSquare() to draw a single maze square. You have to implement the abstract method drawSquare() that Maze defines and that paint() calls in the classes that extend Maze. BlockMaze draws its squares as solid blocks. WallMaze draws walls between squares and leaves the middle of the squares open, except that WallMaze draws squares with walls on all four sides (BLOCKED squares) as solid blocks.

Implementing a circular queue

The breadth-first traverse() code implements the queue[] array as a *circular queue*. A circular queue allows you to continually put squares into one end of the queue and remove squares from the other end without ever running into the end of the queue[] array. If you don't use a circular queue, you have to periodically move the squares from the end of the array back to the beginning. You add squares to the head of the queue like this:

```
queue[qhead][0] = (short)nx;
queue[qhead][1] = (short)ny;
qhead = (qhead + 1) % qsize;
```

You increment qhead to point to the next entry in the queue. The modulo operation % qsize sets qhead to zero if (qhead + 1) equals qsize. (Remember, the modulo operator returns the remainder of dividing the left-hand operand by the right-hand operand — the remainder of dividing (qhead + 1) by qsize in this case.) You use similar code to remove the next square from the tail of the queue.

```
xx = queue[qtail][0];
yy = queue[qtail][1];
qtail = (qtail + 1) % qsize;
```

Using the paint() method

You draw the maze to an offscreen image and then copy this image to the screen. (Chapter 1 shows how to use an offscreen image and override update() for smooth screen updates.) You add the following paint() method and supporting fields to the Maze class:

```
protected Image      offscreenImage;
protected Graphics  offscr;

public synchronized void paint (Graphics g) {
  paintOffscreenImage();
  g.drawImage(offscreenImage, 0, 0, this);
  notifyAll();
}
```

paint() calls paintOffscreenImage() (another method in the Maze class) to do the work of creating the maze image in an offscreen image. You do the work in paintOffscreenImage() rather than in paint() so that the subclasses can override paint() without replacing the code in paintOffscreenImage(). Keeping the offscreen image code out of paint() allows the subclasses to modify how paint() works and still reuse the code in paintOffscreenImage() to generate the maze display. (Chapter 8 shows an example of overriding paint() to display sprites on top of the offscreen maze image.)

The first thing paintOffscreenImage() does is check whether it needs to create the offscreen image and then creates it if necessary.

You allocate the offscreen image from paint() rather than in the Maze() constructor because createImage() can't create the offscreen image until you place the maze canvas on the screen by adding it to a container. And because you can't place the canvas on the screen until you create it, you put the code that allocates the offscreen image in paint(). The Abstract Window Toolkit (AWT) can't call paint() until you add the component to the screen hierarchy, so createImage() is guaranteed to work when paint() calls it.

Next, paintOffscreenImage() loops through all the squares in the range of dirty squares and draws any squares that have the DIRTY bit set in the square. For each DIRTY square, paintOffscreenImage() calls drawSquare() to draw the maze square and then calls drawPathSquare() to draw any path through the square. (The "Displaying a solution" section later in this chapter shows how to implement drawPathSquare().) If the square is the maze's start or finish square, paintOffscreenImage() calls drawTarget() to draw colored circles to mark it.

Finally, you copy the offscreen image to the screen in `paint()` with this statement:

```
g.drawImage(offscreenImage, 0, 0, this);
```

The complete `Maze` class, including the `paintOffscreenImage()` and `drawTarget()` methods, is included on the CD.

Repainting the maze in a thread-friendly manner

Because Java calls `paint()` from a different thread than the thread in which your applet runs, you use `wait()` and `notifyAll()` to wait for `paint()` to draw the maze. (CD Chapter 2 discusses the AWT Interface thread that calls `paint()` and shows how to use `wait()` and `notifyAll()` to control the timing of an animation.) This section shows how you use these techniques to control the animation of a generating maze.

First, notice in the preceding section that before exiting, `paint()` calls `notifyAll()` to wake up any threads that are waiting for the maze to repaint itself. The code waiting to wake up is in `showMaze()`. You call `showMaze()` to `repaint()` the maze and wait for `paint()` to finish. `showMaze()` sleeps long enough after displaying the maze to produce a consistent 30 frames-per-second (fps) animation frame rate. Here is the `showMaze()` method and supporting fields you add to the `Maze` class:

```
protected long timer, maxFrameRate = 30L;  // 30 fps

protected void showMaze (boolean allDirty) {
  if (allDirty  ||  offscreenImage == null)
    repaint();
  else
    repaint(leftOffset + minXdirty * sqWid,
            topOffset + minYdirty * sqHyt,
            sqWid * (maxXdirty - minXdirty + 1) + lineWid,
            sqHyt * (maxYdirty - minYdirty + 1) + lineHyt);
  try { wait(); } catch (InterruptedException e) {}
  long t = System.currentTimeMillis();
  if ((timer -= t - (1000L / maxFrameRate)) > 0)
    try { Thread.sleep(timer); }
    catch (InterruptedException e) {}
  timer = System.currentTimeMillis();
}
```

Calculating where the pixels go

You draw the maze squares at pixel locations determined by the size of the Maze canvas and the grid dimensions of the maze. The pixel locations are the same for wall mazes and block mazes, so you place the code to calculate the pixel offsets and sizes in the Maze class. The drawSquare() methods implemented by the classes that extend Maze use these pixel locations to draw the maze squares.

You calculate the pixel values in resetMaze(). resetMaze() adjusts the pixel width and height of each rectangle in the grid to fit the screen size of the Maze canvas. Maze overrides the reshape() method inherited from Canvas to resize the maze whenever the size of the canvas changes. If reshape() changes the size of the canvas, it calls resetMaze() to calculate the new size of the grid squares. Figure 7-7 and Table 7-2 show the fields that resetMaze() calculates.

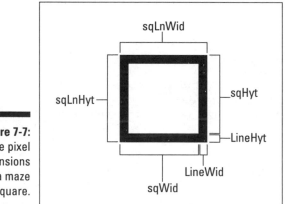

Figure 7-7:
The pixel dimensions of a maze square.

Table 7-2	Pixels Values for Drawing the Maze
Field	*What It Contains*
sqWid, sqHyt	The width and height of a grid square in pixels. These include the lineWid and lineHyt, respectively, of the line on one side of the square.
lineWid, lineHyt	The pixel width and height of the lines separating grid squares. You set these to zero for block mazes.
sqLnWid, sqLnHyt	The pixel width and height of a grid square plus the separating lines.
leftOffset, topOffset	The pixel offsets to center the displayed maze within the canvas. These are the canvas pixel offsets of the upper-left corner of the square maze[0][0].

Knowing that block mazes are simple is half the battle

The squares in a block maze are simple colored rectangles. The type of maze square determines the color of the rectangle. Figure 7-1 earlier in this chapter shows an example of a block maze. You implement the drawSquare() method for the BlockMaze class like this:

```
protected void drawSquare (int xx, int yy) {
   offscr.setColor(maze[xx][yy] == WALL ?
                  Color.gray : Color.white);
   offscr.fillRect(leftOffset + (xx * sqWid),
                  topOffset + (yy * sqHyt), sqWid, sqHyt);
}
```

The expression leftOffset + (xx * sqWid) calculates the pixel offset of the left edge of the maze square and topOffset + (yy * sqHyt) calcu-lates the top pixel offset of the square.

Displaying a wall maze

Each square in a wall maze has 16 different possible combinations of walls, and drawing one such square takes several steps. The first step is to check whether the square has all the walls set, in which case you treat the square as a solid wall. You draw a solid wall by filling the entire square with black. If the square isn't a solid wall, you start by erasing the square to white and then drawing the four sides and four corners depending on which walls the square has set. Figure 7-8 shows the 8 wall sections that you draw and the 16 resulting wall maze squares.

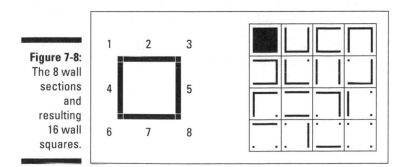

Figure 7-8:
The 8 wall sections and resulting 16 wall squares.

Notice that in Figure 7-8 all 16 squares draw all 4 corner sections of the wall, which happens because `WallMaze` only generates dense mazes with no open areas. If you allow wall mazes with open areas, you only draw a corner if the square on the opposite side of a corner that has any walls set that share the corner, or if the corner of the square is on the edge of the maze.

Figure 7-2 earlier in this chapter shows an example of a wall maze.

The complete `WallMaze` class, including the `drawSquare()` method, is included on the CD.

To reduce the number of `fillRect()` calls that `drawSquare()` has to use in order to draw the maze square, the `fillRect()` calls that draw the wall sides draw both corners as well. For example, the following code draws the top wall and both top corners (sections 1, 2, and 3 in Figure 7-8) in the square:

```
if (top = (sq & TOP) != 0)
    offscr.fillRect(xoff, yoff, sqLnWid, lineHyt);
```

This code also sets the local variable `top` to `true` if it draws the top corners. If `drawSquare()` doesn't draw the `LEFT` side of the square, it checks `top` to determine if it needs to draw the top-left corner of the square. If `top` is `false`, `drawSquare()` didn't draw either the `TOP` or `LEFT` wall, so it draws the corner. You repeat the `TOP` check for the `BOTTOM` wall of the square and repeat the `LEFT` check for the `RIGHT` wall.

Customizing the appearance of a wall maze

You can change the look of a wall maze by either setting the pixel width and height of the grid squares to different values or by changing the thickness of the lines that define the walls. For example, the figure shows a maze with squares that are 16 pixels wide, 8 pixels tall, and have walls that are 6 pixels wide and 6 pixels tall.

You control the pixel sizes of the squares by calling `resize(width, height)` to set the dimensions of the maze canvas, and by calling `setDimensions(squaresWide, squaresHigh)` to set the maze dimensions. To change the default line sizes, you call `setLineSizes()`.

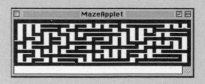

Displaying a solution

A maze stores the current solution path in the path[][] array. The bytes in path[][] have a bit set for each side of the corresponding square in the maze[][] array that has a solution path. The "Solving Mazes" section earlier in this chapter discusses how you set these bits.

You display the solution by drawing each path segment set in path[][]. paintOffscreenImage() calls the drawPathSquare() method in Maze to draw a single path square. Because some subclasses of Maze may want to calculate maze solutions but not display them, paintOffscreenImage() only calls drawPathSquare() if the boolean field displayPath is set.

drawPathSquare() uses pixel sizes and offsets that you initialize in resetMaze(). pWid and pHyt contain the pixel width and height of the displayed path. You set pxoff to the pixel offset within a square of the left edge of a vertical path segment and pyoff to the offset of the top edge of a horizontal segment. You declare these fields in Maze like this:

```
protected int pWid, pHyt, pxoff, pyoff;
```

You initialize these fields by adding the following code to resetMaze():

```
int pw = sqWid - lineWid;
pWid = (pw & 1) == 0 ? Math.max(2, (pw >> 1) & ~1) :
                       Math.max(1, (pw >> 1) | 1);
int ph = sqHyt - lineHyt;
pHyt = (ph & 1) == 0 ? Math.max(2, (ph >> 1) & ~1) :
                       Math.max(1, (ph >> 1) | 1);
pxoff = (sqLnWid - pWid) >> 1;
pyoff = (sqLnHyt - pHyt) >> 1;
```

To center the path in the square, the width of the path must be even if the square width is even and odd if the square width is odd. The following instruction calculates the pixel width of a square:

```
int pw = sqWid - lineWid;
```

You use the pixel width pw to calculate the path width like this:

```
pWid = (pw & 1) == 0 ? Math.max(2, (pw >> 1) & ~1) :
                       Math.max(1, (pw >> 1) | 1);
```

(pw & 1) == 0 is true if the path width is even and false if it is odd. You set an even path width approximately half the width of the square and at least two pixels wide by using Math.max(2, (pw >> 1). You calculate an odd path width at least one pixel wide using Math.max(1, (pw >> 1) | 1).

Figure 7-9 shows what the completed path for a wall maze looks like.

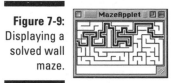

Figure 7-9:
Displaying a solved wall maze.

Putting the maze on the screen

You place a Maze canvas on the screen by adding it to a container, such as an applet. This section shows how to implement the MazeApplet class to display the maze and how to use threads to animate the generation and solving of multiple mazes simultaneously. In fact, the applet can even solve a maze while it is still generating it. Figure 7-10 shows a block maze being solved while it is still being generated.

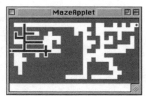

Figure 7-10:
Solving a partially generated maze.

Using a thread to animate, generate, and solve a maze

You spawn a thread to animate, generate, or solve the maze. Because each maze or applet can have more than one thread, you create a thread class to handle the different thread operations.

Because the only function of the class is to execute a thread, you extend the MazeThread class directly from Thread instead of implementing the Runnable interface.

Depending on the solve parameter passed to the MazeThread() constructor, the MazeThread class either generates or solves the maze. Here is the complete MazeThread class:

```
class MazeThread extends Thread {
  private Maze  maze;
  private boolean show, solve;

  MazeThread (ThreadGroup tg, Maze maze,
              boolean show, boolean solve)
  {
    super(tg, solve ? Solve thread  :  Generate thread );
    this.maze = maze;
    this.show = show;
    this.solve = solve;
    start();
  }

  public void run () {
    if (show)
      setPriority(Thread.MIN_PRIORITY + 1);
    if (solve)
      maze.traverse(show);
    else
      maze.generate(show);
  }
} // class MazeThread
```

Notice that if the operation is being animated, the `run()` method sets the thread priority to `MIN_PRIORITY` + 1. Lowering the thread priority makes the user input and screen updating more responsive.

Reviewing parameters in the `MazeApplet` *class*

To make the features of the maze accessible to HyperText Markup Language (HTML), the `MazeApplet` class accepts certain HTML parameters. CD Chapter 1 discusses how to pass parameters to an applet from HTML. `MazeApplet` accepts the following parameters:

Parameter Name	What It Specifies
LINEWIDTH	The width and height of the lines (`lineWid`, `lineHyt`). You only want to specify line width for wall mazes. The line width defaults to zero for block mazes and one for wall mazes.
MAZEWIDTH	The number of grid squares wide to make the maze. The maze width defaults to 30 squares.

Parameter Name	What It Specifies
MAZEHEIGHT	The number of grid squares tall to make the maze. The maze height defaults to 20 squares.
MAZE	The Maze subclass to use. The default maze class is "WallMaze".

For example, you add the following applet tag to your HTML document for a block maze that is 20 squares wide and 15 squares tall:

```
<applet code=MazeApplet width=242 height=182>
<param name= MAZE  value= BlockMaze >
<param name= MAZEWIDTH  value= 20">
<param name= MAZEHEIGHT  value= 15">
</applet>
```

This HTML produces a block maze with squares that are 12 pixels wide and 12 pixels tall with a 1-pixel border around the maze. MazeApplet derives these pixel dimensions from the HTML tag like this:

```
square width = (width / MAZEWIDTH) = (242 / 20) = 12
square height = (height / MAZEHEIGHT) = (182 / 15) = 12
leftOffset = (width % MAZEWIDTH) / 2 = (242 % 20) / 2 = 1
topOffset = (height % MAZEHEIGHT) / 2 = (182 % 20) / 2 = 1
```

MazeApplet generates a new maze when the user clicks the maze with the mouse button. If the user holds the Shift key down while clicking the mouse on the maze and the maze has added the solution square to the maze, the applet solves the maze. mouseDown() spawns a thread to generate or solve the maze. (CD Chapter 2 shows how to spawn threads from event handlers such as mouseDown().)

The MazeApplet class is included on the CD.

Chapter 8

2-D Sprite Maze

In This Chapter

▶ Modeling game elements with sprites

▶ Managing sprites with a sprite engine

▶ Displaying and animating sprites

▶ Detecting and handling sprite collisions

▶ Giving game elements some intelligence

▶ Creating a 2-D maze game using sprites

A sprite is an arbitrarily-shaped (not necessarily rectangular) graphic object that moves nondestructively across a background. A familiar example of a sprite is the mouse cursor — it can be any shape, and it moves around the screen without changing the screen background. You use sprites when you want to minimize redrawing the background.

Sprites are most useful for 2-D games — particularly arcade games where you have a background and various objects moving over it. You use sprites to represent *game elements* that move around the screen, although you can also use sprites for stationary game elements. Game elements can be any object in your game: spaceships, bullets, explosions, little men, obstacles, walls, vicious blobs of slime, or a plumber named Mario.

Movable sprites contain code to move across a game background — which brings up the questions of where and how to move the sprite — so we show you how to give your sprites enough intelligence to answer these questions. Of course, moving sprites can run into the boundaries of the background and other moving and stationary sprites, so we show you how to detect and resolve collisions when they occur.

In short, this chapter shows how to create, display, animate, and most importantly, keep track of and manage sprites with a *sprite engine*. Finally, this chapter puts all the sprite stuff together to make a simple game using sprites and the `BlockMaze` class from Chapter 7.

Gentleman, Start Your Sprite Engines!

Sprite engine is just a fancy term for a data structure that keeps track of sprites and tells them when to perform certain operations such as drawing, moving, or animating. When applied to software, the term *engine* identifies code that stands on it's own and is general enough to be used in a variety of applications. A well-constructed sprite engine (which of course includes the one we present in this chapter) can be extended and used in many games.

A sprite engine manages the sprites in a rectangular *play field*. You can give your sprite engine all kinds of bells and whistles, but the four primary duties of a sprite engine are to

- ✔ **Maintain a list of all the sprites under its control and their positions in the play field**
- ✔ **Draw the sprites from back to front**
- ✔ **Move the sprites**
- ✔ **Detect and resolve collisions between sprites or between a sprite and the edge of the play field**

Actually, detecting and resolving collisions isn't a requirement for a sprite engine. In some of your games, sprites may need to occupy the same space in the play field without triggering a collision. However, for many games, collision detection is the most important service the sprite engine provides, so we include it in our list of primary duties. After all, a shoot-'em-up game wouldn't be much fun if the bullets never hit anything.

To leverage the power of object-oriented programming, your Java sprite engine doesn't actually draw or move the sprites; it simply tells the sprites when to move or draw *themselves*. Because collision detection either involves more than one sprite or involves the sprite and the edge of the play field, the sprite engine takes care of detecting collisions. However, the engine just tells the colliding sprites what happened and lets the sprites determine how to resolve the collision. This division of responsibilities makes the code for both the sprites and the sprite engine fairly simple, yet allows you to build games with hundreds of moving and animating game elements that interact with each other.

Implementing a sprite

A sprite has only a few responsibilities:

- ✔ **It draws itself.**
- ✔ **It updates its state.** This usually involves moving and/or animating the sprite, but it could be anything the sprite needs to do periodically.

⯈ **It defines its *collision box*.** The collision box is a rectangular area that moves with the sprite and functions as the sprite's area of influence, determining where the sprite can collide with other sprites.

⯈ **It handles collisions with other sprites and with the edge of the play field.**

Because game elements that *are* sprites may need to extend classes that *aren't* sprites, you use an *interface* to define the sprite methods. Using an interface allows any class that implements the interface to function as a sprite.

An *interface* is a definition of methods that a class implements in order to do the job that the interface defines.

The sprite interface you use for the game in this chapter, as well as for many other games, is quite simple. You declare the Sprite interface in the file Sprite.java like this:

```
import java.awt.*;
public interface Sprite {
    void      setSpriteEngine (SpriteEngine se);
    boolean   updateSprite ();
    Rectangle drawSprite (Graphics g);
    Rectangle collisionBox ();
    Rectangle collideWith (Object obj);
} // end interface Sprite
```

The sprite engine uses the Sprite interface methods to manage sprites. Table 8-1 shows the responsibilities for each of the five methods the Sprite interface defines.

Table 8-1	The Sprite Interface Methods
Method	**What the Sprite Engine Expects It To Do**
setSpriteEngine()	The sprite engine passes this method a reference to the engine when the sprite is added to the engine, and calls it with null when the sprite is removed from the engine. The sprite uses the reference to call methods in the sprite engine.
updateSprite()	This method is the sprite's heartbeat. The sprite engine calls this method periodically to tell the sprite to update its state. You move, animate, and initiate actions in updateSprite(). updateSprite() returns true if you change the sprite's collision box, false if you don't.

(continued)

Table 8-1 *(continued)*

Method	What the Sprite Engine Expects It To Do
drawSprite()	The sprite engine passes this method a graphics context in which to draw the sprite. It returns a Rectangle representing the region drawn to the screen or null if it didn't draw anything.
collisionBox()	This method returns a Rectangle containing the sprite's collision box. The sprite engine uses the collision box to determine whether the sprite collides with other sprites. collisionBox() returns null to indicate that this sprite doesn't collide with other sprites.
collideWith()	In the event of a collision, the sprite engine passes this method the object with which the sprite collided. After resolving the collision with whatever action is part of your game, collidesWith() returns the possibly changed collision box for the sprite.

The object parameter that the sprite engine passes to the sprite's collideWith() method is usually another Sprite, but can also be one the SpriteBorder constants — NORTH, SOUTH, EAST, or WEST — that SpriteEngine defines to represent collisions with the appropriate edge of the play field. (SpriteBorder is an empty class that SpriteEngine uses to define these object constants so that collideWith() can test for a border collision using the test obj instanceof SpriteBorder.) collideWith() resolves the collision, which may include changing the position of the sprite. collideWith() returns the new collision box or null if the sprite engine must not check for any more collisions with a given sprite during the current update.

Putting sprites in their place

Although some Sprite classes may need to extend a non-Sprite class, the main function of a Sprite class is usually just to be a sprite. In addition, the methods defined by the Sprite interface all have logical default implementations. These two features of sprites often enable you to encapsulate the common code shared between sprites and reduce the amount of code you have to write for each new sprite you create by giving these sprites a common superclass.

The SpriteObject class is exactly this superclass; it implements the Sprite interface. The code to keep track of a sprite's position and collision box is pretty standard for all sprites, so you can implement it in SpriteObject. Here is the SpriteObject class:

```java
import java.awt.*;
public class SpriteObject implements Sprite {
  protected double       x, y;  // center of sprite
  protected int          width, height;
  protected SpriteEngine  spriteEngine;
  public SpriteObject (double x, double y, int w, int h) {
    this.x = x;  this.y = y;  width = w;  height = h;
  }


  public double centerX ()        { return x; }
  public double centerY ()        { return y; }
  public int    spriteWidth ()  { return width; }
  public int    spriteHeight ()  { return height; }


  public void setSpriteEngine (SpriteEngine se) {
    spriteEngine = se;
  }


  public boolean updateSprite () { return false; }
  public Rectangle drawSprite (Graphics g) { return null; }
  public Rectangle collisionBox () {
    return new Rectangle((int)(x - width / 2.0),
                         (int)(y - height / 2.0),
                         width, height);
  }


  public Rectangle collideWith (Object obj) {
    return collisionBox();
  }
}  // end class SpriteObject
```

SpriteObject position sprites with an *anchor point* at the center of the
sprite image. Using the center of the sprite image for the anchor point is a
decision you need to make based on the kinds of actions your sprites need
to be able to perform. You can position sprites from any of the nine locations shown in Figure 8-1. The width and height of a sprite may change as it
is animated, but the anchor point continues to dictate how the sprite
positions itself. You need to choose the anchor point based on how the
sprite anchors itself to the background. We chose the center position as the
default because without any other selection criteria, the center is the best
choice.

However, some sprites may require anchor points at locations other than
the center of the sprite image. For example, an explosion sprite animates
from a small explosion image to a large explosion image. You want the
explosion to grow out from the center, so you use a center anchor point. On
the other hand, if your sprite represents a side view of a worm on the

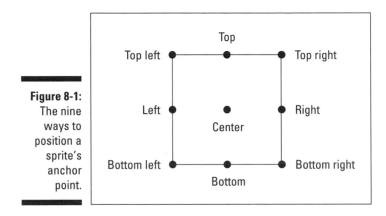

Figure 8-1:
The nine
ways to
position a
sprite's
anchor
point.

ground, you probably want to use a bottom anchor point to anchor the worm to the ground. Using a bottom anchor point, the sprite expands and shrinks from the center as its width changes, but keeps the bottom of the worm anchored to the ground as the height changes. Conversely, you probably want to use a top anchor point when you have a sprite that crawls across a ceiling.

Moving sprites around the play field

Notice that SpriteObject uses double values for the x and y position of the sprite. Given that you can only draw images at integer pixel locations, you may wonder why x and y are floating-point values. The answer lies in the fact that using floating-point values results in much smoother movement. Chapter 1 shows how you use floating-point coordinates and floating-point delta x and y values to smoothly move objects at any speed and in any direction.

You give your sprites motion by changing their position in the method updateSprite(). Here is an example of how you add simple vector motion to your sprite:

```
protected double deltaX, deltaY;  // the vector deltas
public boolean updateSprite () {
  x += deltaX;
  y += deltaY;
  return true;
}
```

Notice that the movement code doesn't need to do any checking to see whether the object moves out of bounds or runs into something because the sprite engine handles all the collision detection. All updateSprite() needs to do is move the sprite.

Resolving collisions

The sprite engine takes care of detecting collisions, but the sprite itself is responsible for handling what happens as a result of the collision. When the sprite engine detects a collision, it calls the collideWith() methods for each sprite involved in the collision. You implement collideWith() to resolve the collision. (The "Implementing a sprite" section earlier in this chapter discusses how the sprite engine calls collideWith().)

The ObjectDetector class extends SpriteObject. It detects when a specific object has collided with it and then notifies the sprite engine's *observers*. (The observers are other objects, such as the SpriteMaze game presented in the "Building on the BlockMaze class" section later in this chapter, that receive messages from the sprites in the engine.) You can trigger an event when a sprite reaches a location in the play field by adding an ObjectDetector sprite for that location to the sprite engine. The section "Sprite events and handling them" later in this chapter discusses how the notification process works. Here is the ObjectDetector class:

```
import java.awt.*;
class ObjectDetector extends SpriteObject {
  private Object target;
  ObjectDetector(int x, int y, int w, int h, Object target){
    super(x, y, w, h);
    this.target = target;
  }


  public Rectangle collideWith (Object obj) {
    if (obj == target)
      spriteEngine.notifyObservers(this);
    return collisionBox();
  }
} // end class ObjectDetector
```

You can use sprite collision detection to do *proximity detection*. Proximity detection is when you want a sprite to know when something is *close* to it *before* it collides. You use proximity detection as an early warning system to allow your sprite to change course, initiate defensive maneuvers, or launch an attack. You give a sprite proximity detection by adding a slave sprite with a collisionBox() that defines the detection perimeter around the master sprite. The slave sprite only needs to implement the collisionBox() and collideWith() methods; you leave the other methods empty like the corresponding methods in the SpriteObject class.

Displaying sprites

You display a sprite by implementing the Sprite method drawSprite().
The sprite engine passes drawSprite() the graphics context in which to
draw the sprite. As an example, the following RoundSprite class draws the
sprite as a colored oval:

```
import java.awt.*;
class RoundSprite extends SpriteObject {
  protected Color color;
  RoundSprite (double x, double y, int w, int h, Color c) {
    super(x, y, w, h);
    color = c;
  }

  public Rectangle drawSprite (Graphics g) {
    g.setColor(color);
    g.fillOval((int)(x - width / 2.0),
               (int)(y - height / 2.0), width, height);
    return collisionBox();
  }
} // end class RoundSprite
```

Notice in the call to fillOval() that drawSprite() translates the sprite's
center anchor point to the upper-left corner of the sprite before drawing to
match the upper-left coordinates that fillOval() expects.

Drawing plain old colored geometric shapes has its place, but what you
really need in order to give your game visual appeal are some colorful
images zippin' around the screen. Here's an ImageSprite class that you can
use to create sprites from loaded images:

```
import java.awt.*;
class ImageSprite extends SpriteObject {
  protected Image image;
  ImageSprite (Image image, double x, double y) {
    super(x, y, 0, 0);
    setImage(image);
  }

  public void setImage (Image img) {
    image = img;
    width = img.getWidth(null);
    height = img.getHeight(null);
  }
```

Transparent GIF images

GIF images come in two formats. The original format, GIF87a or CompuServe GIF, does not support transparency. The more recent format, GIF89a, supports transparency. You often need to use a special procedure or tool to create transparent GIF89a files. Because Web browsers support transparent GIF images, most tools, such as Adobe Photoshop™, that create Web images can create GIF89a files.

When you load a transparent GIF image in Java, the code that loads the image creates an `Image` that contains a transparent color. When you pass this `Image` to `Graphics.drawImage()`, it only draws the nontransparent (opaque) pixels.

```
public Rectangle drawSprite (Graphics g) {
  g.drawImage(image, (int)(x - width / 2.0),
                     (int)(y - height / 2.0), null);
  return collisionBox();
}
} // end class ImageSprite
```

You create an `ImageSprite` by passing an `Image` to the `ImageSprite()` constructor. `ImageSprite()` then calls `setImage()` to set the image the sprite is to display. `setImage()` sets the `width` and `height` of the sprite to be the same as the width and height of the image. You change the sprite's image by passing the new image to `setImage()`.

If you give `ImageSprite` an image that defines a transparent color, `g.drawImage()` doesn't overwrite the pixels in `g` that correspond to the transparent color. You use transparent images to give your sprites a nonrectangular outline. (Remember, a nonrectangular sprite still has a rectangular collision box.)

Animating sprites

If an image is better than a colored shape, certainly an animated image is better still. To animate your sprite, you need to change the image it displays at periodic intervals. The length of the interval is the animation *frame rate*, often expressed in frames-per-second (fps).

Conveniently, the sprite engine periodically calls the sprite's `updateSprite()` method (refer back to Table 8-1 for a refresher). However, because the sprite doesn't have control over *when* the sprite engine calls

TECHNICAL STUFF

Relative versus absolute timing

Using a relative frame rate based on the number of calls to updateSprite() makes the animation rate dependent on the frequency with which the game calls the sprite engine's update() method. Changing the update() frequency changes the animation rate of any animations using a relative frame rate. You may find this change good or bad, depending on what you want to do with your game.

Using a relative frame rate keeps the timing between sprites consistent — a bullet that travels three times faster than the player continues to do so regardless of the rate at which the game calls update(). However, the speed of the entire game, including the animations, changes in relation to the rate that the game calls update(). An alternative is to keep track of real time using System.currentTimeMillis() and base the animation rate on absolute time.

Using an absolute animation rate attempts to maintain a consistent speed for the actions that take place on the screen — a bullet that takes two seconds to cross the play field continues to take approximately two seconds regardless of the rate at which the game calls update().

However, trying to represent absolute time using a discrete timing interval introduces *time aliasing*. If a bullet wants to animate at 15 fps and update() is called 30 times a second, then the bullet animates on every second call to updateSprite(), but if update() is called 20 times a second, then the bullets animate on three out of four calls to updateSprite(), and you may see evidence of the time alias as jittery movement.

updateSprite(), you need to add the following AnimationSprite class so that you can control frame rate in terms of the number of calls to updateSprite() between changes to the image. A frame rate of 1 causes updateSprite() to change the image on every call; a frame rate of 2 causes updateSprite() to change the image every other call, and so on. A larger frame rate causes the sprite to animate slower, kind of like slow-motion video slows down a video playback.

Here is how you extend the ImageSprite class to create AnimationSprite:

```
import java.awt.*;
class AnimationSprite extends ImageSprite {
  protected int     curImage, delay, framerate;
  protected Image[] images;
  AnimationSprite (Image[] images, int framerate,
                   double x, double y) {
    super(images[0], x, y);
    setImages(images, framerate);
  }
```

```
public void setImage (int imageIndex) {
  curImage = imageIndex;
  delay = framerate;
  setImage(images[imageIndex]);
}

public void setImages (Image[] images, int framerate) {
  this.images = images;
  this.framerate = framerate;
  setImage(0);
}

public boolean updateSprite () {
  int w = width, h = height;
  if (--delay <= 0)
    setImage((curImage + 1) % images.length);
  return w != width || h != height;
}
} // end class AnimationSprite
```

If the delay timer has expired, updateSprite() calls the overloaded
setImage(int imageIndex) method to reset the timer and advance to the
next image. But first updateSprite() records the current width and
height in the w and h variables. After calling setImage(), updateSprite()
uses w and h to see whether setImage() changed the size of the sprite and
therefore the collision box (see Table 8-1) and returns the result of this test.

ImageSprite and AnimationSprite follow a similar pattern: Each class
has a method to set the image or images that it displays. You can continue
this pattern and create classes that use multiple arrays of images in order to
give the sprite multiple animations.

You can extend AnimationSprite to create sprites that display different
animations — walking left, walking right, running, shooting, ducking, and so
on — depending on the action the sprite is performing. The subclass calls
setImages() in AnimationSprite to set the animation the sprite displays
in the same manner that AnimationSprite calls ImageSprite's
setImage() method to set the next image in the animation. Chapter 9
shows how to synchronize a sprite's animation with its action.

A Sprite Framework

Sprites are just the first piece in the sprite framework. By themselves,
sprites are about as functional as a fish out of water, so you add a sprite
engine to keep track of and manage the sprites. The third piece of the

framework is the *game* that uses the sprite engine. (Games are, after all, the reason you bought this book, right?) This section shows how to create a sprite engine and how to hook it into your game in order to create a complete sprite framework.

The SpriteEngine *class*

The SpriteEngine class implements the functionality set forth in the section "Gentlemen, Start Your Sprite Engines" at the beginning of this chapter. When you *instantiate* (create) a SpriteEngine, you pass the SpriteEngine() constructor the width and height of the play field (in pixels) and the *depth* of the play field. The depth of the play field determines how many layers of sprites the SpriteEngine supports. (Graphics programs where you can move objects to "front" or to "back" use the same basic layering concept as the play field depth.) Table 8-2 shows the four primary methods that you call to carry out the sprite engine's duties.

Table 8-2	Primary SpriteEngine Methods
Method	**What It Does**
add (Sprite sprite, int depth)	Adds sprite to the play field at the depth sprite layer.
remove (Sprite sprite)	Removes sprite from the play field.
draw (Graphics g)	Draws all the sprites in the play field to the graphics context g from the deepest (highest numbered) sprite layer to the closest (lowest numbered) so that deeper sprites appear to be behind closer sprites. Returns a Rectangle[] array containing all the regions in the play field where sprites drew themselves.
update ()	Calls the updateSprite() method for all the sprites in the engine and then detects and resolves any resulting collisions.

Here is the complete code for the SpriteEngine class. The sections following the code break out and describe how the major functional blocks in the class work.

```
import java.util.*;
import java.awt.*;
```

```
class SpriteBorder extends Object {}
public class SpriteEngine extends Observable {
  public static final SpriteBorder NORTH = new
                                        SpriteBorder();
  public static final SpriteBorder SOUTH = new
                                        SpriteBorder();
  public static final SpriteBorder EAST  = new
                                        SpriteBorder();
  public static final SpriteBorder WEST  = new
                                        SpriteBorder();
  private Vector[]  sprites, addPending;
  private Vector    removePending = new Vector();
  private int       width, height;
  private boolean   updating;

  public SpriteEngine (int width, int height, int depth) {
    this.width = width;  this.height = height;
    sprites = new Vector[depth];
    addPending = new Vector[depth];
    while (--depth >= 0) {
      sprites[depth] = new Vector();
      addPending[depth] = new Vector();
    }
  }


  public synchronized void notifyObservers (Object arg) {
    setChanged();
    super.notifyObservers(arg);
  }


  // adjusts r so that it is contained within the play field
  public final void placeInBounds (Rectangle r) {
    if (r != null) {
      int w = Math.min(width, r.width);
      int h = Math.min(height, r.height);
      int x = Math.min(Math.max(0, r.x), width - w);
      int y = Math.min(Math.max(0, r.y), height - h);
      r.reshape(x, y, w, h);
    }
  }


  public void add (Sprite sprite, int depth) {
    depth = Math.min(Math.max(0, depth), sprites.length-1);
    if (updating) {  // add sprite later
      if (!addPending[depth].contains(sprite))
```

(continued)

(continued)

```
        addPending[depth].addElement(sprite);
    }
    else {  // add sprite now
      sprites[depth].addElement(sprite);
      sprite.setSpriteEngine(this);
    }
}

public void remove (Sprite sprite) {
    if (updating) {  // remove sprite later
      if (!removePending.contains(sprite))
        removePending.addElement(sprite);
    }
    else {  // remove sprite now
      for (int depth = sprites.length;  --depth >= 0; ) {
        if (sprites[depth].contains(sprite)) {
          sprites[depth].removeElement(sprite);
          sprite.setSpriteEngine(null);
          return;
        }
      }
      throw new NoSuchElementException();
    }
}

public Rectangle[] draw (Graphics g) {
    Vector drawRects = new Vector();
    for (int depth = sprites.length;  --depth >= 0; ) {
      synchronized (sprites[depth]) {
        Enumeration enum = sprites[depth].elements();
        while (enum.hasMoreElements()) {
          Rectangle r =
              ((Sprite)enum.nextElement()).drawSprite(g);
          if (r != null)
            drawRects.addElement(r);
        }
      }
    }
    Rectangle[] result = new Rectangle[drawRects.size()];
    drawRects.copyInto((Object[])result);
    return result;
}

public synchronized void update () {
    Vector moved = new Vector();
```

```
try {
  updating = true;
  // Call update() for all the sprites.
  for (int depth = sprites.length;  --depth >= 0; ) {
    Enumeration enum = sprites[depth].elements();
    while (enum.hasMoreElements()) {
      Sprite s = (Sprite)enum.nextElement();
      if (s.updateSprite())
        moved.addElement(s);  // collision rect changed
    }
  }


  // Check for overlapping collision boxes and
  // resolve collisions.
  Enumeration enum = moved.elements();
  while (enum.hasMoreElements()) {
    Sprite movedSprite = (Sprite)enum.nextElement();
    Rectangle cb = movedSprite.collisionBox();
    if (cb != null  &&  cb.x < 0)
      cb = movedSprite.collideWith(WEST);
    if (cb != null  &&  (cb.x + cb.width) > width)
      cb = movedSprite.collideWith(EAST);
    if (cb != null  &&  cb.y < 0)
      cb = movedSprite.collideWith(NORTH);
    if (cb != null  &&  (cb.y + cb.height) > height)
      cb = movedSprite.collideWith(SOUTH);
    for (int depth = 0;
        cb != null && depth < sprites.length; depth++) {
      Enumeration enum2 = sprites[depth].elements();
      while (enum2.hasMoreElements()  &&  cb != null) {
        Sprite s = (Sprite)enum2.nextElement();
        if (s != movedSprite) {
          Rectangle cb2 = s.collisionBox();
          if (cb2 != null  &&  cb2.intersects(cb)) {
            cb = movedSprite.collideWith(s);
            s.collideWith(movedSprite);
          }
        }
      }
    }
  }
}
finally {
  updating = false;
  // Remove pending sprites.
```

(continued)

(continued)

```
    for (int index = removePending.size(); --index >= 0;){
      try {
        remove((Sprite)removePending.elementAt(index));
      }
      catch (NoSuchElementException e) {}
    }
    removePending.removeAllElements();
    // Add pending sprites.
    for (int depth = sprites.length;  --depth >= 0; ) {
      Vector ap = addPending[depth];
      for (int index = ap.size();  --index >= 0; )
        add((Sprite)ap.elementAt(index), depth);
      ap.removeAllElements();
    }
  }
}
}  // end public class SpriteEngine
```

Keeping track of all the sprites

The first responsibility of a sprite engine, as outlined in the "Gentlemen, Start Your Sprite Engines" section earlier in this chapter, is to maintain a list of all the sprites under its control. To fulfill this responsibility, the SpriteEngine class uses Vectors to keep track of the sprites. The sprites[] array contains a vector that stores the sprites for each layer in the play field. As sprites are added to the engine, they are stored in the appropriate vector in the sprites[] array. The SpriteEngine() constructor allocates the sprites[] array and initializes each entry to an empty Vector.

A Vector is a data structure in the java.util package that works like an automatically expanding array; the more stuff you cram into it, the bigger it gets. You use vectors when you want an array, but you don't know how many things you're going to put in it.

You call add() to add sprites to a play field layer, and you call remove() to remove sprites from the play field.

If you look at the code for add() and remove(), you see that these methods check the updating flag and, if it's set (true), they add the sprite to a "pending" vector. The update() method sets the updating flag while update() is calling the sprites' updateSprite() and collideWith() methods. You use the updating flag so that sprites aren't added to or removed from the sprites[] vectors while update() processes the vectors. The addPending[] and removePending vectors hold the sprites until update() finishes processing the vectors. When update() finishes processing the vectors, it clears the updating flag and adds and removes the sprites in the respective pending vectors. Using the pending vectors to delay the add and remove operations prevents update() from attempting to process sprites that you removed or added during the current update.

Drawing sprites layer by layer

The draw() method loops from the highest numbered (deepest, or bottom) layer in the sprites[] array to layer 0 (the closest, or top). It tells each sprite in each layer to draw itself by calling the sprite's drawSprite() method. Drawing the sprites in this order allows sprites in lower-numbered layers to overwrite sprites in higher-numbered layers. This overwriting causes the sprites in the lower-number layers to appear to be in front of the sprites in the higher-numbered layers and creates a sense of depth to your game, with some objects in the background and some in the foreground.

As you draw each sprite, if the rectangle returned from drawSprite() isn't null, you add the rectangle to the drawRects vector using the following code:

```
Rectangle r =
    ((Sprite)enum.nextElement()).drawSprite(g);
if (r != null)
    drawRects.addElement(r);
```

You keep track of the rectangles the sprites draw so that draw() can return the list of rectangles. This list of rectangles tells the code that calls draw() which portions of the play field it needs to copy to the screen. The section "The BackgroundSpriteEngine class" later in this chapter shows how to use the rectangle list returned from draw() to efficiently restore the portions of background image that draw() overwrites.

One more thing to point out about the code in draw(): the code to actually draw each layer is contained inside of this synchronized block:

```
synchronized (sprites[depth]) {
    // code to process layer depth goes here
    }
```

This synchronized block does for draw() the same thing that the updating flag does for update(): It prevents sprites from being added or removed from a vector while draw() is processing the vector. sprites[depth], in this case, is the vector that draw() is processing.

Synchronizing on the sprites[depth] vector makes the code that enumerates the elements in that vector *thread-safe* (protected from data corruption) because the Vector object is already a thread-safe object. The Vector is thread-safe because its addElement() and removeElement() methods are synchronized methods, meaning that no other thread can add or remove elements from the `sprites[depth]` vector while the code in the `synchronized (sprites[depth]) {}` block executes. If the sprite engine's `add()` or `remove()` method is called from another thread while `draw()` is processing the same vector in the current thread, the synchronized block prevents `add()` or `remove()` from changing the vector until `draw()` is finished with it. CD Chapter 2 explains how to make your code thread-safe.

Moving sprites and detecting collisions

`SpriteEngine`'s `update()` method performs three distinct operations:

1. **It calls `updateSprite()` for every sprite in the engine.**

   If `updateSprite()` returns `true` to indicate that it changed the sprite's collision box, `update()` adds the sprite to the `moved` vector.

2. **It checks the collision boxes of every sprite in the `moved` vector to see whether all or part of the collision box is outside the play field.**

   If the sprite is out of bounds, `update()` passes the sprite's `collideWith()` method the appropriate `SpriteBorder` object. Then `update()` checks the collision box of the `moved` vector sprite against the collision box of every other sprite in the engine. If the boxes intersect (overlap), `update()` calls the `collideWith()` method for each sprite.

3. **It adds and removes sprites placed in the respective pending vectors while `update()` is performing Steps 1 and 2.**

One interesting thing about `update()` is how it performs this mysterious collision detection we keep talking about. All `update()` does is get the collision box for each sprite and call the `Rectangle` method `intersects()`. If the collision boxes intersect, `update()` calls the `collideWith()` methods for each sprite.

Improving the accuracy of collision detection

The secondary collision detection techniques presented in this section are advanced techniques that are used by commercial sprite-based arcade games. We describe how the techniques work and when they are used. These techniques aren't used by the `SpriteMaze` game presented later in this chapter and aren't required in order for you to implement a sprite engine or to create a sprite-based arcade game, but rather are used to give your game a final coat of arcade-quality polish.

Collision boxes are rectangular areas. Remember that sprites are graphic objects that you can make any shape you want, so not all sprites are rectangular or necessarily even *close* to rectangular. Collision boxes being rectangular and sprites being any shape means that the collision box intersection test may detect that two sprites collide when they don't appear to on screen. However, you can improve the collision detection by implementing a more precise secondary detection algorithm in the sprites' `collideWith()` method that kicks in when a primary collision box intersection is detected and thus avoid this possible problem of false collision detection. You need to solve two problems to implement improved collision detection:

1. **You need to figure out what portion of the collision box the sprite actually occupies.**

2. **You need to determine whether the portions of each sprite in the intersection of the two collision boxes collide.**

The challenge of secondary collision detection doesn't have one solution that fits every game or even necessarily one solution for every sprite collision in the *same* game. Often you have a trade-off between the precision of the collision detection and the time it takes to perform. You only need collision detection that is precise enough for the collisions to appear logical, fair, and consistent to the player.

Table 8-3 shows some of the solutions you can implement in `collideWith()` to see whether two sprites really collide:

Table 8-3	Techniques for Secondary Collision Detection		
Type of Collision Detection	*Pros*	*Cons*	*To Determine if Two Sprites Collide . . .*
Circular	Fast, easy	Doesn't work for all sprites (not all sprites are round).	Check to see whether the centers of the sprites are closer than their combined radii.
Composite rectangles, multiple rectangles	Easy to customize	Creating rectangles can be a pain.	Check to see whether any of the composite rectangles for one sprite intersect with any of the composite rectangles for the other sprite.
Pixel	Accurate for arbitrary images	Slow, only works for images.	Compare the pixels in the collision box inter-section to see whether both sprites have a nontransparent pixel at the same position.
Bit-mask	Accurate, easy to customize	Masks take up memory and can be a pain to create.	Perform an AND test between the mask-bits in the collision box intersection to check whether both sprites have a collision pixel at the same position.

Circular collision detection is often a good compromise between absolute accuracy and a reasonable speed for the game because this sort of detection is fast to compute and circles tend to do a good job describing the space many objects occupy. Chapter 3 discusses how to calculate the distance between two points so you can determine if the distance between the sprites is less than their combined radii.

Composite rectangles collision detection allows reasonably accurate approximations of arbitrary collision areas and is fairly easy to implement. To use composite rectangles, you have to create a list of rectangles for each sprite; the bottom line is that composite rectangles are a good choice when you don't have too many different sprites.

Pixel collision detection is an accurate way to check collisions between images, but this detection is a slow check to perform. One downside to this approach is that some images, particularly animation images, have parts of the image that you don't want to use in order to determine collisions, and no easy way to ignore these pixels exists. Chapter 12 shows how to use the `PixelGrabber` class to read pixels from an image.

Bit-mask collision detection is the technique most used by commercial arcade games — or at least those that don't have dedicated sprite hardware. Bit-mask collision detection enables you to completely customize the collision region, and bit-mask collision detection is several times faster than pixel collision detection. It requires that you create a *collision mask* for each sprite. Each collision mask is an array of `int` or `long` values with one *bit* in the mask for each pixel in the collision box. You set bits to 1 that correspond to *collision pixels* — pixels in the sprite that collide with other sprites. You perform an AND test between the masks for the bits in the collision intersection for the two sprites using the bitwise (&) operator. If both collision masks contain bits set for the same pixel locations, the AND operation produces a non-zero result to indicate that a collision has occurred.

Selecting a movement frame rate

The frequency with which you call `update()` determines the movement frame rate. The higher the frequency, the more often sprites get to move, and the shorter the distance the sprites have to move for each update in order to move at a given speed across the screen. Typically, you call `update()` at the same rate you call `draw()` so that you have a one-to-one relationship between what the sprites do and what the player sees. However, you may come across situations where you want to call `update()` more frequently than you call `draw()`.

For example, if any sprites are moving fast enough that the x movement is greater than or equal to the sprite's width (`Math.abs(newx - x) >= width`) or the y movement is greater than or equal to the sprite's height

(Math.abs(newy - y) >= height), two sprites can potentially move through each other without colliding, and you don't want that. Chapter 4 explains in lurid detail how two objects can move through each other without colliding when they are allowed to move too far in a single update.

Sometimes missing certain collisions, such as two bullets hitting each other, is acceptable as long as you detect the important collisions, such as the bullet hitting the rampaging monster that's bearing down on you. To figure out how much scrutiny to apply to these various types of sprite collision situations, you add the widths of the two sprites and subtract 1; this operation determines the maximum safe x increment the sprites can move toward each other without passing through each other.

For example, if the rampaging monster is 12 pixels wide and is moving west at 5 pixels per update, how fast can a 2-pixel-wide bullet traveling east move without risk of passing through the monster? The answer is

$(12 + 2 - 1) - 5 = 8$ pixels per update

You prevent the bullet from passing through the monster by restricting its x movement to no more than 8 pixels per call to updateSprite(). You can repeat the calculations for collisions in the y directions by substituting y for x and height for width. You also repeat the calculation for each pair of sprites that you don't want to be able to pass through each other.

Now you can turn the equation around to calculate how frequently you need to call update() in order to allow the bullet traveling at 8 pixels per update to move at a given speed across the screen. For example, if you want the bullet to travel across a 400-pixel-wide playing field in two seconds, how many times a second do you need to call update()? The answer is

$((400 / 2) / 8) = 25$ times per second

Instead of increasing the movement frame rate or restricting the distance a sprite can move on each update, you can give a fast moving sprite one or more *tracer sprites*. Tracer sprites are invisible sprites that follow the fast-moving sprite at fixed intervals. As long as the interval between the sprite and each of its tracer sprites is less than the maximum safe distance the sprite can travel each update, the tracer sprites prevent objects from passing through each other. If a colliding object doesn't hit the fast-moving sprite at exactly the moment update() is called, it hits one of the tracer sprites and still registers a realistic collision. The tracer sprite's collideWith() method then just calls the fast sprite's collideWith() method.

However, be careful not to make the tracer sprite tail too long. Other sprites can run into the tail and collide with it, resulting in erroneous collisions. As long as the tail is short, these erroneous collisions are rare, and it's probably not obvious to the player that they were incorrect.

The BackgroundSpriteEngine *class*

The SpriteEngine class doesn't implement one of the essential aspects of sprites — that of preventing the sprites from changing the background. It just draws the sprites to the graphics context that you pass to draw(). SpriteEngine works this way because sometimes you are redrawing the background each frame anyway, and it wouldn't make much sense to have the sprite engine go to all the work to clean up after itself.

To implement the final required aspect of sprites as we describe early in this chapter — the nondestructive drawing — you extend the SpriteEngine class to accept a background image to draw to. You also override the draw() method to erase any sprites you drew during the previous update before drawing the current list of sprites. The BackgroundSpriteEngine class looks like this:

```java
import java.awt.*;
public class BackgroundSpriteEngine extends SpriteEngine {
  private Image       bgImage;
  private Rectangle[] erase = new Rectangle[0];
  BackgroundSpriteEngine (Image background, int depth) {
    super(background.getWidth(null),
          background.getHeight(null), depth);
    bgImage = background;
  }

  public synchronized Rectangle[] draw (Graphics g) {
    for (int ii = erase.length;  --ii >= 0; ) {
      Rectangle r = erase[ii];
      Graphics clip = g.create(r.x, r.y, r.width, r.height);
      clip.drawImage(bgImage, -r.x, -r.y, null);
      clip.dispose();
    }
    return erase = super.draw(g);
  }
}  // end class BackgroundSpriteEngine
```

Sprite events and handling them

Notice the first line in the SpriteEngine class (from way back in the "The SpriteEngine class" section:

```java
public class SpriteEngine extends Observable {
```

The Observable class that SpriteEngine extends provides methods to allow other Observer classes to receive update notices from the Observable object. The SpriteMaze game presented in the "Building on the BlockMaze class" section later in this chapter implements the Observer interface in order to receive update notices from the sprite engine used by the game. The SpriteEngine class uses this mechanism to create a one-way communication channel from the sprites to the observers. You use this channel to have your sprites notify your game when an event occurs that the game needs to handle. Here is the code you use to send a notification from a sprite:

```
spriteEngine.notifyObservers(this);
```

To receive notifications from sprites, your game implements the Observable interface. The Observable interface defines a single method that your class must implement.

```
public interface Observable {
   void update(Observable observable, Object arg);
}
```

The Observable parameter to update() is a reference to the SpriteEngine object, and arg is the Sprite that sends the notification. If a sprite sends more than one type of notice, update() queries the sprite in order to determine how to handle the event.

The SpriteMaze game at the end of this chapter shows examples of handling sprite notifications.

Sprite control

Your game's responsibilities in the sprite framework are to

- ✔ **Create the sprite engine**
- ✔ **Create sprites and add them to the engine**
- ✔ **Draw the sprites over the background by calling the sprite engine's** draw() **method**
- ✔ **Display the play field on the screen**
- ✔ **Call the sprite engine's** update() **method at regular intervals**
- ✔ **Handle sprite events**

Before you create a sprite engine, you need to decide how many draw layers you need. For example, consider a shoot-'em-up space game where you have nonmoving background sprites, a bunch of aliens, the player's spaceship, bullets, missiles, and explosions. One possible way to assign draw layers to these sprites is as follows:

Draw Layer	Sprites
0	Explosions
1	Bullets and missiles
2	Player's spaceship
3	Aliens
4	Background

These assignments indicate that you need a sprite engine with five draw layers. You create a sprite engine with a 300×200 pixel play field for your game like this:

```
SpriteEngine spriteEngine = new SpriteEngine(300, 200, 5);
```

After creating the sprite engine, you make your game an Observer of the sprite engine so that your game gets the sprite events.

```
spriteEngine.addObserver(this);
```

Now your sprite engine is ready to go. You add sprites to the engine like this:

```
Sprite sprite = new Explosion(x, y, 10);
spriteEngine.add(sprite, 0);
```

This code assumes that a class named Explosion implements the Sprite interface and has an Explosion() constructor that accepts x and y coordinates and an explosion size (10).

You create a thread to call draw() and update() in a loop. CD Chapter 2 shows how to create threads and how to use Thread.sleep() to control the timing of the update loop so that each iteration of the loop takes the same amount of time to execute. The run() method for your game looks something like this:

```
public void run () {
  while (!gameOver) {
    spriteEngine.update();
    spriteEngine.draw(backgroundGraphic);
```

```
    repaint();
    sleepUntilNextFrame();
  }
}
```

The `SpriteMaze` game later in this chapter shows how to put all these steps together to create a game.

Computer Adversaries

In this section, we use the term *adversary* when talking about something or someone in the game that (who) is attempting to keep a player from achieving game goals. We use the term *opponent* when referring to an adversary that isn't just in the way but is also trying to win the game.

One of the most important elements to making your game fun to play is creating adversaries that are challenging and fair. One way to challenge players is to make the adversary another player; human opponents are hard to match as interesting adversaries. Sometimes, though, you need to have the computer provide adversaries, even in a multiplayer game.

The computer is at a definite disadvantage to a human in terms of problem solving, creative thinking, adapting to new situations, and overall knowledge. However, the computer does have some advantages that you can exploit to make the computer adversary seem smarter than it is. This section presents some techniques for creating adversaries that seem to have some characteristics of a human opponent.

Using random intelligence to make adversaries smarter

One of the easiest yet most effective ways to make your computer adversaries seem smart is to make them less predictable. A player can manipulate a completely predictable opponent because the player can figure out how the opponent reacts to any situation (remember the "patterns" arcade wizards came up with for beating Pac-Man™ every time?). Sometimes you want the player to figure out and manipulate the computer adversaries, which is the challenge in playing the game. Often times, however, a predictable computer opponent causes the player to lose interest in the game after playing for a short period. To make your game hold the player's interest longer, you can make your computer opponents less predictable by including random probability in any decisions they make.

Sometimes, random chance causes the computer to make a less-than-optimal choice, yet achieve a better result. For example, you create an alien that always calculates a precise solution to shoot the player along the player's current vector of travel. Players can figure out that they only need to make a small adjustment to their speed and the alien always misses. Instead, have the alien choose the perfect solution 60 percent of the time, shoot a small random distance ahead of the player 20 percent of the time, and behind the player the other 20 percent of the time. Now if players always speed up or slow down, some of the shots still hit them.

As a general rule, if you don't want a predictable computer opponent, you add at least a small random factor to every decision a computer adversary makes.

Using a breadth-first search for adversary navigation

When searching for a path between two points, use a *breadth-first* search to find the shortest path. Following the shortest path makes the computer adversaries look smarter because they move purposefully and efficiently. Chapter 7 shows how to implement a breadth-first maze search.

You also use a breadth-first search to find things that are in the proximity of a computer adversary. An adversary can't react to something until it's aware that the object is there. After the adversary is aware that something is close at hand, the adversary can change tactics, follow the path to get to what it found, or plot another path away from it. Giving your computer adversaries knowledge of their environment allows them to act more intelligently.

Prioritizing adversary goals

A formidable adversary uses multiple strategies, each built from short-term tactics and short-term goals, to achieve its purpose. At any point, the conditions that determine which strategy or tactics the adversary should use can change. The better an adversary exploits these opportunities to shift tactics, the more "intelligent" and formidable that adversary is.

To select a strategy for a computer adversary, you first list the goals that the adversary wants to achieve in order of highest to lowest priority. Next, you assign the conditions that must exist before the adversary can achieve the goal. You also assign the cost — the amount of extra effort or risk — that the adversary "feels" is worth spending to achieve a given goal compared to the next goal in the prioritized list, with the last goal in the list requiring little effort or risk. The relative priorities, conditions, and costs of the goals all change depending on the situation.

For example, assume that you are creating a fantasy role-playing game that takes place in a dungeon maze, and you have a computer adversary that is an archer. The archer's objective is to find arrows and shoot them at the player. The archer settles for punching the player if the archer is close enough or doesn't have any arrows to shoot. The archer also wants to stay alive, so he wants to sustain as little damage as possible while achieving his objective. However, the archer is willing to *risk* sustaining some damage in order to attack the player. You measure the archer's *effort* in terms of how far he has to walk.

The computer archer prioritizes his goals according to several factors. If the archer is injured, the risk involved with attacking the player increases. If the archer has a bunch of arrows, the effort he is willing to expend to collect more arrows decreases. Conversely, if the archer has no arrows, the effort he is willing to spend increases. (You can see how all these goals and risks are interdependent to some degree.) Table 8-4 shows what the prioritized list of goals for a healthy archer with four arrows could look like.

Table 8-4	The Archer's Prioritized List of Goals		
Goal#/Priority	*Distance to Walk*	*Goal*	*Conditions*
1	6	Find a location to shoot arrows at the player	Must have at least one arrow
2	3	Find an arrow to pick up	Must be able to carry more arrows
3	2	Find a location to punch the player	None
4	0	Randomly select a location to move to	None

Notice that we stated all the goals in terms of finding a location from which the archer can accomplish the goal. If the archer selects a goal that he can accomplish from his current location, he does it immediately. Otherwise, he walks to the location where he can accomplish the goal.

The *distance to walk* values in Table 8-4 are cumulative. To satisfy the priority 1 goal, the archer is willing to walk up to 6 squares farther than needed to satisfy the priority 2 goal, up to 9 squares farther than for the priority 3 goal and up to 11 squares beyond the priority 4 goal.

To select the best goal for the archer, you evaluate the goals in order:

1. **Search up to (6 + 3 + 2) = 11 squares away for a location from which to shoot the player.**

   If the search finds a location, set shootDist (a temporary variable used during this goal evaluation) to the distance from the current square to the destination square; otherwise set shootDist to the maximum search distance plus one — (6 + 3 + 2 + 1) = 12 — to allow the archer to search the maximum distance for the other goals.

2. **If shootDist is less than or equal to 6, choose the first goal.**

3. **Search up to (shootDist – 6 – 1) squares for an arrow to pick up.**

   Set arrowDist to the distance or to (3 + 2 + 1) = 6 if no location found.

4. **If arrowDist is less than or equal to 3, choose the second goal.**

5. **If shootDist is less than or equal to (6 + 3) = 9, then choose the first goal.**

6. **Search up to the lesser of (shootDist – 6 – 3 – 1) or (arrowDist – 3 – 1) squares for a location to punch the player from.**

   Set punchDist to the distance, or to (2 + 1) = 3 if not found.

7. **If punchDist is less than or equal to 2, choose the third goal.**

8. **If arrowDist is less than or equal to (3 + 2) = 5, choose the second goal.**

9. **If shootDist is less than or equal to (6 + 3 + 2) = 11, choose the first goal.**

10. **Choose the fourth goal.**

If you look at this sequence carefully, you can see a pattern emerging. You limit each search to no more than the cumulative extra distances of the goal and all lower-priority goals. If any previous search has succeeded, you further limit the search distance to the distance of the successful search minus the cumulative extra distances of the higher-priority goal and any intervening goals minus 1.

Instead of performing separate searches, you can perform a single search looking for multiple goals. Single searches are faster than searching the same area multiple times.

The Sprite Maze Game

Sprite Maze is a simple game that demonstrates the use of a sprite framework. The game is a good example of how you can create relatively sophisticated animated, autonomous game elements with a small amount of code.

The sprite framework makes this possible by taking care of the management and scheduling of the game elements so that all you need to do is add some code to differentiate the various game elements.

The goal in Sprite Maze is to navigate your spinning top from the starting square in the maze to the ending square. You navigate your top by clicking the mouse in the maze. The top moves directly towards the spot where you click. You can hold the mouse button down to continuously control the top's movement.

A game is about overcoming challenges. To make navigating the maze a little more challenging, Sprite Maze adds an enemy top. The enemy top uses breadth-first searching to plot a path to your top. (Chapter 7 shows how to perform a breadth first search.) As it moves toward your top, the enemy top shoots a stream of bullets. If a bullet hits your top, or if the enemy top touches your top, you lose. Figure 8-2 shows the game.

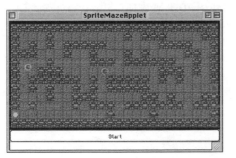

Figure 8-2:
The Sprite
Maze game.

The `SpriteMaze` code shown here uses a `BackgroundSpriteEngine` to automatically erase the sprites before drawing new sprites. A second version of the Sprite Maze game on the CD shows how to use the `SpriteEngine` class and leverage the "dirty" logic for updating the maze that `SpriteMaze` inherits from `BlockMaze`.

Implementing a cast of sprites

`SpriteMaze` uses many of the classes presented earlier in this chapter. It also adds the following custom sprite classes:

- ✔ `Wall`
- ✔ `Runner`
- ✔ `Shooter`
- ✔ `Bullet`

Running into a wall

Sprite Maze marks the wall squares in the sprite play field to take advantage of the collision detection provided by the sprite engine. However, because the `SpriteMaze` class inherits logic from `BlockMaze` to efficiently display the maze, `Wall` sprites don't need to draw themselves. All a `Wall` sprite does is define the boundary of the wall so that other sprites can detect when they run into it. The `Wall` class is

```java
import java.awt.*;
class Wall extends SpriteObject {
  Wall (int x, int y, int w, int h) {
    super(x, y, w, h);
  }
}  // end class Wall
```

Animating maze runners

The main character in the cast of sprites is the `Runner` class. `Runner` serves as not only the class that implements the player's spinning top, but it also serves as the base class for the `Shooter` class. Here is the `Runner` class code:

```java
import java.awt.*;
class Runner extends AnimationSprite {
  static final int NORMAL = 0, DEAD = 1, AT_DEST = 2;
  int state = NORMAL;
  double deltaX, deltaY, destX, destY, lastX, lastY;
  Runner (Image[] imgs, int framerate, int x, int y) {
    super(imgs, framerate, x, y);
  }

  void setDest (double x, double y, double speed) {
    deltaX = ((destX = x) - this.x);
    deltaY = ((destY = y) - this.y);
    if (deltaX != 0 || deltaY != 0) {
      speed /= Math.sqrt(deltaX * deltaX + deltaY * deltaY);
      deltaX *= speed;
      deltaY *= speed;
    }
  }

  public boolean updateSprite () {
    boolean changed = deltaX != 0 || deltaY != 0;
    lastX = x;  lastY = y;
    if (deltaX != 0)
      if (Math.abs(deltaX) >= Math.abs(x - destX)) {
        deltaX = 0;
```

```
      x = destX;
    }
    else
      x += deltaX;
  if (deltaY != 0)
    if (Math.abs(deltaY) >= Math.abs(y - destY)) {
      deltaY = 0;
      y = destY;
    }
    else
      y += deltaY;
  return super.updateSprite() || changed;
}


private double adjust (double last, double cur, int dim,
                       int wpos, int wdim) {
  if (cur > last)  // moving right or down
    return wpos - (cur + dim / 2.0);
  else if (cur < last)  // moving left or up
    return (wpos + wdim) - (cur - dim / 2.0);
  return Double.MAX_VALUE;  // moving at it, don t adjust
}


protected Rectangle slideAlong (Rectangle barrier) {
  double xadjust = adjust(lastX, x, width,
                          barrier.x, barrier.width);
  double yadjust = adjust(lastY, y, height,
                          barrier.y, barrier.height);
  if (xadjust == Double.MAX_VALUE &&
      yadjust == Double.MAX_VALUE) {
    x = lastX;  y = lastY;
  }
  else if (Math.abs(xadjust) <= Math.abs(yadjust))
    x += xadjust;
  else
    y += yadjust;
  return collisionBox();
}


public Rectangle collideWith (Object obj) {
  Rectangle cb = collisionBox();
  if (obj instanceof SpriteBorder) {
    spriteEngine.placeInBounds(cb);
    x = cb.x + width / 2.0;
    y = cb.y + height / 2.0;
```

(continued)

(continued)

```
    }
    else if (obj instanceof Wall)  // slide along wall
        cb = slideAlong(((Wall)obj).collisionBox());
    else if (obj instanceof Bullet ||
                obj instanceof Runner) {
        state = DEAD;
        spriteEngine.remove(this);
        spriteEngine.notifyObservers(this);
        return null;
    }
    return cb;
    }
} // end class Runner
```

Runner extends the AnimationSprite class (presented earlier in this chapter), and so it starts with the capability to animate itself. Runner adds logic to move toward a point. You set the point toward which Runner moves by calling setDest() with the play field x and y coordinates of the point and the speed, measured in pixels per update, to move toward the point. Each time the sprite engine calls updateSprite(), it moves the sprite speed pixels toward the location at destX and destY.

In collideWith(), the Runner class makes sure that the sprite stays in bounds and observes wall squares. If the sprite attempts to move out of the play field, collideWith() calls the sprite engine's placeInBounds() method to move the collision box back into the play field. If the sprite attempts to move through a wall square, collideWith() calls slideAlong(). slideAlong() moves the sprite back along the nearest edge of the wall.

By adjusting either the sprite's x or y position to move the sprite out of the wall (but not both), the sprite ends up sliding along the edge of a wall instead of getting stuck to the wall's edge. This technique is important because it allows players to easily maneuver their spinning tops around the maze.

One other thing that collideWith() does is detect when a bullet hits the sprite. When collideWith() detects a hit, it kills the sprite by removing it from the sprite engine. It then calls spriteEngine.notifyObservers(this) to notify the game that one of the spinning tops died. The "Sprite events and handling them" section earlier in this chapter explains how the notification process works.

Animating an adversary who shoots to kill

The Shooter class implements the computer adversary in the Sprite Maze game. Shooter makes two additions to the Runner class that it extends.

The first addition Shooter makes is to shoot a bullet every fourth call to updateSprite() in the direction the shooter is moving. It uses the bulletTimer variable to keep track of when to shoot the next bullet. It shoots the bullet by creating a new Bullet sprite moving three times as fast as the Shooter and adding it to the sprite engine.

Second, Shooter detects when it has reached the last destX, destY position set by setDest(). When it reaches this position, updateSprite() calls spriteEngine.notifyObservers(this) to notify the game that the shooter needs a new destination. The "Sprite events and handling them" section earlier in this chapter explains how the notification process works.

Here is the Shooter class:

```
import java.awt.*;
class Shooter extends Runner {
  private int bulletTimer;
  Shooter (Image[] imgs, int framerate, int x, int y) {
    super(imgs, framerate, x, y);
  }

  void setDest (double x, double y, double speed) {
    super.setDest(x, y, speed);
    bulletTimer = 4;
  }

  public boolean updateSprite () {
    if (deltaX == 0  &&  deltaY == 0) {
      state = AT_DEST;
      spriteEngine.notifyObservers(this);
    }
    boolean result = super.updateSprite();
    if ((deltaX != 0 || deltaY != 0) && --bulletTimer <= 0){
      bulletTimer = 4;
      spriteEngine.add(new Bullet(x + deltaX, y + deltaY,
                              deltaX * 3, deltaY * 3), 1);
    }
    return result;
  }
} // end class Shooter
```

Whizzing bullets

The Shooter class wouldn't be much fun without bullets to shoot. The Bullet class extends RoundSprite to create red bullets that move in a straight line until they hit something. When the bullet hits something, other than an ObjectDetector, it removes itself from the sprite engine. Here is the Bullet class:

```
import java.awt.*;
class Bullet extends RoundSprite {
  protected double deltaX, deltaY;
  Bullet (double x, double y, double dx, double dy) {
    super(x, y, 2, 2, Color.red);
    deltaX = dx;  deltaY = dy;
  }

  public boolean updateSprite () {
    x += deltaX;  y += deltaY;
    return true;
  }

  public Rectangle collideWith (Object obj) {
    if (obj instanceof ObjectDetector)  // miss the detector
      return collisionBox();
    spriteEngine.remove(this);
    return null;
  }
} // end class Bullet
```

Building on the `BlockMaze` *class*

The main class that implements the game logic is `SpriteMaze`. `SpriteMaze` extends the `BlockMaze` class that Chapter 7 shows how to create. `SpriteMaze`'s primary functions are to

- ✔ Extend `BlockMaze` **to display the maze with images instead of colored rectangles.**
- ✔ **Load the images for the maze and for the spinning tops.**
- ✔ **Start a new game and detect when the game is finished.**
- ✔ **Create a** `BackgroundSpriteEngine` **and spawn a thread to call its** `update()` **and** `draw()` **methods.**
- ✔ **Respond to the mouse input to control the player's spinning top.**
- ✔ **Use the breadth-first search inherited from** `BlockMaze` s `traverse()` **method to tell the enemy top where to go to find the player's top.**

Here is the complete code for the `SpriteMaze` class. The sections following the code describe how `SpriteMaze` implements its primary functions.

```
import java.awt.*;
import java.util.*;
import java.applet.Applet;
```

```
public class SpriteMaze extends BlockMaze
  implements Runnable, Observer
{
  private static Image[] playerImages, shooterImages;
  private static Image   wallImage, floorImage;
  private static boolean imagesLoaded;
  private BackgroundSpriteEngine spriteEngine;
  private Runner         player;
  private Thread         updater;
  private boolean        gameOver, playerDead, mousePressed;
  private int            mouseX, mouseY;

  public static synchronized void loadImages (Applet app) {
    if (!imagesLoaded) {
      MediaTracker mt = new MediaTracker(app);
      java.net.URL url = app.getCodeBase();
      mt.addImage(wallImage =
                  app.getImage(url, WALL.GIF ), 0);
      mt.addImage(floorImage =
                  app.getImage(url, FLOOR.GIF ), 0);
      playerImages = new Image[4];
      shooterImages = new Image[4];
      for (int ii = 1; ii <= 4; ii++) {
        mt.addImage(playerImages[ii-1] =
            app.getImage(url, PLAYER + ii + .GIF ), 0);
        mt.addImage(shooterImages[ii-1] =
            app.getImage(url, SHOOTER + ii + .GIF ), 0);
      }
      try { mt.waitForAll(); }
      catch (InterruptedException e) {}
      imagesLoaded = true;
    }
  }

  public SpriteMaze () {
    displayPath = false;
  }

  private int spriteX (int x) {
   return leftOffset + (x * sqWid) + (sqWid >> 1);
  }
  private int spriteY (int y) {
    return topOffset + (y * sqHyt) + (sqHyt >> 1);
  }
```

(continued)

(continued)

```
  public synchronized void startGame () {
    if (updater != null)
      updater.stop();
    setDimensions(size().width  / wallImage.getWidth(this),
                  size().height / wallImage.getHeight(this));
    generate(false);  // generate a new block maze
    paintOffscreenImage();
Image img = createImage(offscreenImage.getWidth(null),
                            offscreenImage.getHeight(null));
    img.getGraphics().drawImage(offscreenImage, 0, 0, null);
    spriteEngine = new BackgroundSpriteEngine(img, 4);
    for (int xx = 0;  xx < mzWid;  xx++)
      for (int yy = 0;  yy < mzHyt;  yy++)
        if (sqr(xx, yy) == WALL)
          spriteEngine.add(new Wall(spriteX(xx),
                                  spriteY(yy), sqWid, sqHyt), 3);
    player = new Runner(playerImages, 3,
                        spriteX(startX), spriteY(startY));
    spriteEngine.add(player, 2);
    spriteEngine.add(new Shooter(shooterImages, 3,
        spriteX(finishX), spriteY(finishY)), 0);
    spriteEngine.add(new ObjectDetector(spriteX(finishX),
        spriteY(finishY), pWid, pHyt, player), 3);
    spriteEngine.addObserver(this);
    updater = new Thread(this);
    updater.start();
  }

  public void run () {
    playerDead = gameOver = false;
    synchronized (this) { showMaze(true); }
    do {
      if (mousePressed)
        player.setDest(mouseX, mouseY, sqWid / 3.0);
      spriteEngine.update();
      spriteEngine.draw(offscr);
      synchronized (this) { showMaze(true); }
    } while (!gameOver);
    String msg = (playerDead ?  You Lose, Try Again  :
                                You Win! );
    offscr.setFont(new Font( TimesRoman , Font.BOLD, 24));
    offscr.setColor(Color.green);
    FontMetrics fm = offscr.getFontMetrics();
```

```
    offscr.drawString(msg,
      (size().width - fm.stringWidth(msg)) / 2,
      (size().height - fm.getHeight()) / 2 + fm.getAscent());
    repaint();
}


protected void drawSquare (int xx, int yy) {
  Image img = (maze[xx][yy] == WALL ? wallImage :
                                      floorImage);
  offscr.drawImage(img, leftOffset + (xx * sqWid),
                        topOffset + (yy * sqHyt), this);

}


public void update (Observable observer, Object arg) {
  if (observer == spriteEngine)
    if (arg instanceof ObjectDetector ||
        (arg instanceof Runner &&
         ((Runner)arg).state == Runner.DEAD))
    {
      gameOver = true;
      if (arg == player)
        playerDead = true;
    }
    else if (arg instanceof Shooter &&
             ((Shooter)arg).state == Shooter.AT_DEST)
      setShooterDest((Shooter)arg);
}


public synchronized void setShooterDest(Shooter shooter) {
  int sx = (int)shooter.centerX() / sqWid;
  int sy = (int)shooter.centerY() / sqHyt;
  int px = (int)player.centerX() / sqWid;
  int py = (int)player.centerY() / sqHyt;
  if (traverse(sx, sy, px, py, false)) {
    int dir = path[sx][sy];
    do {
      switch (dir) {
        case LEFT:   sx--;  break;
        case RIGHT:  sx++;  break;
        case TOP:    sy--;  break;
        case BOTTOM: sy++;  break;
      }
    } while ((path[sx][sy] & dir) != 0);
    shooter.setDest(spriteX(sx), spriteY(sy), sqWid/6.0);
  }
```

(continued)

(continued)

```
  }

  public boolean mouseDown (Event evt, int x, int y) {
    mousePressed = true;
    mouseX = x;  mouseY = y;
    return true;
  }

  public boolean mouseUp (Event evt, int x, int y) {
    mousePressed = false;
    return true;
  }

  public boolean mouseDrag (Event evt, int x, int y) {
    mouseX = x;  mouseY = y;
    return true;
  }
}  // end public class SpriteMaze
```

Initializing the game

The first thing the `SpriteMaze` class does is load the images the game uses. The `SpriteMazeApplet` (shown at the end of the chapter) calls the static method `loadImages()` to load the images. You call a `static` method to load the images because you only need to do this operation once. `SpriteMaze` keeps track of the images using `static` variables so that all instances of `SpriteMaze` share the same set of images. You also need a reference to the applet in order to call the applet's `getCodeBase()` method to get the Uniform Resource Locator (URL) for the location from which the browser loaded the applet code. You use this URL to load `SpriteMaze`'s images. Chapter 5 discusses using the `MediaTracker` class to load images.

As soon as you load the images, you call the `SpriteMaze()` constructor to create a new `SpriteMaze`. Next you call `startGame()` to generate a new maze and start a game. `startGame()` creates a new `BackgroundSprite Engine` and initializes it with `Wall` sprites for all the walls, a `Runner` sprite for the player at the maze start square, and an enemy `Shooter` sprite at the maze finish square. `startGame()` also adds an `ObjectDetector` sprite that detects when the player reaches the finish square. As soon as the sprite engine is ready to go, `startGame()` spawns a new thread to run the game and returns. (CD Chapter 2 discusses how to spawn threads.)

Overriding `drawSquare()`

To replace the colored rectangles in `BlockMaze` with images, you override the `drawSquare()` method inherited from `BlockMaze`. `drawSquare()` draws either a `floorImage` or a `wallImage` to the `offscreenImage`.

Notice that startGame() calls paintOffscreenImage() — which in turn calls drawSquare() — only once, immediately after startGame() generates the maze. Then startGame() uses the offscreenImage to create a copy of the image that it passes to the BackgroundSpriteEngine constructor, which uses it as the background for the sprite engine's play field. Here is the code:

```
Image img = createImage(offscreenImage.getWidth(null),
                        offscreenImage.getHeight(null));
  img.getGraphics().drawImage(offscreenImage, 0, 0, null);
  spriteEngine = new BackgroundSpriteEngine(img, 4);
```

The first line creates a new image of the same size as offscreenImage. Then the code copies offscreenImage by calling the drawImage() method of the new image's graphics context. After img is complete, the sprite engine uses img in draw() to restore the background of the play field when sprite engine erases sprites.

An ImageProducer is an object that provides the image data for an Image. Chapter 12 shows how to use an ImageProducer and even how to write one yourself.

Using a background image with the BackgroundSpriteEngine class means that SpriteMaze doesn't display changes in the maze. The CD-ROM at the back of this book includes a second version of the Sprite Maze game that uses the SpriteEngine class to leverage the "dirty" logic for displaying changes to the maze.

Giving the player control

You give the player control by overriding mouseDown(), mouseUp(), and mouseDrag() to set the mousePressed, mouseX, and mouseY fields. These fields keep track of the state of the mouse. mousePressed is true after the user presses the mouse button while the mouse cursor is over the SpriteMaze canvas. When the user releases the mouse button, mouseUp() sets mousePressed to false. When mousePressed is true, the fields mouseX and mouseY contain the x and y coordinates of the mouse, relative to the upper-left corner of the SpriteMaze. (CD Chapter 5 discusses how to override the mouse methods and respond to user mouse events.)

At the top of the game loop, the run() method checks to see whether mousePressed is true. If mousePressed is true, it calls the setDest() method for the player's spinning top, which causes the player's top to attempt to move toward the mouse cursor.

Keeping things moving

The heartbeat of the whole game is the run() method in SpriteMaze. run() checks the mouse state and sets the destination of the player's top. Next run() calls the sprite engine's update() method to move the sprites and calls draw() to erase the previous sprites from the background and draw the new sprites. Finally, run() calls showMaze() to call repaint() and wait until paint() draws the maze. showMaze() also waits to return until it's time to display the next maze frame. (See Chapter 7 for a description of how showMaze() works.)

As soon as the game loop terminates, run() displays the game-over message — either "You Lose, Try Again" or "You Win!"

Chasing the player

The SpriteMaze class implements the Observable interface so that it can register with the sprite engine to receive notifications from the sprites. SpriteMaze implements the update() method that the sprite engine calls in order to forward sprite notifications to the game. (The "Sprite events and handling them" section earlier in this chapter explains how the notification process works.)

The update() method handles two different events. One is a signal that the game is over, which occurs when either of the runners has died or when the player has reached the finish square.

The other notice indicates that the enemy top has reached its destination and needs a new destination. update() calls setShooterDest() to set a new destination. setShooterDest() calls traverse() to plot a breadth-first search path from the shooter to the player. The code then traces the search path from the shooter to find the longest straight segment from the shooter's current location and sets this square as the shooter's new destination.

The shooter would actually do a better job of finding the player if setShooterDest() always just set the destination to the next square to move to instead of finding the longest straight path. The reason is that setShooterDest() would compute a new search path after each square. However, the imperfect search strategy is actually an intentional weakness in the enemy top, an example of a behavior that the player can figure out and use to manipulate the enemy top.

Finalizing the Sprite Maze applet

The SpriteMazeApplet is responsible for getting the whole game started. It places a SpriteMaze canvas and a Start button on the screen. When the user presses Start, action() spawns a new thread to call startGame(). action() doesn't call startGame() directly because startGame() takes too long to generate the maze and draw the background image. Also, startGame() spawns a thread, so you don't want to call it from an event method like action(). (CD Chapter 2 explains why you have to be careful spawning threads from an event method and why you don't want to take a lot of time in an event method.)

The code for the SpriteMazeApplet is as follows:

```
import java.awt.*;
public class SpriteMazeApplet extends java.applet.Applet
  implements Runnable
{
  SpriteMaze  spriteMaze;
  Thread      game;
  ThreadGroup appTG;

  public void init () {
    appTG = Thread.currentThread().getThreadGroup();
    SpriteMaze.loadImages(this);
    setLayout(new BorderLayout());
    add( South , new Button( Start ));
    add( Center , spriteMaze = new SpriteMaze(20, 20));
layout();
  }

  public void run () {
    spriteMaze.startGame();
  }

  public boolean action (Event evt, Object arg) {
    if ( Start .equals(arg)) {
      if (game != null)
        game.stop();
      game = new Thread(appTG, this);
      game.start();
    }
    return true;
  }
} // end class SpriteMazeApplet
```

Part III
Seven League Boots

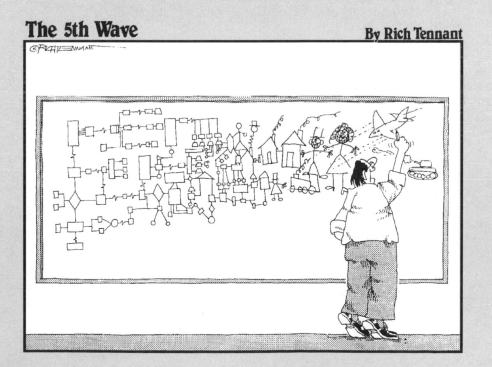

In this part . . .

Only a few years ago most computer games were simple 2-D affairs that hardly taxed the processing power of the typical computer. Then, the 3-D revolution hit with gale-force winds and redefined the meaning of computer games. Today, people judge the processing power of their new computer by how well it runs the latest 3-D games.

The 3-D revolution also seemed to up the ante on the programming skill required to write a cool-looking game. To some people, 3-D programming may seem to require an advanced math degree just to understand how it works. We blast that preconception out of the sky in Part III and show you that the principles that make 3-D games work aren't that hard to understand after all.

In addition, Part III introduces some other cool Java graphics techniques you can use to make exceptionally sharp looking games. Plus, this part presents some advanced code techniques, like timelines and scripts, that can help you write sophisticated, real-time games.

Chapter 9
Modeling the Real World

. . . .

In This Chapter

▶ Scheduling when things happen with a timeline

▶ Scripting animations

▶ Synchronizing animations and actions

▶ Playing sounds

. . . .

*U*nlike the real world, where events happen simultaneously and continuously, a computer program manages events in sequentially ordered, discrete steps.

This chapter shows how to model events that occur in your games so that they appear to happen simultaneously. In essence, the trick is to handle the events sequentially along a timeline that schedules and sequences the events so that you can resolve them one by one and still have them appear "natural" on screen. This chapter also shows how to use animation scripts to model continuous motion using discrete animation frames and how to connect the actions these frames represent to the code for the actions in your game. We also show you how to include sounds in the animation scripts and how to use the limited sound support in Java 1.0 and 1.1. These animation scripts use a data-driven design that allows the artist and the programmer, assuming that they aren't the same person, to work independently of one another.

Making Things Happen at the Right Time with a Timeline

A *timeline* is a data structure that organizes its data according to a chronological sequence. You use a timeline to control the order in which events occur in your game.

A timeline also serves as a way to send messages between game elements. For example, if the player of a dungeon game presses a button on the wall of your dungeon that opens a door, the button adds an event to the timeline that tells the door to open. If a computer adversary presses the button, the same thing happens. Plus, because you use a timeline to sequence events, you may decide to delay 10 seconds after the door button is pushed and before the door opens. You can handle all these situations the same way — by adding an event to the timeline so that the action is carried out at the appropriate time.

Table 9-1 shows the methods in the Timeline class that you use to add and remove events and to search the timeline.

Table 9-1	Timeline Methods
Method	*Call It To...*
void insert (Object obj, int time)	Insert obj into the timeline with the priority time. A *lower* time is a higher priority; that is, you want the event to occur sooner.
Object getNextUntil (int time)	Remove the soonest object from the timeline and return the object if it is <= time. Otherwise getNextUntil() doesn't remove an object and returns null.
boolean remove (Object obj)	Search the timeline for obj and remove the first occurrence found. Returns true if obj found, false if not.
Enumeration elements ()	Return an Enumeration to sequence through the objects in the timeline.

A heap of events

The timeline is just a data structure, similar to a Vector or Hashtable. You don't need to know how to implement a timeline to use one. However, a little knowledge about how a timeline works helps in understanding what timelines do well and what they don't do well.

The complete code to implement a timeline is on the CD. The Timeline class is only about 90 lines.

You use a *priority queue* to efficiently keep track of what you need to do next without the overhead of maintaining a fully sorted list. A priority queue needs to do two things as efficiently as possible:

- ✔ **Add an item to the queue**
- ✔ **Remove the highest priority item from the queue**

You can implement a priority queue that does both of these operations quickly by using a *heap* data structure. A heap organizes its elements into a tree structure, with the highest priority element at the top of the tree. The highest priority element is the *root node* of the tree. The root node has left and right child nodes, each of which is empty, a leaf node (a node with empty left and right children), or the root of a subheap.

The term *heap* has an additional meaning in programming lingo: the region of memory from which chunks of memory are allocated for a program or operating system — this version of *heap* is different from the type presented in this section.

The other important characteristic of a heap is that it fills in from top to bottom and left to right so that you can represent the tree structure using a simple array. You assign the indexes in the same order in which you fill in the tree, so the root node is always at index 0, the root node's left child is at index 1, the right child is at index 2, and so on, until you get to the rightmost child of the final row. Using this scheme, you can calculate the array index for a node's parent and children using truncating integer division like this:

Parent   `(node - 1) / 2`

Left child   `(node * 2) + 1`

Right child   `(node * 2) + 2`

Figure 9-1 shows the numbers 1 through 10, with 1 being the highest priority, arranged in a heap. The figure shows the array indexes below the nodes. Notice that every parent node has a higher priority than its children.

Adding events to the timeline

You add events to the timeline by calling `Timeline.insert()`. The first argument is the event to add. An event can be any object, but if you have more than a few event types, you may want to use a common `TimelineEvent` class or interface to make distinguishing event types easier.

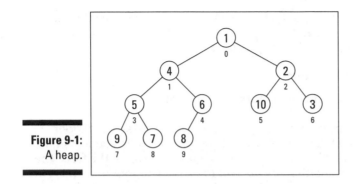

Figure 9-1:
A heap.

All you need in order to use a `switch` statement to process timeline events is a field to identify the event type:

```
class TimelineEvent {
    int eventID;
}
```

You extend `TimelineEvent` to implement your specific event classes. Extending a common class makes event dispatch easier but also requires that you make sure that the various `TimelineEvent` subclasses use unique assignments for `eventID`.

An alternative to using an `eventID` to distinguish events is to use a common `TimelineEvent` interface that defines the method to call in order to process the event. Here is the `TimelineEvent` interface:

```
interface TimelineEvent {
    void processEvent ();
}
```

Your event classes implement the `TimelineEvent` interface and provide a `processEvent()` method to handle the event or dispatch it to another object.

The second parameter to `insert()` is the time the event comes out of the timeline. Typically `time` would either be a real time, such as the number of milliseconds since the game started, or a *frame number* (a count of the number of times the game has processed events in the timeline since the start of the game). If you use a frame number, you may also want to control the order in which your code processes events for a frame. To specify the order within a frame, you separate time into the frame number and the frame time by shifting the frame number left and using the low bits in time for the frame time. (Chapter 7 discusses working with bits and bitwise operators such as the left shift operator.) The following shows how to divide a frame into 256 time segments:

```
int time = (frameNumber << 8) + frameTime;
```

Shifting the frame number eight places to the left reduces the maximum number of frames from around two billion to a mere eight million or so.

Processing events in order

You process timeline events using a loop to extract all the events up until the current time. Event processing is where the `TimelineEvent` class or interface is useful. You call `getNextUntil()` to remove the events from the timeline that extend the `TimelineEvent` class like this:

```
int now = frameNumber;  // or whatever you use for time
Object event;
while ((event = timeline.getNextUntil(now)) != null) {
  switch (((TimelineEvent)event).eventID) {
    // case statements for each event type
  }
}
```

You remove and process events that implement the `TimelineEvent` interface like this:

```
int now = frameNumber;  // or whatever you use for time
Object event;
while ((event = timeline.getNextUntil(now)) != null)
  ((TimelineEvent)event).processEvent();
```

And finally, if you don't use a common event class or interface, you distinguish the event types using the `instanceof` operator, like this:

```
int now = frameNumber;  // or whatever you use for time
Object event;
while ((event = timeline.getNextUntil(now)) != null) {
  if (event instanceof CreatureEvent) {
    // handle creature events
  }
  else if (event instanceof GameEvent) {
    // handle game events
  }
  else . . .
}
```

Changing the future: Removing events before they happen

Sometimes you need to change the future. For example, your extremely dangerous dragon is taking a nap. You have an event in the timeline to wake him up in three hours (game time). Before the three hours are up, the player blasts him with a level 12 fireball and turns your dragon into a month's supply of dragon steaks. Now you have two choices:

- ✔ **Leave the event in the timeline and ignore it when it comes out because the dragon is dead.**
- ✔ **Remove the event from the timeline.**

The first choice is actually the preferred approach. However, if instead of killing the dragon, the level 12 fireball just wakes him up, you may need to get rid of the wake-up event. Otherwise, if the dragon goes down for another nap after eating the player's horse and chasing the player away, the first wake up event may come out before the new wake up event and disturb the dragon's sleep prematurely. (It's very dangerous to disturb a dragon's sleep.)

The reason that leaving the event in the timeline is preferable to removing it has to do with how the `Timeline` class stores events. `Timeline` doesn't have an easy way to find an event; instead, it has to do an exhaustive search for the object it needs to remove. If the timeline is small, this search may not take long, but as the size of your timeline grows, the time for the search increases proportionally and can slow down your game.

Removing events

To alter the future and remove an event before its time, you have to know what the event is. One solution is to have the dragon keep track of its wake-up event. When you know what event object you want to remove from the timeline, you call `Timeline.remove()`. `remove()` just searches the timeline until it finds an object that matches the object you want to remove.

`remove()` uses the `Object.equals()` method to find the object to remove.

Searching the timeline

If you don't already know what event you want to remove or if you just need to see what events are in the timeline, you call `Timeline.elements()` to get an `Enumeration` to search the timeline. Typical code to search the timeline looks like this:

```
Enumeration enum = timeline.elements();
while (enum.hasMoreElements()) {
  Object event = enum.nextElement();
  // code to examine the event goes here
}
```

Enumeration is an interface defined in java.util. The enumeration returned by Timeline.elements() uses a copy of the timeline event list, so you can safely add and remove events from the timeline while using the enumeration.

Playing Sounds

The sound capabilities of Java 1.0.2 and 1.1 are, to say the least, limited. Java only supports a single sound format (see the sidebar "Creating sounds") and only the three AudioClip methods outlined in Table 9-2 for working with sounds.

Table 9-2	AudioClip Sound Methods
Method	*Call It to...*
play()	Play the sound once from beginning to end.
loop()	Loop the sound so that it plays over and over and over. You call loop() to play background sounds.
stop()	Stop the sound if it is playing.

Creating sounds

Java 1.0.2, the version most browsers currently implement, uses a special sound file format called µlaw (myoo-law) that is indicated by the .au file suffix. Some versions of UNIX recognize the sound format µlaw, also known as Sun Audio. However, many sound editing programs for PCs don't handle this file format, so make sure that you have one that does.

The µlaw sound format compresses the dynamic range (the range of volume) of a sound, which makes a sound smaller for downloading but also reduces the quality of the sound. Future versions of Java will support a wider variety of sound file formats and a richer set of controls for playing sounds.

You load sounds using the `Applet` method `getAudioClip()`. `getAudioClip()` returns a `java.applet.AudioClip` object. `getAudioClip()` accepts either a `URL` (a class in the `java.net` package) or a `URL` and a filename to specify the sound.

The following applet loads the sound file "sound.au" from the directory containing the HTML document that invokes the applet and then plays it.

```
import java.applet.*;
public class SoundApplet extends Applet {
  public void init () {
    AudioClip sound;
    sound = getAudioClip(getDocumentBase(), sound.au );
    if (sound != null)
      sound.play();
  }
}
```

When you call `Applet.getAudioClip()`, it doesn't actually load the sound; it just creates a new `AudioClip`. The `AudioClip` loads the sound data the first time you call the `AudioClip`'s `play()` or `loop()` method, which means that a delay inevitably occurs the first time you play a sound. With future versions of Java you should be able to add sounds to a `MediaTracker` so that you can preload the sound, but for now expect an initial, somewhat annoying delay.

The CD-ROM at the back of this book includes some nifty sound creation and conversion utilities to help you add sound to your Java games.

Matching Animations to Game Events with Scripts

If you've ever seen a poorly dubbed movie, you know how important it is to have the words coming out the actors' mouths match the dialog in the soundtrack. When the video and sound don't match, it spoils the whole illusion. Just like a movie, your game needs to synchronize the actions that take place with the display on the screen.

Like a movie, the visual action determines when something happens, not the other way around. When an actor in your game reaches down and picks something off the floor, the animation is what determines when you remove the object from the floor. If you want the object picked up quickly, the animation needs to complete quickly. You can't force the actor to pick up the object more quickly without making the animation match, or your game looks like a poorly dubbed movie — out of sync.

You use an *animation script* to synchronize the animation with changes in the game state — in our example, this occurs when the object is removed from the floor and placed in the actor's hand. The important concept is that the state isn't changed until the actor completes the animation of bending down and grabbing the object, and that you use an animation script to ensure this. The animation script also takes care of sequencing the images needed to show the action taking place.

Interfacing the programmer and the artist

One of the main reasons that synchronizing animations is complicated is because it involves two different creative processes — *art* and *code*. Each of these processes needs to be free to explore new possibilities independently, especially if the artist and programmer aren't the same person.

What you need is an *interface* between the artist and programmer. As long as both sides do their part to conform to the agreed upon interface, both are free to implement their parts of the interface in whatever manner strikes their fancy. The interface in this case is an animation script that specifies the sequence of the animation and identifies the places where the game performs the actions associated with the animation.

The programmer specifies the actions the script must accomplish, and the artist determines the number and sequence of animation frames needed and the frames where the actions take place. The artist creates an animation script to control the art without requiring the programmer to make changes, so the artist can make changes and experiment as often as necessary.

Writing a script

An animation script is a sequence of animation frames. Each frame in the script provides the following:

- ✔ **An image to display**
- ✔ **A sound to play**
- ✔ **The amount of time to display the image (the delay before displaying the next frame)**
- ✔ **The next frame to display after the current one**
- ✔ **The action, if any, associated with the current frame**

To provide some flexibility, you use different types of frames to implement alternative ways of providing these five pieces of information. The frame type is part of the animation script. Here is an example script that displays each of three frames — playing a sound and firing the gun on the second frame — and then terminates:

```
ANIM shoot  ; 3-cycle shooting animation
0  ImageFrame (0  shoot1  3 1)           ; raise gun
1  SoundFrame (1  shoot2   laser.au  3 2) ; fire
2  ImageFrame (0  shoot3  3 -1)          ; recoil
```

A line in an animation script specifies an animation frame that is displayed for one or more *animation ticks*. Typically, an animation tick is the period of time between updates to the game's screen display.

The `AnimScript` class presented later in this chapter reads scripts that use this syntax. The syntax is somewhat arbitrary. You may want to implement a different scheme. The remainder of this section describes the script syntax.

`AnimScript` treats any text on a line following a semicolon (;) as a comment. `AnimScript` ignores all the text from the semicolon to the end of the line. Comments are at least as important in a script as a way to explain what the script does as they are in your code as a way to explain what your code does.

`ANIM` marks the beginning of a new script. Following `ANIM` is the name of the script, in this case `shoot`. Each of the remaining lines in the script defines a frame in the animation.

The initial number in the definition of an animation frame is an optional frame number. `AnimScript` ignores this number; its purpose is to let the person writing the script see the frame numbers more easily. Following the optional frame number is the frame type, which is the name of the class that implements the `AnimFrame` interface. The example script uses two different types of frames: `ImageFrame` and `SoundFrame`. Next come the parameters for the frame type enclosed in parentheses and separated by *white space* (spaces, tabs, and line breaks).

Each frame type has a particular set of parameters it expects. The parameters for `ImageFrame` from left to right are action, image, delay, and next frame. From left to right the parameters for `SoundFrame` are action, image, sound, delay, and next frame.

`AnimScript` understands four types of parameters:

- ✔ **numbers (floating point or integers)**
- ✔ **image names enclosed in double quotes (" ")**
- ✔ **sound filenames enclosed in single quotes (' ')**
- ✔ **arrays of parameters (including nested arrays) enclosed in square brackets ([ ])**

The image names are partial filenames. You supply a set of views that defines the second half of the filename. Doing so allows you to use multiple sets of images with the same animation scripts. For example, you can do any of the following or even a combination of the following:

- ✔ **Use views from different perspectives such as from the front, rear, and side.**
- ✔ **Make a set of 8-bit GIF images and a matching set of 32-bit JPEG images and decide which to use at runtime.**
- ✔ **Add variety by randomly selecting different sets of graphics for different copies of the same animation.**
- ✔ **Use sets of images depicting the animating object after sustaining different degrees of damage.**

Reading scripts from text files

The real power of using scripts comes when you place the scripts in text files. You can change a script in a file without having to do anything to the program. Not only does this feature have advantages when creating your game by making the addition of animations and game elements easy, but it also lets nonprogrammers create the scripts, which opens the creative process to artists, animators, and others who may be programming-impaired.

The `AnimScriptGroup` class presented later in this chapter initializes a set of scripts from an `InputStream`. `AnimScriptGroup` allows multiple animation scripts in the same `InputStream`. You select a script by using the name of the script.

You can create an `InputStream` from a `String` embedded in the code using a `StringBufferInputStream` or from a `File` using a `FileInputStream`, or you can get a stream from a `URL`. This flexibility makes the `InputStream` a general-purpose means of supplying the data to initialize the animation scripts. Add the following code to your game applet to create an `InputStream` for a file called "Script.txt" located in the directory containing your applet class file.

```
URL url = new URL(getCodeBase(), Script.txt );
InputStream stream = url.openStream();
```

Looping an animation

A simple addition to an animation is to have it loop during the action. Loops work well for repetitive actions that you want to display for an indeterminate period of time. Walking, running, flying, and other motion animations are good examples of animations that you can loop. In order to loop the animation, you just set the next frame parameter of the last frame to point back to the first frame of the loop. For example, to loop the `shoot` animation presented earlier in the chapter, you change the last frame loop back to the "fire" frame like this:

```
ANIM shoot  ; 2-cycle continuous shooting animation
0  ImageFrame (0  shoot1  3)           ; raise gun
1  SoundFrame (1  shoot2   laser.au  3) ; fire
2  ImageFrame (0  shoot3  3 1)          ; recoil
```

If you're paying attention, you noticed that there's another change in this version of the `shoot` script. We've removed the last parameter (the one that specifies the next frame) from the first two frames. `ImageFrame` and `SoundFrame` default to going to the next frame in the script if you don't specify a next frame.

Adding random behavior

If all you ever want an animation to do is sequence through a series of images, an animation script is probably overkill. However, if you want to give your animations a little character, you can use animation scripts to do things a little differently each time you run them.

For example, take the nonlooping version of the `shoot` script presented earlier in this chapter. It runs through a straight sequence of three frames to fire a laser. You can do a number of things to spice this script up and give the bad guy firing the laser some character.

1. **Have him shoot with his left or right hand.**

2. **Have his weapon misfire sometimes, so he doesn't get off a shot.**

3. Have him occasionally fire two or three times in a row.

4. Let him select a different weapon.

5. Have his gun malfunction and blow him to pieces.

You can add the first three of these enhancements without making any changes to the game code. The last two enhancements only require that the game implement actions for using other weapons and for blowing the bad guy up. These script techniques give you the tools to give your game those little touches that commercial games have. Here's a modified version of the shoot script that implements enhancements 2 through 5:

```
ANIM shoot  ; shoot, nuke, misfire and malfunction animation
0   BranchFrame([10 13])                    ; nuke!
1   ImageFrame (0  shoot1  3)               ; raise gun
2   BranchFrame([75 7][15 5][4 9][1 11]) ; 1, 2, misfire,
                                         ; malfunction or 3 shots?
3   SoundFrame (1  shoot2   laser.au  3) ; fire
4   ImageFrame (0  shoot3  3)               ; recoil
5   SoundFrame (1  shoot2   laser.au  3) ; fire
6   ImageFrame (0  shoot3  3)               ; recoil
7   SoundFrame (1  shoot2   laser.au  3) ; fire
8   ImageFrame (0  shoot3  3 -1)            ;#recoil
9   ImageFrame (0  miss1  3)                ; misfire
10  ImageFrame (0  miss2  3 -1)             ;#clear gun
11  SoundFrame (0  oops1    blast.au  1) ; malfunction
12  ImageFrame (2  oops2  2 -1)             ;#die
13  ImageFrame (0  nuke1  3)                ; raise nuke
14  SoundFrame (0  nuke2   beep.au  3)   ; arm nuke
15  SoundFrame (3  nuke3   launch.au  3) ; launch nuke
16  ImageFrame (0  nuke4  3 -1)             ;#nuke recoil
```

The first frame of the animation introduces a new type of animation frame: BranchFrame. BranchFrame accepts an arbitrary number of arrays with two numbers in each array. The first number is the probability, expressed as a number from 0 to 100, of selecting the second number as the next frame. So in the first frame (frame 0), there is a 10 percent chance that the script chooses frame 13 next to launch a nuke. If BranchFrame doesn't select any of the listed frames, it defaults to the next frame in the script. So there is a 90 percent chance that the script chooses frame 1 to fire the laser.

BranchFrame sets a delay of zero to tell the AnimScript to immediately execute the next frame. The code that the script controls never knows that the script executed a BranchFrame.

Frame 2 in the example chooses between misfiring, having the weapon malfunction, or firing 1, 2, or 3 shots. The branches evaluate from left to right, so there is a 75 percent chance of firing one shot, a 15 percent chance of firing two shots, a 4 percent chance of the laser misfiring, a 1 percent chance of the weapon malfunctioning, and the remaining 5 percent chance of firing three shots.

In addition to branching, the script returns up to three actions — one for each time it fires the laser in frames 3, 5, and 7. Or when the laser misfires, the script never returns an action. The script also returns action 2 in frame 12 to have the weapon malfunction and blow the shooter up and returns 3 in frame 15 to launch a nuke.

Adding special effects and other goodies

In addition to messing with the next frame and action values returned from an animation frame, you can mess with the image and sound values. Given that there isn't any way to manipulate a sound, all you can do sometimes is choose a different sound. Maybe throw in the occasional taunt, growl, or threat to keep the player alert.

The real fun comes when you start messing with images. You can do more than just return a loaded image. Here are just a few of the things you can do with images in your animation:

✓ **Employ image processing to the returned image, such as flipping, scaling, recoloring, or any of the image tricks that Chapters 11 and 12 discuss.**

✓ **Composite images to get more variety with a smaller number of images.** For example, you may have a base image of a storm trooper and composite a grenade launcher, a laser gun, or bazooka on top of the storm trooper in order to get four different sets of storm trooper images.

✓ **Create special effects such as fading an animation by dithering.**

✓ **Create special wipes to transition from one frame to the next.**

✓ **Render the image from a 3-D model.**

✓ **Do something really wild such as morphing between two images.**

Only your imagination limits the possibilities. To add capabilities to your scripts, you add your own classes that implement the `AnimFrame` interface. The "Implementing an `AnimFrame`" section later in this chapter shows how you add your own classes. To use your new `AnimFrame`, you just add it to your script using the name of the class as the frame type. `AnimScript` passes the parameters you include in the script to the `AnimFrame`'s `init()` method as an array of `Objects`.

An *interface* is a definition of methods a class implements. A class *implements* an interface to do the job the interface defines. You implement an interface by declaring that the class `implements` the interface and by providing the class with the methods that the interface defines.

Understanding the code

The code to implement animation scripts has two primary functions:

- ✔ Translate the script text into script objects
- ✔ Execute the scripts

The code has a hierarchical organization. At the top of the hierarchy is the `AnimScriptGroup` class. An `AnimScriptGroup` contains one or more `AnimScript` objects, which in turn, contain one or more `AnimFrame` objects. Each of these classes participates in both primary functions of the scripts.

Organizing scripts by action

You use an `AnimScriptGroup` to organize all the animations for a game element. You organize the animations by the actions they perform. The `AnimScriptGroup()` constructor takes an `InputStream` to provide the script text. It turns the `InputStream` into a `StreamTokenizer` to take advantage of the tokenizer's text-parsing capabilities. Using the `StreamTokenizer`, `AnimScriptGroup()` finds each animation and creates a new `AnimScript` for it and adds it to the group. If there is a problem parsing the scripts, the `AnimScriptGroup()` constructor throws an `IOException`. See the "Writing a script" section earlier in this chapter for a description of the script syntax.

Parsing text is the process a program uses to translate the characters in a text file into the commands that the program understands. When you compile a program, the first step for the compiler is to parse the text into the commands, statements, and *tokens* the compiler understands. A *token* is simply a sequence of one or more characters that together form the smallest meaningful unit or word that the parser understands.

To use the scripts, you call getScript() with the name of the animation script. Typically, you name the scripts by the actions the script performs. Here is the code to implement AnimScriptGroup:

```java
import java.applet.Applet;
import java.awt.MediaTracker;
import java.util.Vector;
import java.net.URL;
import java.io.*;

public class AnimScriptGroup {
  public AnimScript[] scripts;
  public AnimScript getScript (String name) {
    for (int snum = 0;  snum < scripts.length;  snum++)
      if (scripts[snum].getName().equals(name))
        return scripts[snum];
    return null;
  }

  public AnimScriptGroup (URL url, InputStream stream,
                          String[] views, Applet app)
    throws IOException
  {
    Vector scriptVector = new Vector();
    StreamTokenizer st = new StreamTokenizer(stream);
    MediaTracker tracker = new MediaTracker(app);
    st.ordinaryChar( / );  // don t use / for comments
    st.commentChar( ; );   // use ; to mark a comment
SCRIPT_LOOP:
    while (true) {
      switch (st.nextToken()) {
        case StreamTokenizer.TT_EOF:
          break SCRIPT_LOOP;
        case StreamTokenizer.TT_WORD:
          if (st.sval.toUpperCase().equals( ANIM )) {
            scriptVector.addElement(new
                  AnimScript(st, url, views, app, tracker));
            break;
          }
          // fall thru
        default:
          throw new IOException( Anim: expected  ANIM );
      }
    }
```

```
    try { tracker.waitForAll(); }
    catch (InterruptedException e) {}
    scripts = new AnimScript[scriptVector.size()];
    scriptVector.copyInto((Object[]) scripts);
  }
} // end class AnimScriptGroup
```

Notice that you pass `AnimScriptGroup()` an array of `String`s in the `views[]` parameter. These strings are the second half of the filenames for the "image" arguments in the script that we mentioned in the "Writing a script" section earlier in this chapter. You pass an index into this array as the `view` parameter to `AnimScript.nextFrame()` in order to tell the animation which set of images to use.

Filling a script with frames

The `AnimScriptGroup()` constructor passes the `StreamTokenizer` for the script to the `AnimScript()` constructor in order to continue parsing an individual script. The purpose of most of the code in the `AnimScript` class is to parse the text description of the script. The parsing process initializes the `AnimScript` fields to the values as Table 9-3 shows.

Table 9-3		AnimScript Fields
Type	*Field*	*What* AnimScript *Initializes It To*
String	name	The name that the script specifies following the `ANIM` keyword.
Image[][]	images	The images for all the frames in the script. The first index is the image, and the second index is the view. Regardless of how many times an image appears in the script, `AnimScript` loads the image only once.
AudioClip[]	sounds	The sounds for all the frames in the script. Regardless of how many times a sound appears in the script, `AnimScript` loads the sound only once.
AnimFrame[]	frames	The initialized script frames.

As soon as you initialize the script, you can call the following `AnimScript` methods to execute scripts:

✔ `String getName()`

✔ `FrameData nextFrame (FrameData frame, int view)`

getName() returns the name field. AnimScript.getScript() calls getName() to find the requested script.

You call nextFrame() to advance to the next frame of the script and return the frame information. nextFrame() accepts a view index to choose the set of images to display and uses a FrameData object to hold the frame information. You call nextFrame() with a null frame parameter to execute the first frame of the script and pass the FrameData object it returns to nextFrame() in order to advance to the next frame. Here is the FrameData class and the five pieces of information it holds:

```java
import java.awt.Image;
import java.applet.AudioClip;

public class FrameData {
  public Image      image;
  public AudioClip  sound;
  public int        delay, action, nextFrame;

  FrameData () {}
  FrameData (Image image, AudioClip sound,
             int delay, int action, int next)
  {
    this.image = image;
    this.sound = sound;
    this.delay = delay;
    this.action = action;
    this.nextFrame = next;
  }
} // end class FrameData
```

Your frame classes can keep state information for a frame by extending FrameData to add additional fields.

Here is the complete AnimScript class:

```java
import java.applet.*;
import java.awt.*;
import java.io.*;
import java.util.Vector;
import java.net.URL;

public class AnimScript {
  private String      name;
```

```
private Image[][]  images;  // [image][view]
private AudioClip[] sounds;
private AnimFrame[] frames;

public String getName () { return name; }
public FrameData nextFrame (FrameData frame, int view) {
  if (frame == null)
    frame = new FrameData();
  while (frame.nextFrame >= 0 &&
         frame.nextFrame < frames.length) {
    frame = frames[frame.nextFrame].
              getFrame(frame, images, view, sounds);
    if (frame.delay > 0)
      break;
  }
  if (frame.nextFrame >= frames.length)
    frame.nextFrame = -1;  // no more frames
  return frame;
}

public AnimScript (StreamTokenizer st, URL url,
                   String[] views, Applet app,
                   MediaTracker tracker)
  throws IOException
{
  if (st.nextToken() != StreamTokenizer.TT_WORD)
    throw new IOException( Anim: expected name );
  name = st.sval;
  Vector imgNames = new Vector(), sndNames = new Vector();
  Vector frms = new Vector();
  while (true) {  // parse frames
    if (st.nextToken() == StreamTokenizer.TT_NUMBER)
      st.nextToken();  // discard optional frame number
    if (st.ttype == StreamTokenizer.TT_EOF)
      break;
    if (st.ttype != StreamTokenizer.TT_WORD)
      throw new IOException( Anim: expected frame );
    if (st.sval.toUpperCase().equals( ANIM )) {
      st.pushBack();
      break;
    }
    try {
      AnimFrame af = (AnimFrame)
```

(continued)

(continued)

```
                        Class.forName(st.sval).newInstance();
      af.init(frms.size(),
              (Object[])getArg(st, imgNames, sndNames));
      frms.addElement(af);
    }
    catch (Exception e) {
      throw new IOException( Anim: bad  +name+ :  +e);
    }
  }
  // create the images[][], sounds[] and frames[] arrays
  // and load the Images and AudioClips
  images = new Image[imgNames.size()][views.length];
  for (int ii = 0;  ii < imgNames.size();  ii++)
    for (int v = 0;  v < views.length;  v++) {
      Image img = app.getImage(url,
                  imgNames.elementAt(ii) + views[v]);
      tracker.addImage(images[ii][v] = img, 0);
    }
  sounds = new AudioClip[sndNames.size()];
  for (int ii = 0;  ii < sndNames.size();  ii++)
    sounds[ii] = app.getAudioClip(url,
                      sndNames.elementAt(ii).toString());
  frms.copyInto((Object[])(frames =
                        new AnimFrame[frms.size()]));
}

private Object getArg (StreamTokenizer st,
                      Vector imgNames, Vector sndNames)
  throws IOException
{
  switch (st.nextToken()) {
    case  ( :
    case  [ :
      Object obj;
      Vector array = new Vector();
      while ((obj = getArg(st,imgNames,sndNames)) != null)
        array.addElement(obj);
      Object[] objArray = new Object[array.size()];
      array.copyInto(objArray);
      return objArray;
    case  ) :
    case  ] :
      return null;
```

```
    case StreamTokenizer.TT_NUMBER:
      return new Double(st.nval);
    case    :
      return addUnique(imgNames, st.sval);
    case    :
      return addUnique(sndNames, st.sval);
    }
    throw new IOException( Anim: bad frame arg );
  }

  private Integer addUnique (Vector v, Object obj) {
    int ndx = v.indexOf(obj);
    if (ndx == -1) { // unique object
      ndx = v.size();
      v.addElement(obj);
    }
    return new Integer(ndx);
  }
} // end class AnimScript
```

With the following line, AnimScript() creates new frames from the frame type specified in the script:

```
      AnimFrame df = (AnimFrame)
                Class.forName(st.sval).newInstance();
```

The static Class.forName() method accepts a string containing the name of a class and returns the class's Class object. The newInstance() method of the Class object calls the parameterless constructor for the class and returns the new object instance. You use these two methods together to create an object from the name of a class. The resulting object is of type Object. To get at any methods of the new object beyond those defined in Object, you need to cast the object to a class or interface that contains the desired methods. (Of course, if the object isn't actually an instance of the class or interface to which you cast it, you get a ClassCastException.) In this case, you cast the new object to be an object that implements the AnimFrame interface.

The next line in AnimScript() calls getArg() to parse the frame parameters and place them in an Object[] array:

```
      af.init(frms.size(),
          (Object[])getArg(st, imgNames, sndNames));
```

This code passes the `Object[]` array returned by `getArg()` to the new frame's `init()` method. Notice that `getArg()` converts "image" and 'sound' arguments to integer indexes into the `images[][]` and `sounds[]` arrays, respectively. It doesn't pass the image or sound names.

Implementing an `AnimFrame`

To implement an `AnimFrame`, you create a class that implements this `AnimFrame` interface:

```
import java.awt.Image;
import java.applet.AudioClip;

public interface AnimFrame {
   void      init (int frameNum, Object[] args);
   FrameData getFrame (FrameData frame, Image[][] imgs,
                       int view, AudioClip[] snds);
} // end interface AnimFrame
```

The `init()` method accepts an `int frameNum` parameter containing the frame's frame number and an array of `Object`s containing the parameters from the script. Typically, you retrieve the expected parameters from the array and convert them from generic `Object`s to the parameter types your frame expects.

The `getFrame()` method accepts the current `FrameData` parameter, the set of images for this script, the view parameter you pass to `AnimScript.nextFrame()`, and the set of sounds for this script. `getFrame()` creates a new `FrameData` object, initializes its `image`, `sound`, `delay`, `action`, and `nextFrame` fields, and returns it. Remember, the code passes the returned `FrameData` object back to `getFrame()` in order to get the next frame.

SoundFrame

See the "Writing a script" section earlier in this chapter for a description of how to use the `SoundFrame` class. `SoundFrame` and `ImageFrame` are essentially the same except that `ImageFrame` doesn't accept a `soundIndex` argument in `init()` and always sets the sound to `null` in `getFrame()`. Here is the code for the `SoundFrame` class:

```
import java.awt.Image;
import java.applet.AudioClip;

public class SoundFrame implements AnimFrame {
   private int action, imageIndex, soundIndex, delay, next;
```

```
public void init (int frameNum, Object[] args) {
  try {
    action     = ((Number)args[0]).intValue();
    imageIndex = ((Number)args[1]).intValue();
    soundIndex = ((Number)args[2]).intValue();
    delay      = ((Number)args[3]).intValue();
    if (args.length >= 5)
      next     = ((Number)args[4]).intValue();
    else
      next     = frameNum + 1;
  }
  catch (Exception e) {
    throw new IllegalArgumentException(e.toString());
  }
}


public FrameData getFrame (FrameData last,
      Image[][] images, int view, AudioClip[] sounds) {
  return new FrameData(images[imageIndex][view],
                       sounds[soundIndex],
                       delay, action, next);
}
} // end class SoundFrame
```

BranchFrame

See the "Adding random behavior" section earlier in this chapter for a description of how to use the BranchFrame class. Here is the code for the BranchFrame class:

```
import java.awt.Image;
import java.applet.AudioClip;

public class BranchFrame implements AnimFrame {
  private int       frameNum;
  private double[]  prob;
  private int[]     next;

  public void init (int frameNum, Object[] args) {
    this.frameNum = frameNum;
    try {
      prob = new double[args.length];
      next = new int[args.length];
      for (int ii = 0;  ii < args.length;  ii++) {
        prob[ii] = ((Number)((Object[])args[ii])[0]).
```

(continued)

(continued)

```
                doubleValue();
        next[ii] = ((Number)((Object[])args[ii])[1]).
                  intValue();
      }
    }
    catch (Exception e) {
      throw new IllegalArgumentException(e.toString());
    }
  }

  public FrameData getFrame (FrameData last,
        Image[][] images, int view, AudioClip[] sounds) {
    int    ndx;
    double r = Math.random() * 100;
    for (ndx = 0;
         ndx < prob.length && (r -= prob[ndx]) > 0;  ndx++)
      ;
    return new FrameData(null, null, 0, 0,
                        r > 0 ? frameNum + 1 : next[ndx]);
  }
}  // end class BranchFrame
```

Putting the code to work: The `ScriptSprite` class

Virtually any game element that animates or sequences actions can use an
animation script. One obvious example is the sprites that Chapter 8 describes. Here's a `ScriptSprite` class to replace Chapter 8's
`AnimationSprite` class:

```
import java.awt.*;
class ScriptSprite extends ImageSprite {
  protected AnimScriptGroup anims;
  protected AnimScript      script;
  protected int             view, delay;
  protected FrameData       curFrame;

  ScriptSprite (AnimScriptGroup anims, int view,
            double x, double y) {
    super(null, x, y);
    this.anims = anims;
    setView(view);
    setScript( neutral ); // assume group has  neutral  anim
  }
```

```java
  public void setView (int view) {
    this.view = view;
  }

  public void setScript (String scriptName) {
    script = anims.getScript(scriptName);
    curFrame = null;
    delay = 0;
  }

  protected void doAction (int action) {
    // implement this method to perform the sprite actions
    // in classes that extend this class
  }

  protected void animFinished () {
    spriteEngine.notifyObservers(this);
  }

  protected boolean nextFrame () {
    boolean result = false;
    curFrame = script.nextFrame(curFrame, view);
    delay = curFrame.delay;
    if (curFrame.image != null) {
      int w = width, h = height;
      setImage(curFrame.image);
      result = (w != width || h != height);
    }
    if (curFrame.sound != null)
      curFrame.sound.play();
    doAction(curFrame.action);
    if (curFrame.nextFrame < 0)  // animation finished
      animFinished();
    return result;
  }

  public boolean update () {
    if (script != null  &&  --delay <= 0)
      return nextFrame();
    return false;
  }
} // end class ScriptSprite
```

You can add the following code to your game applet to load the scripts, images, and sounds for a hypothetical spaceship game element. This code loads the spaceship from the same directory containing the game applet's class file:

```
AnimScriptGroup spaceshipAnims;
String[]        spaceshipViews = { .GIF }; // only 1 view
try {
  URL url = new URL(getCodeBase(), spaceship.txt );
  spaceshipAnims =
    new AnimScriptGroup(getCodeBase(), url.openStream(),
                        spaceshipViews, this);
}
catch (IOException e) {
  // get here if there is a problem with the script
}
```

After loading the animation scripts, you create a new spaceship sprite by extending the ScriptSprite class and overriding the doAction() method.

The CD includes an improved version of the SpriteMaze game from Chapter 8, which uses ScriptSprite to animate and control the actions of the sprites.

Chapter 10

3-D Polygon Maze

· ·

In This Chapter

▶ Creating a 3-D maze

▶ Using 3-D shading and lighting effects

· ·

*F*uture versions of Java will include classes with which you can create sophisticated 3-D graphics, but it may be some time before these classes become incorporated into Java-enabled Web browsers. However, you don't need to let that stop you from entering the third dimension on your own, and in this chapter we show you how to roll your own Java 3-D and use it to create a 3-D maze.

Moving into Three Dimensions

When you view a 3-D object on your computer screen, what you actually see is only a *2-D projection* of the 3-D object. You can choose many ways to project a 3-D image onto a 2-D surface, but most often, you want to use a method called *perspective projection* that creates 2-D projections that look a lot like what you get with a camera. For example, if you hold a photograph of a mountain scene, you're holding a flat (2-D) piece of paper, but you can see the 3-D perspective to the image because of the way the camera flattens, or *projects* the image of the scene onto film.

Calculating perspective

The artist Filippo Brunelleschi invented a systematic approach to creating art using perspective projection in the early 1400s. Then, the artist Leono Battista Alberti published the first treatise on perspective in 1435. Finally, the artist Albrecht Dürer created a mathematical way to describe perspective projection using the trigonometric method of similar triangles. Dürer's woodcut "Artist Drawing a Lute" (1525), depicted in Figure 10-1, shows his method in action. Dürer's mathematical approach to drawing might have qualified him as the world's first computer artist, if only he'd had a computer.

Reprinted with permission from *The Complete Woodcuts of Albrecht Dürer* (Dover Publications, Inc., New York).

Figure 10-1: "Artist Drawing a Lute" shows how Dürer used perspective projection to create realistic drawings.

To create a 2-D perspective projection of a 3-D image, you must first pick a *viewpoint.* In Figure 10-1, you can see the artist and his assistant using a string to represent the line from the viewpoint (the hook on the wall to the right) through the screen (the drawing shown in the frame that the artist is holding) and a point on the lute. As the assistant moves the point where the string touches the lute, the point where the string passes through the frame moves, too. The artist records this point on the drawing held on a hinge in the frame.

For your 3-D maze, you need to use a technique similar to the one the artist in the Dürer woodcut is using. Figure 10-2 shows the relationship between the viewpoint, the computer screen, and the 3-D modeled scene. The dotted lines, like the string in the engraving, show how you can project a 2-D representation of a 3-D grid maze onto your computer screen.

You create a 2-D projection of the maze by calculating where the lines from the viewpoint to the maze walls intersect the screen, but instead of string, you can use mathematics and the geometry of similar triangles.

If you think back a bit to high-school geometry class, you may remember that two triangles with the exact same shape are called *similar triangles.* Any two similar triangles, regardless of a difference in size, have the same angles. More importantly, the ratios between any two *sides* of one triangle equal the ratio between the equivalent sides of the other triangle.

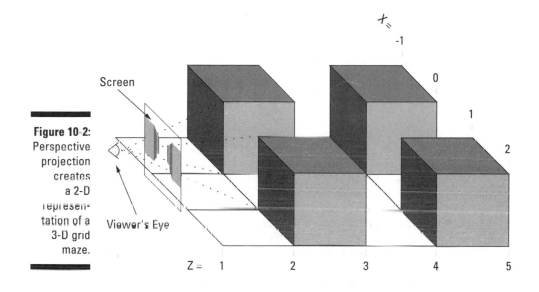

Figure 10-2:
Perspective
projection
creates
a 2-D
represen-
tation of a
3-D grid
maze.

Figure 10-3 shows a side view of the 2-D perspective projection you can use to draw the 3-D maze shown in Figure 10-2. Because Figure 10-3 is a side view, it only shows how to calculate the horizontal lines' intersections on the screen's y axis — that is, the position of the ceiling and the floor of the 3-D maze. However, you can use almost exactly the same technique to draw the walls (the x axis), as explained in the section "Finding the x-axis intersection," later in this chapter.

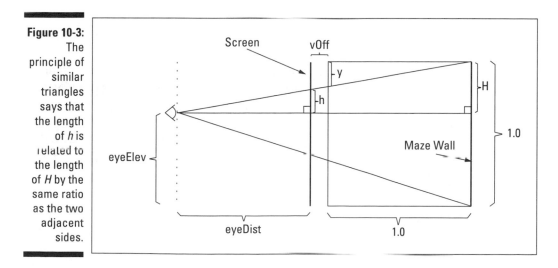

Figure 10-3:
The
principle of
similar
triangles
says that
the length
of *h* is
related to
the length
of *H* by the
same ratio
as the two
adjacent
sides.

Notice that the eye level (eyeElev) of the viewer is even with a point about ²/₃ of the way up the 3-D maze wall. This positioning makes the finished maze look as though it is about the same dimensions as a real room, where an average person's eye level is at about ²/₃ of the height of the room. If you were to design the maze so that the viewer's eye level met closer to the floor of the 3-D maze, the maze would appear to be much larger than normal room dimensions. You can play around with these dimensions to change the look and feel of your maze.

You can construct your maze as a 3-D grid that measures 1.0 unit in height, width, and depth (you use 1.0 as the standard unit just to keep things simple). Figure 10-3 shows how you can calculate the point where a line drawn from the eye of the viewer to the top of the 3-D modeled maze wall intersects the 2-D projection on screen. This point of intersection is represented by the top of the line segment h, as Figure 10-3 shows. The values for eyeElev, eyeDist, and vOff (also shown in Figure 10-3) describe the position of the viewer's eye and the screen relative to the 3-D maze.

The constants vOff and eyeDist control the way the projection of the maze looks on the screen. Changing eyeDist is like zooming a zoom lens in and out, and adjusting vOff is like moving the camera closer to or further from the scene. Try changing these values for yourself to see the different kinds of effects you can create.

Because h and H are two sides of similar triangles, you know that

```
h / H = eyeDist / (eyeDist + vOff + 1)
```

Therefore, you can compute h, like this:

```
h = H * (eyeDist / (eyeDist + vOff + 1))
```

Further, because h and H are sides of right triangles, you know that H equals 1 minus eyeElev. Therefore, you can substitute (1 - eyeElev) in place of H and rewrite the expression like this:

```
h = (1 - eyeElev) * (eyeDist / (eyeDist + vOff + 1))
```

Finally, because the screen height is the same as the height of the wall (1), you can get the y offset from the top of the screen by subtracting h plus eyeElev from 1 like this:

```
y = 1 - (eyeElev + (1 - eyeElev) *
        (eyeDist  / (eyeDist + vOff + 1)))
```

Calculating the height of a wall

The value of y only gives you the location of the top of your 3-D maze wall. You still need to compute the height of the entire wall, not just the portion of the wall given by segment h, so that you can define the top and bottom edges when you draw it. One of the things you calculate to find the length of h is the subexpression

```
(eyeDist / (eyeDist + vOff + 1))
```

This subexpression, (with a little help from the laws of similar triangles), computes the ratio between the size of H and h (refer to Figure 10-3). You can compute the height of the onscreen projection of the maze wall by taking the ratio between H and h and multiplying it by the height of your 3-D maze wall, which you've already set to 1.0, as described in the previous section. And because you already defined the height of the imagined maze wall as 1.0, and multiplying by 1 gives you the same value you started with, you've already computed the height of the onscreen maze wall, and you didn't even know it! Who says math isn't cool?

Finding the x-axis intersection

The calculation to find where the line from the viewpoint to the maze wall intersects the x axis is similar to the calculation for the y intersection, except that you replace the variable eyeElev with the constant .5 and rewrite the code to incorporate the x-axis offset. You use .5 instead of a constant like eyeElev to center the viewpoint in the square.

Expanding the grid into 3 dimensions

Take a look back at Figure 10-2 and notice the numbers that indicate the z and x axes. The z axis describes the distance from the viewer's eye to the forward edge of the rows of maze cubes, as seen from the viewer's position. You can also think of this distance as the *depth*. The x axis describes the lines that separate the different columns of cubes. Using the x and z axes as a reference, you can now write final equations to compute the x and y screen intersection points (vX and vY) and the 2-D projected height of a wall edge at any z depth, like this:

```
height = eyeDist  / (eyeDist + vOff + z - 1)
vY = 1 - (eyeElev + (1 - eyeElev) * height)
vX = .5 + (.5 + x) * height
```

Sizing up the screen

Because vX, vY, and height are values between 0 and 1, you need to convert these values into the actual pixel coordinates in the applet's screen space. You can do this conversion simply by multiplying height and vY by the height of the screen and vX by the width of the screen.

Drawing the Maze

You're now almost ready to start calculating the 2-D projections of the wall faces in the maze so that you can draw them, but you still have a few details to consider. First, you can draw the projected image of a front wall facing the viewer as a simple rectangle using the `Graphics` method `fillRect()`. However, the side wall faces that run parallel to lines away from the view-point aren't rectangular because of the 2-D perspective projection, and so you need to draw these lines with the `Graphics` method `fillPolygon()`.

The painter's algorithm

Also, you can't simply draw the wall faces in any order you choose. As shown in Figure 10-2, the walls of maze cubes closer to the viewer hide portions of the walls that are farther away. Therefore, you need to draw the deeper walls first so that they don't draw over a wall that's closer to the viewer and spoil the image. Other potentially more efficient ways to accomplish this trick exist, but the simplest technique is to draw the walls back to front, using something called the painter's algorithm.

Drawing a wall face at depth Z+1 and then completely obliterating it when you draw a wall in front of it at depth Z may seem wasteful, but the programming complexity added to eliminate this problem is not often worth the time or the code it requires. Java's polygon and rectangle drawing code is quite fast on modern CPUs, so you can take advantage of this speed to simplify the code for your 3-D maze. However, the section "Overriding `drawSq()`" in Chapter 11 describes some of the methods you can use to eliminate this unnecessary drawing.

Draw from the outside in

When `drawSq()` draws a maze cube to the left or right of the viewpoint, you can see both the rectangular front face and also the trapezoid-shaped side face, so `drawSq()` needs to draw both these wall faces. However, this creates a subtle problem. The front face of the center maze cube and the right face of the maze cube to the immediate left of the center cube both draw on top of each other. The same is true for left faces of maze cubes to the right of the center cube.

If you draw the center cube's front face before you draw the right side face of the cube to the left of the center cube, you get a very strange looking wall. Therefore, you need to draw the wall faces of the maze cubes to the left and right of the center cube before you draw the front face of the center cube.

However, if you think about it, this same problem also happens when you draw the side face of the cube, which is to the left of the cube, which is to the left of the center cube. Whew! Ditto for the cube which is to the right of . . . well, you get the idea. The point is that you need to draw cubes so that the front face of a given maze cube is drawn *after* the side face of an adjacent cube. You do this by drawing the cubes starting from the left and right edges and drawing in toward the center cube.

Deeper is wider

As z (the depth of your 3-D maze) increases, the 2-D perspective projection displays more and more wall faces. Your code needs to calculate how many wall faces are visible at each z depth. You can once again use your trusty similar triangles to figure the visible wall faces out.

The diagram in Figure 10-4 shows a top view of the grid maze. Notice that a line drawn from the viewer's eye through the exact left edge of the screen (a distance of .5 from the center) crosses a z line at distance x from the center of the screen.

Because

```
X / .5 = (eyeDist + vOff + z - 1) / eyeDist
```

you know that

```
X = .5 * ((eyeDist + vOff + z - 1) / eyeDist)
```

Rounding the value for x up to the next highest integer value tells you the number of wall cubes that are visible to the left or right of the viewpoint.

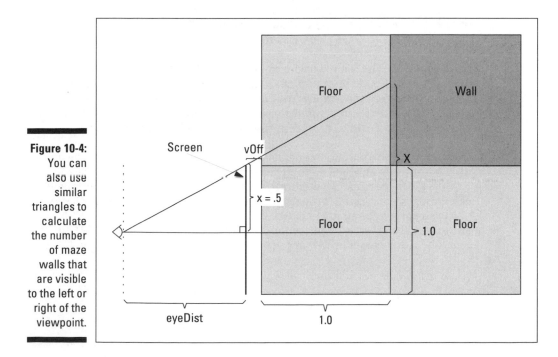

Figure 10-4: You can also use similar triangles to calculate the number of maze walls that are visible to the left or right of the viewpoint.

Creating a Rat's-Eye View

Now, armed with all these fabulous equations, you're ready to write code that can bring your 3-D maze to life. You need to write an applet class called `PolyView` to handle the user input, a 3-D view class called `GridView` where you can use all your new math, and a class called `MazeMap` that processes user input and moves the player around in the maze. Figure 10-5 shows how your completed 3-D maze applet looks.

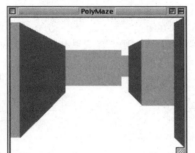

Figure 10-5:
Completed
PolyMaze
applet.

Writing `GridView`

Your `GridView` class needs to contain a constructor that creates a new `GridView` object when given a `Dimension` object called `window` to specify the screen size of the maze and an `int` value called `maxZ` to specify the maximum z depth `GridView` tries to display.

Next, you code the main workhorse method called `drawView()` for `GridView`. You code your applet so that it calls `drawView()` whenever it draws the current maze view. Your applet needs to pass to `drawView()` a `Graphics` context and a pointer to a `MazeMap` object. `MazeMap` is the class you're going to write to represent the overall layout of the 3-D maze.

Your `drawView()` method controls the order in which the maze walls are drawn and uses another method called `drawSq()` to draw the maze squares. `drawSq()`, in turn, calls a method called `getPoint()` to do the perspective calculations and do the 2-D perspective projection to get the wall's faces onto the screen. `drawSq()` also calls the `MazeMap` method `isWall()` to determine if a given square contains a wall. To help enhance the 3-D effect, `drawSq()` draws side-wall faces in a darker color than front-wall faces.

Here's the code for `GridView`:

```java
import java.awt.*;

public class GridView {
  private Dimension    window;
  private float        eyeElev = 0.65f;
  private float        eyeDist = 1.2f;
  private float        vOff = 0.15f;
  private int[]        xx = new int[4];
  private int[]        yy = new int[4];
  private int          maxZ;

  public GridView (Dimension window, int maxZ) {
    this.window = window;
    this.maxZ = maxZ;
  }

  private void getPoint (int idx, int z, int x, boolean b) {
    float height = eyeDist  / (eyeDist + vOff + z - 1);
    float vY = 1f - (eyeElev + (1 - eyeElev) * height);
    float vX = .5f + (.5f + x) * height;
    yy[idx] = (int) (window.height * (b ? height + vY : vY));
    xx[idx] = (int) (window.width * vX);
  }

  private void drawSq (Graphics g, MazeMap map,
                       int x, int z) {
if (map.isWall(x, z)) {
    getPoint(0, z, x - 1, false);
    getPoint(1, z, x, true);
    g.setColor(Color.lightGray);
    g.fillRect(xx[0], yy[0], xx[1] - xx[0], yy[1] - yy[0]);
    if (x != 0) {
      int x2 = x < 0 ? x : x - 1;
      getPoint(0, z, x2, false);
      getPoint(1, z + 1, x2, false);
      getPoint(2, z + 1, x2, true);
      getPoint(3, z, x2, true);
      g.setColor(Color.gray);
      g.fillPolygon(xx, yy, 4);
    }
  }
 }
}
```

(continued)

(continued)

```
public void drawView (Graphics g, MazeMap map) {
  g.setColor(Color.white);
  g.fillRect(0, 0, window.width, window.height);
  for (int zz = maxZ; zz > 0; zz--) {
    int wid = (int) (.5 * ((eyeDist + vOff + zz - 1) /
                           eyeDist)) + 1;
    for (int xx = wid; xx > 0; xx--) {
      drawSq(g, map, -xx, zz);
      drawSq(g, map, xx, zz);
    }
    drawSq(g, map, 0, zz);
  }
  drawSq(g, map, -1, 0);
  drawSq(g, map, 1, 0);
}
}
```

Coding MazeMap

After you've coded GridView, you need to write the companion class
MazeMap. MazeMap contains the code that processes the user events that the
player uses to move around in the maze. MazeMap also contains the
isWall() method that GridView calls when it needs to draw the view at the
player's current location. The isWall() method's main job is to translate
view-relative x and z values into absolute x and y locations in the maze
based on the player's current location and orientation.

The constructor for MazeMap accepts a 2-D byte ([][]) array that specifies a
map of the maze and x, y values that specify the player's starting position in
the maze. The constructor also accepts a dir value that specifies the
player's initial orientation (0 means North, 1 means East, 2 means South,
and 3 means West.)

Here's the code for MazeMap:

```
import java.awt.*;

public class MazeMap {
  public static final byte  FLOOR = 0;
  public static final byte  WALL = 1;
  private byte[][]          map;
  private Point             ploc;
  private int               dir;

  public MazeMap (byte[][] map, int x, int y, int dir) {
    this.map = map;
```

```
      ploc = new Point(x, y);
      this.dir = dir;
   }

   private byte sqType (Point loc) {
      if (loc.y < 0 || loc.y >= map.length ||
         loc.x < 0 || loc.x >= map[loc.y].length)
         return WALL;
      return map[loc.y][loc.x];
   }

   private Point xlate (int x, int z) {
      switch (dir) {
      case 0: return new Point(ploc.x + x, ploc.y - z);
      case 1: return new Point(ploc.x + z, ploc.y + x);
      case 2: return new Point(ploc.x - x, ploc.y + z);
      case 3: return new Point(ploc.x - z, ploc.y - x);
      }
      return ploc;
   }

   public boolean isWall (int x, int z) {
      return sqType(xlate(x, z)) == WALL;
   }

   public void doMove (int key) {
      switch (key) {
      case Event.LEFT:
      case Event.RIGHT:
         dir = (dir + (key == Event.RIGHT ? 1 : -1)) & 3;
         break;
      case Event.UP:
      case Event.DOWN:
         if (!isWall(0, (key == Event.UP ? 1 : -1)))
            ploc = xlate(0, (key == Event.UP ? 1 : -1));
         break;
      }
   }
}
```

Coding PolyMaze

The last step in constructing your 3-D maze is to write the PolyMaze applet
code. This code must define a 2-D byte([][]) array called map and then use
it in order to create a MazeMap object that represents the maze. Then,
PolyMaze creates a GridView object called view to handle the maze display.

Your PolyMaze applet must override update() and paint() and use an offscreen Image to create the image. The paint() method calls GridView's drawView() method to draw the 3-D perspective view. You can create your user interface by overriding keyDown() and passing the key value to MazeMap's doMove() method. doMove() interprets pressing the up- and down-arrow keys as forward and backward moves, respectively, and the left and right arrow keys as left and right turns.

Remember that keyboard events may not work until the player clicks the applet view to get the keyboard focus (see CD Chapter 5 for more on focus). So when you place your 3-D maze applet on a Web page, be sure that you tell your players to click the applet to get it going.

Here's the code for PolyMaze:

```java
import java.awt.*;
import java.applet.Applet;

public class PolyMaze extends Applet {
  private GridView   view;
  private Image      offImg;
  private Graphics   offscr;
  private MazeMap    map;
  private byte[][]   dun = { {0, 0, 0, 0, 0, 0, 0, 0},
{1, 0, 0, 0, 1, 1, 0, 0},
                            {0, 0, 1, 1, 1, 1, 0, 1},
                            {1, 0, 1, 0, 0, 1, 0, 0},
                            {0, 0, 0, 0, 0, 1, 0, 0},
                            {0, 1, 1, 0, 1, 1, 0, 0},
                            {0, 0, 0, 0, 1, 0, 0, 0},
                            {0, 0, 0, 0, 0, 0, 0, 1}};

  public void init() {
    map = new MazeMap(dun, 0, 0, 1);
    view = new GridView(size(), 8);
  }

  public void paint (Graphics g) {
    if (offscr == null) {
      offImg = createImage(size().width, size().height);
      offscr = offImg.getGraphics();
    }
    view.drawView(offscr, map);
    g.drawImage(offImg, 0, 0, null);
  }
```

```
public void update (Graphics g) {
  paint(g);
}

public boolean keyDown (Event evt, int key) {
  map.doMove(key);
  repaint();
  return true;
}
}
```

Adding Shading, Light Effects, and a Reason to Solve the Maze

This first version of your maze applet is nice, but you may notice that the maze doesn't look as truly 3-D as it could. You can improve on this flat appearance by adding code that displays walls at deeper z depths in darker shades of gray. However, displaying shades of gray calls attention to the white floor and ceiling, so you may also want to add code to color the floor and ceiling squares.

Finally, mazes are much more interesting to explore when they have a goal at the end. Even a rat in a maze usually has a little piece of cheese to keep him interested, so why not add code to designate one square in the maze as the goal square?

The following revised GridView class adds the new shading features as well as a red goal square to let players know when they've solved your maze. The new GridView is fairly lengthy, but the changes don't require any new math. Here's the code:

```
import java.awt.*;

public class GridView {
  private Dimension    window;
  private float        eyeElev = 0.65f;
  private float        eyeDist = 1.2f;
  private float        vOff = 0.15f;
  private int[]        xx = new int[5];
  private int[]        yy = new int[5];
  private int          maxZ;
  private Color[]      shades;
```

(continued)

(continued)

```
public GridView (Dimension window, int maxZ) {
  this.window = window;
  this.maxZ = maxZ;
  shades = new Color[maxZ + 4];
  int val = 255 / (maxZ + 3);
  for (int ii = 0, vstep = 255; ii <= maxZ + 3;
       ii++, vstep -= val)
    shades[ii] = new Color(vstep, vstep, vstep);
}

private void getPoint (int idx, int z, int x, boolean b) {
  float height = eyeDist  / (eyeDist + vOff + z - 1);
  float vY = 1f - (eyeElev + (1 - eyeElev) * height);
  float vX = .5f + (.5f + x) * height;
  yy[idx] = (int) (window.height * (b ? height + vY : vY));
  xx[idx] = (int) (window.width * vX);
}

private void drawPoly (Graphics g, Color c1, Color c2) {
  g.setColor(c1);
  g.fillPolygon(xx, yy, 4);
  xx[4] = xx[0];
  yy[4] = yy[0];
  g.setColor(c2);
  g.drawPolygon(xx, yy, 5);
}

private void drawSq (Graphics g, MazeMap map,
                     int x, int z) {
if (map.isWall(x, z)) {
    getPoint(0, z, x - 1, false);
    getPoint(1, z, x, true);
    g.setColor(shades[z + 2]);
    g.fillRect(xx[0], yy[0], xx[1] - xx[0],
               yy[1] - yy[0]);
    g.setColor(Color.black);
    g.drawRect(xx[0], yy[0], xx[1] - xx[0],
               yy[1] - yy[0]);
    if (x != 0) {
      int x2 = x < 0 ? x : x - 1;
      getPoint(0, z, x2, false);
      getPoint(1, z + 1, x2, false);
      getPoint(2, z + 1, x2, true);
      getPoint(3, z, x2, true);
      drawPoly(g, shades[z + 3], Color.black);
```

```
      }
    }
    else
      drawFloorCeil(g, map, x, z);
  }

private void setGrid (int x, int z, boolean floor) {
  getPoint(0, z, x, floor);
  getPoint(1, z + 1, x, floor);
  getPoint(2, z + 1, x - 1, floor);
  getPoint(3, z, x -1, floor);
}


private void drawFloorCeil (Graphics g, MazeMap map,
                            int x, int z) {
  setGrid(x, z, false);
  drawPoly(g, shades[z], shades[z + 1]);
  setGrid(x, z, true);
  drawPoly(g, map.isGoal(x, z) ? Color.red : shades[z],
           shades[z + 1]);
}


public void drawView (Graphics g, MazeMap map) {
  g.setColor(Color.black);
  g.fillRect(0, 0, window.width, window.height);
  for (int zz = maxZ; zz > 0; zz--) {
    int wid = (int) (.5 *
                ((eyeDist + vOff + zz - 1) / eyeDist)) + 1;
    for (int xx = wid; xx > 0; xx--) {
      drawSq(g, map, -xx, zz);
      drawSq(g, map, xx, zz);
    }
    drawSq(g, map, 0, zz);
  }
  drawSq(g, map, -1, 0);
  drawSq(g, map, 1, 0);
  drawFloorCeil(g, map, 0, 0);
  }
}
```

Updating MazeMap

You need to make several small changes to MazeMap to define the red goal
square. First, you need to add a new constant so that you can set a square in
the map to something other than FLOOR or WALL. You can call this new
constant GOAL:

```
public static final byte    GOAL = 2;
```

Next, you need to add a new method to MazeMap called isGoal(). Here's
the code:

```
public boolean isGoal (int x, int z) {
   return sqType(xlate(x, z)) == GOAL;
}
```

Updating PolyMaze

The only change you need to make to the PolyMaze applet is to revise the
map array to include a goal square, like this:

```
private byte[][]  dun = { {0, 0, 0, 0, 0, 0, 0, 0},
                          {1, 0, 0, 0, 1, 1, 0, 0},
                          {0, 0, 1, 1, 1, 1, 0, 1},
                          {1, 0, 1, 0, 0, 1, 0, 0},
                          {0, 0, 0, 0, 0, 1, 0, 0},
                          {0, 1, 1, 0, 1, 1, 0, 2},
                          {0, 0, 0, 0, 1, 0, 0, 0},
                          {0, 0, 0, 0, 0, 0, 0, 1}};
```

Figure 10-6 shows the results of your changes. Notice that the goal square in
the distant rear square.

Figure 10-6:
Revised
PolyMaze
applet with
shaded wall
faces and
a goal
square.

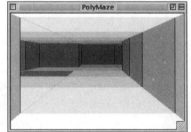

Running a Random Maze

Chapter 7 describes code that you can use to automatically create a 2-D block-style maze. With a few additions, this code works perfectly to create a random map for your new 3-D maze.

Extending from BlockMaze

First, you need to revise your MazeMap class. By revising MazeMap to extend from BlockMaze, you can inherit all the code you need to create a randomly generated block maze. Then, you need to rewrite the sqType(), isWall(), and isGoal() methods and modify the constructor to accept int parameters that set the size of the maze you want to generate. Here's the final revised code for MazeMap:

```
import java.awt.*;

public class MazeMap extends BlockMaze {
  private Point        ploc;
  private int          dir;

  public MazeMap (int wid, int hyt) {
    setDimensions(wid, hyt);
    generate(false);
    ploc = new Point(startX, startY);
    this.dir = (int) (Math.random() * 4);
  }

  private byte sqType (Point loc) {
    if (loc.y < 0 || loc.y >= mzWid  ||
        loc.x < 0 || loc.x >= mzHyt)
      return WALL;
    return (byte) sqr(loc.y, loc.x);
  }

  private Point xlate (int x, int z) {
    switch (dir) {
    case 0: return new Point(ploc.x + x, ploc.y - z);
    case 1: return new Point(ploc.x + z, ploc.y + x);
    case 2: return new Point(ploc.x - x, ploc.y + z);
    case 3: return new Point(ploc.x - z, ploc.y - x);
    }
    return ploc;
```

(continued)

(continued)

```
  }

  public boolean isWall (int x, int z) {
    return sqType(xlate(x, z)) == WALL;
  }

  public boolean isGoal (int x, int z) {
    Point loc = xlate(x, z);
    return loc.x == finishX  &&  loc.y == finishY;
  }

  public void doMove (int key) {
    switch (key) {
    case Event.LEFT:
    case Event.RIGHT:
      dir = (dir + (key == Event.RIGHT ? 1 : -1)) & 3;
      break;
    case Event.UP:
    case Event.DOWN:
      if (!isWall(0, (key == Event.UP ? 1 : -1)))
        ploc = xlate(0, (key == Event.UP ? 1 : -1));
      break;
    }
  }
}
```

Sizing the maze in your HTML

You also need to make a few changes to your PolyMaze applet. You can remove the dun array, because you no longer need it, but you can also add code to PolyMaze's init() method to read the dimensions of the maze from the HTML file. Here's the final code for your revised PolyMaze applet:

```
import java.awt.*;
import java.applet.Applet;

public class PolyMaze extends Applet {
  private GridView    view;
  private Image       offImg;
  private Graphics    offscr;
  private MazeMap     map;
  private int         mwidth, mheight;
```

```
public void init() {
  String  param;

  if ((param = getParameter( MAZEWIDTH )) != null)
    try { mwidth = Integer.parseInt(param); }
    catch (NumberFormatException e) {}
  if ((param = getParameter( MAZEHEIGHT )) != null)
    try { mheight = Integer.parseInt(param); }
    catch (NumberFormatException e) {}
  map = new MazeMap(mwidth, mheight);
  view = new GridView(size(), 8);
}

public void paint (Graphics g) {
  if (offscr == null) {
    offImg = createImage(size().width, size().height);
    offscr = offImg.getGraphics();
  }
  view.drawView(offscr, map);
  g.drawImage(offImg, 0, 0, null);
}

public void update (Graphics g) {
  paint(g);
}

public boolean keyDown (Event evt, int key) {
  map.doMove(key);
  repaint();
  return true;
}
```

Chapter 11

Texture-Mapped 3-D Maze

· ·

In This Chapter

▶ Understanding how texture mapping works

▶ Scaling images

▶ Texture tiling

▶ Bresenham's line drawing technique

▶ Darkening images

· ·

Chapter 10 presents the basics of 3-D graphics by showing you how to use perspective projection to create a 3-D maze. This chapter shows you how you can convert the flat-looking walls in Chapter 10 into more realistic walls using a technique called *texture mapping.*

The complete code for the Texture-Mapped 3-D Maze applet described in this chapter is included on the *Java Game Programming For Dummies* CD-ROM at the back of this book.

Mapping Some Texture

The invention of texture mapping opened a new age in computer graphics. Before texture mapping, most computer-created images showed only the dull, putty-like surfaces of flat-shaded (solid color) techniques, or the shiny, plastic-like surfaces produced by methods, such as Phong shading. (Phong shading tries to simulate how light reflects off surfaces.) However, by modern standards, these images are about as interesting as the interior walls of a freshly painted room.

Surfaces in the real world are more complex than walls painted Navaho white or beige. Real walls are often dirty, damaged, or decorated with pictures, posters, or crayon markings. Computer images that show these details seem more realistic than those that don't. However, trying to convert these features into 3-D polygon coordinates creates a flood of coordinate data and quickly becomes impractical.

The origins of texture mapping

Most computer monitors today display *square pixels,* where the monitor spaces the pixels by the same amount in both the vertical and horizontal directions. If you draw a square on a monitor with square pixels, it looks square. However, on monitors that space the pixels by different amounts vertically and horizontally, when you draw a square, you get a rectangle.

If you're just drawing simple shapes like squares, circles, or polygons, you can compensate for this difference by adjusting the coordinates to stretch the shape along the shorter axis or shrink the shape along the longer axis. However, what if you want to display a photographic image on a monitor with nonsquare pixels?

ASA faced a similar problem in the early 1960s with the images returned by its satellites and space missions. NASA solved the problem with a technique called *image resampling.* Image resampling is a 2-D application of techniques developed to stretch or shrink 1-D waveforms, such as recorded sound waves. The modern electronic instrument called a *digital sampler* uses this technique to stretch or shrink a sound wave and create notes at different frequencies.

You resample an image by interpolating or averaging values so that you can compute a new value in between the values you averaged. Imagine, for example, that you draw a smooth, continuous line to connect the discrete sample values in a 1-D waveform. If you then pick new points from this line that are spaced differently than the original values, you have resampled the waveform.

If you were building a scale model of your bedroom, you could add to the realism of the model by taking pictures of your bedroom walls, reducing the pictures to fit the scale of the model, and then pasting the pictures onto the appropriate model wall. Pasting pictures is a lot easier than trying to draw tiny replicas of real features on the walls of your room. Getting a detailed-looking result without too much work is what texture mapping is all about.

If you haven't already guessed, the *texture* part of texture mapping is really just another word for image. *Mapping* refers to the mathematical idea of connecting points on one surface to points on another surface using a formula that describes how points on one surface connect to the other. For example, you can *map* the points on a 2×2 square A onto a 1×1 square B by using the formulas $B.x = A.x/2$ and $B.y = A.y/2$.

Scaling Images

To create a scaled image B from image A, you write a loop that copies pixels from A to B and uses a mapping formula to decide which pixels to copy. When image B is smaller than image A (scaling down), you have to discard some of the pixels in image A because there image B doesn't have enough room for all of them. When image B is larger than image A (scaling up), you copy some pixels from image A multiple times to fill in the gaps between pixels.

To scale an image to a particular width and height, you use a mapping formula that shrinks or expands an image independently of the width or height. To avoid holes in the scaled image, you write your loop to iterate through all the pixels in the destination image and use your mapping formula to calculate the coordinates of each individual pixel to copy from the source image. You calculate the coordinates of each of the individual pixels in the source image like this:

```
int sx = (int) (dx * ((float) sWid / dWid));
int sy = (int) (dy * ((float) sHyt / dHyt));
```

The code computes a *scale factor* for the x axis that is proportional to the width of the source image (sWid) divided by the width of the destination image (dWid). The code does the same for the y axis by dividing the height of the source image (sHyt) by the height of the destination image (dHyt). Notice that the code casts sWid and sHyt to float values so that the division produces a float result.

Next, the code multiplies the x-axis scale factor by dx and the y-axis scale factor by dy. These calculations produce a floating-point result that gives the coordinate of the source pixel. The code then casts these floating-point values to int values in order to assign the pixel coordinates to sx and sy. (You compute the scale factors as float values so that you can handle noninteger ratios between the width and height of the source and destination images, but you need an int value to index a pixel.)

The x- and y-scale factors are constant for a given pair of source and destination images, so you can calculate them outside the pixel copy loop. Using this approach, here's code for a method called scale() that takes a sWid by sHyt source image specified by the int[] array parameter called src and returns an int[] array containing an image scaled to the size specified by the dWid and dHyt parameters:

```
public int[] scale (int[] src, int sWid, int sHyt,
                    int dWid, int dHyt) {
  // Return a scaled version of the image data in src[]
  int[] buf = new int[dWid * dHyt];
  float scaleX = (float) sWid / dWid;
  float scaleY = (float) sHyt / dHyt;
  for (int dy = 0; dy < dHyt; dy++) {
    for (int dx = 0; dx < dWid; dx++) {
      int sx = (int) (dx * scaleX);
      int sy = (int) (dy * scaleY);
      buf[dy * dWid + dx] = pixels[sy * sWid + sx];
    }
  }
  return buf;
}
```

Then, using `scale()`, you can construct an applet called `ImageScale` to experiment with image scaling. Figure 11-1 shows how the applet enables you to click and drag with the mouse pointer to expand or shrink the image in any direction.

Figure 11-1:
The
ImageScale
applet
demonstrates
scaling an
image to an
arbitrary
size and
shape.

Here's the complete code for `ImageScale`:

```java
import java.awt.*;
import java.awt.image.*;
import java.applet.*;


ublic class ImageScale extends Applet {
 protected Image   img;
 protected int[]   pixels;
 protected int     nx, ny, imgWidth, imgHeight;

 public void init() {
   MediaTracker tracker = new MediaTracker(this);
   img = getImage(getCodeBase(), scale.gif );
   tracker.addImage(img, 0);
   try { tracker.waitForAll(); }
   catch (InterruptedException e) { }
   nx = imgWidth = img.getWidth(null);
   ny = imgHeight = img.getHeight(null);
   // Extract pixel data using PixelGrabber
   pixels = new int[imgWidth * imgHeight];
   PixelGrabber pg = new PixelGrabber(img, 0, 0, imgWidth,
                                       imgHeight, pixels, 0,
                                       imgWidth);
   try { pg.grabPixels(); }
   catch (InterruptedException e) { }
 }
```

```java
public int[] scale (int[] src, int sWid, int sHyt,
                    int dWid, int dHyt) {
  // Return a scaled version of the image data in src[]
  int[] buf = new int[dWid * dHyt];
  float scaleX = (float) sWid / dWid;
  float scaleY = (float) sHyt / dHyt;
  for (int dy = 0; dy < dHyt; dy++) {
    for (int dx = 0; dx < dWid; dx++) {
      int sx = (int) (dx * scaleX);
      int sy = (int) (dy * scaleY);
      buf[dy * dWid + dx] = pixels[sy * sWid + sx];
    }
  }
  return buf;
}


public void paint (Graphics g) {
  int[] buf = scale(pixels, imgWidth, imgHeight, nx, ny);
  Image sImg = createImage(new MemoryImageSource(nx, ny,
                                        buf, 0, nx));
  g.drawImage(sImg, 0, 0, null);
  g.setColor(Color.white);
  g.fillRect(nx, 0, size().width - nx, ny);
  g.fillRect(0, ny, size().width, size().height - ny);
}

public void update (Graphics g) {
  paint(g);
}

public boolean mouseDown (Event evt, int x, int y) {
  nx = x;
  ny = y;
  repaint();
  return true;
}

public boolean mouseDrag (Event evt, int x, int y) {
  return mouseDown(evt, x, y);
}
```

The code for `ImageScale` uses Java's `PixelGrabber` class to read the data from an image file and convert it to pixel data in the `int[]` array `pixels`. For more information on `PixelGrabber`, see the "Using `PixelGrabber`" section in Chapter 12.

Tiling Textures

As Figure 11-2 shows, you can endlessly tile texture map images if they are constructed so that the left and right edges and the top and bottom edges blend smoothly with each other. Constructing tiling texture maps is somewhat difficult if you have to draw them by hand, but you can purchase commercial software, such as the "Texture Explorer" filter (included in Kai's Power Tools 3.0 from MetaCreations), that can produce these types of images with little effort.

Figure 11-2:
A tiled
image.

You can experiment with texture tiling by changing to this code the `paint()` method in the `ImageScale` demo applet:

```
public void paint (Graphics g) {
  int[] buf = scale(pixels, imgWidth, imgHeight, nx, ny);
  Image sImg = createImage(new MemoryImageSource(nx, ny,
                                            buf, 0, nx));
  for (int xx = 0; xx < size().width; xx += nx) {
    for (int yy = 0; yy < size().height; yy += ny) {
      g.drawImage(sImg, xx, yy, null);
    }
  }
}
```

Texture Mapping a 3-D Maze

Chapter 10 shows how to draw a 3-D perspective maze, but the code in that chapter draws the surfaces of the maze walls as plain, filled polygons. You can create a much more realistic maze if you instead use texture mapping to draw the walls. You can use the ideas from the earlier "Scaling Images" section to draw the rectangular front wall faces as texture-mapped surfaces and scale them to fit the dimensions of the face.

Side-wall faces, however, are not rectangular (remember Albrecht Dürer and his perspective stuff in Chapter 10), which means that you have to use a different approach to scale an image to fit them: Instead of copying the pixels into a rectangular destination area, you need to warp the image to fit the trapezoidal shape of a side wall.

Start by thinking of the trapezoid-shaped side wall as a series of pixel-wide columns stacked side by side, as shown in Figure 11-3. You texture map each column by stretching or shrinking a tasty, pixel-wide slice of texture to fit the height of each column. When you repeat this process for each column you get a fully texture-mapped side wall.

Figure 11-3:
Fit your texture to the trapezoid-shaped side walls by individually stretching or shrinking a pixel-wide slice of texture to fit each column.

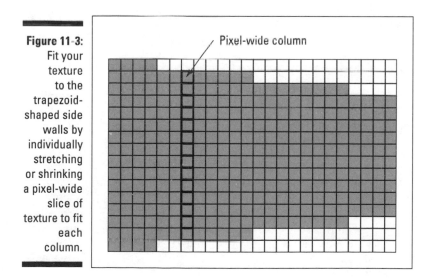

Pixel-wide column

The tricky part here is writing the code to compute the top and bottom position of each column of texture. However, you can easily take advantage of the lines that define the top and bottom edge of the side wall. The GridView class, described in the section "Writing GridView" in Chapter 10, includes code that computes the points that define the four corners of a side-wall face. Starting from these four points, you can move along the top and bottom edge lines and compute the positions of each pixel-wide column's top and bottom pixel.

Introducing Mr. Bresenham

You can trace sloping lines in a variety of ways, but the most accurate and widely-used approach was invented in the mid-sixties by a researcher named Jack Bresenham at IBM.

Prior to Bresenham's invention, people drew lines by coding a loop to step by one along one axis, either x or y, and then step along the other axis by adding a fractional increment proportional to the slope of the line. This approach is called the *Digital Differential Analyzer,* or DDA for short. For example, to draw a line from x=0, y=0 to x=6, y=3, the DDA approach uses code like this:

```
float y = 0;
for (int x = 0; x <= 6; x++) {
  plotPoint(x, (int) y);
  y += 3f / 6f;
}
```

This approach works fine when you can accurately represent the fractional increment in a float, or double value. However, you cannot accurately represent some fractions, such as 1/3, as binary values. Therefore, each time you add such a fraction, you make the value that represents the line's position on the fractional axis increasingly inaccurate. In some cases this error accumulates to the point that the line is off by an entire pixel by the time the code draws the last pixel (and results in a pretty funky-looking wall).

Bresenham realized that you can completely avoid this problem if you step by rational fractions. Rather than step by the truncated decimal .33333, Bresenham created a way to step by the rational fraction 1/3, much the way a carpenter would compute the position of the points. When drawing a line from x=0, y=0 to x=7, y=2, for example, Bresenham realized that you can think of the y position as increasing by $^2/_7$ for each step by 1 along the x axis. This approach produces the following values for x and y:

$$(0, 0), (1, 2/7), (2, 4/7), (3, 6/7), (4, 8/7), (5, 10/7), (6, 12/7), (7, 14/7)$$

Then when you round each fraction to its nearest integer, you get

$$(0, 0), (1, 0), (2, 1), (3, 1), (4, 1), (5, 1), (6, 2), (7, 2)$$

However, notice that the y value increases when the numerator crosses a multiple of n × 7 + 7/2. In the example, the y value increases at 7/2 and 7 + 7/2 or, expressed decimally, 3.5 and 10.5. With Bresenham's approach you get rid of the .5 in 3.5 and 10.5 by the simple trick of doubling the numbers. Instead of counting the fractions as increasing by 2/7, you count them increasing by 4/14. Then, you check for the numerator crossing a multiple of n × 14 + 14/2 rather than n × 7 + 7/2.

Bresenham also realized that an easier way to check whether the numerator has crossed a multiple of n × 14 + 14/2 is instead to subtract 14 from the numerator whenever it becomes greater than or equal to 7. He also realized that he could then forget about the denominator in the fraction and let the algorithm increase the value of y whenever it decides to subtract 14 from the numerator. Using Bresenham's approach, you can draw a line from x1=0, y1=0 to x2=7, y2=2 with the following code:

```
int num = 0;
int inc = (y2 - y1) * 2;
int dec = (x2 - x1) * 2;
int y = y1;
for (int x = x1; x <= x2; x++) {
  plotPoint(x, y);
  num += inc;
  while (num >= x2) {
    num -= dec;
    y++;
  }
}
```

You normally write Bresenham-based line-drawing code to step along the longest axis and fractionally step along the other axis. This approach draws lines without gaps. It also means that the `while` loop in the previous code can be replaced with an `if` statement because y can then never increment by more than 1 in any pass through the `for` loop. However, for your texture-mapped maze you always want to step by 1 along the x axis, so you need the `while` loop to handle cases where y steps more than one pixel for each x axis step.

Experimenting with Bresenham

You can easily convert the code from the previous section, "Introducing Mr. Bresenham," into an example named `Bresenham` that demonstrates how the algorithm works. Figure 11-4 shows the result. You can click on any square to select a new endpoint for the line.

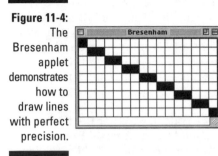

Figure 11-4:
The
Bresenham
applet
demonstrates
how to
draw lines
with perfect
precision.

Here's the code for the `Bresenham` applet:

```
import java.awt.*;
import java.applet.Applet;


/  Note: this applet should be sized in the HTML to a
/  multiple of grid + 1 in both width and height.  For
/  example, 257 x 145 for a desired grid of 256 x 144.

ublic class Bresenham extends Applet {
  int    x1 = 0, y1 = 0, x2, y2, gWid, gHyt, grid = 16;

ublic void init () {
    x2 = (gWid = size().width / grid) - 1;
    y2 = (gHyt = size().height / grid) - 1;
  }

ublic void paint (Graphics g) {
    g.setColor(Color.white);
    g.fillRect(0, 0, size().width, size().height);
    g.setColor(Color.black);
    for (int yy = 0; yy < gHyt; yy++)
      for (int xx = 0; xx < gWid; xx++)
        g.drawRect(xx * grid, yy * grid, grid, grid);
    if (x1 != x2) {
      int num = 0;
      int inc = (y2 - y1) * 2;
      int dec = (x2 - x1) * 2;
      int y = y1;
      for (int x = x1; x <= x2; x++) {
        g.fillRect(x * grid + 1, y * grid + 1,
```

```
           grid -1, grid - 1);
      num += inc;
      while (num >= x2) {
        num -= dec;
        y++;
      }
    }
  }
}


public boolean mouseDown (Event evt, int x, int y) {
  x2 = x / grid;
  y2 = y / grid;
  repaint();
  return true;
}
```

Extending a `TexView` class from `GridView`

Most of the code you need for your texture-mapped 3-D maze is contained in the `GridView` class described in Chapter 10. However, you need to extend a new class from `GridView` called `TexView` so that you add code to load the texture maps and draw texture-mapped wall faces instead of the flat-shaded walls used in Chapter 10.

Loading textures

`TexView` ultimately creates images of texture-mapped wall faces that you can draw into the 3-D view, but `TexView` does all its internal texture scaling using raw pixel data. You could use `PixelGrabber` to extract the pixel data from an image, as described earlier in the "Scaling Images" section. However, a better way is to use the `ImageBytes` class (described in Chapter 12) to load indexed color images, such as GIF files, and keep them in their original indexed form. Indexed color images use less memory because they represent each pixel as a `byte` rather than as an `int`. The section "Modifying GIF Images" in Chapter 12 describes the `ImageBytes` class in more detail.

Overriding `drawSq()`

`TexView` overrides the `GridView` method `drawSq()` so that it can substitute code to draw a texture-mapped wall rather than solid color walls. Here's the new code for `drawSq()`:

```
protected void drawSq (Graphics g, MazeMap map,
                       int x, int z) {
  if (map.isWall(x, z)) {
    ix = map.isOdd(x, z) ? 0 : 1;
    if (z > 0  && !map.isWall(x, z - 1))
      textureFront(g, x, z);
    if (x != 0  && !map.isWall(x < 0 ? x + 1 : x - 1, z))
      textureSide(g, x, z);
  }
  else
    drawFloorCeil(g, map, x, z);
}
```

Drawing texture-mapped walls takes more CPU time than drawing solid filled walls, so the new `drawSq()` code does checks to reduce the number of walls it draws that are subsequently covered from view by walls closer to the viewer. `drawSq()` reduces the number of front faces it draws by checking whether the square just in front of a square in question (relative to the viewpoint) is also a wall square. If the square in front is a wall square, it skips drawing the wall behind it, because that wall would be covered anyway.

The code does a similar check for side-wall faces. For left-facing side walls, it skips drawing the side wall if the square to the immediate left is a wall. Likewise, for right-facing walls, it skips drawing the side wall if the square to the immediate right contains a wall.

Alternating wall textures

The constructor for `TexView` (see the later section "Shading the walls") loads two different textures maps. You could code `TexView` to use only a single texture map, but a single texture map creates a subtle aesthetic problem: If you were to move down a long corridor in a maze, you would notice that the side-wall texture never changes. This unchanging texture happens because the single texture pattern would repeat every maze square, so each step forward would show an identical-looking side wall.

With two texture maps you can assign the textures to the maze walls in a checkerboard pattern so that the walls repeat every other square rather than every square. This pattern is less obvious when moving down corridors and gives the player more of a realistic sense of motion. The method `isOdd()` is a new method you need to add to the `MazeMap` class. You call `isOdd()` to determine which texture to use for a given square. Here's the code for `isOdd()`:

```
public boolean isOdd (int x, int z) {
  Point loc = xlate(x, z);
  return (loc.x & 1) == (loc.y & 1);
}
```

If creating one texture map that tiles seamlessly is hard, creating two texture maps that seamlessly tile with each other and with themselves can be a real trick. However, if one texture map is simply a horizontal flip of the other, the two resulting texture maps are guaranteed to work together.

Drawing front walls

drawSq() calls a method called textureFront() to draw the front faces of a wall square. The code for textureFront() is a loop that draws column slices from the left edge of the wall to the right. For each slice of texture, textureFront() calls a method called frontOff() to compute the location of the slice in the source texture. frontOff() returns a number that ranges from 0 to just less than 1 that represents the horizontal offset into the texture.

Calculating the front wall's texture offset

It may seem that this texture offset value is simply proportional to the position of the pixel column in the destination image, but that isn't exactly true. Walls further to the left or right of the viewpoint are slightly narrower than the walls in the center of the viewpoint due to the perspective projection. Perspective projection also causes the texture slices to be spaced *slightly* closer together the further the slices are from the center of the viewpoint. You could ignore this effect and map the texture as if the columns were evenly spaced, and you may not even notice the subtle difference. However, deep in your heart, you would know that you just didn't do it exactly right, and if you're like us, you may toss and turn in bed until you correct the situation.

The correct way to compute the texture offset uses a variation on the formula used in the section "Deeper is wider" in Chapter 10. This formula, coded in the frontOff() method, calculates where a line drawn through a screen column specified in frontOff()'s x parameter crosses the maze grid at a depth specified by the z parameter. In the section "Deeper is wider," this value is rounded to the next highest integer to find how many wall faces are visible to the left or right of the viewpoint at a given z depth. However, if you instead discard the integer part and keep only the fraction, you have the texture offset you need!

Here's the code for frontOff():

```
protected float frontOff (float x, int z) {
    float height = ((eyeDist + vOff + z - 1) / eyeDist);
    return (((x + .5f) / window.width) - .5f) * height + .5f;
}
```

`textureFront()` extracts the fraction part of the value returned from `frontOff()` using Java's mode operator (%) and assigns it to a variable called `tx`. However, because `tx` represents the distance from the center of the viewpoint, you need to adjust its value before you use `tx` as a texture offset. Walls to the right of the viewpoint use `tx` unchanged, but walls to the left of the viewpoint must use `1-tx` as the texture offset. Here's the code for `textureFront()`:

```
protected void textureFront (Graphics g, int x, int z) {
  getPoint(0, z, x - 1, false);
  getPoint(1, z, x, true);
  int height = yy[1] - yy[0];
  int width = xx[1] - xx[0];
  byte[] dst = new byte[width * height];
  for (int ii = 0; ii < width; ii++) {
    float tx = Math.abs(frontOff(xx[0] + ii, z)) % 1f;
    colSlice(dst, ii, x < 0 ? 1f - tx : tx, width, height);
  }
  g.drawImage(makePic(dst, width, height, z),
              xx[0], yy[0], null);
}
```

Creating the front wall image

`textureFront()` allocates a `byte[]` array called `dst` to receive the texture-mapped pixels and calls a method called `makePix()` to convert these pixels into an `Image` object. It then uses `drawImage()` to draw the newly created wall face image into the 3-D view. `makePic()` is described in more detail in the later section "Darkening the walls."

Clipping to the view

The `getPoint()` method (introduced in Chapter 10) computes the location of the four corners of a wall's face, but some of the points it computes fall outside the bounds of the 3-D view. This boundary issue isn't a problem when you use `fillRect()` and `fillPolygon()` to draw the wall faces because these AWT methods automatically *clip* the draw so that only the region inside the 3-D view are drawn. However, there's no point in using the CPU's limited resources in creating any portion of a texture-mapped image that you don't draw to the screen. Therefore, you need to override `getPoint()` with new code that properly clips (removes) all points it computes that appear outside the 3-D view. Here's the code:

```
protected void getPoint (int idx, int z, int x, boolean b) {
  super.getPoint(idx, z, x, b);
  yy[idx] = Math.max(0, Math.min(window.height, yy[idx]));
  xx[idx] = Math.max(0, Math.min(window.width, xx[idx]));
}
```

Slicing a column of texture

In the earlier section "Scaling Images," you used floating-point values to compute the scale factors (ratios) for the x and y axis. You can also use Bresenham's ideas to compute the same type of scaling ratios. With Bresenham's approach, you can avoid the same type of accumulating floating-point errors that can affect line drawing. In texture scaling, these errors can cause the scaled texture to be off by a pixel at the end of the stepping loop.

The `colSlice()` method used by `textureFront()` only needs to scale a column of pixels, so you can use a slight variation on the Bresenham line-drawing code to scale a slice of texture. In the Bresenham line-draw example, you step by 1 along one axis while you fractionally step along the other. To scale a slice of texture, you step by 1 across the pixels in the destination column slice while you fractionally step through the pixels in the source texture.

You now know how to use Bresenham's algorithm to trace the top and bottom lines of the face of a side wall. You can also use his ideas to replace the scale factor values you use to scale a texture map in the earlier "Scaling Images" section. As you trace the top and bottom edges of a side-wall face, you need to copy a slice of texture to every pixel in the column between the top and bottom position. Here's how you can copy the column pixels using Bresenham's approach:

```
protected void colSlice (byte[] dst, int dstIdx,
                         float texOff, int width,
                         int height) {
  int sIdx = (int) (texOff * iData[ix].width);
  byte[] src = iData[ix].iData;
  int sWidth = iData[ix].width;
  int sHeight = iData[ix].height;
  int end = dstIdx + width * height;
  int sNum = 0;
  int sInc = sHeight * 2;
  int sDec = height * 2;
  for (int ii = dstIdx; ii < end; ii += width) {
    dst[ii] = src[sIdx];
    for (sNum += sInc; sNum > height; sNum -= sDec)
      sIdx += sWidth;
  }
}
```

This code uses a simple coding trick to make the Bresenham code more compact. See the later section "Tracing the side-wall edges" for more details.

Drawing side walls

When `drawSq()` needs to draw a side-wall face, it calls `TexView`'s `textureSide()` method. The code in `textureSide()` uses Bresenham's method to trace the top and bottom edges of the wall and calls `colSlice()` to fill in the texture in each pixel column in the destination image. Here's the code for `textureSide()`:

```
protected void textureSide (Graphics g, int x, int z) {
  int x2 = x < 1 ? x : x - 1;
  getPoint(0, z, x2, false);      // top front
  getPoint(1, z + 1, x2, false);  // top rear
  getPoint(2, z + 1, x2, true);   // bottom rear
  getPoint(3, z, x2, true);       // bottom front
  int wallX = Math.min(xx[0], xx[1]);
  int wallY = Math.min(yy[0], yy[1]);
  int width = Math.abs(xx[1] - xx[0]);
  int height = yy[3] - yy[0];
  byte[] dst = new byte[width * height];
  // Setup ratio counters
  int dec = width * 2;
  int topNum = 0;
  int topInc = (yy[1] - yy[0]) * 2;
  int botNum = 0;
  int botInc = (yy[3] - yy[2]) * 2;
  int top = yy[0] - wallY;
  int bot = height + top;
  int topStep = 1;
  int botStep = -topStep;
  for (int ii = 0; ii < width; ii++) {
    int dx = x < 0 ? ii : width - ii - 1;
    float tx = sideOff(x < 0 ? xx[0] + ii :
                    window.width - xx[0] + ii, z);
    colSlice(dst, dx + top * width, x < 0 ? tx : 1f - tx,
          width, bot - top);
    for (topNum += topInc; topNum > width; topNum -= dec)
      top += topStep;
    for (botNum += botInc; botNum > width; botNum -= dec)
      bot += botStep;
  }
  g.drawImage(makePic(dst, width, height, z + sDark),
          wallX, wallY, null);
}
```

The main `for` loop in `textureSide()` steps through the pixel columns from left to right for walls to the left of the viewpoint and from right to left for walls to the right of the viewpoint. Thus, the `for` loop forces walls on the right to mirror walls on the left, which is needed to make the textures match correctly. The variable dx is set to the correct column index for left or right walls at the top of the loop.

Calculating the side wall's texture offset

Inside the for loop, the code calls sideOff() to compute the offset into the source texture. sideOff() also adjusts for the perspective projection, but sideOff() needs to include the z depth in its calculations. Fortunately, as shown in Figure 11-5, you can use similar triangles to compute the texture offset for a side wall from the texture offset for the front wall adjacent to the side wall. Using this approach, here's the code for sideOff():

```
protected float sideOff (float xOff, int z) {
    float sRatio = eyeDist / (Math.abs(xOff - hWidth) /
                                  window.width);
    return (Math.abs(frontOff(xOff, z)) * sRatio) % 1f;
}
```

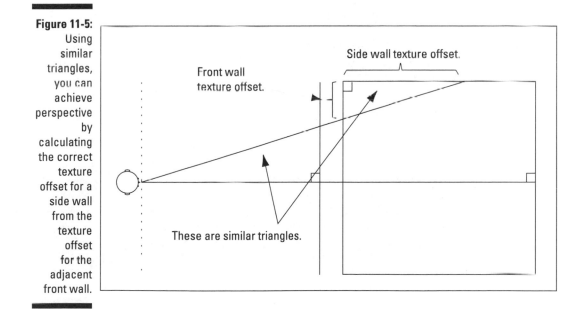

Figure 11-5:
Using similar triangles, you can achieve perspective by calculating the correct texture offset for a side wall from the texture offset for the adjacent front wall.

Side wall texture offset.

Front wall texture offset.

These are similar triangles.

Tracing the side-wall edges

textureSide( )'s main for loop also contains code that traces the lines forming the top and bottom edges of the side wall. This code uses Bresenham's technique, but it uses a simple code trick to make checking and updating the numerator value and the y axis value more compact. The code trick replaces this:

```
botNum += botInc;
while (botNum > width) {
  botNum -= width;
  bot += botStep
}
```

with this:

```
for (botCnt += botInc; botCnt > width; botCnt -= width)
  bot += botStep;
```

Masking the side walls

After slicing all the texture columns into the destination pixel array, textureSide( ) converts the pixel data into an Image using the same method described earlier in "Drawing front walls." However, remember that the code never copies any data into the pixels above and below the tops and bottoms of each texture slice. Is this a problem? No. Because GridView draws the wall faces in the way described in the section "Draw from the outside in" in Chapter 10, the code in GridView that draws the floor squares simply draws over these extra pixels. Problem solved and no new code required!

Darkening the walls

You may want to darken the texture images when you draw walls at greater z depths in the maze (see Chapter 10 for an explanation of z depth) to create the same sort of shading and lighting effects with texture maps as are described for flat shaded walls in the section " Adding Shading, Light Effects, and a Reason to Solve the Maze" in Chapter 10.

Computing a darkened color table

You can darken an IndexColorModel image simply by changing the color table attached to the image. Being able to darken an IndexColorModel image means that you can precompute a set of color tables that change from light to dark and then use these color tables to set the proper darkness for each wall image. Here's the code for a method called darker( ) that takes an IndexColorModel object passed in the pal parameter and a float value called `inten` and returns a new `IndexColorModel` object. If the `inten` parameter is set near 1, `darker()` returns `IndexColorModel` objects near the original intensity of the `pal` object. As the values of `inten` decrease toward 0, `darker()` returns progressively darker color tables.

Here's the code for `darker()`:

```
protected IndexColorModel darker (IndexColorModel pal,
                                  float inten) {
  int colors = pal.getMapSize();
  byte[] reds = new byte[colors];
  byte[] grns = new byte[colors];
  byte[] blus = new byte[colors];
  for (int ii = 0; ii < colors; ii++) {
    int rgb = pal.getRGB(ii);
    int red = (rgb >> 16) & 0xFF;
    int grn = (rgb >> 8) & 0xFF;
    int blu = rgb & 0xFF;
    // Convert to HSB to darken and then back to RGB
    float[] vals = Color.RGBtoHSB(red, grn, blu, null);
    rgb = Color.HSBtoRGB(vals[0], vals[1], vals[2] * inten);
    reds[ii] = (byte) (rgb >> 16);
    grns[ii] = (byte) (rgb >> 8);
    blus[ii] = (byte) rgb;
  }
  return new IndexColorModel(8, colors, reds, grns, blus);
}
```

`darker()` uses a loop to extract each color from the input color table. Then it converts each color from Red, Green, Blue (RGB) to a different color representation called Hue, Saturation, and Brightness (HSB) using the `Color` class method `RGBtoHSB()`. Colors represented in HSB can be easily darkened by modifying the brightness component. `darker()` adjusts the brightness of each color by multiplying the HSB brightness values by `inten`. Then, `darker()` converts the darkened color back to RGB using the `Color` method `HSBtoRGB()`.

Shading the walls

The constructor for `TexView` is a convenient place to initialize the array of color tables you use to darken the wall images. The new constructor also takes three new parameters that weren't required in `GridView`. Two image parameters called `wA` and `wB` pass references to wall images for two different wall textures, and the Applet parameter `ap` passes a reference to the Component that displays the `TexView`'s 3-D view image. Here's the code for the new constructor:

```
public TexView (Dimension window, int maxZ,
                Image wA, Image wB, Component ap) {
  super(window, maxZ);
  iData[0] = new ImageBytes(wA);
  iData[1] = new ImageBytes(wB);
  this.ap = ap;
  hWidth = window.width / 2f;
  // Generate array of darkened color tables
  int steps = maxZ + sDark + 1;
  shades = new IndexColorModel[2][steps];
  for (int jj = 0; jj < 2; jj++) {
    for (int ii = 0; ii < steps; ii++)
      shades[jj][ii] =
            darker((IndexColorModel) iData[jj].cModel,
                (float) (steps - ii) / steps);
  }
}
```

TexView's makePic() method needs the ap parameter because it needs to call the Component method createImage(). Only objects that extend from the Component class can call createImage(). Here's the code for makePic():

```
protected Image makePic (byte[] buf, int width, int height,
                         int z) {
  return ap.createImage(new MemoryImageSource(width, height,
                        shades[ix][z], buf, 0, width));
}
```

Notice that makePic() creates the new Image using an IndexColorModel object it selects from the shades[] array based on the ix parameter (described in the earlier section "Alternating wall textures") and the depth parameter z.

Shading the side walls

To increase the 3-D illusion, the code in textureSide() adds a constant value to the z depth to make side walls look slightly darker than front walls. Darker side walls simulates the real-world effect that light reflects back more easily off surfaces perpendicular to the line of sight (assuming that the light travels in the same direction.)

The complete code for the TexView class, as well as all the other code you need to construct the Texture-Mapped 3-D maze, is contained on the *Java Game Programming For Dummies* CD-ROM. In addition, the CD-ROM contains a small set of additional texture map images you can use to customize your 3-D maze.

Assembling the Pieces

The final piece of code you need to write in order to produce the result shown in Figure 11-6 is the `TexMapMaze` applet. `TexMapMaze` is based on Chapter 10's `MazeMap` applet but includes code to load the texture map images. Here's the complete code for `TexMapMaze`:

```
import java.awt.*;
import java.applet.Applet;


ublic class TexMapMaze extends Applet {
  private GridView   view;
  private Image      offImg, wallA, wallB;
  private Graphics   offscr;
  private MazeMap    map;
  private byte[][]   dun = { {0, 0, 0, 0, 0, 0, 0, 0},
                             {1, 0, 0, 0, 1, 1, 0, 0},
                             {0, 0, 1, 0, 1, 1, 0, 1},
                             {1, 0, 0, 0, 0, 1, 0, 0},
                             {0, 0, 0, 0, 0, 1, 0, 0},
                             {0, 1, 1, 0, 1, 1, 0, 0},
                             {0, 0, 0, 0, 1, 0, 0, 2},
                             {0, 0, 0, 0, 0, 0, 0, 1}};

ublic void init() {
    map = new MazeMap(dun, 0, 0, 1);
    MediaTracker tracker = new MediaTracker(this);
    wallA = getImage(getCodeBase(), "wallA.gif");
    wallB = getImage(getCodeBase(), "wallB.gif");
    tracker.addImage(wallA, 0);
    tracker.addImage(wallB, 0);
    try { tracker.waitForAll(); }
    catch (InterruptedException e) { ; }
    view = new TexView(size(), 8, wallA, wallB, this);
  }

  public void paint (Graphics g) {
    if (offscr == null) {
      offImg = createImage(size().width, size().height);
      offscr = offImg.getGraphics();
    }
    view.drawView(offscr, map);
    g.drawImage(offImg, 0, 0, null);
  }
```

(continued)

(continued)

```
public void update (Graphics g) {
  paint(g);
}


public boolean keyDown (Event evt, int key) {
  map.doMove(key);
  repaint();
  return true;
}
}
```

Figure 11-6:
The completed 3-D texture-mapped maze. Notice that the walls in the distance are darker.

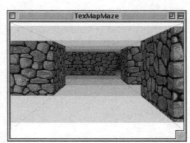

Chapter 12
Advanced Imaging

● ●

In This Chapter

▶ Unleashing the *alpha channel*

▶ Antialiasing with alpha

▶ Creating images with `MemoryImageSource`

▶ Using the `ImageConsumer` and `ImageProducer` interfaces

● ●

*T*he basics of graphics and color are covered in CD Chapters 3 and 4, but what do you do if you want to create truly stunning graphics with Java? What if you want to create antialiased text for your title screens? Or, what if you want to create a translucent ghost to inhabit your 3-D texture-mapped maze? Or, what if you want to increase the variety of images in your game by remapping the colors of one image to create a rainbow of variations?

You may think that advanced effects like antialiased text or translucency are all but impossible with the sparse methods provided in the Graphics class. Think again, fancy pants — this chapter shows you how.

In addition to the three color components — Red, Green, and Blue, or *RGB* for short — Java also provides an additional component called *alpha*. You use the alpha component to blend colors you draw into colors you've already drawn. Imagine that each pixel has a tiny little louvered blind in front of it. Then imagine that you can paint the blind any color you want and that you can also paint the space behind the blind any color.

If you close the blind on a pixel, you only see the color of the blind. Likewise, if you open the blind fully, you only see the color of the space behind. If you open the blind just a bit, you see a blend of the color of the blind and the color of the space behind the blind. Of course, in an actual window blind, you see stripes, but in the tiny world of pixels, you see mixed colors.

The alpha value provides you with a control similar to the imaginary louvered blinds. Whenever you draw an image on top of another image, Java uses the alpha information to decide how to blend the colors of the two images.

The term *alpha channel* has other meanings on other systems, but as far as Java is concerned, the alpha channel cannot be used for any purpose other than to control transparency when one image is drawn onto another. This may be different from what you are used to with the alpha channel in many graphics software packages. The bottom line is don't consult your graphics software documentation for Java alpha channel information.

Drawing Partially Transparent Images

The default value of alpha (255) in an image specifies that all pixels in the image completely replace the value of the old pixel so that new images completely cover old images. You can also set a pixel's alpha value to make a pixel completely transparent (a value of 0), or you can set it to a value between transparent and opaque and create an image that is partially transparent. However, the alpha value must be individually set for each pixel in an image.

Creating new images with MemoryImageSource

With Java, you can't change the alpha values in images that are already loaded, but you can set the alpha values in images that you create from scratch using the Java class `java.awt.MemoryImageSource`. To use `MemoryImageSource`, you start by creating an array of numeric values, which `MemoryImageSource` takes and converts into a Java image. `MemoryImageSource` has a number of different constructors with which you can create images from arrays of both `int` and `byte` values; creating images from `int` arrays is probably the easiest way to go.

When you create an image in an `int` array, you need to construct value for each pixel in your array by using the << (left shift) operator to pack the alpha, red, blue, and green component values into an `int` value using the following formula:

```
pixel = (alpha << 24) + (red << 16) + (blue << 8) + green;
```

The values `alpha`, `red`, `blue`, and `green` are `int` values that range from 0 to 255. The composite formed in `pixel` is called an ARGB value (for Alpha, Red, Green, and Blue).

You can convert an array of ARGB values into an image using the `MemoryImageSource` class. `MemoryImageSource` contains code that implements a special interface called the `ImageProducer` interface. The `ImageProducer` interface is an internal mechanism that Java uses to copy image data from one object to another.

When you create a new `MemoryImageSource` object by passing it a reference to your array of pixel data, you get back a reference to an object that implements the `ImageProducer` interface. However, to get an `Image` object, you need to pass the `ImageProducer` reference to a method in the `Component` class called `createImage()`. This may seem a little convoluted, but it's not that hard to code.

For example, assume that you create an `int[]` array called `buf` and record the size of this image in the `int` variables `wid` and `hyt`. Following is the code you need in order to convert the `buf[]` array into an `Image`:

```
ImageProducer ip = new MemoryImageSource(wid, hyt, buf, 0, wid);
Image img = createImage(ip);
```

Coding an `AlphaGradient`

Here's a simple demo called `AlphaGradient` that shows how to use `MemoryImageSource` and also demonstrates how the alpha value works. The demo first draws a checkerboard pattern of white and gray. Then `AlphaGradient` creates a pixel array and sets its RGB values to black but varies the alpha values from fully transparent on the left to fully opaque on the right.

Next, `AlphaGradient` draws this constructed image onto the checkerboard pattern it has already drawn. The alpha information causes the black to mix into the checkerboard only lightly on the left but to increase gradually to strongly black on the right. The effect, as Figure 12-1 shows, creates a light to dark gradient from left to right.

Figure 12-1: The alpha value creates a gradient fade.

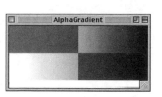

The code for the `AlphaGradient` applet is as follows:

```
import java.awt.*;
import java.applet.Applet;
import java.awt.image.*;
```

(continued)

(continued)

```
public class AlphaGradient extends Applet {
 private int   width, height;
 private Image  gradient = null;

 public void init() {
  width = size().width;
  height = size().height;
 }

 public void paint (Graphics g) {
  int  x2 = width >> 1;
  int  y2 = height >> 1;
  g.setColor(Color.gray);
  g.fillRect(0, 0, x2, y2);
  g.fillRect(x2, y2, width - x2, height - y2);
  g.setColor(Color.white);
  g.fillRect(x2, 0, width - x2, height - y2);
  g.fillRect(0, y2, x2, y2);
  if (gradient == null) {
                          int pcount = width * height;
   int[] buf = new int[pcount];
   for (int jj = 0; jj < height; jj++) {
    for (int ii = 0; ii < width; ii++)
     buf[ii + (jj * width)] =
             ((ii * 256) / width) << 24;
   }
   gradient = createImage(new MemoryImageSource(width,
             height, buf, 0, width));
  }
  g.drawImage(gradient, 0, 0, this);
 }
}
```

Unfortunately, not all Java implementations properly support the alpha value. For example, many of the examples presented in this chapter don't function correctly with the Mac versions of Netscape Navigator 4.03 and Communicator 4.03. Most work correctly under Mac Navigator 3.01, but you need to be careful not to assume that code that modifies alpha values works on a particular Java implementation until you test it.

Blending the edges of images with alpha masking

Chapter 8 shows you how to use transparent GIF images to draw one image onto another. However, transparent GIF images limit you to a single transparent color, which can result in blocky, pixelated edges that don't blend smoothly into the background image. What you really want to do is find a way to make images with smooth edges. If you've ever used Adobe Photoshop to draw a vector outline image, such as one created by Adobe Illustrator, into a bitmap image, you've seen how Photoshop can perform a bit of pixel magic called *antialiasing*.

Antialiasing works by pretending that an image has more pixels per inch than it really does. For example, Photoshop can pretend that each pixel in an image is broken up into 256 subpixels arranged in a 16-subpixel by 16-subpixel grid. When Photoshop draws the vector format picture into the bitmap, it draws it at 16 times the resolution of the real bitmap.

Then — and here's the magic part — after Photoshop has drawn the image, it counts up all the subpixels in a pixel and converts this count into an alpha value. Using this alpha information, Photoshop can compute how to blend the pixels together to simulate a smooth edge. Photoshop uses the subpixels as a way to compute the percentage of subpixels that cover a whole pixel.

The Java class libraries don't provide a means to load images from Photoshop that preserve its alpha channel information. Photoshop can store images in a proprietary format that has an alpha channel, but Java doesn't provide built-in code to read Photoshop files. The current implementations of Java do provide code that can load transparent GIF images, but transparent GIF images provide only a simple on/off type of transparency.

However, by using some simple Photoshop tricks, you can use grayscale values to encode alpha information into a GIF or a JPEG image that Java can load. Then you can write Java code to convert the grayscale image into a solid-color, antialiased image with a Java alpha channel.

Creating alpha information from a GIF image

First, you use Photoshop, or a similar program, to create an image that encodes the alpha information as grayscale values. Photoshop can automatically antialias a vector image when you draw it into a bitmap. So, by starting with a vector image created in Adobe Illustrator, or an outline font, or any other vector image, you can use Photoshop to easily create an antialiased, grayscale image.

Your goal is to create an image drawn in white that antialiases to black, like the greatly magnified view of the an antialiased letter *T* shown in Figure 12-2. You can create this type of image in Photoshop by setting the draw color to white and then using Photoshop's Type Tool to draw text into an image prefilled with black. By checking the antialias box in Type Tool, Photoshop will automatically antialias the image it draws.

Figure 12-2:
Magnified view of an antialiased image of the letter *T*.

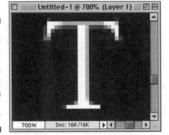

By using appropriate code, you can load this image, extract the grayscale values, and convert them into alpha values. Drawing a white image into a black background is a trick that lets you use the red, green, or blue channel as the alpha channel. This works because white is composed of equal parts of red, green, and blue. Therefore, the values in the red, green, or blue channels will all be the same.

Using `PixelGrabber`

The next step is to load the image and then use a special class called `java.awt.image.PixelGrabber` to convert the image's pixels into ARGB values in an `int` array.

Here's the code for a class called `AlphaImage` that uses `PixelGrabber` to convert an `Image` that encodes alpha information as grayscale values into a new `Image` with a true alpha channel. `AlphaImage` recolors the image to any color you specify in the parameter `clr`. Also, you can use the `trans` parameter to create a translucent image. Setting `trans` to 255 tells `alphaImage()` to return an opaque `Image`. Decreasing `trans` makes the image progressively more transparent until you reach 0, at which point you create a fully transparent image.

```
import java.awt.*;
import java.awt.image.*;

public class AlphaImage {
  static ImageProducer alphaImage (Image src, Color clr,
                    int trans) {
    int wid = src.getWidth(null);
```

```
int hgt = src.getHeight(null);
int rgb = clr.getRGB() & 0xFFFFFF;
int pixels = wid * hgt;
int[] buf = new int[pixels];
PixelGrabber pg = new PixelGrabber(src, 0, 0, wid,
                 hgt, buf, 0, wid);
try {pg.grabPixels();} catch (InterruptedException e){}
for (int ii = 0; ii < pixels; ii++) {
  int alpha = (((buf[ii] & 0xFF) *
       trans) << 16) & 0xFF000000;
  buf[ii] = (buf[ii] & 0xFF) != 0 ? alpha | rgb : 0;
  }
  return new MemoryImageSource(wid, hgt, buf, 0, wid);
  }
}
```

To use PixelGrabber, you must first create a PixelGrabber object. Then you can use this object to read the data from an Image. Although the constructor for PixelGrabber takes parameters that specify an Image, PixelGrabber doesn't read the image data until you call its grabPixels() method. Also, you must allocate an array to receive the pixel data before you call grabPixels().

Here's the code for a small applet called AntialiasDemo that uses your new AlphaImage class to load and draw an antialiased image:

```
import java.awt.*;
import java.applet.Applet;
import java.awt.image.*;

public class AntialiasDemo extends Applet {
 private Image  img, imgA, imgS;
 private int    width, height, offX, offY;

 public void init() {
  width = size().width;
  height = size().height;
   MediaTracker tracker = new MediaTracker(this);
   tracker.addImage(img = getImage(getCodeBase(),
               Java.GIF ), 0);
   try { tracker.waitForAll(); }
   catch (InterruptedException e) { ; }
offX = (width - img.getWidth(null)) / 2;
   offY = (height - img.getHeight(null)) / 2;
   imgA = createImage(AlphaImage.alphaImage(img,
            Color.black, 255));
```

(continued)

(continued)

```
    imgS = createImage(AlphaImage.alphaImage(img,
            Color.darkGray, 127));
  }

  public void paint (Graphics g) {
    int x2 = width >> 1;
    int y2 = height >> 1;
    g.setColor(Color.gray);
    g.fillRect(0, 0, x2, y2);
    g.fillRect(x2, y2, width - x2, height - y2);
    g.setColor(Color.white);
    g.fillRect(x2, 0, width - x2, height - y2);
    g.fillRect(0, y2, x2, y2);
    g.drawImage(imgS, offX + 8, offY + 8, this);
    g.drawImage(imgA, offX, offY, this);
  }
}
```

When you run this demo, you see a result similar to Figure 12-3. Pay particular attention to the shadow beneath the image and note that the shadow is translucent, as the places where it crosses between the light and dark areas of the checkerboard pattern show.

Figure 12-3:
The
Antialias
demo
shows how
you can
draw
antialiased
and
translucent
images
(note the
shadow).

Some Java implementations simulate alpha transparency by *dithering* the images, meaning that individual pixels of various colors are combined in a pattern to simulate a blended color. For example, if the color gray is dithered, it may be created using pixels of black and white in a tiny checkerboard pattern, which from a distance looks acceptably gray. However, dithering can look pretty bad in some cases — for example, a thin dithered gray line on a black background appears to be a dotted white line. You're most likely to see dithering when a Web browser displays an image on a monitor that is set to use only 256 colors and so has to approximate colors outside its 256-color palette by combining (dithering) colors it knows how to display. Dithered images can look okay, but they can also look fairly crummy when you use alpha values to blend the edges of images. The best thing to do is test your code on different screen settings to make sure that you get an acceptable image.

Antialiasing in Java

One of the strange omissions in Java's Graphics class is a means to draw antialiased shapes or text. Anything you draw with Java's Graphics class comes out looking ragged around the edges. However, now that you know about using alpha values to antialias images, you can use a technique similar to Photoshop's subpixel rendering (explained in the section "Blending the edges of images with alpha masking" earlier in this chapter) to draw antialiased lines, shapes, and text. The trick is simulating Photoshop's subpixel rendering in Java.

Before you get started, be aware that this method uses features of the Java class library that may not work correctly with all implementations of Java. In particular, some Java implementations, such as many of the Mac versions of Netscape browsers, don't support using `PixelGrabber` to read from an offscreen `Image`.

Rendering to subpixels

Photoshop can render up to 256 levels of alpha but can get good-looking edges on text and other filled and line graphics using only four levels of alpha, as shown in Figure 12-4. You can create four levels of alpha by breaking each pixel up into a 2×2 subpixel grid. Java doesn't provide any means to draw to subpixels, but you can achieve the same result by drawing your image twice as large as your desired result, treating each pixel as if it were a subpixel, and then shrinking the image back down.

Obviously, text and graphics look better when antialiased, as shown in Figure 12-4, but subpixel rendering has other uses, too. For example, antialiasing can preserve details, such as closely spaced, parallel, diagonal lines, that would be difficult to see otherwise. Subpixel rendering takes more CPU time, but in many cases you can create all the antialiased images before the game starts to avoid this penalty.

Figure 12-4:
By rendering to an offscreen image that is 200 percent larger than the size of your final image, you can use the AlphaShrink class to create antialiased text.

Reading from offscreen images

You create your double-sized images by drawing them to an offscreen Image and then using PixelGrabber to convert them into an int[] array of pixel data. You then write code to scan the pixel data while making a regular-sized copy of the pixels, with alpha, in a second int[] array. The idea is that every group of four pixels from the double-sized image (the subpixels) becomes one pixel in the final result. For example, a group of four subpixels with one white and three black pixels will have an alpha value that corresponds to 25 percent opaque, or a value of 63.

Although this process may sound complicated, the code to accomplish all these steps is quite simple. Here's the code for a class called AlphaShrink that does just that:

```java
import java.awt.*;
import java.awt.image.*;


public class AlphaShrink {
  static final int[] vals = {0, 0x66, 0x99, 0xCC, 0xFF};

static ImageProducer shrink (Image src, Color clr,
                int trans) {
  int wid = src.getWidth(null);
  int hyt = src.getHeight(null);
```

```
wid += wid & 1;
hyt += hyt & 1;
int rgb = clr.getRGB() & 0xFFFFFF;
int[] buf = new int[wid * hyt];
PixelGrabber pg = new PixelGrabber(src, 0, 0, wid, hyt,
                   buf, 0, wid);
try {pg.grabPixels();} catch (InterruptedException e) {}
int awid = wid / 2;
int ahyt = hyt / 2;
int[] abuf = new int[awid * ahyt];
for (int yy = 0; yy < ahyt; yy++) {
  for (int xx = 0; xx < awid; xx++) {
    int ii = xx * 2 + yy * 2 * wid;
    int alpha = 0;
    alpha += (buf[ii] & 0xFF) != 0 ? 1 : 0;
    alpha += (buf[ii + 1] & 0xFF) != 0 ? 1 : 0;
    alpha += (buf[ii + wid] & 0xFF) != 0 ? 1 : 0;
    alpha += (buf[ii + wid + 1] & 0xFF) != 0 ? 1 : 0;
    alpha = ((vals[alpha] * trans) << 16) & 0xFF000000;
    abuf[yy * awid + xx] = alpha + rgb;
  }
}
return new MemoryImageSource(awid, ahyt, abuf, 0, awid);
}
}
```

Okay, maybe the code is a little tricky. However, if you break down the steps, you're sure to understand how it works — read on.

The code starts by using PixelGrabber to convert the image into an int array of pixels. Then, it computes the values awid and ahyt to hold the size of the destination, antialiased image, which is one-half the width and height of the source image. The code also allocates the int[] array abuf to receive the antialiased pixels.

Next, shrink() uses two nested for loops to calculate all the pixels of the destination image. Inside the inner for loop, shrink() computes an index into the double-sized source image in the value ii, which indexes the upper-left subpixel in the source image. Then shrink() tests each of the four subpixels to see if the subpixels contain a non-zero value. If a subpixel is non-zero, the corresponding test increments the variable alpha by 1.

After testing all four subpixels, alpha will contain a value in the range 0–4. This value is converted into a value in the range 0–255 by indexing the vals array. This value fetched from vals is multiplied by the value trans to globally adjust the transparency of all the alpha channel values according to the value passed to shrink(). Then, the alpha value is shifted left an additional 16 bits and masked with the value 0xFF000000 to create the alpha channel value for this pixel. Finally, the code adds the alpha value to the value rgb to create the final, antialiased pixel which is copied into the abuf array.

Shrinking text

Here's the code for a demo applet called AntialiasText that calls to AlphaShrink and creates the image shown back in Figure 12-4:

```
import java.awt.*;
import java.applet.Applet;
import java.awt.image.*;

public class AntialiasText extends Applet {
  private Image   img, imgA, imgS;
  private Graphics offscr;
  private int     width, height, offX, offY;

  public void init() {
    width = size().width;
    height = size().height;
    String msg = Antialiased ;
    Font fnt = new Font( TimesRoman , Font.BOLD, 96);
    FontMetrics fm = getGraphics().getFontMetrics(fnt);
    int sWidth = fm.stringWidth(msg);
    int sHeight = fm.getHeight();
    int base = fm.getAscent();
    img = createImage(sWidth, sHeight);
    offscr = img.getGraphics();
    offscr.setFont(fnt);
    offscr.setColor(Color.black);
    offscr.fillRect(0, 0, sWidth, sHeight);
    offscr.setColor(Color.white);
    offscr.drawString(msg, 0, base);
    imgA = createImage(AlphaShrink.shrink(img, Color.black,
                         255));
    imgS = createImage(AlphaShrink.shrink(img,
                         Color.darkGray,
127));
    offX = (width - imgA.getWidth(null)) / 2;
    offY = (height - imgA.getHeight(null)) / 2;
  }
```

```
public void paint (Graphics g) {
  int x2 = width >> 1;
  int y2 = height >> 1;
  g.setColor(Color.gray);
  g.fillRect(0, 0, x2, y2);
  g.fillRect(x2, y2, width - x2, height - y2);
  g.setColor(Color.white);
  g.fillRect(x2, 0, width - x2, height - y2);
  g.fillRect(0, y2, x2, y2);
  g.drawImage(imgS, offX + 8, offY + 8, this);
  g.drawImage(imgA, offX, offY, this);
  }
}
```

Drawing Direct

If you're an experienced code jockey, you may have heard of a technique called *direct draw,* with which you can write pixel data directly to the screen. Java, however, doesn't seem to offer any means to get at screen pixel data. You can write individual pixels in Java using 1 pixel by 1 pixel fillRect() calls, but this is horrendously slow. Using the code in this section will give you a much faster way to draw individual pixels.

Implementing direct draw in Java isn't something you need for every game project, but there are certain types of games that are difficult to code without it. For example, if you want to write games that use a more advanced type of texture mapping to create smooth, fluid movement through a 3-D maze, you need to use direct draw techniques to do it. Also, if you're interested in adapting any public domain C or C++ game code to Java, you may need to write pixels directly.

As discussed in the earlier section "Creating new images with MemoryImageSource," you can use MemoryImageSource to create images from raw pixel data. However, you need to construct a new MemoryImageSource object *each time* you want to update an Image. Because of this limitation, using MemoryImageSource for direct draw animation is a pain in the neck. However, as this section shows, you can build your own custom replacement for MemoryImageSource that is both fast and easy to use.

The `ImageProducer` *interface*

You may remember that `MemoryImageSource` doesn't return an `Image` object directly but, instead, returns a reference to an `ImageProducer`. An `ImageProducer` is an interface that `MemoryImageSource` uses to do a bit of behind-the-scenes magic required to convert raw pixels into images. The `ImageProducer` lets you tap into some of Java's low-level code and inject pixel data directly into images.

You can't use the `ImageProducer` interface to modify pictures that you load, but you can use it to create new images from pixel data. The really neat part is that you can continue to update the pixel data in any images you create this way, meaning that you can allocate an `int[]` array and draw into it *as if* you were drawing directly to the screen. You can then use the `ImageProducer` to copy the new data to the screen whenever you want.

Coding an `ImageProducer`

The `ImageProducer` interface defines five methods you need to write to implement it, as described in Table 12-1.

Table 12-1	`ImageProducer` **Methods**
Method	*What the Method Does*
`addConsumer()`	Tells your `ImageProducer` that an object wants to read its pixel data and registers this object with your `ImageProducer` so that you can send it any new pixel data
`isConsumer()`	Checks whether an object is already registered to receive image updates
`removeConsumer()`	Removes an object from your `ImageProducer`'s list of registered objects
`startProduction()`	Tells your `ImageProducer` to send its pixel data
`requestTopDown` `LeftRightResend()`	Requests that your `ImageProducer` resend its pixel data in left to right, top to bottom order

The `ImageProducer` interface works in combination with another interface called, appropriately, the `ImageConsumer` interface. The `ImageConsumer` interface defines a set of six methods that `ImageProducer` can call in order to deliver the pixel data to an `Image`, as listed in Table 12-2.

Table 12-2	ImageConsumer **Methods**
Method	*What the Method Does*
imageComplete()	ImageProducer calls this method to notify the ImageConsumer that all the pixel data has been sent.
setColorModel()	ImageProducer calls this method to define the color model for your pixel data.
setDimensions()	ImageProducer calls this method to specify the width and height of the Image.
setHints()	ImageProducer calls this method to specify the order in which it sends the pixel data.
setPixels()	ImageProducer calls this method to send the pixel data to the ImageConsumer.
setProperties()	ImageProducer calls this method to define properties for the image.

Dancing the ImageProducer *tango*

In looking over the list of methods in Tables 12-1 and 12-2, you may be tempted to move on to a new chapter and forget all about the ImageProducer interface. We have to admit that writing an ImageProducer isn't a simple undertaking. But the code isn't that complicated to understand after you've seen a working example. And if you construct a class to hide all the details (that is, copy the one we wrote!), you can then write code to use an ImageProducer without bothering with the details ever again.

The class you need to write is called DirectImage. The constructor for DirectImage takes two parameters that specify a width and height, like this:

```
DirectImage dimg = new DirectImage(width, height);
```

This code does all the work of constructing an ImageProducer and gives you back an object that you can use almost exactly like the object returned by MemoryImageSource. For example, you can create an Image from this reference by calling createImage() like this:

```
Image img = createImage(dimg);
```

However, the fun has only just begun. Inside the dimg object is an int[] array called pixels. This array is public, so you can read and write directly to it, like this:

```
dimg.pixels[x * dimg.width + y] = 0xFF0000FF;
```

As shown, you can also reference copies of the width and height data that was stored when the object was created. Here's the code for DirectImage:

```
import java.awt.image.*;
import java.awt.*;
import java.util.*;

class DirectImage implements ImageProducer {
 public int[]  pixels;
 public int    width, height;
 private ColorModel model = ColorModel.getRGBdefault();
 private Vector   consumers = new Vector();
 private Image   img = null;

 DirectImage (int width, int height) {
  this.width = width;
  this.height = height;
  pixels = new int[width * height];
 }

 public synchronized void addConsumer (ImageConsumer ic) {
  if (isConsumer(ic))
   return;
  consumers.addElement(ic);
  ic.setHints(ImageConsumer.TOPDOWNLEFTRIGHT |
       ImageConsumer.SINGLEPASS);
  ic.setDimensions(width, height);
  ic.setProperties(new Hashtable());
  ic.setColorModel(model);
 }

 public synchronized boolean isConsumer (ImageConsumer ic) {
  return consumers.contains(ic);
 }

 public synchronized void removeConsumer (ImageConsumer ic)
  {
consumers.removeElement(ic);
 }
```

```
public void startProduction (ImageConsumer ic) {
 addConsumer(ic);
 Enumeration e = consumers.elements();
 while (e.hasMoreElements()) {
  ImageConsumer icl = (ImageConsumer)e.nextElement();
  icl.setPixels(0, 0, width, height, model, pixels,
       0, width);
  icl.imageComplete(ImageConsumer.SINGLEFRAMEDONE);
 }
}


public void requestTopDownLeftRightResend (ImageConsumer ic)
 {

 }
}
```

When an ImageConsumer wants to receive pixels from an ImageProducer, it must first register with the ImageProducer by calling the ImageProducer's addConsumer() method. The code for DirectImage uses a Vector object called consumers to record all the ImageConsumers that call addConsumer(). addConsumer() then calls various ImageConsumer methods to tell each registering consumer the width, height, and other parameters of the image it produces. The method isConsumer() checks the consumers Vector's contains() method to see whether the consumer ic has already been registered. The removeConsumer() method uses the Vector method removeElement() to unregister an ImageConsumer.

The startProduction() method performs the real work in DirectImage. Each time you call startProduction(), startProduction() checks the list of currently registered consumers and calls each ImageConsumer's setPixels() method to deliver the pixel data. Then it calls each ImageConsumer's imageComplete() method to signal that the update is complete.

Demoing DirectImage

You're probably eager to see how DirectImage works, so here's code for a demo applet called DirectDraw that uses DirectImage to draw a side-scrolling sine wave display, as shown in Figure 12-5.

```
import java.applet.*;
import java.awt.image.*;
import java.awt.*;
```

(continued)

(continued)

```
public class DirectDraw extends Applet implements Runnable {
  private DirectImage  bitmap;
  private Image        bitImg;
  private int          xs, ys;
  private int          width, height;
  private Thread       ticker;
  private boolean      running = false;

  public void init () {
    width = size().width;
    height = size().height;
    bitmap = new DirectImage(width, height);
    bitImg = createImage(bitmap);
  }

  public void paint (Graphics g) {
    bitImg.flush();
    g.drawImage(bitImg, 0, 0, null);
  }

  public void update (Graphics g) {
    paint(g);
  }

  public void run () {
    int off = 0;
    while (running) {
      waveForm(off += 4);
      repaint();
      try {
        ticker.sleep(1000 / 30);
      } catch (InterruptedException e) { ; }
    }
  }

  public void waveForm (int off) {
    for (int ii = 0; ii < bitmap.pixels.length; ii++)
      bitmap.pixels[ii] = 0xFF000000;
    int base = (height >> 1);
    double twoPI = Math.PI * 2;
    double scale = (double) height * 0.75;
    for (int x = 0; x < width; x++) {
      double rad = ((x + off) * twoPI) / width;
```

```
    int y = ((int) (Math.sin(rad) * scale) / 2) + base;
    bitmap.pixels[y * bitmap.width + x] = 0xFFFFFFFF;
    }
  }


public void start () {
  if (ticker == null || !ticker.isAlive()) {
   running = true;
   ticker = new Thread(this);
   ticker.setPriority(Thread.MIN_PRIORITY + 1);
   ticker.start();
  }
 }


public void stop () {
  running = false;
 }
}
```

Be sure to note the call to `Image.flush()` in `DirectDraw`'s `paint()` method, which is the special trick that makes the `ImageProducer` so useful. Normally, the AWT only calls the `ImageProducer` once to create an image and then caches these images in its internal memory so that it can *redraw* them without needing to *re-create* them. However, you *want* the images to be re-created from scratch, so you have to call the image's `flush()` method in order to discard the old cached copy and regenerate a new image.

Figure 12-5:
The
`DirectDraw`
demo
applet
uses the
`DirectImage`
class to
draw an
animated
sine wave
directly into
an `int[]`
array of raw
pixel data.

Modifying GIF Images

One annoying limitation of Java's `PixelGrabber` class is that it converts any image type it reads into an `int[]` array. CD Chapter 4 discusses using indexed color images, such as GIF files, but `PixelGrabber` doesn't provide a way for you to directly read the raw data in a GIF image or to read the *indexed color table* (color palette) used by that image. However, by coding your own `ImageConsumer`, you can tap into GIF image data and extract it yourself.

Getting at the raw image data with the `ImageConsumer` *interface*

The section "Coding an `ImageProducer`" earlier in this chapter briefly introduces the `ImageConsumer` interface, so you may already know that an `ImageConsumer` receives the raw pixel data produced by an `ImageProducer`. Java's `Image` class provides a method called `getSource()` that returns a reference to an `ImageProducer` for any `Image` that you load. By connecting this `ImageProducer` to a custom `ImageConsumer`, you can ask the `ImageProducer` to make the raw data available.

Although connecting `ImageProducer`s to `ImageConsumer`s may sound complicated, the code to do this is fairly simple (and again, we provide it for you to copy and use). To make this code convenient, you need to package it in a new class called `ImageBytes`. Then, whenever you want to read the pixel data in a GIF Image, you can use this new class to construct an `ImageBytes` object, like this:

```
ImageBytes iBytes = new ImageBytes(img);
```

This code invokes the constructor for `ImageBytes` to create the new `iBytes` object. As a side effect, the code in the constructor allocates a `byte[]` array called `iData` in the new `iBytes` object. Then, the constructor code reads all the indexed pixel data from the source image `img` into the `iData` array. After it's constructed, the newly created `iBytes` object contains public variables with which you can read the `width` and `height` of the pixel data and also read the indexed color table for the `Image`. The `iBytes` object also contains a variable called `cModel` that records a reference to the `ColorModel` for `img`. The `ColorModel` for an `Image` isn't normally accessible, so this gives you a way to read the color palette data in addition to the pixel data.

Here's the complete code for the `ImageBytes` class:

```
import java.awt.*;
import java.awt.image.*;
import java.util.*;

public class ImageBytes implements ImageConsumer {
 public int       width, height;
 public byte[]      iData;
 public ColorModel   cModel = null;
 private ImageProducer  pro;

 ImageBytes (Image img) {
  synchronized (this) {
   pro = img.getSource();
   pro.addConsumer(this);
   pro.startProduction(this);
   try { wait(); } catch (InterruptedException e) { }
  }
 }

 public synchronized void imageComplete (int status) {
  pro.removeConsumer(this);
  notify();
 }

 public void setColorModel (ColorModel model) {
  if (model instanceof IndexColorModel && cModel == null)
   cModel = model;
 }

 public void setDimensions (int width, int height) {
  this.width = width;
  this.height = height;
  iData = new byte [width * height];
 }

 public void setHints (int hintflags) {
 }

 public void setPixels (int x, int y, int w, int h,
            ColorModel model, byte pixels[],
            int off, int scansize) {
  int doff = (y * width) + x;
  if (w == scansize && w == width) {
   System.arraycopy(pixels, off, iData, doff, h * w);
  }
```

(continued)

(continued)

```
  else {
   for (int row = 0; row < h; row++) {
    System.arraycopy(pixels, off, iData, doff, w);
    doff += width;
    off += scansize;
   }
  }
 }

 public void setPixels (int x, int y, int w, int h,
          ColorModel model, int pixels[],
          int off, int scansize) {
 }

 public void setProperties (Hashtable props) {
 }
}
```

Note that you don't need to write code for all the methods specified in the
ImageConsumer interface. For example, you don't need to implement the
methods setHints() and setProperties() in ImageBytes. In addition,
because ImageBytes is designed to read indexed color GIF files only, you
need to code only the version of setPixels() that is designed to accept
byte data.

The way ImageBytes works is fairly simple to understand. The constructor
starts the process by calling the getSource() method so that it can talk to
the ImageProducer for the source image. Then it calls the
ImageProducer's addConsumer() method in order to register to receive
image data. Finally, it calls the ImageProducer's startProduction()
method in order to ask the ImageProducer to start delivering the pixels to
the ImageConsumer's setPixels() method.

The ImageProducer calls the methods setDimensions() and
setColorModel() first so that the ImageConsumer can allocate an array in
which to receive the pixel data and save the color model information. Then
the ImageProducer calls the setPixels() method to deliver the pixel data.
Note that setPixels() may be called multiple times, so don't assume that
it receives the data in a single call; interlaced GIF images are especially likely
to cause multiple calls to setPixels().

When all the pixel data has been delivered, the ImageProducer calls the
ImageConsumer s imageComplete() method. Your code should then set
the boolean flag done and call notifyAll() to let the constructor's wait()
call know that the image is loaded.

Recoloring a GIF Image

You can use your new `ImageBytes` class for a whole bunch of operations. One idea is to use `ImageBytes` to read a GIF image, modify its indexed color table, and then use `MemoryImageSource` to create a new image using the modified color table — a useful way to create a variety of images from a single source image. For example, you can recolor the sprite graphics in Chapter 8 to create more enemies. Or you can recolor the wall graphics in Chapter 11 to create earthy brown walls or slimy green walls. By recoloring the same graphic, you save the time it would take to download the extra images that you can, instead, create.

Here's the code for a simple applet called `ModifyGIF` that reads a GIF image and changes all the reds to green, greens to blues, and blues to reds, as is shown in Figure 12-6:

```java
import java.awt.*;
import java.applet.Applet;
import java.awt.image.*;

public class ModifyGIF extends Applet {
  Image   img, src;

  public void init() {
    IndexColorModel  nmod, imod;

    MediaTracker tracker = new MediaTracker(this);
    tracker.addImage(src = getImage(getCodeBase(), note.gif ), 0);
try { tracker.waitForAll(); }
    catch (InterruptedException e) { ; }
ImageBytes pix = new ImageBytes(src);
    imod = (IndexColorModel)pix.cModel;
    int colors = imod.getMapSize();
    byte[] reds = new byte[colors];
    byte[] grns = new byte[colors];
    byte[] blus = new byte[colors];
    imod.getReds(grns);
    imod.getGreens(blus);
    imod.getBlues(reds);
    nmod = new IndexColorModel(imod.getPixelSize(), colors,
               reds, grns, blus,
               imod.getTransparentPixel());
    img = createImage(new MemoryImageSource(pix.width,
               pix.height, nmod, pix.iData,
               0, pix.width));
  }
```

(continued)

(continued)

```
public void paint (Graphics g) {
  g.drawImage(src, 10, 10, null);
  g.drawImage(img, 42, 42, null);
 }
}
```

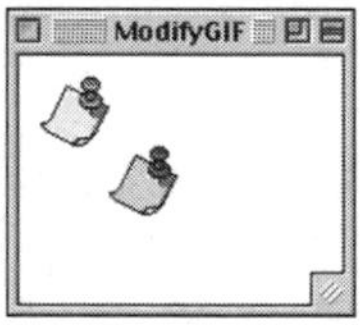

Figure 12-6:
The
ModifyGIF
demo
applet
uses the
ImageBytes
class to
read a GIF
image,
remap the
color table,
and create
a new
image that
uses the
remapped
colors.

Part IV
The Part of Tens

The 5th Wave   By Rich Tennant

"MISS LAMONT, WILL YOU GET ME TECHNICAL SUPPORT AT STRIPOC INTERACTIVE PLEASE?"

In this part . . .

Part IV helps you tackle some of the finer points of game design and style and shows you how to write better Java code. However, the points mentioned in this part are all things that can take time to master. Therefore, you should probably read this section again a few months after reading it the first time. You may be surprised to find that a little time and some experience help you see some of the points discussed in this part in a new light.

Chapter 13

Ten Secrets for Making Fun Games

In This Chapter

▶ Giving the players what they want

▶ Creating games that don't get boring

▶ Making sure your games are ready for the world

*T*his chapter reveals the deep dark secrets known previously only to the inner circle of famous game designers. Be warned that sharing these secrets with mere mortals seriously endangers your chances of membership in this most exclusive of clubs.

Knowing What Players Want

You may be tempted to believe that whatever you think is fun is also fun to everyone else, but different people often have different ideas about what fun is. Some players like games that reward manual dexterity and quick reflexes. Other players prefer games that favor careful analysis over lizard-brain reaction time. Some players even delight in finding ways to beat the system and take their enjoyment from ferreting out weaknesses in the rules of the game or in its code.

People also play games for different reasons. Some people play games to unwind after a stressful day at work or school. Others play games to escape from boredom or to experience a fantasy that could never exist in the real world. Still others play games as a competitive challenge to attain a higher score than anyone else, or at least a score higher than their best friend's highest score.

The challenge in designing a new game is to find ways to make your game appeal to these different types of players. Obviously, you're never going to be able to create games that appeal to absolutely everyone. However, this doesn't mean you can't try. One secret is simply to talk to people who play games and ask them to name their favorite game and, more importantly, ask them to tell you why they enjoy that game. It sounds obvious, but it's easy to forget that other people are your audience.

Internet newsgroups (try `rec.games.*` with just about any game out there as the * part) are a great resource as well. Make it a habit to read what people say about newly released games. However, try to spend most of your time reading about what people *like,* not what they *dislike.* Positive opinions are frequently more informative and well thought-out than pointless ramblings about why some particular game *sucks.*

Understanding What Makes a Game Addictive

When you're having fun, you know it. Whatever you're doing, you almost certainly wish it could go on forever. Playing an addictively fun game creates the same feeling. Even when the player stumbles, an addictive game draws the player right back in. In an exceptionally addictive game, even failure can be exhilarating because the player enjoys savoring how, next time, it's the computer's turn to lose.

The key to creating an addictive game is knowing how to push a player right up to the limit of their skills and no further. An addictive game makes a player feel in control and powerful but demands the player's full attention. When the player makes a mistake or fails to keep up in a challenging game, rather than blame the game for being too hard, the player immediately thinks "Oh, man! I wasn't paying attention. I want to try that again."

Start Easy and Then Increase Difficulty

One way to increase the chances that the player becomes addicted to your game is to ease them in to the action or the plot. In an action game, give the player time to get oriented and master the controls before you start attacking. In a puzzle-based game, make sure that the player has plenty of clues at the start and that the player can solve the initial puzzles in a reasonable amount of time.

As the game advances, slowly increase the difficulty. Make sure that you increase the variety of the challenges as well. For example, instead of making an action game harder by firing more missiles at a player, introduce new types of missiles. An alternate way to increase the difficulty in an action game is to make it harder and harder for the player to find cover, fresh ammo, or a good defensive position.

The best way to increase the difficulty of a game is to give the player more and more to think about. Putting time pressure on the player to make decisions faster as the game progresses further increases the difficulty.

Should I go left or right? Should I have my gun ready or my chain saw? Is something going to ambush me around the next corner? Is that tiny hole in the wall something I should examine more closely, or is it a ruse to lure me into the corner of the room?

Making It Easy to "Step In"

A poor interface design can easily spoil an otherwise well-conceived game. A truly great game, however, has an interface that is nearly invisible to the player. To a champion tennis player, the racket becomes an invisible extension of her hand and arm. The professional race car driver melds with his car, and driving becomes as automatic as thinking his way around a curve.

Game players want the same experience in a game. They want to be able to focus on the game while thinking as little as possible about the computer. If the interface does its job properly, the player forgets about operating a computer and mentally steps into the game world.

Interface design is as much an art as a science, but the most important design goal is simplicity. This sounds obvious, but it's not. Adding just one more feature to your interface design can be sooo tempting. You may only intend these interface add-ons as special features for advanced players, but without realizing it, each new feature you add is as much dead weight as enhancement. Resist the temptation.

Instead, seek to master the art of interface reduction. Step back and look at your interface and ask yourself, "How can I replace two controls with a single control." Even better, ask, "How can I replace three, four, or five controls with one control." If you need inspiration, compare the cockpit of a professional race car with the interior of a consumer sedan; the race car looks spartan by comparison.

Enhancing the Player's Suspension of Disbelief

Suspension of disbelief is a term fiction writers use to describe the trust that readers place in the author to create a believable story. It's the fiction writer's job to craft a story where the details and descriptions seem so believable that you temporarily allow yourself to be convinced that the story is utterly real. However, the reader's suspension of disbelief is a fragile trance, and even a single mistake by the writer may remind the reader that it's only a story.

Games are similar to stories. The key to making believable games is to take the game's central premise seriously. If the game is a mythological fantasy game, don't inject modern weapons or contemporary references. If the game is a military simulation, be sure that you carefully research what weapons and tactics are appropriate to each situation. If you don't take your own creation seriously, the player won't either.

Making the Player Feel Smart

Good puzzle games work on the *Aha!* principle, where the player can easily solve the puzzle after they realize how the materials at hand fit the situation they are trying to solve. For example, when the player realizes that *kcol* and *yek* are spelled backwards, she won't have any problem knowing what to do with them. These flashes of insight into the puzzle's solution make a player feel smart. Players love games that make them feel smart.

Bad puzzle games force the player to guess at solutions or to know facts only the puzzle's designer thinks are obvious. For example, some players may know the Japanese words for lock and key, but the majority of players aren't likely to figure out such a hint. Instead, they solve the puzzle by trial and error. These types of puzzles make the player feel stupid, and no one likes to feel stupid.

What Did I Do Wrong? The Player Should Always Know

When the edge of the cliff crumbles beneath Wile E. Coyote as his latest scheme for catching the Road Runner unravels, he doesn't immediately drop into the canyon. Instead, he experiences that brief "Uh, oh" moment that freezes time just long enough for him to realize he's made a serious mistake. Wile E. Coyote never really gets a chance to catch his mistakes before suffering the consequences, but the player must always have a chance, if even a slim one, to save himself from every potential pitfall.

Games that violate this rule treat the player unfairly. Unfair games make players feel as if the game tricked them into defeat, like losing money to a rigged carnival game. In contrast, if players feel that your game is fair, they may even *enjoy* losing. It's okay to be outfoxed by a clever opponent because, after all, the opponent really played well.

Although designing games to be both challenging and fair is difficult, following some simple rules can help. First, don't exceed the player's reaction time. Missiles that seem to come out of nowhere and hit before even a skilled player can react are definitely unfair. As Chapter 5 points out, you also need to maintain *flow* by making sure that the game is responsive to the player's input. Failing to quickly respond to the player's input is almost as unfair as expecting the player to have lightning reflexes.

Second, foreshadow events to give the player a chance to *anticipate* the coming challenges and opportunities. Computer games sometimes unintentionally foreshadow events with predictable behavior, but used correctly, a little predictability can be a good thing. For example, if the computer bad guys have to stop and reload occasionally, the game gains a bit of realistic predictability.

Cheating Spoils the Fun

Don't let players cheat. If one player gets a high score by cheating the game, it cheapens the accomplishment of players who get the same score without cheating. Players wonder whether other players believe their high score or simply think that they cheated to get it, which can be the kiss of death to a competitive game.

Creating a 100 percent cheat-proof game is impossible, but you can make cheating more difficult. First, don't leave in debugging code that some players may accidentally — or intentionally — discover. Second, consider adding internal checks to try and detect whether players try to cheat by altering the game's code or data. Finally, test your game thoroughly to make sure that you haven't unintentionally programmed some fatal weakness.

Your Friend, Mr. Random Number

If the player can reliably predict the actions of a computerized opponent, defeating the computer is easy. The game may be fun for a few rounds, and the player may momentarily enjoy having outsmarted the machine, but it quickly becomes boring. A human would make an ideal opponent, but programming a computer to act as unpredictably as a human is surprisingly difficult.

As Chapter 13 points out, a simple solution, and one that is surprisingly effective, is to make sure that you always build a random component into your game's strategy engine. You may think that you've invented the next breakthrough in artificial intelligence, but players are amazingly good at finding ways to make computer opponents self-destruct.

Randomizing the randomness helps too. For example, make a random percentage of the monsters stupid by making them only partially effective at navigating mazes and let the remaining monsters be smart by using your full maze search strategy (see Chapter 13). The smart monsters will probably find a better route to attack the player than the stupid monsters, which makes it harder for the player to anticipate the direction from which the monsters will attack

Playtesting

Thorough playtesting is probably the single most important thing you can do to increase your chances of making a hit game. However, knowing what you can expect to discover from playtesting and what you can't is important. Just as too many cooks can spoil the broth, trying to accommodate every request from a playtester can inflict a fatal wound on a good game.

Getting complete strangers to test your code is vitally important — this is the essence of true playtesting. Don't simply rely on friends and family, because they'll be tempted to tell you what want to hear to avoid hurting your feelings. Also, stay out of the room when other people are playing your game. Your presence will influence how they play. Setting up a camcorder to tape the action for later viewing is workable, but it may still make some people uncomfortable.

Your primary goal in playtesting is to discover any fundamental flaws that you need to rethink at the design level. Sometimes it's difficult to recognize that a dozen "minor" complaints may really be a design flaw in disguise. To identify design flaws, sort problem reports into categories and then ask yourself if all the problems in each category may result from some common mistake the playtesters are making. If you answer yes, your game probably needs some redesign.

Chapter 14
Ten Ways to Say "Game Over"

In This Chapter

▶ Baiting players to play again

▶ Giving credit where credit is due

▶ Creating instant replays and other animation

*P*layers expect to see more than "You Win" at the conclusion of a hard fought battle for control of the world. Likewise, most players don't appreciate having a defeat rubbed in with a message like "You Lose, Bozo!" A well-designed game needs to display a bit more class in how it handles the end of a game. This chapter discusses these issues and also talks about ending animations, scoring, consolation messages, and, of course, credits.

Fading to Black

The simplest way to signal game over, especially when the player has lost, is to freeze the action and slowly fade the screen to black. Then, after a respectful pause, in commemoration of all the time the player has invested trying to win, it's okay to fade up a tactful, "The End." But unless you want to get nasty e-mail, resist the temptation to taunt the player with insulting messages.

You have a variety of ways to code a screen fade. Chapter 12 shows how to use the alpha channel to fade graphics between opaque and fully transparent. Apply this effect on top of a black background image and you have an instant fade to black. You may also try a dither fade, which randomly erases pixels from the screen until the screen is completely erased.

Rolling the Credits

Forcing the player to wait through a list of credits before he can start to play the game is a big no-no. Immediately jumping to a list of credits the moment the game has ended is also slightly rude. Sure, you deserve to display your name and the names of everyone who helped create the game, but you need to do it with *style*.

Start by including a respectful moment of silence after the game has ended. Then, bring up the credits at a reasonable reading speed. (If you want anyone to have a chance of remembering your name, you have to give them time to read it.) You can check the timing by reading the credits aloud.

You're also more likely to get people to read the credits if you add in a bit of entertainment. The old Monty Python TV episodes and films, for example, used a variety of comedy gags, such as listing humorously fake credits to keep viewers interested in reading them. If comedy isn't your style, you can roll the credits on top of memorable graphics taken from the game so that the player can remember some of the more exciting moments in the game while reading the credits.

The CD contains a simple example applet that demonstrates how to combine the text centering code from CD Chapter 3 with the animation code from Chapter 1 to create scrolling text.

Providing an Instant Replay

Many players enjoy watching an instant replay of the moments leading up to victory. The *Virtual World* location-based entertainment centers, for example, provide players with a post-battle *debriefing* where they can watch an accelerated replay of the game.

If you plan your code properly, you can record the data you need to provide a replay using the same code the game uses to display the game. You can also display the game replay in a small inset window and roll the credits at the same time.

For example, you can use a Vector object to record the moves a player makes through the 3-D perspective maze described in Chapters 10 and 11. Then, after the player has solved the maze, you can show a replay of the player's moves on a 2-D display, like that shown in Chapter 7.

Scoring and Points: The Competitive Obsession

Although points and scoring aren't for everyone, some players *strongly agree* with Vince Lombardi's line, "Winning isn't everything. It's the *only* thing." Competitive players may also strongly agree with the axiom, "If you're not keeping score, you're only practicing." For these players, a good score is more of a reward than winning, and the only thing better is getting a higher score next time.

Competitive players expect a game to compute scores accurately and fairly, and they prefer to understand how the game computes the scores so that they can play for maximum points. Carefully check all code that computes scores for errors and omissions. A competitive player may tolerate a glitch in the graphics or a hiccup in the sound, but a mistake in computing the score is just *unforgivable!*

Point scores help players quantify their progress and give them an objective measure of what they've accomplished. For some players, improving a previous high score by even a few points can boost them to try even harder the next time. And don't just flash the score for a few seconds — leave it on screen so that players can show it off to the family, a few friends, the neighbors, and anyone else they can round up.

Marking Levels of Achievement

If a numerical score doesn't quite fit the style of your game, reward players by bestowing titles to indicate general levels of achievement. For example, in a military flight simulation, you can reward the player by awarding titles that parallel military rank. Alternately, in a role-playing simulation, you could establish increasing levels of skill, such as novice, apprentice, master, and so on.

You can also enhance the game play if you code these levels so that they grant the player more than just a fancy title. For example, allow a high-ranking player to fly more advanced types of aircraft in your military flight simulation. Or in your fantasy dungeon game, give the player access to magical powers after attaining some advanced skill level.

Achievement levels give players alternate ways to measure their advancement and can help pull them into the game's fantasy world. Some types of games, such as computer role-playing games and puzzle-based adventure games, take hours or days of playing time to win. Earning a few titles along the way helps motivate players to press on to ultimate victory.

Ranking One Player against Another

If getting a high score is fun, getting a score higher than your arch rival is even more fun. You can help players squeeze an extra bit of enjoyment from a victory if you tell them something about how their score compares to other players.

One way to show such a comparison is to maintain a list of high scores and simply tell them where their score places them on the list. However, this list won't mean much if it only contains that player's previous scores. Therefore, consider compiling a list of scores from your playtesters and include these scores as the initial values in the list of a new game.

You may also want to consider recording other factors and statistics in your list, such as the total playing time required to attain a given high score, the total number of hits or misses, or the total number of rounds fired. Using this data, you can compute all sorts of new ways to rank players. You can report, for example, that the player is the first player to break 10,000 points in less than 10 minutes of total play. Keeping additional statistics also gives the player other goals to shoot for and other ways to play the game.

Reusing Game Code to Make an Ending Animation

Game-ending animations can be complex and time-consuming to create because players expect a reward commensurate with the time they invest in playing a game. In truth, few ending animations ever do justice to what players imagine is their just reward for winning. However, don't get stuck on the idea that the only solution is creating some fantastic animation using a state-of-the-art 3-D rendering program. Improving the game play is a better way to invest your hours. Instead, consider using your game code as the source of your ending animation. With a few extra graphics you can create a nice ending sequence.

For example, say you've used the Texture-Mapped 3-D Maze code from Chapter 11 to create your own dungeon-style adventure game. The game ends when the player locates the power amulet hidden in the maze. However, simply flashing some "You Win" text on the screen is pretty boring. Instead, you can add a bit of code to make the walls of the maze vanish one by one until the player is left standing in a completely open area. Then, after this tiny bit of drama, you can flash up a more thematic message, such as "Your skill has destroyed the maze!" Okay, the example's a bit corny, but you get the idea.

Offering a Practice Round

In arcade-style games the player usually has to complete lower levels to challenge the next level. When the game ends, the player has to start all over and work back up through the lower levels in order to try and complete the level that beat him the last time through. You can lessen the player's frustration by offering the player a practice round at the new level. Doing so gives the player a chance to get familiar with the layout of the new level and encourages the player to try again.

Losing Should Even Be Fun

Although there may be other reasons people play games, people do expect a game to be fun. Occasionally, however, some game designer gets it in his or her head that the purpose of a game is to demonstrate the designer's prowess at crafting a game that is exceptionally difficult to win. This is egomania without redeeming social value.

Although the goal of a good game designer is to help people have fun, your skill as a game designer is tested not when someone wins your game, but when they lose. If you've done your job right, losing players sigh and then laugh and say to themselves, "I gotta try that again."

Thanking Players for an Enjoyable Game

"Thank you for an enjoyable game" is how HAL, the sentient computer in Stanley Kubrick's classic film *2001,* attempts to console astronaut Frank Poole after besting him in a game of chess. However, even though HAL tries to simulate human politeness and concern, his attempts seem hollow and slightly creepy. Computers are not people, and attempts to make them act human often fall flat.

Although you may be tempted to try to make a player feel better by printing messages like "Nice try!" or "You almost had me that time," don't. Hardly anyone is impressed by this phony display of feigned encouragement. Some players think that it's corny, and others find it downright obnoxious.

A better strategy to encourage the player is to report objective facts that can induce the player to try again. For example, instead of the trite phrase "You almost had me that time," tell the player how close, in points or time or percentage of puzzles solved, the player came to winning.

Chapter 15

Ten Ways to Optimize Your Java Code

. . . .

In This Chapter

▶ Profiling your code to see where it spends its time

▶ Using faster methods and variables

▶ Coding a faster loop

▶ Using a few tricks to take the bite out of synchronizing your code

▶ Making your applet download faster by keeping it small

. . . .

Frequently, the difference between a fun game and one that is painful to play is how fast the game runs. If the game doesn't keep up with the player, the player isn't likely to stick with the game. The best way to make sure that your game's performance is up to snuff is to use a good design and efficient algorithms. No amount of optimizing can overcome a bad design or algorithm.

As soon as your game *works* and you're confident that your design and algorithms are sound, you're ready to look for that extra performance tweak to push the pedal to the metal. This chapter outlines some techniques to make your game run an extra 5 to 20 percent faster.

Code Profiling: Finding Where the Time Goes

As a general rule, a game spends 90 percent of its time executing 10 percent of its code. Optimizing the other 90 percent of the code that accounts for only 10 percent of the execution time has no noticeable effect on performance. If you make that 90 percent of the code execute twice as fast, the program only runs 5 percent faster. So the first task in optimizing code is to identify the part of the program that consumes most of the execution time, which isn't always where you expect it to be.

A *code profiler* is a program that monitors your code as it executes and records statistics about where it spends its time and how many times it calls each method or constructor.

To find out where your game is spending its time, invoke the Java profiler (included with the Java Development Kit [JDK] on the CD at the back of this book) from the DOS or other operating system command line, like this:

```
java_g -prof sun.applet.AppletViewer myApplet.html
```

Where `myApplet.html` is the name of the Hypertext Markup Language (HTML) document that invokes your game applet. (Unfortunately, the Macintosh doesn't have a command line from which to invoke the Java interpreter, so this option isn't available.)

The profiler keeps track of the time your game spends in each method and writes the information to the text file called java.prof.

The profiler for Java 1.0.2 is buggy and you may have problems running it or getting useful results. The Java 1.1 profiler is better behaved.

A Shifty Divide

A simple technique to speed up your code is to accomplish the same result with an instruction that executes faster. On most processors, division is the slowest arithmetic operation — sometimes more than 20 times slower than addition. If you only do an occasional division here or there, it's no big deal. However, if you divide lots of integers by constants that are a power of two (2, 4, 8, 16, ...), it's faster to replace the division with a right shift.

Each bit you shift the value right by divides the value by two. So to divide by 8 ($2 \times 2 \times 2$), you shift right by 3:

```
(val >> 3) == (val / 8)
```

You can do the same thing with multiply, but the speed improvement is less. A left shift is anywhere from 0 to 4 times faster than a multiply on most modern processors:

```
(val << 3) == (val * 8)
```

Chapter 7 includes a sidebar with additional discussion of these types of operations, known as *bitwise operations*.

Inline Methods with the Compiler

The javac compiler that comes with the JDK provides a simple optimization that *inlines* certain small methods in your class files. The compiler can inline `private`, `static`, or `final` methods.

The compiler *inlines* a method by replacing the code that calls the method with the code that the method executes. Instead of calling the method, the inlined code executes the method directly.

To inline methods between all classes in the current directory, invoke the compiler from the DOS or other operating system command line like this:

```
javac -O *.java
```

A bug in the Java 1.0.2 compiler — fixed in version 1.1 — inlines methods that access nonpublic members of the class that the JVM doesn't allow the calling method to access. When the Java Virtual Machine (JVM) executes improperly inlined code, it throws an `IllegalAccessError`. If you get this error, recompile the files without the optimization. Note that you can always safely optimize your files by compiling them one at a time with the optimization on; only calls that occur between classes cause the problem.

If you are using an integrated development environment (IDE), such as Symantec Café or Metrowerks CodeWarrior, you need to enable the Java optimizations in the IDE.

The `javac -O` (minus O — as in the letter O) option also removes the debugging information from your class file that tells the debugger what line in your source file generates each instruction. Eliminating this information reduces the size of the class file but also eliminates the source file and line-number information printed by an exception.

Do Once, Use Often

Don't do something twice when you can do it once. This maxim may seem obvious, but you can violate it easily when writing code. Can you spot the five operations that the following code repeats unnecessarily?

```
if (p instanceof Point && Math.sqrt(x) < ((Point)p).x) {
    d = Math.sqrt(x) * x * y - ((Point)p).y / limit);
    y *= x;
    buf[i] = buf[i] + ((Point)p).y / limit);
}
```

Most people can spot one or two of the repeated operations, but even highly skilled programmers are likely to miss at least one. The five repeated operations are as follows:

- ✔ **The expressions to calculate both** d **and** buf[i] **perform the operation** ((Point)p).y / limit).

- ✔ **Both the** if **test and the expression to calculate** d **perform the operation** Math.sqrt(x).

- ✔ **The expressions to calculate both** d **and** y **perform the operation** x * y.

- ✔ **The expression to calculate** buf[i] **performs the array load operation** buf[i] **twice.**

- ✔ ((Point)p) **casts** p **to a** Point **three times. Even after fixing the duplicate** ((Point)p).y / limit)**, the code still casts** p **twice. Casting takes longer than storing the result in a local variable, so this is an unnecessarily repeated operation.**

The optimized version of this code is

```
if (p instanceof Point) {
    Point pt = (Point)p;
    double sqrtX = Math.sqrt(x);
    if (sqrtX < pt.x) {
        int ylim = pt.y / limit;
        y *= x;
        d = sqrtX * y - ylim;
        buf[i] += ylim;
    }
}
```

Faster Variables

A variable's scope and type determine its performance. Local method variables are the fastest scope of variables, and object references and ints are the fastest types of variables, so local ints are a good choice for fast variables.

A variable's *scope* is the range of code that can access the variable. For example, method parameters and local variables have less scope than a private field, which has less scope than a public static field.

The JVM performs operations on `byte`, `short`, and `char` values as `int`s; assigning the results to a variable of the corresponding type requires an explicit cast. In the following example, you have to cast the `int` value (`b + c`) in order to assign it to a `byte` variable.

```
byte a, b, c;
a = (byte) (b + c);
```

This cast requires an extra bytecode instruction, which is another penalty for using smaller types. Use an `int` unless you have a clear reason to use one of the smaller integral types.

The Java compiler turns your source files into class files. The code instructions in the class file are called *bytecodes* because they occupy a byte (0 to 255).

A Faster Loop

Your basic `for` loop looks like this:

```
for (i = 0; i < N; i++) {
    // do something
}
```

If the code inside the loop doesn't need the loop variable `i` to count from 0 to `N-1`, restructure the loop to use a more efficient test:

```
for (i = N; --i >= 0; ) {
    // do something
}
```

Rather than comparing `i` against `N` at each iteration, which requires the JVM to load `N`, the restructured loop takes advantage of the efficient checks against 0. Comparing against zero is almost always more efficient in *any* language because the processor bases the underlying tests on $< 0, <= 0, == 0, != 0, >= 0,$ and > 0.

Depending on the JVM, the instruction to decrement the variable `i` in the second example may perform a free comparison of the result against zero. In this case, no additional code is executed to compare `i` against zero.

Faster Methods

Three factors determine the speed of a method invocation:

- ✔ **Is the method** `synchronized?` Synchronized methods take longer to invoke — up to 50 times longer on some Java runtimes — because the JVM has to obtain the lock for the object. See CD Chapter 2 for a description of synchronized methods and locks.

- ✔ **Can the compiler *statically* resolve the class for the method or does the JVM have to *dynamically* resolve the class?** In order to statically resolve a method, the compiler must be able to determine absolutely which method to invoke. The compiler can resolve methods declared as `static`, `private`, and `final`, as well as all constructors. Dynamically resolved method calls are slower because the runtime code has to look at the object to determine whether to call an overridden version of the method.

- ✔ **Is the reference used to invoke the method an interface?** Interface methods take longer to invoke because the JVM has to look at both the object and the interface declaration to figure out which method to call.

Not only is it good programming practice to declare methods as `private` that you only call from within a class, but it makes your code faster as well. (This is one of those rare instances where good style and optimization go hand-in-hand.)

Declare methods that you don't need to override as `final`; you can also declare the entire class `final` if you don't need to subclass it. Declaring a class `final` implicitly declares all the methods in the class as `final`. However, take care not to hinder your ability to extend your game in the future by declaring methods `final` that you may want to override later.

Don't get overly ambitious removing synchronization from methods just to make them faster. You can too easily introduce subtle and hard-to-find bugs in multithreaded code by failing to synchronize code that needs it. CD Chapter 2 discusses how to tell which methods you need to synchronize.

Reduce the Cost of Synchronizing

After you have the lock for an object, you don't need to synchronize on the object again. If you have a heavily synchronized class that calls lots of synchronized methods from other synchronized methods, have the synchronized methods delegate the work to private nonsynchronized methods in order to avoid the overhead of reacquiring the lock. For example,

```
class ThreadSafe {
    public synchronized void setStuff () {
        doSetStuff();
    }

    private doSetStuff () {
        // setStuff code goes here
    }

    synchronized void doLotsOfStuff () {
        doSetStuff();  // instead of calling setStuff()
        // do more stuff...
    }
}
```

Beware of Large Array Initializers

When using arrays in Java, remember how the compiler implements an array *initializer*. The compiler produces code to initialize the array at runtime one element at a time. For example, the compiler translates this array initializer:

```
byte[][] myData = {{1, 2}, {3, 4}};
```

into the same bytecodes produced by this version:

```
byte[][] myData = new byte[2][];
myData[0] = new byte[2];
myData[0][0] = 1;
myData[0][1] = 2;
myData[1] = new byte[2];
myData[1][0] = 3;
myData[1][1] = 4;
```

This array initialization has a couple of ramifications:

  ✔ **It can bloat your class files to embed data in arrays.** The code to initialize the array can take up to five times more space in your class file than the data, so a 10K array of bytes can add up to 50K to the size of your class file! For data of any significant size, loading the data from a separate file is faster.

✔ **A local variable array initializer executes all this code** *each time you call the method,* **which increases the time the method takes to execute.** Declare the array as a static or instance member in order to eliminate the initialization for each method call. Even if you need a fresh copy of the array each time you call the method, for nontrivial arrays, storing and making a copy of a single initialized array is faster.

The Fastest Way to Copy Arrays

Call `System.arraycopy()` to copy more than a few array elements.

```
int[] a = new int[50], b = new int[50];
System.arraycopy(a, 0, b, 0, a.length);
```

Remember that Java doesn't have true multidimension arrays — only arrays of arrays. Both `System.arraycopy()` and `clone()` do only a shallow copy of the outermost dimension of a multidimension array. The original array and the copy share the internal arrays unless you individually copy or clone them, like this:

```
int[][] a = new int[50][20], b = new int[50][20];
for (int i = a.length;  --i >= 0; )
    System.arraycopy(a[i], 0, b[i], 0, a[i].length);
```

Appendix

What's on the CD-ROM

On the CD-ROM:

▶ The Java Development Kit (JDK), a bare-bones development environment for creating Java programs

▶ Microsoft Internet Explorer, a Java-capable Web browser for viewing and running Java applets

▶ Five bonus chapters on the fundamental aspects of Java programming

▶ The games and applets found in this book plus several cool bonus applets

▶ Various sound utilities for creating, tweaking, and converting sounds to the sound file format used by Java programs

System Requirements

Make sure that your computer meets the minimum system requirements listed below. If your computer doesn't match up to most of these requirements, you may have problems in using the contents of the CD.

✔ A PC with a 486 or faster processor, or a Mac OS computer with a 68040 or faster processor. For best performance, we recommend a PC with a Pentium or 586 processor, or a Mac OS computer with a PowerPC processor.

✔ Microsoft Windows 95 or later, Microsoft Windows NT 4.0 or later, or Mac OS system software 7.5.5 or later. For Macintosh, Mac OS 7.6.1 or later is needed and Mac OS 8 is recommended in order to install the latest version of Java.

✔ At least 16MB of total RAM installed on your computer. For best performance, we recommend that your computer have at least 32MB of RAM installed.

✔ If you already have Java installed on your computer's hard drive, then you need at least 50MB of hard drive space available to install the other software from this CD. (You need less space if you don't install every program.)

If you need to install Java, then you need an additional 22MB of hard drive space for the Windows version of Java, or an additional 4MB for the Macintosh version. (Mac OS 8 includes most of what you need for Java.)

✔ A CD-ROM drive.

✔ A sound card for PCs. (Mac OS computers have built-in sound support.)

✔ A monitor capable of displaying at least 256 colors or grayscale. For best performance, we strongly recommend a color monitor.

If you need more information on the basics, check out *PCs For Dummies,* 4th Edition, by Dan Gookin; *Macs For Dummies,* 4th Edition by David Pogue; or *Windows 95 For Dummies,* 2nd Edition, by Andy Rathbone (all published by IDG Books Worldwide, Inc.).

Using the CD with Microsoft Windows 95 or NT 4.0

1. **Insert the CD into your computer's CD-ROM drive.**

   Give your computer a moment to take a look at the CD.

2. **When the light on your CD-ROM drive goes out, double click on the My Computer icon. (It's probably in the top-left corner of your desktop.)**

   This action opens the My Computer window, which shows you all the drives attached to your computer, the Control Panel, and a couple other handy things.

3. **Double-click the icon for your CD-ROM drive.**

   Another window opens, showing you all the folders and files on the CD.

4. **Double-click the file called License.txt.**

   We're sure you'll want to use the CD, and by using the CD you agree to abide by the license agreement, so read through the license agreement and nod your head. When you are done reading the license, close the program — most likely Windows Notepad — that displayed the file.

5. **Double-click the file called Readme.txt.**

   This file contains instructions about installing the software from this CD. You may find it helpful to leave this text file open while you are using the CD.

6. **Follow the instructions in the "Getting to the Content" section in this appendix.**

Using the CD with Mac OS

To install the items from the CD to your hard drive, follow these steps.

1. **Insert the CD into your computer's CD-ROM drive.**

   In a moment, an icon representing the CD you just inserted appears on your Mac desktop. Chances are, the icon looks like a CD-ROM.

2. **Double-click the CD icon to show the CD's contents.**

3. **Double click the file called License.txt.**

   We're sure you'll want to use the CD, and by using the CD you agree to abide by the license agreement, so read through the license agreement and nod your head. When you are done reading the license, close the program — most likely SimpleText — that displayed the file.

4. **Double-click the Read Me First icon.**

   This text file contains information about the CD's programs and any last-minute instructions you need to know about installing the programs on the CD that we don't cover in this appendix.

5. **To install most programs, just drag the program's folder from the CD window and drop it on your hard drive icon.**

6. **Some programs come with installer programs—with those you simply open the program's folder on the CD, and double-click the icon with the words "Install" or "Installer."**

7. **Follow the instructions in the "Getting to the Content" section in this appendix to start browsing the CD for the applets and other stuff.**

Getting to the Content

This section describes how to access the Java applets described in this book, a variety of bonus applets, the source code for these applets, and the bonus CD chapters. In order to use the Java applets, you need to have a Java-capable Web browser installed on your computer. (Java-capable browsers include Netscape 4.0 and Microsoft Internet Explorer 4.0.) In order to read the CD chapters, you need to have Adobe Acrobat Reader installed. See the "What You'll Find" section later in this appendix for descriptions of the CD content and specifics about accessing the particular items.

If you don't yet have a Java-capable browser or Adobe Acrobat Reader, you're in luck: The CD includes both Microsoft Internet Explorer 4.0 and Adobe Acrobat Reader for both Mac OS and Windows 95 and NT. If you use a PC, skip to the section, "Installing Programs," to find out how to install these programs. If you use a Mac, go back to Step 5 in the "Using the CD with Mac OS" section.

1. **Insert the CD into your computer's CD-ROM drive.**

2. **Launch your Web browser (be sure that it's Java-capable and that the Java options are turned on).**

3. **Click File⇨Open (Internet Explorer) or File⇨Open File (Netscape).**

   A File open dialog box appears.

4. **Browse to the CD-ROM drive.**

5. **Double-click the file JGPFD.HTM in the root directory of the CD-ROM.**

   The *Java Game Programming For Dummies* Web page appears in your browser complete with links to all the applets discussed in the book, some additional applets, the applet code, the bonus CD chapters, links to Internet Web sites, and more.

6. **Explore the Web page to your heart's content.**

   After you have installed the programs that you want, you can eject the CD. Carefully place it back in the plastic jacket of the book for safe-keeping.

Installing Programs

This section provides instructions on how to install the various programs included on the CD.

1. **Follow the instruction in the previous section, "Getting to the Content."**

2. **Click the Extras icon on the Java Game Programming For Dummies page (JGPFD.HTM).**

   Browse the Extras page to learn about the software on the CD and for links to the Web sites for the software authors and vendors.

3. **To install the software, browse the CD using Windows Explorer or the Mac's Finder.**

   Each program has a folder on the CD. For the exact path and installer file name, see the descriptions of the programs on the Extras page or in the "What You'll Find" section of this appendix.

   After you have installed the programs that you want, you can eject the CD. Carefully place it back in the plastic jacket of the book for safekeeping.

What You'll Find

Here's a summary of the software on this CD.

The Java Development Kit

For Windows and Mac OS. In case you don't have a Java programming environment, the CD includes the Java Development Kit (JDK) from Sun Microsystems, the creator of Java. The JDK contains everything you need to compile and test Java applets and applications. JDK 1.1.5 is included for Windows and JDK 1.0.2 for Mac OS.

On the Windows version of the JDK, you run the tools (such as the compiler) from the DOS command-line interface. On the Mac version of the JDK, you drag the files you want to compile or run on top of the appropriate application.

For more information and updates of the JDK, visit Sun Microsystem's Java Web site: http://java.sun.com. The JDK is © 1997 by Sun Microsystems, Inc. 2550 Garcia Ave., Mtn. View, CA 94043-1100 USA. All rights reserved.

The JDK is a minimal environment for creating Java programs. There are several commercial Integrated Development Environments (IDEs) for Java that you may want to check out. An IDE integrates the editor, compiler, debugger, project management and other tools into a single environment to boost your programming productivity. Metrowerks CodeWarrior and Symantec Café are both excellent Java IDEs that offer versions for both Windows and Mac OS.

The Macintosh version of the JDK included on the CD is version 1.0.2 from Sun Microsystems. Although JDK 1.0.2 is all you need to compile and run the applets in this book and on the CD, this is an old (in Java terms) version of the JDK. Since version 1.0.2, Apple Computer has assumed the task of creating Mac OS versions of Java. Mac OS 8 and later come with Macintosh Runtime for Java (MRJ) and include everything you need to run Java programs. To develop and compile Java programs, Apple provides the MRJ SDK (Software Development Kit). You can get a more recent version of Java by downloading the latest version of the MRJ SDK from http://applejava.apple.com. Note that only MRJ SDK 2.0.1 and later include a compiler.

To install the JDK for Windows, open the JDK115 folder on your CD and run JDK115.EXE. You can also browse the JDK documentation in the JDK115/DOCS folder. If you have trouble viewing the files in the DOCS folder, you can run the self extractor JDKDOCS.EXE and copy all of the documentation (10MB) to your hard drive.

To install the JDK for Macintosh, open the JDK1.0.2 folder and run the JDK-1_0_2-MacOS.sea. To use the documentation, run JDK API Documentation.sea.

Microsoft Internet Explorer 4.0

For Windows and Mac OS. Internet Explorer 4.0 is a free Java-capable Web browser that you can use to run all of the applets in this book and on the CD. Separate versions for Windows and Mac OS are included on the CD.

Netscape Navigator (not included on the CD) is another free Web browser that you can also use to run Java applets on either Windows or Mac OS. You can download the latest version of Netscape Navigator from http://home.netscape.com/download/index.html.

To install IE4, open the MSIE4 folder and run IE4SETUP.EXE for Windows, or IE 4.0 Full 68K Installer or IE 4.0 Full PPC Installer for the Mac.

Adobe Acrobat Reader

For Windows and Mac OS. Adobe Acrobat Reader is a free program for reading Portable Document Format (PDF) files, many of which are included on the CD. You need to use this program to read the CD Chapters.

To install Acrobat Reader, open the ACROBAT folder, and run AR32E301.EXE in Windows, or Acrobat Reader 3.01 Installer on the Mac.

CD Bonus Chapters

The CD contains five additional chapters on Java Fundamentals that just wouldn't fit in this book. The CD Chapters are stored in Adobe Acrobat PDF format and can be viewed using the Adobe Acrobat Reader.

To view the Bonus chapters, you must have Adobe Acrobat Reader installed. Launch the Reader, then click File⇨Open. The Bonus chapter files are located in the BONUS folder on the CD, and are called CDCHAP#.PDF, where # is the CD chapter number.

CD Chapter 1: An Applet a Day

This chapter shows you how to create applets and add them to an HTML document. It discusses the life-cycle of an applet and the important applet methods called by the Web browser. This chapter also discusses how to pass parameters from HTML and then read the parameters from an applet.

CD Chapter 2: Using Threads

This chapter shows you how to use Java's built-in multithreading capabilities to create programs that do more than one thing at a time. It includes an in-depth discussion of special issues related to using threads in applets, and how to avoid some common pitfalls of multithreaded programming. The applets in the rest of this book make heavy use of Java's multithreading capabilities and consequently contain many references to this chapter which explains thread concepts in easy-to-understand terms.

CD Chapter 3: Getting Savvy with Graphics

This chapter discusses how to use the Abstract Window Toolkit (AWT) Graphics class to perform basic draw operations, such as drawing lines, circles, and rectangles.

CD Chapter 4: Adding Color to Cool

This chapter shows how to specify colors in Java for drawing. It explains the RGB color format and why the same RGB color looks different on different computers. This chapter also reveals the secrets of the 216-color browser-safe palette that you can use to make your game look the same (or at least as close as you can get) on most player's computer screens.

CD Chapter 5: User Input

This chapter explains how to respond to mouse and keyboard events. It discusses the important concept of *focus,* which you need to understand in order to use the keyboard to control your games. This chapter also includes a complete roadmap to where and how to catch and respond to any event generated by any of the AWT components.

Applets and More Applets

To see these applets in action, start your Web browser and open the file JGPFD.HTM, located at the root of the CD. This file contains a visual index, arranged by chapter, of every applet and game presented in this book and in the CD Chapters, plus several bonus applets. Each applet is presented on its own Web page accessed by a link from the JGPFD.HTM index page. The source code for the applets is located in the AUTHOR folder, and can be viewed by clicking on the links to the source files included in the applet HTML files.

 In Windows, if you have trouble viewing the files within the AUTHOR folder, or loading the applets from the CD, you probably still have a 16 bit driver for your CD-ROM drive. We have included a self-extractor, JGPFD.EXE, at the root of the CD. Running the self extractor will copy all of the files from the AUTHOR folder as well as JGPFD.HTM to your hard drive, to a folder called C:\JGPFD, and avoid this drive problem. Alternately, you can probably find and download an updated driver from the Microsoft Web site or the Web site of your CD-ROM drive manufacturer.

CD Chapter 1	HelloWorld
	HelloMessage
CD Chapter 2	Blink — Bonus Applet!
	Radar — Bonus Applet!
CD Chapter 3	DrawMethods
	CenterText
CD Chapter 4	WebColors
	WebColorPicker — Bonus Applet!
CD Chapter 5	ActionEvents
Chapter 1	Ball
Chapter 2	Ponglet
Chapter 3	HoleInOne
Chapter 4	JavaPool
	Intersect — Bonus Applet!
Chapter 5	Puzzle
Chapter 6	ColoredApplet
	ScoreLabel
	ListEntry
	ImageButton
	FlowLayout
	BorderLayout
	GridLayout
	Blackjack
Chapter 7	BlockMaze
	WallMaze
Chapter 8	SpriteMaze
	SpriteMaze (changeable maze) — Bonus Applet!
Chapter 9	Timeline Demo — Bonus Applet!
	ScriptMaze — Bonus Applet!
Chapter 10	PolyMaze
	PolyMaze (shaded)
	PolyMaze (shaded, maze generation)
Chapter 11	ImageScale
	ImageTile
	Bresenham
	TexMapMaze
Chapter 12	AlphaGradient
	AntiAliasDemo
	AntiAliasText
	ModifyGIF
	DirectDraw
Chapter 14	ScrollText — Bonus Applet!

Chinese Checkers for Java

This applet is a multiplayer Java version of the popular board game. This game was created by programmer Miltiadis Mitrakas, and is included on the CD-ROM with his kind permission.

To run Chinese Checkers for Java, launch your Java-enabled browser, and open the file CCJPAGE.HTM in the CHECKERS folder. If you have trouble accessing the files in the CHECKERS folder in Windows, you can run the self extractor CHECKERS.EXE from the CD and move the files to your hard drive.

GoldWave 3.24

For Windows 95. GoldWave 3.24 is a nifty shareware program for Windows written by Chris Craig. GoldWave 3.23 can open and play the .au files used by Java and some Web pages, and can convert to and from many sound formats. Special effects such as Doppler, distortion, echo, flange, and transpose can alter and enhance your audio files to create new and unique sounds.

GoldWave 4.0 is a commercial version of the product that allows full digital editing of sounds. You can get it at www.goldwave.com.

To install GoldWave, open the GOLDWAVE folder and run GWAVE324.EXE.

SoundForge XP 4.0d Demo

Windows 95 and NT. SoundForge XP 4.0d Demo is a demo program from Sonic Foundry, Inc. for Windows that can open and play the μlaw files used by Java and on Web pages. SoundForge XP also includes sophisticated digital sound filters and effects. You can upgrade from the demo to the commercial product at www.sonicfoundry.com.

To install SoundForge, open the SOUNDFRG folder and run XPD4DX86.EXE.

SoundApp 2.4.4

Mac OS. SoundApp 2.4.4 is a great freeware program written by Norman Franke for Mac OS that can convert between dozens of sound formats, including of course, the Java μlaw sound format. SoundApp is a very well written program — it's amazing what you can get for free. SoundApp is constantly being updated; you can check for more recent versions at www-cs-students.stanford.edu/~franke/SoundApp/index.html.

To install SoundApp, copy the SoundApp68K or SoundAppPPC folder to your hard drive.

SoundHack 0.872

Mac OS. SoundHack 0.872 is a shareware program written by Tom Erbe for Mac OS that converts between most sound formats, including once again the Java sound format. In addition, SoundHack performs many utility and esoteric sound processing functions that are quite possibly available nowhere else. You can learn more about the program at `http:// shoko.calarts.edu/~tre/SndHckDoc/`

To install SoundHack, copy the SoundHack folder to your hard drive.

If You've Got Problems (Of the CD Kind)

The two likeliest problems are that you don't have enough memory (RAM) for the programs you want to use, or you have other programs running that are affecting installation or running of a program. If you get error messages like `Not enough memory` or `Setup cannot continue`, try one or more of these methods and then try using the software again:

- ✔ **Turn off any anti-virus software that you have on your computer.** Installers sometimes mimic virus activity and may make your computer incorrectly believe that it is being infected by a virus.

- ✔ **Close all running programs.** The more programs you're running, the less memory is available to other programs. Installers also typically update files and programs. So if you keep other programs running, installation may not work properly.

- ✔ **Have your local computer store add more RAM to your computer.** This is, admittedly, a drastic and somewhat expensive step. However, if you have a Windows 95 PC or a Mac OS computer with a PowerPC chip, adding more memory can really help the speed of your computer and enable more programs to run at the same time.

If you still have trouble installing the items from the CD, please call the IDG Books Worldwide Customer Service phone number: 800-762-2974 (outside the U.S.: 317-596-5430).

Index

• Numbers & Symbols•

" (double quotes), 227
; (semicolon), 226
' (single quotes), 227
[] (square brackets), 227
2-D Maze applet
  calculating pixel place-ment for, 166–167
  creating the Maze class for, 138–141
  customizing the appearance of, 168
  displaying a 2-D maze with, 163–170
  displaying solutions for, 169–170
  finding the shortest path using breadth-first searching, 159–163
  generating a maze with, 142–146
  left-handed/right-handed rule for, 157–159
  repainting, 165–166
  representing the solution for, 156–157
  solving, 156–163
3-D polygon Maze applet
  basic description of, 243–262
  calculating wall height for, 247
  creating a rat's-eye view for, 250–255
  drawing the maze for, 248–249
  light effects for, 255–258
  reasons to solve, adding, 255–258
  running a random maze in, 259–261
  shading for, 255–258
  sizing mazes with, 260–261
3-D texture-mapped Maze applet
  assembling the code for, 283–284
  basic description of, 263–284
  darkening the walls for, 280–282
  drawing front walls for, 275–277
  drawing side walls for, 278–280
  offset textures and, 279–280
  reusing code from, 320
  shading for, 280–281

•A•

About the CD, 331–340
abstract classes, 138
abstract method, 138, 139, 144
accessing CD files, 333–334
achievement, marking levels of, 319
Acrobat Reader (Adobe), 333, 336
action method, 108–111, 134, 212, 213
ACTION_EVENT, 108
add method, 107, 184, 188
addConsumer method, 298, 301, 306
addElement method, 189
addictiveness of games, 312
addImage method, 78
addLayoutComponent method, 123
addToBankroll method, 134
addVec method, 36, 39, 46
Adobe Systems
  Acrobat Reader, 333, 336
  Illustrator, 289
  Photoshop, 181, 289, 290, 293
advanced imaging. *See also* images
  antialiasing and, 289–293, 293–297
  basic description of, 285–308
  direct draw technique and, 297–308
adversary
  creating an, 197–200
  goals, prioritizing, 198–200
  navigation, using breadth-first searches for, 198
  Shooter class and, 201–202, 204–205
  use of the term, 197
Alberti, Leo Battista, 243
algorithms, 142–143, 157–159, 248
aliasing
  anti-, 289–293, 293–297
  time, 182
alignment, of components, 119
alpha channels, 285–293, 317
AlphaGradient applet, 287–288
alphaImage method, 290
AlphaShrink class, 294–295

anchor points, 177–178
and operator, 141
AND tests, 192
AniFrame frame, 230–231
animation(s). *See also*
    scripts; sprites
    ending, reusing game
        code for, 320
    ticks, 226
    scripts, implementing,
        231–242
AnimationSprite class,
    182–183, 240–242
AnimFrame frame, 238–240
AnimScript class, 226–227,
    229, 234–238
AnimScriptGroup class,
    231–233
anti-virus software, 340
AntialiasDemo applet,
    291–292
antialiasing, 289–293,
    293–297
AntialiasText applet,
    296–297
Apple Computer, 107
<APPLET> tag, 10
appletText method, 110
arg parameter, 108
ARGB (Alpha, Red, Green,
    and Blue) color
    values, 286
array(s)
    copying, 330
    initializers, large, 329–330
arraycopy method, 330
audio
    creating, 223
    playing, 223–224
    software for handling,
        339–340
    sound cards, 332
    writing animation scripts
        and, 225–227
AudioClip field, 233
AudioClip sound
    methods, 223–224

• B •

backgrounds, 16, 173
BackgroundSpriteEngine
    class, 194–195, 201
Ball applet, 10–14
Ball class, 9–14, 23, 37–41,
    62, 67
bd parameter, 39
Billiards applet
  assembling, 68–69
  basic description of,
      51–70
  calculating ball-to-ball
      collisions for, 52–53
  calculating distances to
      collisions for, 54–55
  calculating position over
      time for, 53–54
  checking combinations
      for, 61
  coding collisions for,
      62–63
  conserving momentum
      for, 63–68
  solving for time with,
      56–60
  timing and order for,
      60–61
binary (base 2) numbers,
    138, 141
bit(s)
  basic description of, 138
  bit–mask collision
      detection, 191–192
bitwise operators, 141,
    192, 324
Blackjack applet
  arranging the user
      interface for, 117–136
  basic description of,
      93–136
  converting cards to
      strings for, 102–103
  creating a deck of cards
      for, 96–106
  customizing the appear-
      ance of, 112–114

customizing the deck for,
    105–106
  dealing cards with, 97–99
  displaying a hand of cards
      with, 114–117
  dividing the screen for,
      123–124
  playing, 94–95
  rules, 94–95
  shuffling cards with,
      97–99
  top-level applet for,
      124–125
BlackjackHand class,
    114–117
BlockMaze class, 138–140,
    144, 151, 155–156,
    160, 167, 173, 179,
    206–212, 259
boolean flags, 40
boolean parameters, 144
boolean remove method,
    218
boolean variables, 8, 27
BorderLayout layout
    manager, 118–120,
    123–124, 130
bounce method, 63, 69
brackets ([]), 226
BrainTeaser applet
  basic description of,
      73–92
  digital stamp pads and,
      75–79
  drawing the board for,
      90–91
  images for, 74–79, 81
  laying out the game board
      for, 79–81
  reading image height/
      width for, 81, 83
  selecting puzzle pieces
      for, 85–86
  sliding action in, 87–89
  solving, 91–92
  winning, 91–92
BranchFrame class,
    239–240

BranchFrame frame, 229, 239–240

breadth-first searches, 159–163, 198

Bresenham, Jack, 270–273

Bresenham applet, 270–273, 277

browser(s)
  browser-safe palettes, 76
  Internet Explorer browser, 333, 336
  Netscape Navigator browser, 107, 288

Brunelleschi, Filippo, 243

Bullet class, 201, 205–206

ButtonPeer class, 107

buttons
  Blackjack applet and, 93, 106–108
  creating/placing, 107–108

byte variable, 327

bytecode, 327

• *C* •

Canvas component, 112–117

Card class, 99–106

CardLayout layout manager, 118–119

carriage return character (\r), 112

case statements, 19

CD (*Java Game Programming For Dummies*)
  About the CD, 331–340
  applets on, list of, 337
  bonus chapters on, 336–337
  files on, accessing, 333–334
  files on, installing, 334–335, 339
  installing, 332–334
  problems with, troubleshooting, 340

system requirements for, 331–332

using, with Windows 95 or Windows NT, 332–333

centerText method, 29

centrifugal force, 42

cheating, 315

checkerboard pattern, 292

checkReturn method, 23–24

Chinese Checkers applet, 339

Circle class, 36–38, 43, 62

Circular collision detection, 191–192

circular queues, 163

classes (listed by name)
  AlphaShrink class, 294–295
  AnimationSprite class, 182–183, 240–242
  AnimScript class, 226–227, 229, 234–238
  AnimScriptGroup class, 231–233
  BackgroundSpriteEngine class, 194–195, 201
  Ball class, 9–14, 23, 37–41, 62, 67
  BlackjackHand class, 114–117
  BlockMaze class, 138–140, 144, 151, 155–156, 160, 167, 173, 179, 206–212, 259
  BranchFrame class, 239–240
  Bullet class, 201, 205–206
  ButtonPeer class, 107
  Card class, 99–106
  Circle class, 36–38, 43, 62
  Deck class, 96–106
  DirectImage class, 299–301
  Explosion class, 196

GridView class, 250–252, 255, 269–270, 273–275, 281

Hole class, 42–43

Image class, 81

ImageButton class, 112–114

ImageBytes class, 273, 304–306

ImageSprite class, 182–183

Maze class, 138–141, 144, 156–157, 165, 166–167

MazeApplet class, 170–172

MazeThread class, 170

MediaTracker class, 77–79, 104

MemoryImageSource class, 286–287, 297–298, 307

ObjectDetector class, 179

Observable class, 195, 212

Paddle class, 24

Piece class, 82–85, 88, 89

PixelGrabber class, 192, 268, 273, 290–291, 293–296, 304

PlayerHandLayout class, 121–122

PolyView class, 250

Rectangle class, 82, 87–88

RoundSprite class, 180

Runner class, 201, 202–204

ScriptSprite class, 240–242

Shooter class, 201, 202, 204–205, 210

SpriteEngine class, 184–193

SpriteMaze class, 206–212

SpriteObject class, 176–177, 179

(continued)

classes *(continued)*
  Sqr class, 149
  TexView class, 273–275,
    278–282
  Thread class, 7–8
  Timeline class, 218–223
  TimelineEvent class,
    219–221
  Vec2D class, 35–39, 42–43,
    46, 67–68
  Wall class, 201–202, 210
  WallMaze class, 138,
    140–141, 143–147, 158,
    163, 168
clearHand method,
  117, 139
clipping regions, 104
clipRect method, 105
clone method, 330
clr parameter, 290
code
  optimizing, 323–330
  profiling, 323–330
  repeated, 325–326
  reusing, 320–321
collide method, 67–68, 69
collideWith method, 176,
  179, 188, 190, 193, 204
collision detection
  for the Ball applet,
    12–14, 18
  for the Billiards applet,
    51–63
  improving the accuracy
    of, 190–191
  sprites and, 174, 175,
    179–180, 190–192
collision masks, 192
collisionBox method,
  176, 179
color. *See also* shading
  dithered, 292–293
  in GIF images, 307–308
  information on, in the CD
    bonus chapters, 337
  palettes, 76
  RGB color, 281, 285, 287

colSlice method, 277, 278
columns, of texture, 277
compilers, 325, 328
component(s)
  aligning, 119
  creating new, 112–117
  lightweight, 114
  peers, 107
composite images, 103–
  104. *See also* images
composite rectangle
    collision detection,
    191–192. *See also*
    collision detection
CompuServe GIF format,
  181. *See also* GIF
  (Graphics Interchange
  Format)
conservation of momen-
  tum, 63–68
Container component,
  109
Control Panel, 332
coordinates, 9, 11, 104, 178
  3–D polygon Maze
    applet and, 245–247,
    249–250
  Billiards applet and,
    53–60
  Ponglet applet and, 23
  texture-mapped 3–D
    maze applet and, 271
CPUs (central processing
    units)
  advanced imaging and,
    293
  drawing code and, 248
  optimizing code and, 324
  system requirements and,
    331–332
  texture-mapping and,
    274, 276
Craig, Chris, 339
create method, 105
createImage method, 85,
  164, 282, 287, 299–300
credits, 318
crossing points, 52–53

• D •

darker method, 280–281
data corruption, 189
DDA (Digital Differential
  Analyzer), 270
deal method, 99, 117, 130
debriefing, 318
decel method, 38–40
deceleration, 32–42
decimal (base 10)
  numbers, 141
Deck class, 96–106
dHyt parameter, 265
diag field, 156
difficulty, of games,
  312–313
dir parameter, 153
direct draw technique,
  297–308
DirectDraw applet,
  301–303
DirectImage applet,
  299–303
DirectImage class,
  299–301
DIRTY flag, 138, 140, 164
dirtySquare method,
  144, 148
disbelief, suspension of,
  313–314
dispose method, 105
dist method, 37, 41–42, 46
distance formula, 54–55
distance to walk
  values, 199
distance-over-time
  equations, 56–60
dithering, 76, 292–293
doAction method, 242
doDraw method, 104
doMove method, 254
Doom, 137
dotProd method, 66
double data type, 178
double quotes ("), 226

downloading
drawing while, 77
images, 103
draw method, 10, 14–15, 43,
83, 90–91, 104, 184,
189–190, 190, 192,
194–196, 206, 211, 212
drawCardBack method,
104
drawImage method,
28, 75–77, 105, 181, 211
drawPathSquare method,
164, 169
drawSprite method, 176,
180, 189
drawSq method, 248–250,
273–274, 275, 278–280
drawSquare method, 163,
166–168, 210–211
drawTarget method, 164
drawView method, 250, 254
Dürer, Albrecht,
243–244, 268
Dungeon Master, 137
dWid parameter, 265

• *E* •

EAST constant, 176
edgeIntercept method,
62, 63, 69
elements method, 223
else statement, 30
ending games, 317–322
Enumeration interface,
218, 222–223
equals method, 88–89, 103
equations, polynomial,
57–60
Erbe, Tom, 340
errors
illegal access, 325
related to the CD, 340
event modeling. *See also*
events

basic description of,
217–242
matching animations to
game events, 224–242
with timelines, 217–223
events. *See also* event
modeling
adding, to timelines,
219–221
removing, before they
happen, 222–223
processing, in order, 221
exceptions, 78
exclusive-or operator, 141
Explosion class, 196
extruded polygon maze,
137
eyeDist constant, 246

• *F* •

fictitious force, 42, 43–44
FIFO (First In First Out)
data structure, 160
file(s)
filenames, partial, 227
on the CD, accessing,
333–334
on the CD, installing,
334–335, 339
fill3DRect method, 75
fillOval method, 10, 180
fillPolygon method,
248, 276
fillRect method, 15, 74,
168, 248, 276, 297
final method, 325, 328
Finder, 334
flicker, 15–16
float data type, 9, 10, 21,
178, 264, 280–281
float parameter, 36
FlowLayout layout man-
ager, 118–119

flush method, 303
fontHeight value, 29
FontMetrics object, 29
for loops, 278–279, 280, 327
forName method, 237
frame(s)
implementing, 238–240
initializing, 233
numbers, 220–221
rates, 181–182, 192–193
filling scripts with,
233–234
of reference, 66
writing animation scripts
and, 225–227
friction parameter, 39
frontOff method, 275

• *G* •

generate method, 144,
145, 149, 151
getArg method, 237, 238
getAudioclip method,
224
getCodeBase method, 75
getDocumentBase
method, 75
getFrame method, 238
getGraphics method, 85
getHand method, 134
getImage method,
75, 77, 78
getName method, 234
getNextUntil method,
221
getPoint method, 276
getScript method,
232, 234
getSelectedText
method, 110
getSource method, 306
getText method, 110

GIF (Graphics Interchange Format). *See also* images
advanced imaging and, 304–308
alpha masking and, 289–293
in animation scripts, 227
for the Blackjack applet, 104, 105–106
CompuServe GIF format, 181
GIF87a format, 181
GIF89a format, 181
modifying, 304–308
for the Sliding Blocks Brain Teaser applet, 74, 76, 79
recoloring, 307–308
for the texture-mapped 3-D maze applet, 273
transparent, 181, 289
GoldWave, 339
Golf (HoleInOne) applet
basic description of, 31–50
decelerating the ball for, 38–39
completing the putting interface for, 48–49
digging a hole for, 42–48
drawing the ball for, 41–42
drawing the green for, 49–50
gravitating toward the center in, 43–44
JavaPool applet and, 68–69
keeping the ball in bounds for, 39–40
modelling the deceleration of a ball for, 32–42
moving the ball for, 39
putting the ball in, 40–41
simulating a hole for, 36–38
sinking the putt for, 47

grabPixels method, 291
graphics. *See also* GIF (Graphics Interchange Format); sprites
backgrounds, 16, 173
clipping regions for, 104
composite, 103–104
height/width of, 81, 83, 184, 247
information on, in the CD bonus chapters, 337
loading, 77–79, 210
offscreen, reading from, 294–296
resampling, 264
scaling, 264–268
scripts, 225–227, 230–231
special effects for, 230–231
Sliding Blocks Brain Teaser applet and, 74–79, 81
SpriteMaze applet and, 181, 210–211
texture-mapped 3-D maze applet and, 264–268
transparent, 181, 286–293, 317
writing animation scripts and, 225–227
gravity, simulating, 43–44
grid parameter, 90
GridBagLayout layout manager, 118–119, 124
GridLayout layout manager, 118–119, 120
GridView class, 250–252, 255, 269–270, 273–275, 281
gridX variable, 79–81, 83, 84
gridY variable, 79–81, 83, 84
gstate variable, 20, 24–26
GWON state, 19, 26

• H •

hard drive space, 331–332
hashCode method, 103
hCol variable, 63
heap data structure, 219
height/width
of images, 81, 83, 184, 247
of play fields, 184
of walls, 247
hexadecimal numbers, 141
hitEdge flag, 40
Hole class, 42–43
HoleInOne (Golf) applet
basic description of, 31–50
decelerating the ball for, 38–39
completing the putting interface for, 48–49
digging a hole for, 42–48
drawing the ball for, 41–42
drawing the green for, 49–50
gravitating towards the center in, 43–44
JavaPool applet and, 68–69
keeping the ball inbounds for, 39–40
modeling the deceleration of a ball for, 32–42
moving the ball for, 39
putting the ball in, 40–41
simulating a hole for, 36–38
sinking the putt for, 47
HSB (Hue, Saturation, Brightness) color model, 281
HSBtoRGB method, 281
HTML (HyperText Markup Language),
<APPLET> tag, 10
information on, in the CD bonus chapters, 336

loading the Blackjack
applet with, 130
Maze applet and, 171–172
optimizing code and, 324
parameters, 171–172
sizing mazes in, 260–261
sound applets and, 224
hypotenuse, 34

• *I* •

IBM (International Business Machines), 270
icons, used in this book, 4
IDE (integrated development environment), 325
IDG Books Worldwide Customer Service, 340
Illustrator (Adobe), 289
image(s). *See also* GIF (Graphics Interchange Format); sprites
advanced imaging, 285–308
backgrounds, 16, 173
clipping regions for, 104
composite, 103–104
height/width of, 81, 83, 184, 247
information on, in the CD bonus chapters, 337
JPEG images, 76, 227, 289
loading, 77–79, 210
offscreen, reading from, 294–296
resampling, 264
scaling, 264–268
scripts, 225–227, 230–231
special effects for, 230–231
Sliding Blocks Brain Teaser applet and, 74–79, 81
SpriteMaze applet and, 181, 210–211

texture-mapped 3-D maze applet and, 264–268
transparent, 181, 286–293, 317
writing animation scripts and, 225–227
Image class, 81
Image field, 233
Image object, 75, 76
ImageButton class, 112–114
ImageBytes class, 273, 304–306
imageComplete method, 299, 306
ImageConsumer interface, 298, 301, 304–306
ImageFrame frame, 226, 228
ImageObserver interface, 77
ImageProducer interface, 286–287, 298–301, 304
ImageScale applet, 266–268
ImageSprite class, 182–183
imaging, advanced. *See also* images
antialiasing and, 289–293, 293–297
basic description of, 285–308
direct draw technique and, 297–308
immutable (unchangeable) attributes, 103
in variable, 79
IndexColorModel object, 280–281
indexed color table (color palette), 304
influence method, 46
init method, 13–14, 28–29, 69, 83–85, 118–119, 130, 231, 238, 260

initGraphics method, 104
initialization, of arrays, 329–330
initSq method, 139
inline methods, 325
insert method, 220
insertText method, 110
inside method, 86
installing
the CD, 332–334
files on the CD, 334–335, 339
instanceof operator, 221
instant replay, 318
interfaces
basic description of, 231
between artists and programmers, 225
implementing, 231
Internet Explorer browser, 333, 336
intersects method, 87–88, 190
invalidate method, 119
isAlive method, 8
isConsumer method, 298, 301
isGoal method, 259
isOdd method, 274–275
isOpen method, 144, 145, 151, 154–155
isWall method, 250, 252, 258, 259

• *J* •

java.awt (Abstract Window Toolkit) package, 276, 303
advanced imaging and, 286–287
Blackjack applet and, 93, 106, 112–113, 120
information on, in the CD bonus chapters, 337
layout managers and, 120
Maze applet and, 164

java.net package, 224
java.util package, 32, 117, 188, 223
JavaPool applet, 68–69
JDK (Java Development Kit), 324–325, 335–336
JPEG images, 76, 227, 289
JVM (Java Virtual Machine), 105, 325, 327, 328

• K •

keyDown method, 254

• L •

Label component, 108, 109
layout managers, custom, 120–122
layout method, 107
layoutcontainer method, 122
LayoutManager method, 118–123
left shift operator, 141
leftOffset field, 166
License.txt, 332
light effects, for the 3–D polygon Maze applet, 255–258
lightweight components, 114
limit method, 86–87
line separators, 112
linefeed character (\n), 112
lineHyt field, 166
lineWid field, 166
LINEWIDTH parameter, 171
ListEntry applet, 111
loadImages method, 210
Lombardi, Vince, 319
loop method, 223–224
loops
  faster, 327
  for loops, 278–279, 280, 327

texture–mapped 3–D maze applet and, 271, 280, 281, 279
while (running) loops, 19, 87, 271

• M •

Macintosh OS, 107, 332–334
mag method, 36
magnitude, of vectors, 33
makePic method, 282
Mathematica, 56
MAX_SCORE, 26
Maze applet (2-D)
  calculating pixel placement for, 166–167
  creating the Maze class for, 138–141
  customizing the appearance of, 168
  displaying a 2-D maze with, 163–170
  displaying solutions for, 169–170
  finding the shortest path with, using breadth-first
searching, 159–163
  generating a maze with, 142–146
  left-handed/right-handed rule for, 157–159
  repainting, 165–166
  representing the solution for, 156–157
  solving, 156–163
Maze applet (3-D polygon)
  basic description of, 243–262
  calculating wall height for, 247
  creating a rat's-eye view for, 250–255
  drawing the maze for, 248–249

light effects for, 255–258
reasons to solve, adding, 255–258
running a random maze in, 259–261
shading for, 255–258
sizing mazes with, 260–261
Maze applet (3-D texture–mapped)
  assembling the code for, 283–284
  basic description of, 263–284
  darkening the walls for, 280–282
  drawing front walls for, 275–277
  drawing side walls for, 278–280
  offset textures and, 279–280
  reusing code from, 320
  shading for, 280–281
Maze class, 138–141, 144, 156–157, 165, 166–167
MAZE parameter, 172
MazeApplet class, 170–172
MAZEHEIGHT parameter, 172
MazeMap applet, 250, 252–253, 257–258, 259–261, 274
MazeThread class, 170
MAZEWIDTH parameter, 171
MediaTracker class, 77–79, 104
memory, 103, 331–332, 340
MemoryImageSource class, 286–287, 297–298, 307
method(s). *See also* methods (listed by name)
  faster, 328
  interfaces as definitions of, 175

methods (listed by name).
See also methods
abstract method, 138, 139, 144
action method, 108–111, 134, 212, 213
add method, 107, 184, 188
addConsumer method, 298, 301, 306
addElement method, 189
addImage method, 78
addLayoutComponent method, 123
addToBankroll method, 134
addVec method, 36, 39, 46
alphaImage method, 290
appletText method, 110
arraycopy method, 330
boolean remove method, 218
bounce method, 63, 69
centerText method, 29
checkReturn method, 23–24
clearHand method, 117, 139
clipRect method, 105
clone method, 330
collide method, 67–68, 69
collideWith method, 176, 179, 188, 190, 193, 204
collisionBox method, 176, 179
colSlice method, 277, 278
create method, 105
createImage method, 85, 164, 282, 287, 299–300
darker method, 280–281
deal method, 99, 117, 130
decel method, 38–40
dirtySquare method, 144, 148
dispose method, 105
dist method, 37, 41–42, 46

doAction method, 242
doDraw method, 104
doMove method, 254
dotProd method, 66
draw method, 10, 14–15, 43, 83, 90–91, 104, 184, 189–190, 190, 192, 194–196, 206, 211, 212
drawCardBack method, 104
drawImage method, 28, 75–77, 105, 181, 211
drawPathSquare method, 164, 169
drawSprite method, 176, 180, 189
drawSq method, 248–250, 273–274, 275, 278–280
drawSquare method, 163, 166–168, 210–211
drawTarget method, 164
drawView method, 250, 254
edgeIntercept method, 62, 63, 69
elements method, 223
equals method, 88–89, 103
fill3DRect method, 75
fillOval method, 10, 180
fillPolygon method, 248, 276
fillRect method, 15, 74, 168, 248, 276, 297
final method, 325, 328
flush method, 303
forName method, 237
generate method, 144, 145, 149, 151
getArg method, 237, 238
getAudioclip method, 224
getCodeBase method, 75
getDocumentBase method, 75
getFrame method, 238

getGraphics method, 85
getHand method, 134
getImage method, 75, 77, 78
getName method, 234
getNextUntil method, 221
getPoint method, 276
getScript method, 232, 234
getSelectedText method, 110
getSource method, 306
getText method, 110
hashCode method, 103
HSBtoRGB method, 281
imageComplete method, 299, 306
influence method, 46
init method, 13–14, 28–29, 69, 83–85, 118–119, 130, 231, 238, 260
initGraphics method, 104
initSq method, 139
insert method, 220
insertText method, 110
inside method, 86
intersects method, 87–88, 190
invalidate method, 119
isAlive method, 8
isConsumer method, 298, 301
isGoal method, 259
isOdd method, 274–275
isOpen method, 144, 145, 151, 154–155
isWall method, 250, 252, 258, 259
keyDown method, 254
layout method, 107
layoutContainer method, 122
LayoutManager method, 118–123

(continued)

methods *(continued)*
limit method, 86–87
loadImages method, 210
loop method, 223–224
mag method, 36
makePic method, 282
minimumSize method,
   118
mouseDown method,
   48–49, 85, 113, 172, 211
mouseDrag method,
   48–49, 85–87, 211
mouseEnter method, 27
mouseExit method, 27
mouseMove method, 27
mouseUp method, 48–49,
   89–90, 211
move method, 11–14, 23,
   39, 118
placeInBounds method,
   204
play method, 223–224
preferredLayoutSize
   method, 123
preferredSize method,
   118
private method, 325, 328
processEvent method,
   220
putt method, 41, 48
Rectangle method, 190
remove method, 184, 188,
   190, 222–223
removeConsumer
   method, 298, 301
removeElement method,
   189, 301
removeLayoutComponent
   method, 123
repaint method, 8, 85,
   165, 212
replaceText method,
   110
requestTopDownLeft
   RightResend
   method, 298

resetMaze method, 166
reshape method, 122, 166
reshuffle method, 106
resize method, 118, 168
RGBtoHSB method, 281
rnd method, 21
rndInt method, 21
run method, 8, 18–20, 48,
   113–114, 130, 196,
   211–212
scale method, 265, 266
select method, 150
setActive method, 117
setBet method, 134
setButtons method, 130
setClip method, 105
setColor method, 10, 15
setColorModel method,
   299, 306
setDest method,
   204, 205, 211
setDimensions method,
   299
setEditable method,
   110
setHints method,
   299, 306
setImage method, 183
setLabel method, 107
setLayout method, 118,
   120
setLineSizes method,
   168
setPixels method, 299,
   306
setProperties method,
   299, 306
setSpriteEngine
   method, 175
setText method, 110
setVec method, 36, 38, 41
showMaze method, 148,
   165, 212
shrink method, 295
shuffle method, 97–99
sideOff method, 279

sleep method, 7, 19
slide method, 87–90
snap method, 90
sqType method, 259
start method, 8
startGame method,
   210–213
startProduction
   method, 298, 301
static method, 325, 328
stop method, 8, 223–224
subVec method, 36, 38
textureFront method,
   275–276, 277
textureSize method,
   278, 280, 282
toString method,
   102–103
touches method, 40–41
translate method, 89
traverse method,
   157–159, 160, 163, 206
tryDir method,
   151, 153, 154
union method, 88–89
unitVec method, 36, 38
update method, 16–17,
   164, 182, 184, 188–190,
   192, 195–196, 206,
   211–212, 254
updateBalls method,
   61, 69
updateSprite method,
   175, 178, 181–183,
   188, 193, 204–205
validate method,
   107, 119
void insert method, 218
wait method, 130, 165, 306
waitForAll method, 78
waitForID method, 78
microprocessors
advanced imaging and,
   293
drawing code and, 248
optimizing code and, 324

system requirements and, 331–332
texture-mapping and, 274, 276
minimumSize method, 118
mode operator, 276
ModifyGif applet, 307–308
momentum, conservation of, 63–68
mouse. *See also* mouse methods
control pad, drawing, 30
cursor, as a sprite, 173
HoleInOne (Golf) applet and, 40–41
Sliding Blocks Brain Teaser applet and, 85–90
SpriteMaze applet and, 211
tracking, for the Ponglet applet, 27
mouse methods
mouseDown method, 48–49, 85, 113, 172, 211
mouseDrag method, 48–49, 85–87, 211
mouseEnter method, 27
mouseExit method, 27
mouseMove method, 27
mouseUp method, 48–49, 89–90, 211
move method, 11–14, 23, 39, 118
mulVec method, 36, 38
mx parameter, 41
My Computer, 332
my parameter, 41
myApplet.html, 324

• N •

NASA (National Aeronautics and Space Administration), 264

Netscape Navigator browser, 107, 288
newInstance method, 237
Newton, Isaac, 32, 63
nextFrame method, 234
nextHand method, 130, 134
noDiag method, 155
NORTH constant, 176
"Not enough memory" errors, 340
Notepad, 332
notify method, 130
notifyAll method, 165, 306
null layout managers, 118

• O •

ObjectDetector class, 179
Observable class, 195, 212
offscreen Image, 15–16, 28
open method, 150
opponent, use of the term, 197
optimizing code, 323–330
overloaded methods, 99

• P •

packSize method, 106
Paddle class, 24
paint method, 14–15, 17–18, 28–29, 49–50, 85, 92, 114, 138, 163–165, 212, 254, 268, 303
paintOffscreenImage method, 144, 164, 165, 169
pal parameter, 280–281
panels, 123–124, 131–132
parsing text, 231
pathIntercept method, 62, 69
peek method, 99
perspective, 243–247

PGUTTER state, 19, 24–25
Photoshop (Adobe), 181, 289, 290, 293
picked variable, 86
Piece class, 82–85, 88, 89
pieceHeight variable, 79–81, 84
pieceWidth variable, 79–81, 83, 84
Ping–Pong (Ponglet) applet
basic description of, 17–30
changing states for, 24
code for Paddle objects in, 22–26
creating an opponent for, 24–25
displaying the state for, 28–30
returning serves in, 23–24
scoring in, 26, 29
state-drive design and, 17–20
tracking user input for, 27
winning in, 26, 29–30
pixel(s)
alpha values and, 295–296
collision detection and, 191–192
GIF images and, 181
placement of, for the Maze applet, 166–167
SpriteMaze applet and, 181, 191–192, 196
square, 264
sub-, rendering to, 293–296
texture-mapped 3–D maze applet and, 264, 268, 273
PixelGrabber class, 192, 268, 273, 290–291, 293–296, 304
placeInBounds method, 204

play fields
  basic description of, 174
  displaying, 195
  height/width of, 184
  moving sprites around,
    178–179
play method, 223–224
PlayerHandLayout class,
    121–122
players
  control of, providing, 211
  designing games for,
    311–316
  ranking, 320
  thanking, for an enjoyable
    game, 321
playtesting, 316
Point object, 41, 48
Point parameter, 29
polygon Maze applet
  basic description of,
    243–262
  calculating wall height
    for, 247
  creating a rat's-eye view
    for, 250–255
  drawing the maze for,
    248–249
  light effects for, 255–258
  reasons to solve, adding,
    255–258
  running a random maze
    in, 259–261
  shading for, 255–258
  sizing mazes with,
    260–261
polynomial equations,
    57–60
PolyView class, 250
Ponglet (Ping–Pong)
    applet
  basic description of,
    17–30
  changing states for, 24
  code for Paddle objects
    in, 22–26

creating an opponent for,
    24–25
displaying the state for,
    28–30
returning serves in, 23–24
scoring in, 26, 29
state-drive design and,
    17–20
tracking user input for, 27
winning in, 26, 29–30
practice rounds, 321
preferredLayoutSize
    method, 123
preferredSize method,
    118
prefix increment operator,
    26
priority queues, 219
private field, 326
private method, 325, 328
processEvent method,
    220
processors
  advanced imaging and,
    293
  drawing code and, 248
  optimizing code and, 324
  system requirements and,
    331–332
  texture-mapping and,
    274, 276
pruning paths, 159
PSCORE state, 26
public static field, 326
putt method, 41, 48
PWON state, 19, 26
Pythagorus, 33

• Q •

quadratic formula, 58
quotes, 226

• R •

RAM (random-access
    memory), 103,
    331–332, 340
random numbers, 315–316
Read Me First icon, 333
Readme.txt, 332
Rectangle class, 82, 87–88
Rectangle method, 190
recursion, 88
remove method, 184, 188,
    190, 222–223
removeConsumer method,
    298, 301
removeElement method,
    189, 301
removeLayoutComponent
    method, 123
repaint method, 8, 85,
    165, 212
replaceText method, 110
requestTopDownLeftRightResend
    method, 298
resetMaze method, 166
reshape method, 122, 166
reshuffle method, 106
resize method, 118, 168
RETURN state, 24–25
reusing code, 320–321
RGB color, 281, 285, 287
RGBtoHSB method, 281
right shift operator, 141
rnd method, 21
rndInt method, 21
RoundSprite class, 180
run method, 8, 18–20, 48,
    113–114, 130, 196,
    211–212
Runner class, 201, 202–204

• S •

samplers, digital, 264
scale method, 265, 266
scaling images, 264–268

scope, 326
scores, 29, 29, 109, 319
screen(s)
  dividing, for the Black-
    jack applet, 123–124
  flicker, 15–16
  sizing, 117, 247
script(s)
  adding random behavior
    to, 228–230
  adding special effects to,
    230–231
  filling, with frames,
    233–234
  implementing, 231–242
  initializing, 227–228
  matching animations to
    game events with,
    224–242
  organizing, by action,
    231–232
  reading, from text files,
    227–228
  writing, 225–227
ScriptSprite class,
  240–242
Script.txt, 228
scrollable text areas,
  110–111
sdir field, 156
searches, breadth-first,
  159–163, 198
select method, 150
semicolon (;), 226
SERVE state, 24, 25
setActive method, 117
setBet method, 134
setButtons method, 130
setClip method, 105
setColor method, 10, 15
setColorModel method,
  299, 306
setDest method, 204, 205,
  211
setDimensions method,
  299
setEditable method, 110

setHints method, 299, 306
setImage method, 183
setLabel method, 107
setLayout method,
  118, 120
setLineSizes method,
  168
setPixels method,
  299, 306
setProperties method,
  299, 306
setSpriteEngine method,
  175
setText method, 110
"Setup cannot continue"
  errors, 340
setVec method, 36, 38, 41
shading
  for the 3-D polygon Maze
    applet, 255–258
  for the texture–mapped
    3-D maze applet,
    280–281
shoot script, 228–230
Shooter class, 201, 202,
  204–205, 210
showMaze method, 148,
  165, 212
shrink method, 295
shuffle method, 97–99
side field, 156
sideOff method, 279
single quotes ('), 226
sleep method, 7, 19
slide method, 87–90
Sliding Blocks Brain
  Teaser applet
  basic description of,
    73–92
  digital stamp pads and,
    75–79
  drawing the board for,
    90–91
  images for, 74–79, 81
  laying out the game board
    for, 79–81

reading image height/
  width for, 81, 83
selecting puzzle pieces
  for, 85–86
sliding action in, 87–89
solving, 91–92
winning, 91–92
sLoc value, 21
snap method, 90
Sonic Foundry, 339
SoundApp, 339
SoundForge, 339
SoundFrame frame, 226,
  228, 238–239
SoundHack, 340
sound(s)
  cards, 332
  creating, 223
  playing, 223–224
  software for handling,
    339–340
  writing animation scripts
    and, 225–227
SOUTH constant, 176
special effects, adding,
  230–231
sprite(s)
  animating, 181–183
  basic description of,
    138, 173
  control, 195–196
  displaying, 180–181
  drawing, layer by layer,
    189–190
  events, 194–195
  frameworks, 183–197
  height/width of, 177
  implementing, 174–176,
    201–206
  keeping track of, 188–189
  moving, 178–179, 190–191
  tracer, 193
  updating, 174
Sprite interface, 175–178
SpriteEngine class,
  184–193

SpriteMaze applet
  basic description of,
      173–214
  building the BlockMaze
      class for, 206–212
  chasing the player in, 212
  finalizing, 212–213
  implementing a cast of
      sprites for, 201–206
  initializing, 210
SpriteMaze class, 206–212
SpriteObject class,
      176–177, 179
sqHyt field, 166
sqLnHyt field, 166
sqLnWid field, 166
Sqr class, 149
sqType method, 259
square brackets ([]), 226
square pixels, 264. *See also*
      pixels
sqWid field, 166
start method, 8
startGame method,
      210–213
startProduction method,
      298, 301
state-driven design, 17–20
static method, 325, 328
status, displaying, 109
stop method, 8, 223–224
string(s)
  concatenation, 79
  converting cards to,
      102–104
  system-dependent, 112
String field, 233
subVec method, 36, 38
Sun Audio, 223
Sun Microsystems Web
      site, 335
sunk flag, 38, 46
switch statements, 19, 220
synchronizing, reducing
      the cost of, 328–329
system requirements, for
      the CD, 331–332

• T •

text
  areas, scrollable, 110–111
  files, reading scripts from,
      227–228
  parsing, 231
  reading/displaying, in
      the Blackjack applet,
      108–112
text component, 93, 108
TextArea component, 108
TextComponent compo-
      nent, 109
TextField component,
      108, 109–111
texture. *See also* texture–
      mapped 3–D maze
      applet
  alternating wall, 274–275
  loading, 273
  mapping, 263–284
  origins of, 264
  tiling, 268
texture–mapped 3–D
      maze applet. *See also*
      texture
  assembling the code for,
      283–284
  basic description of,
      263–284
  darkening the walls for,
      280–282
  drawing front walls for,
      275–277
  drawing side walls for,
      278–280
  offset textures and,
      279–280
  reusing code from, 320
  shading for, 280–281
textureFront method,
      275–276, 277
textureSize method,
      278, 280, 282

TexView class, 273–275,
      278–282
thanking players, 321
this parameter, 78
thread(s)
  information on, in the CD
      bonus chapters, 337
  Maze applet and, 165–166,
      170–171
  repainting and, 165–166
  thread-safe vectors, 189
Thread class, 7–8
thru field, 156
time aliasing, 182
Timeline class, 218–223
TimelineEvent class,
      219–221
timelines
  adding events to, 219–221
  basic description of,
      217–223
  removing events from,
      222–223
  searching, 222–223
timing, relative versus
      absolute, 182
tokens, 231
topOffset field, 166
toString method, 102–103
touches method, 40–41
tracer sprites, 193. *See also*
      sprites
translate method, 89
transparent GIFs, 181, 289.
      See also GIF (Graphics
      Interchange Format)
transparent images, 181,
      286–293, 317
traverse method, 157–159,
      160, 163, 206
triangles, 244, 249, 279
troubleshooting, 340
try/catch blocks, 78
tryDir method,
      151, 153, 154

• U •

union method, 88–89
unit vectors, 34–35, 66.
    See also vectors
unitVec method, 36, 38
update method, 16–17,
    164, 182, 184, 188–190,
    192, 195–196, 206,
    211–212, 254
updateBalls method,
    61, 69
updateSprite method,
    175, 178, 181–183, 188,
    193, 204–205
URLs (Uniform Resource
    Locator), 75, 210

• V •

validate method, 107, 119
variables
  faster, 326–327
  initializing, 81
vCol variable, 63
Vec2D class, 35–39, 42–43,
    46, 67–68
vector(s)
  adding, to sprites, 178
  basic description of,
    32–35
  Billiards applet and,
    64–68
  classes, creating, 35–36
  HoleInOne applet and,
    32–36, 44–45
  instant replay and, 318
  magnitude of, 33
  math, 32
  unit, 34–35, 66
vel vector, 38, 41, 44,
    47–48, 68
velocity, as momentum, 64
viewpoints, selecting, 244
viruses, 340
vOff constant, 246

• W •

wA parameter, 281
wait method, 130, 165, 306
WAIT value, 20, 21, 26–27
waitForAll method, 78
waitForID method, 78
Wall class, 201–202, 210
WallMaze class, 138, 140–141,
    143–147, 158, 163, 168
Web browser(s)
  browser-safe palettes, 76
  Internet Explorer
    browser, 333, 336
  Netscape Navigator
    browser, 107, 288
WEST constant, 176
while (running) loop, 19,
    87, 271
white space, 226
width/height
  of images, 81, 83, 184, 247
  of play fields, 184
  of walls, 247
winLocation object, 91–92
Wizardry, 137
Wolfram Research, 56

• X •

x/y coordinates, 9, 11, 104,
    178
  3-D polygon Maze
    applet and, 245–247,
    249–250
  Billiards applet and,
    53–60
  Ponglet applet and, 23
  texture-mapped 3-D
    maze applet and, 271

Java™ Development Kit Version 1.0.2 (Mac OS) 1.1.5 (Windows) Binary Code License

This binary code license ("License") contains rights and restrictions associated with use of the accompanying software and documentation ("Software"). Read the License carefully before installing the Software. By installing the Software you agree to the terms and conditions of this License.

1. **Limited License Grant**. Sun grants to you ("Licensee") a non-exclusive, non-transferable limited license to use the Software without fee for evaluation of the Software and for development of Java™ compatible applets and applications. Licensee may make one archival copy of the Software. Except for the foregoing, Licensee may not re-distribute the Software in whole or in part, either separately or included with a product. Refer to the Java Runtime Environment Version 1.1 binary code license (http://www.javasoft.com/products/JDK/1.1/index.html) for the availability of runtime code which may be distributed with Java compatible applets and applications.

2. **Java Platform Interface**. Licensee may not modify the Java Platform Interface ("JPI", identified as classes contained within the "java" package or any subpackages of the "java" package), by creating additional classes within the JPI or otherwise causing the addition to or modification of the classes in the JPI. In the event that Licensee creates any Java-related API and distributes such API to others for applet or application development, Licensee must promptly publish an accurate specification for such API for free use by all developers of Java-based software.

3. **Restrictions**. Software is confidential copyrighted information of Sun and title to all copies is retained by Sun and/or its licensors. Licensee shall not modify, decompile, disassemble, decrypt, extract, or otherwise reverse engineer Software. Software may not be leased, assigned, or sublicensed, in whole or in part. **Software is not designed or intended for use in on-line control of aircraft, air traffic, aircraft navigation or aircraft communications; or in the design, construction, operation or maintenance of any nuclear facility. Licensee warrants that it will not use or redistribute the Software for such purposes.**

4. **Trademarks and Logos**. This License does not authorize Licensee to use any Sun name, trademark or logo. Licensee acknowledges that Sun owns the Java trademark and all Java-related trademarks, logos and icons including the Coffee Cup and Duke ("Java Marks") and agrees to: (i) to comply with the Java Trademark Guidelines at http://java.com/trademarks.html; (ii) not do anything harmful to or inconsistent with Sun's rights in the Java Marks; and (iii) assist Sun in protecting those rights, including assigning to Sun any rights acquired by Licensee in any Java Mark.

5. **Disclaimer of Warranty**. Software is provided "AS IS," without a warranty of any kind. ALL EXPRESS OR IMPLIED REPRESENTATIONS AND WARRANTIES, INCLUDING ANY IMPLIED WARRANTY OF MERCHANTABILITY, FITNESS FOR A PARTICULAR PURPOSE OR NON-INFRINGEMENT, ARE HEREBY EXCLUDED.

6. **Limitation of Liability**. SUN AND ITS LICENSORS SHALL NOT BE LIABLE FOR ANY DAMAGES SUFFERED BY LICENSEE OR ANY THIRD PARTY AS A RESULT OF USING OR DISTRIBUTING SOFTWARE. IN NO EVENT WILL SUN OR ITS LICENSORS BE LIABLE FOR ANY LOST REVENUE, PROFIT OR DATA, OR FOR DIRECT, INDIRECT, SPECIAL, CONSEQUENTIAL, INCIDENTAL OR PUNITIVE DAMAGES, HOWEVER CAUSED AND REGARDLESS OF THE THEORY OF LIABILITY, ARISING OUT OF THE USE OF OR INABILITY TO USE SOFTWARE, EVEN IF SUN HAS BEEN ADVISED OF THE POSSIBILITY OF SUCH DAMAGES.

7. **Termination**. Licensee may terminate this License at any time by destroying all copies of Software. This License will terminate immediately without notice from Sun if Licensee fails to comply with any provision of this License. Upon such termination, Licensee must destroy all copies of Software.

8. **Export Regulations**. Software, including technical data, is subject to U.S. export control laws, including the U.S. Export Administration Act and its associated regulations, and may be subject to export or import regulations in other countries. Licensee agrees to comply strictly with all such regulations and acknowledges that it has the responsibility to obtain licenses to export, re-export, or import Software. Software may not be downloaded, or otherwise exported or re-exported (i) into, or to a national or resident of, Cuba, Iraq, Iran, North Korea, Libya, Sudan, Syria or any country to which the U.S. has embargoed goods; or (ii) to anyone on the U.S. Treasury Department's list of Specially Designated Nations or the U.S. Commerce Department's Table of Denial Orders.

9. **Restricted Rights**. Use, duplication or disclosure by the United States government is subject to the restrictions as set forth in the Rights in Technical Data and Computer Software Clauses in DFARS 252.227-7013(c) (1) (ii) and FAR 52.227-19(c) (2) as applicable.

10. **Governing Law**. Any action related to this License will be governed by California law and controlling U.S. federal law. No choice of law rules of any jurisdiction will apply.

11. **Severability**. If any of the above provisions are held to be in violation of applicable law, void, or unenforceable in any jurisdiction, then such provisions are herewith waived to the extent necessary for the License to be otherwise enforceable in such jurisdiction. However, if in Sun's opinion deletion of any provisions of the License by operation of this paragraph unreasonably compromises the rights or increase the liabilities of Sun or its licensors, Sun reserves the right to terminate the License and refund the fee paid by Licensee, if any, as Licensee's sole and exclusive remedy

IDG Books Worldwide, Inc., End-User License Agreement

READ THIS. You should carefully read these terms and conditions before opening the software packet(s) included with this book ("Book"). This is a license agreement ("Agreement") between you and IDG Books Worldwide, Inc. ("IDGB"). By opening the accompanying software packet(s), you acknowledge that you have read and accept the following terms and conditions. If you do not agree and do not want to be bound by such terms and conditions, promptly return the Book and the unopened software packet(s) to the place you obtained them for a full refund.

1. **License Grant.** IDGB grants to you (either an individual or entity) a nonexclusive license to use one copy of the enclosed software program(s) (collectively, the "Software") solely for your own personal or business purposes on a single computer (whether a standard computer or a workstation component of a multiuser network). The Software is in use on a computer when it is loaded into temporary memory (RAM) or installed into permanent memory (hard disk, CD-ROM, or other storage device). IDGB reserves all rights not expressly granted herein.

2. **Ownership.** IDGB is the owner of all right, title, and interest, including copyright, in and to the compilation of the Software recorded on the disk(s) or CD-ROM ("Software Media"). Copyright to the individual programs recorded on the Software Media is owned by the author or other authorized copyright owner of each program. Ownership of the Software and all proprietary rights relating thereto remain with IDGB and its licensers.

3. **Restrictions on Use and Transfer.**

   (a) You may only (i) make one copy of the Software for backup or archival purposes, or (ii) transfer the Software to a single hard disk, provided that you keep the original for backup or archival purposes. You may not (i) rent or lease the Software, (ii) copy or reproduce the Software through a LAN or other network system or through any computer subscriber system or bulletin-board system, or (iii) modify, adapt, or create derivative works based on the Software.

   (b) You may not reverse engineer, decompile, or disassemble the Software. You may transfer the Software and user documentation on a permanent basis, provided that the transferee agrees to accept the terms and conditions of this Agreement and you retain no copies. If the Software is an update or has been updated, any transfer must include the most recent update and all prior versions.

4. **Restrictions on Use of Individual Programs.** You must follow the individual requirements and restrictions detailed for each individual program in the "About the CD-ROM" section of this Book. These limitations are also contained in the individual license agreements recorded on the Software Media. These limitations may include a requirement that after using the program for a specified period of time, the user must pay a registration fee or discontinue use. By opening the Software packet(s), you will be agreeing to abide by the licenses and restrictions for these individual programs that are detailed in the "About the CD-ROM" section and on the Software Media. None of the material on this Software Media or listed in this Book may ever be redistributed, in original or modified form, for commercial purposes.

5. **Limited Warranty.**

   (a) IDGB warrants that the Software and Software Media are free from defects in materials and workmanship under normal use for a period of sixty (60) days from the date of purchase of this Book. If IDGB receives notification within the warranty period of defects in materials or workmanship, IDGB will replace the defective Software Media.

   (b) **IDGB AND THE AUTHOR OF THE BOOK DISCLAIM ALL OTHER WARRANTIES, EXPRESS OR IMPLIED, INCLUDING WITHOUT LIMITATION IMPLIED WARRANTIES OF MERCHANTABILITY AND FITNESS FOR A PARTICULAR PURPOSE, WITH RESPECT TO THE SOFTWARE, THE PROGRAMS, THE SOURCE CODE CONTAINED THEREIN, AND/OR THE TECHNIQUES DESCRIBED IN THIS BOOK. IDGB DOES NOT WARRANT THAT THE FUNCTIONS CONTAINED IN THE SOFTWARE WILL MEET YOUR REQUIREMENTS OR THAT THE OPERATION OF THE SOFTWARE WILL BE ERROR FREE.**

   (c) This limited warranty gives you specific legal rights, and you may have other rights that vary from jurisdiction to jurisdiction.

6. **Remedies.**

   (a) IDGB's entire liability and your exclusive remedy for defects in materials and workmanship shall be limited to replacement of the Software Media, which may be returned to IDGB with a copy of your receipt at the following address: Software Media Fulfillment Department, Attn.: *Java Game Programming For Dummies,* IDG Books Worldwide, Inc., 7260 Shadeland Station, Ste. 100, Indianapolis, IN 46256, or call 800-762-2974. Please allow three to four weeks for delivery. This Limited Warranty is void if failure of the Software Media has resulted from accident, abuse, or misapplication. Any replacement Software Media will be warranted for the remainder of the original warranty period or thirty (30) days, whichever is longer.

   (b) In no event shall IDGB or the author be liable for any damages whatsoever (including without limitation damages for loss of business profits, business interruption, loss of business information, or any other pecuniary loss) arising from the use of or inability to use the Book or the Software, even if IDGB has been advised of the possibility of such damages.

   (c) Because some jurisdictions do not allow the exclusion or limitation of liability for consequential or incidental damages, the above limitation or exclusion may not apply to you.

7. **U.S. Government Restricted Rights.** Use, duplication, or disclosure of the Software by the U.S. Government is subject to restrictions stated in paragraph (c)(1)(ii) of the Rights in Technical Data and Computer Software clause of DFARS 252.227-7013, and in subparagraphs (a) through (d) of the Commercial Computer–Restricted Rights clause at FAR 52.227-19, and in similar clauses in the NASA FAR supplement, when applicable.

8. **General.** This Agreement constitutes the entire understanding of the parties and revokes and supersedes all prior agreements, oral or written, between them and may not be modified or amended except in a writing signed by both parties hereto that specifically refers to this Agreement. This Agreement shall take precedence over any other documents that may be in conflict herewith. If any one or more provisions contained in this Agreement are held by any court or tribunal to be invalid, illegal, or otherwise unenforceable, each and every other provision shall remain in full force and effect.

Installation Instructions

For information on installing the software from the CD-ROM included with this book, see Appendix. Use of the included Sun Microsystems Java™ Development Kit software is subject to the Binary Code License terms and conditions on page 356. Read the license carefully. By opening the package, you are agreeing to be bound by the terms and conditions of this license from Sun Microsystems, Inc.

YOUR ONLINE RESOURCE

WWW.DUMMIES.COM

Discover Dummies Online!

The Dummies Web Site is your fun and friendly online resource for the latest information about ...*For Dummies*® books and your favorite topics. The Web site is the place to communicate with us, exchange ideas with other ...*For Dummies* readers, chat with authors, and have fun!

Ten Fun and Useful Things You Can Do at www.dummies.com

1. Win free ...*For Dummies* books and more!
2. Register your book and be entered in a prize drawing.
3. Meet your favorite authors through the IDG Books Author Chat Series.
4. Exchange helpful information with other ...*For Dummies* readers.
5. Discover other great ...*For Dummies* books you must have!
6. Purchase Dummieswear™ exclusively from our Web site.
7. Buy ...*For Dummies* books online.
8. Talk to us. Make comments, ask questions, get answers!
9. Download free software.
10. Find additional useful resources from authors.

Link directly to these ten fun and useful things at
http://www.dummies.com/10useful

WWW.DUMMIES.COM

For other technology titles from IDG Books Worldwide, go to
www.idgbooks.com

Not on the Web yet? It's easy to get started with *Dummies 101*®: *The Internet For Windows*®*95* or *The Internet For Dummies*,® 4th Edition, at local retailers everywhere.

IDG BOOKS WORLDWIDE™

Find other ...*For Dummies* books on these topics:
Business • Career • Databases • Food & Beverage • Games • Gardening • Graphics • Hardware
Health & Fitness • Internet and the World Wide Web • Networking • Office Suites
Operating Systems • Personal Finance • Pets • Programming • Recreation • Sports
Spreadsheets • Teacher Resources • Test Prep • Word Processing

The IDG Books Worldwide logo and Dummieswear are trademarks, and Dummies Man and ...For Dummies are registered trademarks under exclusive license to IDG Books Worldwide, Inc., from International Data Group, Inc.

IDG BOOKS WORLDWIDE BOOK REGISTRATION

Register This Book and Win!

We want to hear from you!

Visit **http://my2cents.dummies.com** to register this book and tell us how you liked it!

- Get entered in our monthly prize giveaway.

- Give us feedback about this book — tell us what you like best, what you like least, or maybe what you'd like to ask the author and us to change!

- Let us know any other ...*For Dummies®* topics that interest you.

Your feedback helps us determine what books to publish, tells us what coverage to add as we revise our books, and lets us know whether we're meeting your needs as a ...*For Dummies* reader. You're our most valuable resource, and what you have to say is important to us!

Not on the Web yet? It's easy to get started with *Dummies 101®: The Internet For Windows® 95* or *The Internet For Dummies®,* 4th Edition, at local retailers everywhere.

Or let us know what you think by sending us a letter at the following address:

...*For Dummies* Book Registration
Dummies Press
7260 Shadeland Station, Suite 100
Indianapolis, IN 46256-3945
Fax 317-596-5498

BUSINESS AND GENERAL REFERENCE BOOK SERIES FROM IDG

COMPUTER BOOK SERIES FROM IDG